PLURALISM IN SELF PSYCHOLOGY

Progress in Self Psychology
Volume 15

Progress in Self Psychology
Editor, Arnold Goldberg, M.D.

Progress in Self Psychology invites articles relevant to psychoanalytic self psychology to be submitted for publication. Send the original manuscript (double-spaced, including references, footnotes, quoted passages, and dialogue) and three copies to:

Arnold Goldberg, M.D.
122 South Michigan Avenue
Chicago, IL 60603-6107

If the article is accepted, a diskette will be required as well. All submissions are refereed. Papers will not be returned if unacceptable.

PLURALISM IN SELF PSYCHOLOGY

Progress in Self Psychology
Volume 15

Arnold Goldberg
editor

 THE ANALYTIC PRESS

1999   Hillsdale, NJ   London

ISBN 0-88163-312-7
ISSN 0893-5483

Printed in the United States of America
10 9 8 7 6 5 4 3 2 1

Acknowledgment

We would like to thank Ms. Christine Susman, who provided secretarial and editorial assistance.

Contents

III KLEIN AND KOHUT

IV CASE STUDIES

V AFFECTS

     Model Integrating Silvan Tomkins's Affect- and Script
     Theory Within the Framework of Self Psychology
          Jon T. Monsen and Kirsti Monsen   287
21. The Self and Its Past: On Shame and the
     "Biographical Void"
          Martin Gossmann   307
22. Death and the Self
          Charles B. Strozier   321

     Author Index   343

     Subject Index   347

Contributors

George E. Atwood, Ph.D. is a Professor of Psychology at Rutgers University and Founding Faculty Member, Institute for the Psychoanalytic Study of Subjectivity, New York.

Doris Brothers, Ph.D. is Co-Founder, Faculty, and Training and Supervising Analyst, The Training and Research Institute for Self Psychology, New York City and Member, Board of Advisors, Institute for the Advancement of Self Psychology, Toronto.

Peter Buirski, Ph.D. is Dean, Graduate School of Professional Psychology, University of Denver; Training Analyst and Supervisor, Colorado Center for Psychoanalytic Studies.

Linda A. Chernus, M.S.W. is Professor of Clinical Psychiatry at the University of Cincinnati College of Medicine and Faculty Member, International Center for the Study of Psychoanalytic Self Psychology, Cincinnati, Ohio.

William J. Coburn, Ph.D. is a Faculty Member at the Institute of Contemporary Psychoanalysis in Los Angeles.

James M. Fisch, M.D. is Faculty, Chicago Institute for Psychoanalysis and Training and Supervising Analyst, Israel Institute for Psychoanalysis.

James L. Fosshage, Ph.D. is Founding Faculty Member of the Institute for the Psychoanalytic Study of Subjectivity, New York City, and Clinical Professor of Psychology, New York University Postdoctoral Program in Psychotherapy and Psychoanalysis.

Mark J. Gehrie, Ph.D. is Faculty, Training and Supervising Analyst, Chicago Institute for Psychoanalysis; Visiting Professor, Division of General Studies, University of Chicago.

Martin Gossmann, M.D. is in private practice in Berlin, Germany.

James S. Grotstein, M.D. is Clinical Professor of Psychiatry, UCLA School of Medicine; Training and Supervising Analyst, Los Angeles Psychoanalytic Society Institute and the Psychoanalytic Center of California, Los Angeles.

Pamela Haglund, Psy.D. is Adjunct Assistant Professor, Graduate School of Professional Psychology, University of Denver; Jefferson Center for Mental Health.

Alan Kindler, MBBS is a Training Analyst with the Toronto Institute of Psychoanalysis and a Board and Faculty Member of the Institute for the Advancement of Self Psychology in Toronto.

Dorthy M. Levinson, M.S.W. is Senior Supervisor, National Institute for the Psychotherapies and Faculty and Supervisor, New York Institute for Psychoanalytic Self Psychology.

Ellen Lewinberg, C.S.W. is Director, Faculty, and Supervising Analyst, The Institute for the Advancement of Self Psychology, Toronto; Faculty and Supervisor, the Toronto Child Psychotherapy Program.

Barry Magid, M.D. is Senior Supervisor, Postgraduate Center for Mental Health and Supervisor, Institute for Contemporary Psychotherapy, both in New York.

Jon T. Monsen, Ph.D. is Research Director and Associate Professor, Center for Research in Clinical Psychology, Department of Psychology, University of Oslo.

Kirsti Monsen, Cand. psychol., is Research Fellow and Assistant Professor, Center for Research in Clinical Psychology, Department of Psychology, University of Oslo.

Anna Ornstein, M.D. is Professor Emerita, University of Cincinnati and Co-Director, International Center for the Study of Psychoanalytic Self Psychology, Department of Psychiatry, University of Cincinnati.

Paul H. Ornstein, M.D. is Professor Emeritus, University of Cincinnati and Co-Director, International Center for the Study of Psychoanalytic Self Psychology, Department of Psychiatry, University of Cincinnati.

Craig Powell, M.B., B.S., F.R.A.N.Z.C.P. is Faculty, Sydney Branch, Australian Psychoanalytical Society and is a psychoanalyst in private practice in Sydney, Australia.

Crayton E. Rowe, Jr., M.S.W. is Founding Member and Faculty, the New York Institute for Psychoanalytic Self Psychology; Past Chair and Founder, the National Membership Committee on Psychoanalysis in Clinical Social Work.

Allen M. Siegel, M.D. is Faculty, Chicago Institute for Psychoanalysis and Chair, Kohut Memorial Fund.

Robert D. Stolorow, Ph.D. is Faculty Member and Training and Supervising Analyst, Institute of Contemporary Psychoanalysis, Los

Angeles; Faculty Member, Institute for the Psychoanalytic Study of Subjectivity, New York City.

Charles B. Strozier, Ph.D. is Professor of History, John Jay College and the Graduate Center, CUNY; Training and Supervising Analyst, TRISP, New York City.

Introduction

James M. Fisch

In his final paper, "Introspection, Empathy, and the Semi-Circle of Mental Health" (Kohut, 1982), written just before his death, Kohut ended with the statement that, for analysis to stay alive and reach its destiny, "It must turn from the study of Freud to the study of man" (p. 405). Now, some 18 years since those words were written, there are some who would say that, for self psychology to stay alive and reach its destiny, it must turn from the study of Kohut to the study of the self. The nature of that self and how it can best be studied is the central theme that runs through this volume of *Progress in Self Psychology.*

In that same paper, Kohut fired his final broadside at Freud, whom he referred to as the ultimate maker of psychoanalytic myths, the foremost one being the myth of a universal oedipal neurosis. After recasting the Oedipus story in self psychological terms as the story of an abandoned child, Kohut then playfully offered his own countermyth. He told the story of Odysseus and how he saved the life of his infant son, Telemachus, at great cost to himself. The Odysseus myth, he argued, was closer to the true nature of normal human psychology. Human beings are motivated by a deep need to preserve and sustain the next generation, not by infanticide, patricide, and incest. Kohut had no illusions that his Odysseus myth would replace Freud's Oedipus, but he did nonetheless leave us with a powerful legacy: the legacy of a central motivating structure and internal program, the nuclear self.

Another legacy Kohut left us is the idea that our most precious analytic theories, including his own, are also forms of mythology. Today, when a new idea is advanced, the prior model is referred to as a myth, for example, "the myth of the isolated mind" (Stolorow and Atwood,

1992). Are there any basic ideas that the majority of self psychologists working today would hold to be basic truths and above the level of myth? Reading through this volume, it seems that just about everyone, from every perspective, employs the term *selfobject* although often in a different context. For some, it is a general term describing a background phenomenon where the patient and therapist are in sync and the patient feels vitalized, similar to the positive transference. For others, *selfobject* describes a specific developmental experience along the trajectory of self-development and is foreground, rather than background. Another difference is the extent to which *selfobject* is employed with more emphasis on the relational and less on the intrapsychic. Those who emphasize the relational, intersubjective, and motivational aspects of selfobject experience refer to changes in the sense of self and self with other. Those who emphasize the intrapsychic refer to selfobject transferences and changes in psychic structure. One can then ask, "Does this difference in emphasis and whether one refers to selfobject transferences or not really matter?" Aside from mattering greatly to those identified with the particular models, I think a fair answer might be that the struggle over whether the self is a relational (two-person) concept or a structural (one-person) concept is a struggle over the very soul of self psychology. I do not believe we are on the verge of a religious war, but at one extreme end of these positions, patient and therapist are curing each other; at the other end, the patient of necessity creates the same selfobject transference with that therapist that would develop with any therapist. In between these two poles, which is where most clinicians live, clinical practice involves (1) a mixture of selfobject experience for both patient and therapist (archaic for the patient, mature for the therapist), (2) a deepening understanding of the nature of the patient's self structure gained through analysis of the selfobject transferences, and (3) a highly sensitive intersubjective context that fluctuates with changes in the relational field.

The reader will find sharp debate in this volume regarding the question of how the self is best studied and the nature of therapeutic process. Rowe, Siegel, Gehrie, Chernus, and Paul Ornstein argue that the essential work of analysis is the analysis and working through of the selfobject transferences. This debate is particularly clear in the case of Joanna Churchill, presented by Alan Kindler, where an unsanitized case, "warts and all," is presented with discussions by Stolorow, Fosshage, and Ornstein. The different perspectives—intersubjective, motivational systems, and self–selfobject—are nowhere more clearly illustrated as applied to clinical material. By carefully studying this material, it is possible to look beyond the political positioning of each proponent and see how different terminology may be employed with the same meaning and also how different perspectives arrive at the same destination. Are the differences in language and degree of abstraction of the three perspectives differences of substance or style? Although no definitive answer is given, the exercise provides an ideal vehicle for studying the question.

Aside from the ongoing theoretical debates, this volume contains a rich harvest of the progress in self psychology, including comparisons with Kleinian theory, a clinical study of the sense of agency, a discussion of how current cultural attitudes affect parenting, a relational view of the therapeutic partnership, the application of self psychology to psychotherapy research, and the study of history. Finally, there are more letters from the Kohut archives, as well as a deeply moving account of Kohut's struggle with his own death.

The search for a new mythology goes on, as does progress in self psychology. It may be that we will be better off without a new mythology and, instead, just devote ourselves to the continuing study of the self.

REFERENCES

Kohut, H. (1982), Introspection, empathy, and the semi-circle of mental health. *Internat. J. Psycho-Anal.*, 63:395–407.

Stolorow, R. & Atwood, G. (1992), *Contexts of Being: The Intersubjective Foundations of Psychological Life.* Hillsdale, NJ: The Analytic Press.

Chapter 1

From the Kohut Archives

Charles B. Strozier

This second installment of "From the Kohut Archives" publishes a range of letters from Kohut to his close colleagues between 1966 and 1981. The selection also includes a letter expressing his concern for the care of his mother after she was admitted to a nursing home in 1970, two letters from Michael Franz Basch to Kohut, and a letter to Anita Eckstaedt that is relevant to the story of "The Two Analyses of Mr. Z." These letters show Heinz Kohut's ambivalence about his mother (as well as hints about how psychotic she became before she died in 1972), his deep involvement in the lives of his junior colleagues and followers, his irritation with Eckstaedt over the case of Mr. X, and some hints about his self-presentation to his less friendly colleagues in psychoanalysis.

October 17, 1966

Dear Paul [Ornstein]:

Welcome back! I shall try to arrange for a continuation of your consultations with me regarding your patient and you may, of course, attend my seminar. Concerning the latter, however, I think that it would be proper that you get also Dr. [Joan] Fleming's permission.

If you want to attend my seminar on those occasions when it does not fall on the last Friday of the month, I suggest that you see me on Friday at 7:30 A.M. on November 11 and December 9. The seminar

1

is from 8:30 to 10:00. If you wish I can also see you this Friday, October 21, at 7:30 A.M. (I am, however, not teaching the new seminar afterwards but am participating in L-511 for a discussion of my narcissism paper). We would thus have a minimum of three sessions in 1966 and could continue on that basis in 1967, i.e., on every Friday on B-weekends[1] which does not come as the last of the month. If additional consultations seem desirable we can use other Fridays and make ad hoc arrangements for them. I am sorry to have to add that my fee has gone up a bit; it is now $30.00.

Please let me know as soon as you can about this schedule, especially about this Friday.

Sincerely,

Heinz Kohut, M.D.

October 3, 1970

James M. Goldinger, M.D.
10552 South Oakley Avenue
Chicago, Illinois 60643

Dear Jim,

First of all my warm thanks for taking care of my poor mother and for allowing us to spend a wonderful and very rewarding vacation in Europe.[2]

Secondly, please write a one-sentence statement that my mother (Mrs. Else L. Kohut) had to be transported by ambulance form Billings to Monticello, put it into the enclosed envelope and mail it.

Thirdly: is there anything that we could do to make my mother's life more comfortable? I know that her complaints have often not much to do with reality, but occasionally I believe that a little more help while she is eating, etc. might make life easier for her. She seems indeed to have recovered no function on her left side and her hemianopic and

---

[1] The Chicago Institute alternated its curriculum between A and B weekends. The first two years met on one Friday and Saturday morning, and the other two years on the other Fridays and Saturdays during the academic year.

[2] Kohut's mother, Else Kohut, had been admitted to the nursing home where Dr. Goldinger worked.

otherwise diminished eye-sight is of very restricted use to her. Please let me know if there is anything that we could do without disturbing the hospital routine that could help her.

I am off again for a week in Europe (this time it's business not pleasure) but I will be back again on October 11. Betty [Elizabeth Kohut], of course, who joins me in her thanks to you, is available.

With warm regards,

Sincerely yours,

Heinz Kohut, M.D.
5805 S. Dorchester Avenue
Chicago, Illinois 60637

Telephone: MUseum 4-1994

April 18, 1972

Michael Franz Basch, M.D.
180 North Michigan Avenue
Chicago, Illinois 60601

Dear Mike:

Your letter gave me great pleasure and I felt instructed and helped by it. How all this is to be applied in my own work, I don't know. At the moment I feel no urge to go beyond the conceptual means at my disposal when I try to formulate and to communicate my findings and ideas. I did think, however—although I intentionally refrained from saying so—that [Roy] Schafer was not fair in taking me to task about my formulations, especially in those instances when I had gone out of my way to explain that I wanted to be evocative and that I was not theoretical. Schafer does not know my last paper (I wonder actually whether he has read much beyond my "Forms and Transformations of Narcissism")[Kohut, 1966]—but how would you evaluate the contrasting formulations of "shame" and "rage" in "Thoughts on Narcissism and Narcissistic Rage"? [Kohut, 1972]

Warm regards,

Heinz Kohut, M.D.

September 4, 1973

Dear Doctor Kohut,

Carol [Basch] and I thank you for your card from Rome. It sounds as if you had a fine vacation and I hope that the rest of your summer will be as rewarding. I'll be very interested to hear what you have been working on when you get back to Chicago. Just in case you have not seen it, I am enclosing a review of *"The Analysis of the Self"* in "Psychiatric Annals," although in itself this little publication is of little consequence it is widely distributed gratis to the general psychiatrists and I think it is significant that your work continues to excite attention in such a wide circle.

My summer has been busy, rewarding and a little tiring. We all went to Europe for three weeks. Though we went to Paris we spent more time sight seeing than attending the convention. We stopped in London for about a week and saw some relatives of mine, some of whom I had not seen for 34 years. This was emotionally more significant for me than our stop in Berlin where I revisited the site of my childhood home as well as other places that played a part in my childhood life. I think this was quite meaningful for my children and they seem to be impressed by what they saw. While in Berlin visited with Dr. Maetze who spent a day with us and was a wonderful host to my whole family.

We also went to Vienna. Freud's apartment was the highlight of our visit there. It was really a thrill, not just for me but for Carol and the children. After the ornate palaces, the National Library, the imposing statues etc. to come into these simple, charming rooms where the world was changed was a contrast that made a deep impact on all of us. The curator is a delightful fellow and spent a lot of time with us; he really knows his subject and obviously loves it. It is a good thing that this "museum" has been established.

Before going home we spent a few days in Lucerne and really relaxed for the first time. Didn't have to run around so much to make sure we saw all we wanted to, but, instead, could enjoy the food and the accommodations that the Swiss know how to provide so well.

At the moment I am working my way back into the practice, preparing the classes and trying to finish off a chapter on some theoretical considerations in the area of depression for a book that T. [Teresa] Benedek and J. [James] Anthony are planning to publish.

Be glad you are in California, though I am not suffering thanks to hyposensitization I understand it's a terrible year for ragweed!

My very best regards to Betty and best wishes to both of you in which Carol joins me.

Cordially yours,

Mike Basch

April 17, 1974

Dr. Michael F. Basch
180 North Michigan Avenue
Chicago, Illinois 60601

Dear Mike:

I am working very hard on two manuscripts and have, therefore, not devoted the attention to your extensive reaction to the pages which continue the manuscript (on the resisters; the tragic hero of drama and religion; the history of the analysis of the patient who strove to realize an aspect of his nuclear self) which I read to you and the rest of the group some time ago.[3] I read your critique with great interest, am grateful for the time that you spent on it, and I admire your scholarship and intelligence.

On first sight—but really only on first sight!—I can see that you are right in many details. I cannot grasp yet why you see these speculations as so disastrous to my work and why you plead with me to discard them. I have the impression that a number of comparatively minor changes should be sufficient to avoid the dangers of which you speak—but I will reserve my judgment until can really think about it concentratedly, which I surely will—perhaps even, if you are willing, through direct interchange with you. Before we do that, however, I would first like you to read the manuscript of a paper—it is almost finished—in which I am examining the empirical basis of my work and am discussing the way in which I come to set up and evaluate certain hypotheses, including the one about Guilty and Tragic Man. I would want you to read this manuscript first before we tackle your objections together.

In the meantime, many thanks for your analysis of these pages of my work. I know the deep protective concern which is the motivation of your critical admonitions.

Warmly,

Heinz Kohut, M.D.

---

[3] The paper Kohut was referring to was "On Courage" (see Strozier, 1985). [I deleted the case of Mr. R, to which Kohut refers in this sentence, from the original version of the paper, while Paul Ornstein, the editor of the *Search* series, re-inserted it into the paper in *Search*, volume 3]. The "some time ago" when Kohut read the paper in draft form to "the group" (his close colleagues in Chicago) is not entirely clear but was probably sometime in 1969 when the first group took shape but just as quickly went out of existence until it was revived in 1974. See chapter 11 of my forthcoming *Heinz Kohut: His Life and Work*.

[handwritten on Michael Franz Basch M.D. letterhead]

4/17/74

Dear Doctor Kohut,
Thanks so much for your note, I am relieved that you understand my motives in writing as I did. I knew you would, of course, you always have.
Needless to say, when the time comes and if you should still wish it, I'd be very happy to discuss further the points I made and your reactions to them to whatever extent you would find useful.
I am honored and very pleased that you will have me read your new manuscript when it is completed. I am looking forward to the opportunity!

Cordially yours,

Mike

April 18, 1975

Michael F. Basch, M.D.
233 North Michigan Avenue
Chicago, Illinois 60601

Dear Mike,
Thank you for the xerox of the panel discussion at the meeting of the American Psychoanalytic Association. I agree with you that [Kurt] Eissler's opinion misses the mark. [August] Aichorn fostered a therapeutic alliance by play-acting the role of a super-delinquent; then he analyzed the Oedipus complex. There is little resemblance between the discovery of this technical device in the treatment of juvenile delinquents and the discovery of the cohesive narcissistic transferences and their analysis.
Thank you also for your valuable comments concerning my letter to Dr. [Norman] Litowitz who compared my work with that of [Donald W.] Winnicott.[4] I have not yet had the time to think about all the issues

---

[4] This "letter" was read by Kohut at two consecutive meetings of the Wednesday Research Seminar at the Chicago Institute for Psychoanalysis in January 1975, and published as, "Remarks About the Formation of the Self: Letter to a Student Regarding Some Principles of Psychoanalytic Research" (Ornstein, 1978, Vol. 2, pp. 737–770).

which you raise. Some of your points strike me as excellent (e.g., the advisability of stressing the fact that I am studying narcissistic transferences, that I am using the psychoanalytic method, that my experiences are open to consensual validation by others in the psychoanalytic situation); others are less convincing to me (e.g., that I should I omit the remarks about my own road from disconnected insights to systematic presentation).

May I send a xerox of your letter to Paul Ornstein? Or, even better: could you send a copy to Paul? Your remarks should be helpful to him in his preparation of my papers for publication.

Warm regards,

Cordially yours,

Heinz Kohut, M.D.

[handwritten on Kohut's letterhead . . . 'From the desk of HEINZ KOHUT, M.D. . . .']

December 12, 1975

Dear Arnold [Goldberg],

Here is the present version of Chapter 6 [of the manuscript of *The Restoration of the Self*] and the passage from my letter to [illegible] about the "self" and "identity."

I spoke with Paul O. [Ornstein] last night—a long talk, part of it similar to our recent discussion. He agreed to a meeting and we agreed tentatively on Sat. January 3. This is not a good date for Paul; I think he would prefer January 10. One of my reasons for having preferred January 3 was that I thought I would meet the Institute Curriculum Committee on Tuesday, January 6. I now just learned that this meeting will be on January 13—thus *our* meeting on January 10 would still give me the benefit of our discussion in preparation for my appearance at the C.C [Curriculum Committee]. I am telling you all this because Paul O. will try to talk with you in New York and discuss the meeting with you.

I thought further about your feeling that I did you an injustice by saying that you brought up the topic of selection in a belligerent way. I am sorry about that and I understand the situation better now. I am familiar with the frustration and the rage that are created by brush-offs from representatives of institutions. Still, if at all possible, one must learn to retain (or regain) calmness. To *show* one's narcissistic rage is deleterious to one's cause—one must learn to use it constructively, amalgamated to a wisdom that has learned to accept institutionalized conceit as an almost unavoidable and at any rate expectable aspect of the human condition.

Warmly,

Heinz

March 26, 1977

Dr. med. Anita Eckstaedt
Schmiedebergerstrasse 31
6242 Kronberg/T.S. 1
Germany (B.R.D.)

Dear Dr. Eckstaedt:

In response to your letter of March 22 let me tell you that no definite decision has been reached concerning a German translation of my new book; and if it is decided to translate it, it will take quite a while until this is achieved. We are thus under no pressure to come to a decision quickly.[5] Now to particulars.

You say that the transposition of the analysis to Chicago is improper—yet it is you who made that choice. On October 11, 1975, I said (I am translating my German letter in English) that I "would change the material in the text in such a way that the patient was treated in Germany (that I would, however, not mention directly that the patient is a theologian and that I will change the external features sufficiently so that a complete disguise of the identity of the patient is achieved)." You did not accept this suggestion but decided on the other possibility I had offered to you, namely that I will leave the material in the text just as it is at the present time (i.e., as if it were a patient that had been treated in Chicago by a Chicago colleague, a woman [Kollegin] . . .).

---

[5] Anita Eckstaedt was the analyst of the patient described in *The Restoration of the Self* (Kohut, 1977) as Mr. X (pp. 199–219). Kohut had heard her present the case in Germany during a visit in the early 1970s and was immediately taken with it. He got her permission to use the case in heavy disguise for *Restoration,* which appeared in the spring of 1977. Eckstaedt raised new concerns, however, in connection with the German translation of the book. In the end, Kohut cut out the case from the translation and substituted Mr. Z. For a more complete discussion of these issues, see Strozier (forthcoming).

During the past twenty-five years I have used dozens of clinical cases in my psychoanalytic writings—cases of my own and cases treated by colleagues—in order to illustrate various theoretical points. I have always disguised these reports carefully, in some instances even by ascribing my own cases to others. I have not upset the patients' post-analytic equilibrium by telling them that some of the lessons learned in their analyses (directly or indirectly, i.e., via the report of the analyst to me), including some relevant data from the analysis, will appear in a scientific publication. (The only exceptions concern material of patients who were themselves psychoanalysts.) This has worked well for me. But I have no quarrel with a colleague who sees his obligations toward a former patient differently.

At present I think we should leave things in abeyance. If a German translation should be prepared, I will decide whether I should include this illustration or whether I should delete it or use some substitutive material. Should I decide to include it, I will be glad to have you look over the relevant passages, in order to make sure that no identifiable data have been overlooked.

Sincerely yours,

Heinz Kohut, M.D.

[handwritten on Kohut's letterhead . . . 'From the desk of HEINZ KOHUT, M.D. . . .']

May 4, 1981

Dear Marian [Tolpin],

Although you are now far away in Greece, taking in the sights and the bright lights of today & reverberating to the [illegible] from the cultural glory of 2000 years back in time, I want to say hello and thank you for the warm birthday letter you dropped into my mailbox just before you left. It was good to read it—to see this evidence of your active mind and of your responsive heart.

Our party[6] went well—everybody was there, and we all thought for a little while of the two of you in Greece when I gave everyone a little gift (including one for both of you) after the birthday cake. The many

---

[6] Kohut made it a custom to have a party for himself on his birthday, May 3.

thanks to both of you for your part in the beautiful (and generous) gift that I received. It has found a good place (over) in our living room, looking out from under some branches in a nearby vase, and the light shining through its perfect body.

Betty & I are looking forward to seeing you after your return. The very best to Paul from both of us.

Affectionately,

Heinz

[handwritten on Kohut's letterhead . . . 'From the desk of HEINZ KOHUT, M.D. . . .']

5/6/81

Arnold [Goldberg]

I love Sarah's work of art.[7] You, like all of us, must sometimes wonder, what life is all about, whether it is worth the pain & anxieties. But seeing Sarah's colors and focus wipes all questions away.

Thanks,

Heinz

REFERENCES

Kohut, H. (1966), Forms and transformations of narcissism. In: *The Search for the Self: Selected Writings of Heinz Kohut: 1950–1994,* Vol. 1, ed. P. Ornstein. New York: International Universities Press.

———— (1972), Thoughts on narcissism and narcissitic rage. *The Psychoanalytic Study of the Child,* 27:360–400. New Haven, CT: Yale University Press.

———— (1977), *The Restoration of the Self.* New York: International Universities Press.

Ornstein, P., ed. (1978–1994), *The Search for the Self: Selected Writings of Heinz Kohut: 1950–1994,* 4 volumes. New York: International Universities Press.

---

[7] Sarah Goldberg, then three years old.

Strozier, C. B. (1985), Kohut's "On Courage." In: *Self Psychology and the Humani-ties: Reflections on a New Psychoanalytic Approach,* ed. C. B. Strozier. New York: Norton.

———— (forthcoming), *Heinz Kohut: His Life and Work.* New York: Farrar, Straus & Giroux.

I

The Clinical
Situation

Chapter 2

The Selfobject Transferences Reconsidered

Crayton E. Rowe, Jr.

Kohut's concluding remarks in his 1984 posthumously published work was a clear reminder that the central focus of self psychology was its attention to the development and analysis of the transferences: "Self psychology does not advocate a change in the essence of analytic technique. The transferences are allowed to unfold and their analysis— the understanding of the transference reactions, their explanation in dynamic and genetic terms—occupies, now as before, the center of the analyst's attention" (p. 208). Kohut has emphasized that it is through this process that the patient's arrested development can be set in motion and come to completion.

While Kohut has clearly demonstrated the significance of continued exploration and understanding selfobject transferences as the central focal point of treatment, there has been a number of recent self psychological treatment contributions that have shifted the emphasis away from the analysis and development of the selfobject transferences as the primary focus of treatment. This chapter examines four major conceptual shifts and their potential consequences on the understanding of the patient's selfobject needs and the development of the selfobject transferences.

Finally, I will present a brief summary of the progress that has been made in advancing the understanding of selfobject transferences.[1]

---

[1] Permission was given by The Analytic Press, Human Science Press, and Jason Aronson for the use of material quoted and summarized in this chapter.

KOHUT'S DEFINITION OF TRANSFERENCE

Kohut's definition of transference is a broadly based structural definition that defines transference as the amalgamation of unconscious repressed material with preconscious and conscious contents of the mind. This definition can be contrasted to the commonly held clinical meaning of transference as unconscious distortions of the analyst through the displacement of childhood parental representations. Rather than the analyst being experienced as distorted transference figures, there is a mobilization of unrequited self needs for idealizing; for recognition of exhibitionistic expressions of ideas, talents, and abilities; and for experiencing alikeness with others. These needs emerge as strivings toward establishing self-cohesion and continue to unfold and develop in the treatment as mature forms of selfobject transferences (Kohut, 1979, 1984).

Kohut's fundamental discoveries of selfobject needs and selfobject transferences were born out of an attunement to the patient's experience (1959, 1968a, b, 1977, 1981, 1984). He taught that it was only through prolonged immersion in his patients' experience that the analyst could arrive at an awareness and an understanding of the unique complexities of the patient's selfobject needs and allow for their development as selfobject transferences. As the transferences unfold, the analyst must be able to differentiate their various forms in order to understand the specific developmental needs of the patient:

> The ability to differentiate between various types of selfobject transferences also gives us the opportunity to study in greater detail the developmental line characteristically associated with the archaic form of a particular self–selfobject relationship—from the archaic state that is revived at the beginning of the transference to the mature state which, as a result of the systematic and patiently pursued working-through process, may be attained at the end of successful analyses [1984, p. 202].

THEORETICAL SHIFTS FROM THE CONCEPT OF SELFOBJECT TRANSFERENCES AS THE PRIMARY FOCUS OF TREATMENT

Emphasis on Motivational Systems

Lichtenberg, Lachmann, and Fosshage (1992, 1996) evolved a theory of psychoanalytic technique that shifts the emphasis from the analysis and development of the selfobject transferences as conceptualized by Kohut to selfobject experiences as being integral to understanding motivational systems.

The proposed theory of technique includes the concepts of motivational systems earlier formulated by Lichtenberg (1989): (1) the need for psychic regulation of physiological requirements, (2) the need for attachment and later affiliation, (3) the need for exploration and assertion, (4) the need to react aversively through antagonism or withdrawal (or both), and (5) the need for sensual enjoyment and sexual excitement.

Lichtenberg et al. (1992) contend: "Mirroring, twinship, and idealization are central to the development of the attachment motivational system" (p. 136). These authors consider other selfobject experiences, mentoring and sponsoring, rivalry and competition, and dependent/altruistic and romantic love, to convey significant vitalization to attachment.[2]

In their 1992 work the authors provided a clinical vignette of an ongoing psychoanalysis (approximately two and a half years into the analysis) to illustrate the interventions that have evolved from their formulations.[3] I will present only the beginning and end of the vignette as an effort to highlight their approach to treatment. The vignette includes a brief interchange between the analyst and patient as well as the analyst's description and assessment of his interventions.

The patient was a 28-year-old woman, who had been married and was the mother of a young son. She had just terminated a psychoanalysis after three years. The treatment helped her curtail the use of drugs and alcohol, as well as her promiscuous behavior. However, she became depressed during the last year of her analysis. Most problematic was her need to know that her analyst "cared" about her.

It was learned that the patient grew up in a large family with a tyrannical father and deeply religious mother. She suffered intense

---

[2] In 1996, Lichtenberg et al. formulated ten principles of technique which can be summarized as follows: (1) establishing a frame of friendliness and reliability and an ambiance of safety; (2) systematic application of the empathic mode of perception; (3) discerning a patient's specific affect to appreciate the patient's experience and discerning a patient's affect experience being sought to appreciate the patient's motivation; (4) considering that the patient's message contains the message; (5) obtaining information to grasp the patient's narrative; (6) wearing the patient's attributions; (7) jointly constructing model scenes; (8) considering aversive motives (resistance, reluctance, defensiveness) as a communicative expression to be explored like any other message; (9) intervening in three ways: (a) selecting and focusing, highlighting and questioning, and articulating subtle affects and states, including spelling out transference implications of the patient's associations; (b) illuminating a recognizable pattern, or communicating feelings, appraisals, or impressions from the analyst's own perspective; (c) maintaining disciplined spontaneous engagements between analyst and patient; and (10) following the sequence of our interventions and the patient's responses to them to evaluate their effect.

[3] This case was previously discussed elsewhere (Fosshage, 1990a, b). See P. H. Ornstein's (1990) extensive discussion of this case from a self psychological point of view.

feelings of emotional abandonment by her mother but was able to connect with her through periodic religious and psychological discussions. Her father viewed her as "his special one," but she felt severely humiliated and crushed on occasions when in public he denied their special connection. She often looked to God in response to these profound disappointments.

Opening Moments of the Vignette

P: [in a dejected mood] I don't like the additional session.
A: No? [p. 100]

After this very brief opening moment, the analyst gives the following assessment for the reader:

THE SEQUENCE BEGINS WITH AN INTERVENTION THAT ACKNOWLEDGES THE COM-PLAINT, UNDERSCORES A REFLECTIVE INTEREST, AND ATTEMPTS TO ENGAGE THE PATIENT IN A SHARED EXPLORATION OF HER AVERSIVENESS [Lichtenberg et al., 1992, pp. 100–101].

Here, the analyst has determined that the patient's motivation is the need to react aversively, which is considered to be a resistance to uncovering underlying material. The focus is to engage the patient in an exploration of her aversiveness in order to get to the underlying material. Therefore, while the analyst was aware that the patient was experiencing a depressed emotional state (a dejected mood), he does not attempt to further his attunement to her experience of dejection to gain an understanding of her emotional life.

The patient then responds to the analyst's inquiry ("No?").

P: I'm not sure. Well, it causes all kinds of problems at home.
A: With E [her son] [p. 101].

At this point the analyst assesses his response for the reader:

THE ANALYST IS TOO EAGER TO ENGAGE P AND GUESSES INCORRECTLY, BUT HIS INQUIRY SERVES BOTH TO REFLECT KNOWLEDGE AND INTEREST IN P AND TO FUR-THER THEIR EXPLORATION [p. 101].

Here we see that the analyst's treatment focus was to continue his exploration of what is considered to be the patient's aversive motivation. As a result of the focus, there was no effort to become attuned to the patient's experience as she revealed that she had difficulty at home ("it causes all kinds of problems at home").

P: No, well, that's not what I meant. My mother . . . that's not why I don't like to come. You asked me last week why I felt ambivalent about it, and I wasn't sure why, but I think it's just too hard to generate material. I get very annoyed and resentful about such things. I don't think I can generate enough, so that's part of the problem.

A: So you feel that you have to generate material here that interferes with your freedom just to *be* here.

The analyst gives the following assessment:

THE BRIEF PRIOR INTERVENTIONS MAY HAVE ENABLED P TO SHIFT HER AMBIVA-LENCE FROM HOME TO THE ANALYTIC SITUATION. SHE RELATES HER AMBIVALENCE ABOUT THE ADDITIONAL SESSION SPECIFICALLY TO FEELING A BURDENSOME PRES-SURE TO GENERATE MATERIAL. THE ANALYST REFLECTS THIS AMPLIFICATION, CON-NECTS IT TO A PRIOR THEME, 'FREEDOM TO BE HERSELF,' AND SPELLS OUT THAT THIS INTERFERES WITH HER INCREASED EXPANSIVENESS AND ASSERTIVE MOTIVA-TION [p. 101].

Here we see that the analyst's focus was on what was understood as evidence of an assertive motivation. Again, and as result of the focus, there was no attempt to become attuned to what the patient was experiencing even though in this sequence the patient verbalized her feelings that she felt it was too hard to generate material and that she was likely to get annoyed and resentful. It can be suggested that attunement may well have led to an unfolding and understanding of other levels of the patient's emotional life, for example, feelings of inadequacy, help-lessness, and the like.

Near the end of the vignette, the analyst gives the following assess-ment having to do with the patient's idealization:

P NOTED THAT THE IDEALIZATION OF THE ANALYST AND HERSELF IN A WORLD OF SPECIALNESS PROTECTED HER FROM THIS TRAUMATIC CONFIGURATION AS DESCRIBED IN RELATION TO BOTH HER PARENTS. SHE WONDERED, WITH A NOTE OF IRONY, WHY SHE HAD GIVEN UP THIS IDEAL WORLD "TO GET INTO THIS EXTRA STUFF." WITH FURTHER EXPLORATION A MUTUAL PLAYFULNESS WAS EMERGING AROUND THE NOTION THAT IT CERTAINLY WAS UNDERSTANDABLE TO WANT TO RETURN TO THE IDEALIZED WORLD IN THE FACE OF THE POTENCY OF THIS "EXTRA STUFF" [pp. 115–116].

(By "extra stuff" the patient was referring generally to feelings of being overwhelmed by the expected repetitious traumatic experiences with her parents.)

In this assessment we clearly see that the patient's idealization was considered a defensive interference against exploring underlying trau-mata. Idealization was seen by both patient and analyst as something to give up in order to face the potency of her earlier traumatic life situations. Therefore, the idealizing selfobject transference was not al-lowed to develop.

Summary and Implications

In these brief excerpts, focusing on aversive and assertive motivational systems led to missed opportunities for in-depth attunement to the patient's experience. We, therefore, do not know the needs that were overlooked and might have emerged and developed as selfobject transferences as the patient felt understood. If the selfobject transferences had been allowed to develop and worked through, it is likely that the patient would have felt strengthened and, therefore, less reluctant to explore painful experiences.

In sum, the opportunities for the development of selfobject transferences were thwarted and with it the structure building process that occurs through transmuting internalization.

Pairing Selfobject Transferences with Object-Related Transferences

Stolorow and Lachmann (1981, 1984/85) have formulated a specific treatment model that pairs selfobject transferences with object-related transferences through the postulation of a figure and ground relationship. The selfobject transference often provides the background. They stated:

> Kohut's work has illuminated the unique therapeutic importance of understanding and transforming those transference configurations in which the selfobject dimension is figure—in which, that is, the restoration or maintenance of self-organization is the paramount psychological purpose motivating the patient's specific tie to the analyst. Even when this is not the case, however, and other dimensions of experience and human motivation—such as conflicts over loving, hating, desiring, and competing—emerge as most salient in structuring the transference, the selfobject dimension is never absent. So long as it is undisturbed, it operates silently in the background, enabling the patient to confront frightening feelings and painful dilemmas [1984/85, pp. 30–31].[4]

According to Stolorow and Lachmann (1981), an important implication of their conceptualization is that the analyst must be able to

---

[4] Lichtenberg et al. (1992) add the following to the perception of foreground–background relationships: "The shift to an emphasis on selfobject experiences and an understanding of motivational systems changes dramatically the perception of foreground–background relationships. Selfobject experiences triggered by needs and desires being met in any motivational system may dominate the foreground of experience at any moment" (p. 138). Also see Lachmann and Beebe (1992, 1995a, b) for a discussion of figure–ground dimensions of the transference, which include a selfobject dimension and representational configurations.

assess the shifting figure–ground relationships to determine the content and timing of the transference interpretations.

The authors summarized a treatment example of what they consider to be a transference shift from a selfobject tie with the analyst to an oedipal transference. In their summary they stated that the analyst:

> had become less an archaic selfobject and more a separate and whole object. . . . In short, the treatment had moved, by way of transmuting internalizations of an archaic selfobject tie and the concomitant consolidations of psychological structure, to what increasingly took on the character of a more or less classical analysis of an oedipal transference neurosis. . . . Even during the oedipal transference phase of the treatment Mary often required a feeling of union with the analyst as an idealized *paternal* selfobject in order to restore or maintain her sense of self-esteem [pp. 315–316].

In speaking of the termination phase, the authors concluded:

> The termination phase of Mary's treatment was ushered in when she decided to "give up hope" that her romantic and sexual wishes, now expressed openly and with passion, would ever find fulfillment with the analyst in reality. . . . On the one hand, she experienced the ending as a profound oedipal defeat. . . . Even more painful for Mary, however, was her experience of losing the analyst as a paternal selfobject. . . . She voiced fears that without the bond with him her life would become empty and devoid of meaning. . . . She spoke of plans for graduate work in literature and became immersed in writing an autobiographical novel—both an oedipal baby *and* transitional selfobject which helped her to give up *and* symbolically continue her oedipal *and* selfobject attachments to the analyst [pp. 317–318].

Summary and Implications

The pairing of selfobject transferences with object-related transferences precluded consideration of the patient's movement in treatment from what was described as an archaic selfobject tie, as being evidence of a developing selfobject transference without an interrelationship with an object-related transference. It can be suggested that the painful loss and "profound oedipal defeat" the patient suffered during termination, as well as her attempts to maintain the connection with treatment after termination through the writing of her autobiography, were confirmations that the analysis was incomplete as the patient was continuing to struggle with unrequited selfobject needs.

It can be further suggested that both the perception and understanding of the patient's selfobject needs were interrupted by the analyst's shift to a classical conceptualization. As a consequence, the analysis did not lead to the unfolding and development of the selfobject transference and to the transmuting of the patient's unrequited selfobject needs.

Redefining the Concept of Selfobject Transferences as a Class of Invariant Organizing Principles

From an intersubjective point of view, selfobject transferences are only one of many unconscious ways of organizing activity. They represent "one of a multiplicity of unconscious, automatic, and repetitive ways that patients organize their experience of the analyst. Selfobject transferences, in other words, are a class of invariant organizing principles" (Trop, 1994, p. 79). The patient comes to identify and understand the unconscious organizing principles as they emerge in the treatment. Successful psychoanalytic treatment is seen as facilitating the patient's establishment and consolidation of alternative organizing principles through new relational experiences with the analyst and through self-awareness (Stolorow and Atwood, 1992). Empathic inquiry is redefined as a method of investigating and illuminating the unconscious organizing principles (Stolorow, 1993).

The following interchange (Trop, 1994) is an example where the analyst attempts to help the patient establish an alternative organizing principle. In this case the patient's severe upset in his relationship with a woman friend was considered to be a deleterious replication of the way he unconsciously organized his experiences of abandonment:

> David came to a session in an acute state of agitation and rage. . . . Ruth had told him the night before that she was taking a walk and would be back in 10 minutes, but she actually returned in an hour. . . . She had never seen him so angry and she broke down in tears. . . . She had told him that she had been transfixed by the moon and the stars and had lost all concept of time, because the air and the stars were so beautiful. He looked at me intensely and said, "Can you believe that?!"' [p. 86].

In summarizing this interchange for the reader, the analyst concluded:

> He clearly was turning vigorously to me for support. He felt extremely upset . . . and wanted my validation for the correctness of his experience . . . I had always felt that David and I had developed a good rapport. . . . He had developed an idealizing transference. . . . I wondered if our tie would be damaged if I conveyed my perception of his vulnerability. Could David tolerate my communicating to him my understanding of the episode, which was distinctively different from

his? . . . I told David that I could certainly agree that what Ruth had done was an act of unreliability. I also said that it seemed clear that he wanted my support, not only as a confirmation that what she had done was unreliable, but for his perception that this meant there was something centrally flawed about Ruth. I told him that I was reluctant to support this perception because I felt there were feelings underlying his rage that would be valuable to explore. I said . . . that it felt to me that he was reacting as if she had chosen to be with the stars and had not chosen him . . . that his rage seemed to be an attempt to recover his equilibrium and that his anger had been codetermined by her thoughtlessness and by his automatically and unconsciously organizing her lateness to mean that he was not compelling and special to her. . . . Anything that engaged Ruth and took her away from him was experienced as a confirmation of some defect in himself. He smiled ruefully and asked plaintively, "Will this always sneak up on me; will I ever be free of this?" I replied that I was confident that he would come to recognize this pattern, but that I also thought there were aspects of his reactions that awaited further understanding [pp. 86–87].

After further exploration of the events leading to the organization of his experience, the analyst concluded:

He increasingly was able to recognize how he automatically assimilated Ruth's enthusiastic interest in other things as a confirmation of his defectiveness. . . . David now understood his reactions to Ruth as replicating the way he unconsciously organized his experiences of abandonment by both his mother and his father. . . . He has continued to develop a greater capacity for affect tolerance and self-reflection through our work together [pp. 88–89].

Summary and Implications

The analyst considered that the patient established an idealizing transference. He attempted to preserve the idealization as an effort to safeguard the treatment alliance by supporting his patient's belief that his friend's action was an unreliable one. Sensing that the treatment alliance was secure, the analyst then communicated his understanding of the organizing principle. The patient accepted the explanation but was concerned that he would never be free of his pattern. The analyst was confident that the patient would be free with further recognition of his pattern and with an understanding of his reactions. We learned that the patient eventually developed a greater capacity for affect tolerance and self-reflection, which were the major goals for treatment (Stolorow, 1993).

Since selfobject transferences were understood as a class of invariant organizing principles and the value of treatment was in the identification of and understanding the organizing principles, it followed that the patient's idealizing transference had no significance other than ensuring a treatment alliance for the purpose of elucidating the organizing principle. Therefore, there was no attention to the development and working through of the idealizing selfobject transference.

Since empathic inquiry was redefined as an investigation for the purpose of illuminating the organizing principle, there was no experience-near immersion to gain an awareness and understanding of the patient's selfobject needs and to allow for the working through and unfolding of the selfobject transferences. We, therefore, do not know what other selfobject transferences might have otherwise emerged and developed. Thus, it can be suggested that the patient was deprived of the growth process that takes place through this development. Had this growth process taken place, it can be further suggested that the patient's vulnerability and concern about being free of his characteristic reaction pattern would likely have diminished, as would his continuous need for affect tolerance.[5]

Redefining the Concept of Selfobject as an Object Relations Concept

In an earlier paper (Rowe, 1994) I suggested that there have been efforts at reformulating Kohut's concept of selfobject. Reformulations were directed at shifting the meaning of selfobject as the experience of the function that is provided by the analyst to the experience of the analyst as the provider of the function. This object relations conceptualization assumes that the direction of the patient's experience necessarily is to the object/analyst and by its assumption, disallows an unrestricted direction-free attunement to the patient's experience necessary to perceive, understand, and allow for the development of the selfobject transferences.

The reformulation of the concept of selfobject was clearly seen in Bacal's (1990) statement: "Self psychological theory has, in effect, focused on the experience of selfobject *function*, and has lost sight of the *object* that provides that function and of the importance of the *relationship* for the patient. Thus, I would add to Stolorow's caveat

---

[5] P. H. Ornstein (1995) makes a similar point in his discussion of Trop's 1994 paper. He stated: "Attending to the selfobject transferences results in the increase in self-cohesion that makes self-reflection possible and lessens the need for the repetitive deployment of the maladaptive 'invariant organizing principles' in new situations" (p. 75).

that the selfobject should be conceived of as a dimension of experiencing an object, that this experience is also embodied in a significant object" (p. 202). Bacal was referring to Stolorow's (1986) statement: "Thus, when we use the term 'selfobject,' we refer to an object experienced subjectively as serving selfobject functions" (p. 274).

In this chapter, I presented a treatment session where I made the assumption that the direction of my patient's experience was to me as an object. Briefly, my patient, Mr. Y, frequently suffered agonizing feelings of emptiness and depletion especially when pressured to fulfill work responsibilities within a specific time limit.

Mr. Y was late for his session and angrily described himself as feeling like a "dead man." He had overslept and did not have time for breakfast. He felt trapped and wanted to leave.

I was concerned that Mr. Y's feeling trapped was evidence of his feeling pressure by me to be on time. My reasoning was buttressed by my patient's earlier complaints that he felt pressured by me to keep regularly scheduled appointments and by my policy of charging when he missed. Because I thought it important to explore his reaction, reasoning that it could become a source of escalating resistance, I said, "I know we spoke about your feeling pressured by me to come to sessions—my being unfair. I wonder if that trapped feeling has something to do with me?" Mr. Y paused, sat up on the couch, and said, "I cannot believe you said that. I'm telling you that my guts are hanging out—a dead man—and you wonder about yourself. Now I think I really have to leave. Damn analysts! Everything has to revolve around the God analyst. Do you realize how difficult it is to tell you how bad I feel this morning? It's not just this morning but my whole life. You don't know that, do you? I never told anybody as much as I've told you." Mr. Y then stood and started to walk toward the door. He stopped and said, "I really have to think about this; this is not like you."

I was aware that shifting my focus from what Mr. Y was experiencing to myself as the object of his experience seriously disrupted the idealizing selfobject transference that had been established. This shift of focus prevented me from gaining the experience-near data that he was revealing, namely, a painful state of emptiness and hopelessness that permeated his life and transcended any specific experience. As we came to understand, this breach in the empathic process was especially devastating because it was a repeat of the relentless traumatic unempathic experiences he suffered throughout his childhood.

While my patient was able to respond to my understanding and continued treatment, the traumatic effects made it difficult for him to analyze his response and reestablish the idealizing selfobject transference.

CONCLUSION

If we are to appreciate fully the growing number of contributions emerging within self psychology, we must be able to delineate the distinctions between its theories (Rowe, 1996).

This chapter has highlighted theoretical and clinical distinctions inherent in recent contributions from those formulations of Kohut in terms of the effect on the understanding of the patient's selfobject needs and the development of the selfobject transferences. It has attempted to show how shifts in emphasis away from the selfobject transferences as the focal point of treatment seriously limits the patient's development.

Kohut (1984) acknowledged that there are varieties of selfobject transferences yet to be discovered: "that there are still transferences— probably varieties of selfobject transferences—that have not yet been discovered and which, therefore, remain unanalyzed" (p. 209). If we deemphasize the selfobject transferences as the focus of treatment, we are unlikely to discover these yet to be discovered transference needs. Therefore, if self psychology is to benefit fully from Kohut's foundational contribution to psychoanalysis, we must redouble our efforts to be alert to the patient's selfobject needs. This requires the following.

Furthering the Explorations of the Selfobject Transferences

Some of those explorations undertaken are as follows: the archaic forms of selfobject transferences (Goldberg, 1978b; Shapiro, 1985; Rowe and MacIsaac, 1989; Rowe, 1992), the resolution of a mirror transference (Goldberg, 1978a), the mirror transference in arrested development (Goldberg, 1978c), the mirror transference in the etiology of sexualization (Goldberg, 1993), pathognomic mirroring (Slade and Moskowitz, 1988), the idealizing transference (A. Ornstein, 1983; Hall, 1985), confrontation and the selfobject transference (London, 1983), the role of the selfobject transference in the process of desomatization (Brickman, 1992), alterego selfobject transference (Detrick, 1985), and the working-through process (Muslin, 1986; P. Ornstein, 1990).

Refining the Experience-Near Mode of Observation to Enhance the Perception of Selfobject Transferences

Thus far, discoveries of new forms of selfobject transferences have been limited. For example, with the exception of the introduction of the adversarial selfobject transference (Wolf, 1976, 1980), which has been largely neglected (Lichtenberg, 1990), there has been little in the literature that has fully illustrated new paradigms of selfobject needs.[6]

Discoveries of new forms of selfobject transferences are dependent upon our ability to perceive selfobject experiences that are not familiar and new editions of those selfobject experiences that are familiar. We must be able to perceive their developmental aspects in order to justify new classifications (Kohut, 1984).

The discovery process is not an easy one. It requires prolonged immersion into the patient's experience to become aware of intricacies of the patient's selfobject needs. This requirement necessarily exacerbates the analyst's anxieties through lengthy periods of tolerating the unfamiliar and at times diverse directions of the patient's experience. Dread of helplessness and inactivity can solidify resistances to in-depth exploration (Kohut, 1959).[7] Perhaps it is the difficulty of these requirements that account for the lack of attention in the literature to refining the observational process.[8]

Kohut's concept of selfobject and selfobject transferences are foundational to self psychology. However, it is only through continuing clinical exploration can we fully realize the import of his discovery.

REFERENCES

Bacal, H. (1990), Does an object relations theory exist in self psychology. *Psychoanal. Inq.*, 10:197–220.

Brickman, B. (1992), The desomatizing selfobject transference: A case report. In: *New Therapeutic Visions: Progress in Self Psychology, Vol. 8*, ed. A. Goldberg. Hillsdale, NJ: The Analytic Press, pp. 93–108.

Detrick, D. (1985), Alterego phenomena and the alterego transferences. In: *Progress in Self Psychology, Vol. 1*, ed. A. Goldberg. New York: Guilford Press, pp. 240–256.

Fosshage, J. (1990a), Clinical protocol. *Psychoanal. Inq.*, 10:461–477.

——— (1990b), The analyst's response. *Psychoanal. Inq.*, 10:601–622.

---

[6] Lachmann has described how adversarial experiences can serve selfobject functions (1986). Wolf also considered the vitalization-attunement experience, introduced by Stern (1985) as "vitality affects," a selfobject experience (Hunter, 1992).

[7] Kohut (1981), in his final extemporaneous address at the Fifth Conference on Self Psychology at Berkeley, California, in October 1981, expressed his concern about the persistent misinterpretation and the devaluation of empathy as merely being supportive.

[8] Dr. David MacIsaac and I (Rowe and MacIsaac, 1989; Rowe, 1997) have attempted to contribute to the refining of the experience-near mode of observation through developing a form of receptivity, which we have termed "expanding attunement."

Goldberg, A. (1978a), The resolution of a mirror transference: Clinical emphasis on the termination phase. In: *The Psychology of the Self: A Casebook,* ed. A. Goldberg. New York: International Universities Press, pp. 13–120.

───── (1978b), Transformation of archaic narcissism. In: *The Psychology of the Self: A Casebook,* ed. A. Goldberg. New York: International Universities Press, pp. 121–163.

───── (1978c), Analysis of a mirror transference in a case of arrested development. In: *The Psychology of the Self: A Casebook,* ed. A. Goldberg. New York: International Universities Press, pp. 263–296.

Goldberg, C. (1993), The peripheral position of sex in a psychotherapy: An illustrative case of a mirror transference. *Clin. Soc. Work J.,* 21:365–373.

Hall, J. (1985), Idealizing transference: Disruptions and repairs. In: *Progress in Self Psychology, Vol. 1,* ed. A. Goldberg. New York: Guilford Press, pp. 109–146.

Hunter, V. (1992), An interview with Ernest Wolf part II: The analytic years to 1990. *Psychoanal. Rev.,* 79:481–507.

Kohut, H. (1959), Introspection, empathy, and psychoanalysis: An examination of the relationship between mode of observation and theory. In: *The Search for the Self, Vol. 1,* ed. P. Ornstein. New York: International Universities Press, 1978, pp. 205–232.

───── (1968a), Introspection and empathy: Further thoughts about their role in psychoanalysis. In: *The Search for the Self, Vol. 3,* ed. P. Ornstein. Madison, CT: International Universities Press, 1990, pp. 83–101.

───── (1968b), The psychoanalytic treatment of narcissistic personality disorders: Outline of a systematic approach In: *The Search for the Self. Vol. 1,* ed. P. Ornstein. New York: International Universities Press, 1978, pp. 477–509.

───── (1977), *The Restoration of the Self.* New York: International Universities Press.

───── (1979), Four basic concepts in self psychology. In: *The Search for the Self, Vol. 4,* ed. P. Ornstein. Madison, CT: International Universities Press, 1991, pp. 447–470.

───── (1981), On empathy. In: *The Search for the Self, Vol. 4,* ed. P. Ornstein. Madison, CT: International Universities Press, 1991, pp. 525–535.

───── (1984), *How Does Analysis Cure?* ed. A. Goldberg & P. Stepansky. Chicago: University of Chicago Press.

Lachmann, F. (1986), Interpretation of physic conflict and adversarial relationships: A self- psychological perspective. *Psychoanal. Psychol.,* 3:341–355.

───── & Beebe, B. (1992), Representational and selfobject transferences: A developmental perspective. In: *New Therapeutic Visions: Progress in Self Psychology, Vol. 8,* ed. A. Goldberg. Hillsdale, NJ: The Analytic Press, pp. 3–15.

───── & ───── (1995a), Self psychology today. *Psychoanal. Dial.,* 5:375–384.

───── & ───── (1995b), Self psychology: Later, the same day: Response to editors' follow-up questions. *Psychoanal. Dial.,* 5:415–419.

Lichtenberg, J. (1989), *Psychoanalysis and Motivation.* Hillsdale, NJ: The Analytic Press.

───── (1990), Rethinking the scope of the patient's transference and the therapist's counterresponsiveness. In: *The Realities of the Transference: Progress in Self Psychology, Vol. 6,* ed. A. Goldberg. Hillsdale, NJ: The Analytic Press, pp. 23–33.

——— Lachmann, F. & Fosshage, J. (1992), *Self and Motivational Systems: Toward a Theory of Psychoanalytic Technique*. Hillsdale, NJ: The Analytic Press.

——— ——— & ——— (1996), *The Clinical Exchange: Techniques Derived from Self and Motivational Systems*. Hillsdale, NJ: The Analytic Press.

London, N. (1983), Confrontation and selfobject transference: A case study. In: *Reflections on Self Psychology*, ed. J. Lichtenberg & S. Kaplan. Hillsdale, NJ: The Analytic Press, pp. 247–267.

Muslin, H. (1986), On working through in self psychology. In: *Progress in Self Psychology, Vol. 2*, ed. A. Goldberg. New York: Guilford Press, pp. 280–298.

Ornstein, A. (1983), An idealizing transference of the oedipal phase. In: *Reflections on Self Psychology*, ed. J. Lichtenberg & S. Kaplan. Hillsdale, NJ: The Analytic Press, pp. 135–148.

——— (1990), Selfobject transferences and the process of working through. In: *The Realities of Transference: Progress in Self Psychology, Vol. 6*, ed. A. Goldberg. Hillsdale, NJ: The Analytic Press, pp. 41–58.

Ornstein, P. H. (1990), How to "enter" a psychoanalytic process conducted by another analyst: A self psychology view. *Psychoanal. Inq.*, 10:478–497.

——— (1995), Critical reflections on a comparative analysis of "self psychology and intersubjectivity theory." In: *The Impact of New Ideas: Progress in Self Psychology, Vol. 11*, ed. A. Goldberg. Hillsdale, NJ: The Analytic Press, pp. 47–77.

Rowe, C. (1992), Development from archaic to mature selfobject transferences. *Clin. Soc. Work J.*, 20:31–45.

——— (1994), Reformulations of the concept of selfobject: A misalliance of self psychology with object relations theory. In: *A Decade of Progress: Progress in Self Psychology, Vol. 10*, ed. A. Goldberg. Hillsdale, NJ: The Analytic Press, pp. 9–20.

——— (1996), Introduction: Notes on the integration, reformulation, and development of Kohut's contributions. In: *Basic Ideas Reconsidered: Progress in Self Psychology, Vol. 12*, ed. A. Goldberg. Hillsdale, NJ: The Analytic Press, xiii–xxii.

——— (1997), Expanding attunement: A contribution to the experience-near mode of observation. In: *Empathy Reconsidered*, ed. A. Bohart & L. Greenberg. Washington, D.C.: American Psychological Association, pp. 265–278.

——— & MacIsaac, D. (1989), *Empathic Attunement: The "Technique" of Psychoanalytic Self Psychology*. Northvale, NJ: Aronson.

Shapiro, S. (1985), Archaic selfobject transferences in the analysis of a case of male homosexuality. In: *Progress in Self Psychology, Vol. 1*, ed. A. Goldberg. New York: Guilford Press, pp. 164–177.

Slade, D. & Moskowitz, L. (1988), Pathognomic mirroring and the organization of experience: A developmental factor in self pathology. In: *Frontiers in Self Psychology: Progress in Self Psychology: Vol. 3*, ed. A. Goldberg. Hillsdale, NJ: The Analytic Press, pp. 177–194.

Stern, D. (1985), *The Interpersonal World of the Infant*. New York: Basic Books.

Stolorow, R. (1986), On experiencing an object: A multidimensional perspective. In: *Progress in Self Psychology, Vol. 2*, ed. A. Goldberg. New York: Guilford Press, pp. 273–279.

——— (1993), Thoughts on the nature and therapeutic action of psychoanalytic interpretation. In: *The Widening Scope of Self Psychology: Progress in Self*

Psychology, Vol. 9, ed. A. Goldberg. Hillsdale, NJ: The Analytic Press, pp. 31–43.

———— & Atwood, G. (1992), Contexts of Being: The Intersubjective Foundations of Psychological Life. Hillsdale, NJ: The Analytic Press.

———— & Lachmann, F. (1981), Two psychoanalyses or one? Psychoanal. Rev., 68:307–319.

———— & ———— (1984/85), Transference: The future of an illusion. The Annual of Psychoanalysis, 12/13:19–37. New York: International Universities Press.

Trop, J. (1994), Self psychology and intersubjectivity theory. In: The Intersubjective Perspective, ed. R. Stolorow, G. Atwood & B. Brandchaft. Northvale, NJ: Aronson, pp. 77–91.

Wolf, E. S. (1976), Ambience and abstinence. The Annual of Psychoanalysis. 4:101–115. New York: International Universities Press.

———— (1980), On the developmental line of selfobject relations. In: Advances in Self Psychology, ed. A. Goldberg. New York: International Universities Press, pp. 117–130.

Chapter 3

The Selfobject Function of Interpretation

Peter Buirski
Pamela Haglund

Critics of self psychology mistakenly assume that the therapeutic action of self psychology is primarily found in the provision of empathy. Thus, they conclude, somewhat dismissively, that self psychology is a superficial therapy because it is merely another version of the discredited corrective emotional experience. One of the reasons for the failure of critics to appreciate the richness and depth of the self psychological approach to treatment has been the difficulty for self psychology of incorporating the role of interpretation into the theory of selfobject functioning. The aim of this chapter is to locate interpretation firmly within the theory of selfobject functioning.

Traditionally, psychoanalytic theoreticians have sought the therapeutic action of psychoanalysis in various activities of the analyst. The Freudian school has located the therapeutic action in interpretation, conceptualized primarily as cognitive processes whereby the analyst transmits new knowledge or insight to the patient. Relational theorists have emphasized that the therapeutic action resides in the new experience that analyst and patient construct together out of their relationship. For self psychology, the therapeutic action is generally believed to derive from the provision of selfobject functions that mobilize thwarted developmental needs.

Interpretation is a term burdened with history. It derives from the classical literature where the focus was on making the unconscious conscious through attaching word cathexes to preconscious thoughts

(Freud, 1915). Freud (1900) used *interpretation (Deutung)* to describe his procedures for discerning the unconscious meanings of dreams and parapraxes. As Freud (1913a) explained, "The interpretation of dreams has as its object the removal of the disguise to which the dreamer's thoughts have been subjected" (p. 210). "Interpretation" here is being used in the sense of finding a "solution" to the puzzling mental phenomenon (Freud, 1913b). In the sense that it is generally used, *interpretation* refers to the analyst's communication of the "solution" to the patient. The emphasis is placed squarely on the analyst's promoting cognitive insight by conveying new cognitive knowledge to the patient about the contents of the patient's unconscious longings or defenses against such knowing. Within this tradition, Arlow (1987) regards "the principle function of the psychoanalyst to be the giving of interpretations" (p. 69). From this perspective, the transmission of the analyst's cognitive insights into the mental functioning of the patient, through the verbal procedure of interpretation, is the principle therapeutic action of ego psychology, even if the insight forms in the mind of the analyst as an outgrowth of his/her relationship with the patient. There seems to be agreement that for the cognitive component to have therapeutic impact, it must resonate emotionally for the patient (Neubauer, 1980).

From the perspective of self psychology, Kohut (1984) articulated a transitional position, retaining, at least in theory, the role of the analyst as objective observer, while simultaneously emphasizing the primary importance of understanding gained through an empathic bond. Others have discussed the confusion in Kohut's writings between the use of empathy as an observational stance and as a description of the relationship that facilitates therapeutic action (Stolorow, Brandchaft, and Atwood, 1987). Kohut (1984) recognized that a therapeutic intervention consists of two interdependent steps: the analyst's empathic understanding of the patient and communication of this understanding to the patient through explanation (p. 94). Following from the self psychological tradition, Stolorow's (1994) definition of a psychoanalytic interpretation as "an act of illuminating *personal* meaning" (p. 43) is a formulation broad enough to be acceptable to most psychoanalytic schools of thought. Where psychoanalytic schools may differ is on how personal meanings can be best illuminated.

The two poles of the debate on the therapeutic action of psychoanalysis are represented on the one hand by ego psychology, which emphasizes the transmission of new cognitive understanding and on the other hand by self psychology, which stresses that the therapeutic action is to be found in the new selfobject experiences that come from feeling understood. Atwood and Stolorow (1984) have suggested that both are important and indivisible: "Every transference interpretation that successfully illuminates for the patient his unconscious past simultaneously crystallizes an illusive present—the novelty of the therapist as an understanding presence. Perceptions of self and other are perforce transformed and reshaped to allow for the new experience" (p. 60). In other words, whenever new cognitive knowledge is accepted by the patient as a meaningful formulation of his/her inner experience, the patient also has a new experience of feeling understood. Therefore, interpretations work on two levels: the level of cognitive understanding, where new knowledge is assimilated, and the developmental level, where needed selfobject functions are experienced through the therapist's affect attunement. The tendency to dichotomize the therapeutic action into a cognitive component and an affective component is seemingly resolved by this stance that accurate transference interpretations convey both (Terman, 1989). But the emphasis still seems to be that new cognitive knowledge provided through interpretation has therapeutic effect largely *because* it is packaged with the selfobject experience of feeling emotionally understood.

In contrast to Kohut's (1977, 1984) view of the curative process, which invoked optimal frustration and transmuting internalization, Bacal (1990) has suggested that the curative process involves a corrective selfobject experience. The notion here is that psychopathology results from archaic developmental longings being disrupted by a failing selfobject relationship with the caregivers. By restoring a needed selfobject tie, thwarted developmental longings will be remobilized in the safety of the attuned selfobject relationship. Hence, "the internalization of the cohesion-fostering selfobject tie constitutes the essence of what is the therapeutic, or 'corrective' experience in analysis" (Bacal and Newman, 1990, p. 258).

We would like to further the discussion of the locus of the therapeutic action in self psychology by pulling together the three themes in the debate: enhanced cognitive understanding, the experience of feeling understood, and selfobject functioning. We propose that any interpretation that conveys new cognitive understanding finds its therapeutic action in the selfobject functions that it provides. That is, new cognitive understanding not only satisfies the longing to be understood, but the function of making sense of the totality of one's life experience also promotes self-understanding, self-delineation, self-continuity, and self-cohesion. Furthermore, new self-understanding contributes to the construction of new organizations of experience.

Patients respond to the analyst's verbal communications in varied and complex ways. To us, the words chosen by the analyst, in and of themselves, have significance. As human beings, we have unique capacities for language and for construing meaning. It is precisely the potential selfobject function of the analyst's verbal communication that we address in this chapter.

In examining what we refer to as the selfobject function of interpretation, we favor Donna Orange's formulation of selfobject experience occurring within the context of selfobject relatedness. According to Orange (1995), "Selfobject relatedness is the person's experience, at any age, of a significant human other or attachment figure as support for the establishment, development, and maintenance of continuous, cohesive, and positive self-experience" (p. 177). The subjective experience of the analyst and his or her interpretive activities provides vitally needed capacities that are missing from the patient's psychological makeup. Subjective experience and the associated meaning made of it by the patient form the basis for the largely unconscious organizing principles the patient constructs. These organizing configurations and affects associated with them become the focus of the therapist's sustained empathic inquiry. We propose that verbal interpretations of such complex, affectively charged configurations are subjectively experienced as providing selfobject functions, specifically through promoting the experience of self-understanding. New self-understanding promotes the sense of historical self-continuity that one's current organization of experience is meaningfully connected to past experience. In this case, the selfobject function of interpretation derives from the patient's ability to use the interpretation to further self-understanding. The importance of self-understanding to the articulation of new organizations of experience has not previously been fully appreciated.

Traditionally, interpretation derived from a one-person stance in which the analyst is the authority on the truth of the patient's inner experience (Fosshage, 1995). As such, the term *interpretation,* as used in modern relational thinking, is anachronistic; it is a derivative of the myth of the isolated mind (Stolorow and Atwood, 1992). Postmodern thinking emphasizes the co-construction of personal meaning. In referring to "interpretation," we are specifically addressing the verbal component of putting into words the analyst's understanding of the patient's subjective experience as acquired through the process of sustained empathic inquiry.

Since Freud, analysts have questioned whether words alone produce therapeutic effects. Ego psychologists accept that, for new cognitive meanings to be assimilated, the verbal interpretation needs to connect with some affective charge. We would like to refine this notion by proposing that verbal interpretations will convey cognitive and affective understanding only within the context of primary selfobject relatedness (Orange, 1995). Verbal interpretations are an important part of the process that allows for the conscious recognition and reevaluation of archaic organizations of experience and the emergence of new organizing principles. By putting the patient's subjective experience into words, the analyst provides vital selfobject functions that promote self-cohesion and the integration of affect into experience.

Humans are meaning makers, and as Orange (1995) has pointed out, "The urge to make sense is distinctively human" (p. 6). According to Orange, "Healthy humans have a developing and lifelong propensity to reflect, to organize experience variously, and especially to wonder and to converse about meanings. . . . Psychoanalysis is a special conversation about meaning; it is an attempt of analyst and patient to make sense together of the patient's emotional life" (p. 7). As humans we have a unique capacity for symbolic representation. At approximately 18 months the human child develops the capacity for language and, with the acquisition of language, memory, communication, and organization of experience, are irrevocably altered. Not only is linear, secondary processing acquired, but through the maturation of the frontal cortex and associational pathways, primary process representation becomes accessible (Lichtenberg, Lachmann, and Fosshage, 1996, p. 82).

Levin (1991) discusses at length many possible ways of understanding the effectiveness of psychoanalysis (particularly transference interpretations) in terms of the emerging knowledge about functional neuroscience. According to Levin, metaphorical language, used spontaneously by an analyst, may serve as a bridge among multiple levels of neurological functioning. For example, an interpretation framed as a metaphor may link modalities of touch, hearing, and sight; it can bridge past and present experiences simultaneously; it might connect affect with a narration of experience; and it could allow for associations among different developmental levels of cognitive processing (such as preverbal sensorimotor experiences and, later, more advanced levels of symbolic representation). The ambiguity of the metaphor and its implicit comparison between that which is similar and yet not identical allows for simultaneous multiple processing in the brain by which new associations and therefore new understandings can emerge.

Children suffering from alexithymia present another instance of the developmental imperative of putting words to feelings. By verbally labeling emotional experience, children can be helped to identify and think about their feelings, thereby promoting the organization and integration of affect. According to Reckling and Buirski (1996), "Without the capacity to think about feelings, children will not develop the ability to identify and verbally express affect and will likely continue to express affect somatically. The caregivers' inadequate articulation of their child's affect states interferes with the child's development of a capacity to desomatize and identify affects" (p. 85).

Our position is not that verbal interpretations of the patient's archaic organizing principles are the primary or even necessary component of therapeutic action. We have certainly been impressed with Lachmann and Beebe's (1996) demonstration of the importance of nonverbal interaction on therapeutic growth. What we are trying to emphasize is that putting into words the patient's developmental dynamics has the selfobject function of promoting self-understanding— the understanding of one's organization of experience in the context of one's personal development. Such self-understanding promotes a sense of self-delineation, self-continuity, and self-cohesion. Understanding how one's experience has become organized and the developmental context and constraints in which this organization took shape gives coherence to one's life. For example, through verbal interpretation, an adult male patient developed the awareness that his anger, which served as a shield to ward off hurtful disregard by his parents and formed a protective armor against a threatening world, while vital to his survival as a child, now functions to keep potential good objects at a distance. This understanding now provides the patient with a template against which to assess the dangers of new relationships, as well as a signpost to his self-protective behavior. He understands that, when he finds himself enraged, behind this lurks an archaic conviction of his vulnerability to the presently perceived threat of retraumatization.

Building on our formulation that interpretations given in the context of a primary selfobject relationship provide important selfobject functions, we would now like to explore the question of the accuracy or exactness of interpretations. It is in just this arena that the different perspectives of historical truth and narrative truth collide.

Freud pursued historical truth. Using the archeological metaphor, he sought to excavate the buried unconscious layers and unearth veridical memories of past experience. The important tool in excavating the past was interpretation or genetic reconstruction. According to Freud (1937),

> The path that starts from the analyst's construction ought to end in the patient's recollection; but it does not always lead so far. Quite often we do not succeed in bringing the patient to recollect what has been repressed. Instead of that, if the analysis is carried out correctly, we produce in him an assured conviction of the truth of the construction which achieves the same therapeutic result as a recaptured memory [pp. 265–266].

For Freud, the 19th-century positivist, "an assured conviction of the truth" referred to his belief in the objectivity of truth, as opposed to the postmodern view of the relativity of truth. In this vein then, Freud stressed the therapeutic importance of the accuracy of the construction, even while acknowledging that the therapist arrives at the accurate construction through successive approximations.

As much as Freud stressed the therapeutic importance of accurate interpretations or constructions, he minimized the effect of inaccurate ones. As he clearly stated (1937),

> No damage is done if, for once in a way, we make a mistake and offer the patient a wrong construction as the probable historical truth. . . . A single mistake of the sort can do no harm. What in fact occurs in such an event is rather that the patient remains as though he were untouched by what has been said and reacts to it with neither a "Yes" nor a "No". . . . If nothing further develops we may conclude that we have made a mistake and we shall admit as much to the patient at some suitable opportunity without sacrificing any of our authority. Such an opportunity will arise when some new material has come to light which allows us to make a better construction and so to correct our error. In this way the false construction drops out, as if it had never been made. . . . The danger of our leading a patient astray by suggestion, by persuading him to accept things which we ourselves believe but which he ought not to, has certainly been enormously exaggerated [pp. 261–262].

Glover (1931) in his famous paper, "The Therapeutic Effect of Inexact Interpretation" (published six years before the Freud paper quoted earlier), takes the opposite position. Glover's view is that an incorrect or inexact interpretation is utilized by the patient as a "displacement-substitute" (p. 356). Such substitutes act like suggestions; they may "bring about improvement in the symptomatic sense at the cost of refractoriness to deeper analysis" (p. 356).

Modern relational thinking discards the notion of historical truth in favor of a hermeneutics/constructivist approach (Mitchell, 1993). As Mitchell summarizes it, "The patient's experiences, associations, and memories can be integrated or organized in innumerable ways. The organizational scheme arrived at is a dual creation, shaped partly by the patient's material but also inevitably shaped by the analyst's patterns of thought, or theory. The 'meaning' of clinical material does not exist until it is named—it is not uncovered but created" (p. 58).

From this perspective, it is meaningless to apply the criterion of accuracy or exactness to an interpretation or construction. An interpretation, given by an analyst to a patient, represents the analyst's experience of the patient's subjectivity, filtered through the analyst's subjectivity, which includes the analyst's theoretical system. It is an outgrowth of the context in which it forms in the mind of the analyst.

Thus, an interpretation is not an expression of some objective truth about the patient's experience. It is the way in which the analyst has organized his/her understanding of the patient at this moment, in this place, in this immediate context. This particular organization of experience will necessarily change with the changes in the context of the therapeutic relationship. Interpretations, within the hermeneutic/constructivist perspective, are not successive approximations of the truth about the patient's past but are constructions about the patient's current subjective organization of experience. The meaningfulness of the interpretation to the patient depends on the selfobject functions provided by the formulation. We judge the clinical usefulness of an interpretation or construction, not by its proximity to some criterion of truth, but by whether or not the patient finds the interpretation personally meaningful. A personally meaningful interpretation is one that leads the patient to new ways of organizing his/her experience, that is, new self-understanding that is growth enhancing.

We have all probably encountered patients for whom belief in God is a profoundly organizing experience. Questions about the existence of God are irrelevant to the therapeutic enterprise. Belief in God helps organize these patients' experiences of themselves in the world. Other belief systems have similar effects. Interpretations, being constructed out of the experiences of both patient and analyst, are another form of belief system. The patient accepts the analyst's interpretation because the patient experiences it as personally meaningful and because it helps organize the patient's experience, or the patient may reject the interpretation because it is experienced as nonorganizing or, at worst, disorganizing. Such understandings or ways of organizing experience are not fixed but are subject to being modified or replaced as newer understandings or organizations of experience are constructed.

Even though we are dispensing with the notion of true or accurate interpretations, we nevertheless believe that some misuses of interpretation or reconstruction can ultimately be hurtful to the patient's development. Interpretations or constructions that move beyond a focus on illuminating the patient's subjective experience, relational configurations, and affect but aim instead to reconstruct memories of actual events presumed to have taken place in the patient's past and reside in the patient's unconscious are potentially very destructive. Such interpretations as "Your dream is the dream of someone who has been sexually abused by her father" is the type of destructive interpretation that purports to reconstruct some piece of real experience out of the cloth of subjective experience. One cannot derive objective reality from subjective experience. This is the flaw in the archeological analogy. Freud believed that, by sifting through the strata of the unconscious, one could unearth real artifacts of a patient's buried past. Take for example Freud's (1918) analysis of the Wolf Man's dream. Freud reconstructed that his patient had literally observed his parents having intercourse *a tergo*, three times, at five o'clock in the afternoon (Buirski and Haglund, 1998). Objective reality can only be known through applying the scientific method of empirical observation, not from psychoanalytic exploration of personal meanings.

On a television news magazine program some time ago, a patient in "past lives therapy" and his therapist were being interviewed. The therapist reported that the patient, who had come for treatment because of his fear of water, had, under hypnosis, been regressed back to a prior life. It was uncovered that in the 17th century, the patient had drowned in a shipwreck. The patient reported that recovering the memory of this prior life experience had been extremely helpful, and he experienced relief from his fear of water.

Following the line of thought we have been developing, the recovery of the prior life experience offered the patient a new way of understanding himself and organizing his experience. The new understanding grew out of a primary selfobject relationship that facilitated the patient's receptivity to it. What is critical is that the formulation functions as a selfobject experience, providing patients with a new understanding of themselves that structures their organization of experience in a new way. However, this kind of interpretation, while organizing on one level, fosters defensive rigidification rather than promoting growth and self-development.

Many of the ideas put forth in this chapter represent themes dramatically interwoven in the False Memory Syndrome controversy (see the "Symposium on 'False Memory' Controversy" in *Psychoanalytic Dialogues*, 1996, 6 [2]). While a complete discussion of the controversy is not possible in the context of this chapter, the relativity of "truth" in the co-constructed understanding developed in psychoanalytic treatment between patient and analyst must be considered. From the intersubjective perspective, the personal meaning of memories, fantasies, and experiences is the focus of analytic inquiry, and such meaning is not assumed to correspond to observable events, past or present. However, it seems imperative that patient and analyst explicitly discuss the subjective nature of their constructions. Harris (1996) articulates a position with which we concur:

> We need to assert the importance of provisional knowing, of inquiry, and of creating climates of respect and support. . . . This attention to the potential for distorted listening does not rule out the importance of validating the patient's experience where possible; but when the

analyst moves beyond or beneath the experience of the patient, the grounds for doing so must be open for shared inquiry and meaning making [pp. 183–184].

Verbal interpretations always occur within an intersubjective field, and the patient's subjective experience of receiving interpretations can be as complex as the therapist's motives for giving them. They may be experienced as blaming or gratifying, loving or destructive, genuine or manipulative, depending on the particular intersubjective context. But for verbal interpretations to generate meaningful cognitive and emotional understanding, they must be given within the context of a primary selfobject relationship. Interpretations convey the selfobject functions of self-understanding, self-delineation, self-cohesion, and self-continuity. In the clinical material that follows, we will try to illustrate these points.

CLINICAL MATERIAL

The patient is a 36-year-old woman with a history of hospitalizations for suicidality, who came for treatment to a clinic associated with a training program. Her current symptoms include head-banging and cutting on herself. To illustrate the selfobject function of verbal interpretations, we have chosen to follow three themes over the course of the initial two consultation sessions. The cumulative effect of putting the patient's experience into words appears to have helped make her past and her present more comprehensible to her and, therefore, we suggest, contributed to her understanding of herself in a way that enhanced a cohesive and continuous sense of self. While this chapter is not intended to demonstrate the feasibility of short-term treatment, we have chosen only to use material from the first two consultation sessions in order to illustrate the power of interpretations delivered within the context of a quickly forming selfobject relationship.

In the opening remarks of session #1, responding to the analyst's invitation to describe what brought her into treatment, the patient begins:

Patient: (describing her experience of hospitalization the previous year)
            . . . Some issues within myself which are not resolved. I didn't
            feel on kilter, not who I really am. Does this make sense? I feel
            hopeless. I get a black feeling inside myself that wells up, very
            black.
Analyst: Is it related to feelings that led to your hospitalization?
Patient: Yes, I think so. . . . I have trouble differentiating what is
            really happening. . . . I have difficulty expressing myself well
            and making myself understood.

In this summary of the first exchanges between analyst and patient, three themes have been articulated by the patient that the analyst will track and clarify with her over the two sessions: first, her experience that she does not "make sense," that she cannot make herself understood; second, her unstable sense of self, that she is "not who she really is"; and third, her description of a black feeling inside her, which is connected with such extensive personal disruption that she has required hospitalization in the past. Of course, these themes have been artificially separated in order to simplify illustration of the subsequent effect of the analyst's responses.

This patient goes on to express her subjective experience of a lack of a cohesive sense of self in the absence of mirroring selfobject reflection. The patient presents a developmental dilemma which she reveals by repeatedly asking, "Does this make sense?" Through this question, the patient is raising the possibility that, if the analyst can understand her, then perhaps she can grasp who she is. Tracking the theme of making sense, the analyst responds to her statement that she has difficulty making herself understood:

Analyst: You're awfully worried about making sense. Have you had the experience of being misunderstood?
Patient: I find that I have difficulty expressing myself well, to get my meaning across.
Analyst: You're feeling that it's your problem in communicating, rather than people's problem in listening?
Patient: Must be.
Analyst: Must be (with a smile). (The nonverbal communication conveys that the analyst is leaving open to question that her problem is an inability to communicate.)

At this point the patient blames herself for her inability to communicate; she identifies the problem as one of her manner of delivery and expression. However, as the analyst invites her to explore with whom and in what contexts she feels she fails to communicate well, the patient reveals that the problem is almost exclusively manifested in close personal relationships, such as with both her present and former husbands and her mother. For example, with her mother and sisters who did not visit her during her hospitalization:

Analyst: You were hurt by that.
Patient: I was hurt by that because I have pretty much gone out of my way for everybody, and . . . that's my role in the family.
Analyst: Your role is to help everybody else.
Patient: Right (said with surprise). I basically was (sighs), when people had problems they would come and dump them on me, and I would help them, or listen to them and . . .

Analyst: But nobody listens to you.

Patient: Right. . . . At that point when I knew I was not together mentally. . . . (She describes how her sister tried to get her to take care of her children and became indignant when the patient expressed unwillingness to take on that responsibility.)

Analyst: She wasn't hearing you.

Patient: Right. Exactly.

Analyst: She wasn't hearing what you needed.

Patient: Right. Right. Exactly. I think, I have a problem with my family. They don't hear me. They definitely don't hear me. I have a picture, as a matter of fact, that I drew in art therapy. It was really weird because I'm a little girl, kneeling. And my family . . . it's just their heads, and they're real huge, and they're looking away from me. And none of them have ears.

Analyst: So they're not hearing you and they're not seeing you.

From this point in the session, the patient focuses in-depth on her relationship with her current husband and how, in her wish to meet his needs, she has lost some respect for herself. As she tried to communicate her experience to her husband, he did not respond. She feels unable to make things change, unable to stop the course that their relationship is taking.

Patient: . . . I feel like I can't talk to him, you know. I mean, you reach a point. . . . At least I've reached the point where when I feel like it doesn't matter what I say . . . there's no point in trying to say anything.

Analyst: He's not going to hear you.

The patient moves now to exploring an area in which she does not feel hopeless, her relationship with her children. She contrasts these relationships to her relationship with her own mother, and again the theme of listening and being heard emerges.

Analyst: And they (her children) can listen to you?

Patient: Yeah . . . That, too. That, too. I try not to be like my mom was. My mom was definitely, "Listen to me. Listen to me. Be my friend." I try not to be that. I try to listen to the things that they have to say. I try to learn . . .

And the session ends with the following exchange.

Analyst: Do you have any thoughts about our meeting today?

Patient: Yeah . . . It's intense. I don't really talk about this stuff very much.

Analyst: It stirred up a lot of feelings.
Patient: Yeah, pretty much. I get jumbled and I jump around . . . pretty much.
Analyst: I think I've been able to follow you.
Patient: (Laughs) I appreciate that. It's an accomplishment.

The second session begins with the patient's thoughts about the previous week's session.

Patient: . . . I thought about the part where we talked about me not being heard. And I think that is pretty much true. Yeah. Very much true. I don't seem to have that problem communicating to people that I'm not in a close relationship with.

At this point the patient develops an extensive description of an incident earlier in the week in which she and her husband argued about the behavior of his 18-year-old son and the son's thoughtless use of a car that is her only means of transportation. Relating the incident and her subsequent efforts to get support from her husband, she states:

Patient: You know, after a while, when you try to talk to somebody and they're not hearing you, you give up. What is the point of even trying?
Analyst: You feel it's hopeless to get him to hear you?
Patient: Yeah, because, it's like, I'm in a no-win situation. . . . And he just doesn't listen to me at all.

From this point in session #2 the patient produces material that illuminates her unwillingness to continue trying to make herself understood. Her first husband was physically abusive to her, and she associates her attempts to assert herself and her position with her second husband and stepson with the past violence. Furthering her associations, she relates feelings of being alone and unsupported and in physical danger in her efforts to deal with her stepson.

Patient: I can never stand up for myself. It's like that is my lot in life. Do you know what I'm saying? And this has been my whole life. And I don't want to be like that. It's Hell to live in your own home, and not be free. . . .
Analyst: So, the safest course is not to be seen, not to be heard.
Patient: That's pretty much it. Which really sucks, because I feel like (crying and sighing deeply). . . . For a while I had been in a coma, for ten years or so. You know, I mean, my *self*. Because I started finally thinking of myself as a person instead of, "I need to do this for this person, this for this person, I need to take care of my mother, I need to do this for my

husband, and I need to be there for my kids. . . ." And I
finally started thinking "well, I don't do anything for myself."
And I started just taking a little time for myself. I felt like I was
waking up, the "inner me," who I am, not who anybody else
needs me to be. I don't know how to hang on to it (crying).

Analyst: It seems like in the face of (husband and stepson's) criticism,
it's hard to hold on to who you are.

In the above interchange, the patient shifts from the initial theme of
not being understood to the second, not knowing who she is. The
analyst has consistently put into words her immediate experience of
not being heard and in doing so, has apparently identified one pervasive dynamic of her intimate relationships, a core organizing principle—
that people close to her do not listen to her or hear her. By putting
words to this organizing principle, the analyst has both provided an
experience in which she does feel heard and understood and simultaneously has provided her the *understanding* that while she has not
felt heard or understood by important people in her life, it is not the
fault of any deficiency in her ability to communicate. From this new
position, she is willing to move into a slightly different kind of "making
sense," the area of identity.

Patient: I don't even know what to be. I don't know how to be.
Analyst: You want to please him?
Patient: Yeah. I don't know. I'm too aggressive; I'm not aggressive
enough. I'm subservient.
Analyst: It sounds like you feel that he doesn't approve of you however
you are. You never get it right.
Patient: Maybe that's it.
Analyst: You're always feeling disapproved of?
Patient: I guess not when I'm what he wants me to be. But I never
know exactly. . . . It's like, sometimes you get it. But that's
not me. Does that make sense?
Analyst: So he approves of you when you're the way he wants you to
be. . . .
Patient: Right. Which is never consistent.
Analyst: It's not always clear to you what that is.
Patient: Right. That's . . . right. Right.

The patient moves with the analyst more deeply into her internal
process as she begins to lose her sense of herself in the face of conflict
with her husband, especially conflict in which she feels she is not being heard.

Patient: My husband can tell me "I know that it's not just you," but
he's not saying anything to his son, so it's all just me. Does

that make sense? He may say, "I know that," but for him to only address me. . . .

Analyst: It's like saying that *you're* the problem. And you don't feel strong enough to know inside that it's not you.

Patient: Right. I don't. For a while there I thought it wasn't me. And now I don't know . . . , and I'm, uh . . .

Analyst: You get confused.

The patient reveals the experience she referred to in the initial exchange of the first session, the black feeling that wells up within her. In Session #1 she identified this feeling:

Patient: It's just a really awful, awful feeling. It's awful to almost the point of feeling vile. Does that make sense?

When she picks up this theme late in Session #2 she relates

Patient: I just have to hurt myself to feel better . . . and I don't like that. . . .

Analyst: But that's something you do.

Patient: Yeah. It's like there's nothing. . . . It's just a very alone feeling. It's not like loneliness; it's just totally alone.

Analyst: Isn't that the black feeling you talked about last week?

Patient: That's part of it. That's not entirely it. It's like a self-destructive thing. . . . It's like, if I can make myself hurt enough, then I can quit feeling like that inside.

Analyst: Can you say something about how hurting yourself or injuring yourself makes the hurt inside go away?

Patient: (Lengthy pause) I don't know if it overshadows it or just makes it dissipate.
(Explains that if there is enough pain, she begins to feel "fuzzy" and can gain equilibrium.)

Analyst: "Fuzzy" makes you forget how hurt you've been by your husband?

Patient: Exactly. That's it. That's it. (And a little later) It's like, if I can make myself hurt enough, then I can quit feeling like that inside (vile).

The patient connects this pattern of harming herself to remove herself from painful feelings of hurt and estrangement with her previous material about not being sure of who she is. She asserts that she has needs of her own which she should rightfully present to her husband.

Patient: It's like, OK, once you're a victim, you have this tattoo that says "victim" here (points to her forehead), and like, only weirdos can see it. . . . It's like a magnet.

Analyst: It sounds like you feel that you somehow invite these attacks on you . . . but I think that must be because you've been attacked so much. And you've come to think it must be you.

Patient: Well, yeah. (pause). I don't have any other explanation.

Analyst: You've never had a different kind of relationship.

Patient: In some ways all of my relationships end up, well maybe not, like, yelled at, and treated like I'm, you know, made to feel like I'm stupid and worthless, but. . . . Giving more than I want to give. Feeling forced into giving more than I want to give.

Analyst: They haven't been reciprocal relationships where you got as much as you gave.

Patient: No. That's like my M.O. (laughs). Yeah, it's like, it's almost like I seek that out, and I don't . . . I don't intentionally. I don't. But I've noticed that I get into relationships with people I don't like (laughs). That's weird, I think . . . I think that if I met my husband now, and I saw him how he is with me now, there's no way that I would get married to him.

She develops this theme until, at the close of the session, she reveals an intense interest in writing and a wish to share her writing publicly at a small reading.

Patient: . . . I don't feel like I can go [to the reading] without him. I don't feel like I can . . . I don't even feel like I can approach him about that.

Analyst: But writing is something you feel good about.

Patient: Yeah. That's me when I do that.

Analyst: And you want to be able to go and read.

Patient: Right. I would love that. I would love to do a reading.

Patient and analyst have illuminated the personal meaning of much of what the patient revealed in the initial moments of the first meeting. By carefully putting words to her pervasive experience in close relationships that she has not been heard, the patient has both felt heard and understands that others, although perhaps not her mother or husband, can hear her. From that calmed and more secure position, her feelings of identity confusion and self-fragmentation became available to be talked about. By attending closely to the patient's evolving self-experience when in conflict with her husband, the analyst articulated the way in which the patient loses herself in her attempts to stay related to her husband. This verbalization and the understanding conveyed by it then allowed the patient to begin a tentative exploration of the third theme, her emptiness and self-abusive behavior as symbolized by the "black hole." As the analyst closely tracked her associations, carefully putting into words the feelings and experiences she expressed, she found her way to a part of herself that felt real and positive—her ability to express herself in her writing and her wish to have her writing heard, her openness to trusting the hearing power of an audience. Clearly, more working through of these themes would be expected to occur throughout the course of treatment. However, the work accomplished in these two sessions has given the patient the language tools to pursue further understanding of these themes.

CONCLUSION

In the case material, the female patient appeared to integrate the analyst's interpretation that she was someone who had not been "heard" in her close personal relationships. This verbalization captured her experience; that is, she understood herself in a new way. Once she grasped the pervasiveness of this dynamic, she presented several manifestations of enhanced self-understanding. For example, she asserted that she had legitimate needs in her marital relationship and that she believed that she had a right to present them to her husband and to have them acknowledged. This assertion appears to illustrate a more solid, cohesive sense of self. Additionally, by the close of the second session, she revealed that she would like to be "heard" by reading some of her writing to others in a formal setting. She fantasied doing this independently, without her husband, and explored the emotional and relational implications of such a move. These fantasies demonstrate a shift toward increased self-delineation. She understands that her concerns about her communications are historically rooted in the experience of not being "heard." This connection between her childhood experience and the present supports a developing sense of self-continuity. She ended the second session in an optimistic state, one that suggested the possibility that her improved self-understanding might free her to explore new ways of experiencing herself. Although the clinical material covers only two sessions, we believe that it illustrates the concept that verbal interpretations provide the selfobject function of self-understanding.

In this chapter we sought to illustrate that among selfobject functions provided by an analyst's attuned verbal interpretations is that of self-understanding. In other words, earlier discussions of the locus of therapeutic action of interpretation implied that the benefit for the patient was either in new or enhanced cognitive understanding or in a selfobject experience of feeling understood. We propose that verbal interpretations provide not only both of the previously mentioned experiences for the patient but that, additionally, such interventions provide the potential for self-understanding. For the patient, when the elusive past and the troublesome present become comprehensible, through language, in the context of a primary selfobject relationship, the possibility for new organizations of experience arises.

REFERENCES

Arlow, J. A. (1987), The dynamics of interpretation. *Psychoanal. Quart.*, 56:68–87.

Atwood, G. E. & Stolorow, R. D. (1984), *Structures of Subjectivity: Explorations in Psychoanalytic Phenomenology.* Hillsdale, NJ: The Analytic Press.

Bacal, H. (1990), The elements of a corrective selfobject experience. *Psychoanal. Inq.*, 10:347–372.

———— & Newman, K. M. (1990), *Theories of Object Relations: Bridges to Self Psychology.* New York: Columbia University Press.

Buirski, P. & Haglund, P. (1998), The Wolf Man's subjective experience of his treatment with Freud. *Psychoanal. Psychol.*, 15:49–62.

Fosshage, J. L. (1995), Interaction in psychoanalysis: A broadening horizon. *Psychoanal. Dial.*, 5:459–478.

Freud, S. (1900), The interpretation of dreams. *Standard Edition,* 4 & 5:1–625. London: Hogarth Press, 1953.

———— (1913a), On psycho-analysis. *Standard Edition,* 12:205–211. London: Hogarth Press, 1958.

————(1913b), On beginning the treatment. *Standard Edition,* 12:121–144. London: Hogarth Press, 1958.

————(1915), The unconscious. *Standard Edition,* 14:166–215. London: Hogarth Press, 1957.

———— (1918), From the history of an infantile neurosis. *Standard Edition,* 17:7–122. London: Hogarth Press, 1955.

————(1937), Constructions in analysis. *Standard Edition,* 23:255–269. London: Hogarth Press, 1964.

Glover, E. (1931), The therapeutic effect of inexact interpretation. In: *The Technique of Psycho-analysis.* New York: International Universities Press, 1955.

Harris, A. (1996), False memory? False memory syndrome? The so-called false memory syndrome? *Psychoanal. Dial.*, 6:155–187.

Kohut, H. (1977), *The Restoration of the Self.* New York: International Universities Press.

———— (1984), *How Does Analysis Cure?* ed. A. Goldberg & P. Stepansky. Chicago: University of Chicago Press.

Lachmann, F. M. & Beebe, B. (1996), The contribution of self- and mutual regulation to therapeutic action: A case illustration. In: *Basic Ideas Reconsidered: Progress in Self Psychology, Vol. 12,* ed. A. Goldberg. Hillsdale, NJ: The Analytic Press, pp. 123–140.

Levin, F. M. (1991), *Mapping the Mind.* Hillsdale, NJ: The Analytic Press.

Lichtenberg, J. D., Lachmann, F. M. & Fosshage, J. L. (1996), *The Clinical Exchange: Techniques Derived from Self and Motivational Systems.* Hillsdale, NJ: The Analytic Press.

Mitchell, S. A. (1993), *Hope and Dread in Psychoanalysis*. New York: Basic Books.

Neubauer, P. B. (1980), The role of insight in psychoanalysis. In: *Psychoanalytic Explorations of Technique: Discourse on the Theory of Therapy*, ed. H. P. Blum. New York: International Universities Press, pp. 29–40.

Orange, D. M. (1995), *Emotional Understanding: Studies in Psychoanalytic Epistemology*. New York: Guilford Press.

Reckling, A. E. & Buirski, P. (1996), Child abuse, self-development, and affect regulation. *Psychoanal. Psychol.*, 13:81–99.

Stolorow, R. D. (1994), The nature and therapeutic action of psychoanalytic interpretation. In: *The Intersubjective Perspective*, ed. R. D. Stolorow, G. E. Atwood, & B. Brandchaft. Northvale, NJ: Aronson, pp. 43–55.

———— & Atwood, G. E. (1992), *Contexts of Being: The Intersubjective Foundations of Psychological Life*. Hillsdale, NJ: The Analytic Press.

———— Brandchaft, B. & Atwood, G. E. (1987), *Psychoanalytic Treatment: An Intersubjective Approach*. Hillsdale, NJ: The Analytic Press.

Terman, D. (1989), Therapeutic change: Perspectives of self psychology. *Psychoanal. Inq.*, 9:88–100.

Chapter 4

The Optimal Conversation: A Concern About Current Trends Within Self Psychology

Allen M. Siegel

Self psychology is witness to an ongoing conversation that addresses the question: "What is optimal in the clinician's response that will facilitate the hoped-for cure?" The persistence of this troublesome question, despite 100 years of psychoanalytic study, suggests that the central curative elements of analytic treatment remain unclear, or at least they remain in dispute among and between the various psycho-analytic camps. Kohut, in the provocative title of his posthumously published book, *How Does Analysis Cure?* (1984), posed a variant of this perplexing query. Kohut's seemingly straightforward question is not so simple when one realizes that the "how" of his question can be read either from the perspective of therapeutic process, in which case the query asks, "By what process does analysis cure?" or it can be read in terms of therapeutic action whereby the query asks, "By what action does the analyst facilitate the analytic cure?" The former reading asks the developmental–theoretical question, while the latter gives voice to the technical-clinical question. I believe that the current conversation in self psychology has become mired in the untenable predicament of separating its clinical technique from a rational underlying developmental theory. This separation is evident in the very form of the conversation's central question, "What is optimal in the clinician's response?" This is a technical question that cannot be answered without considering the developmental theory that informs its therapeutic rationale. Self psychology is especially vulnerable to theoretical confusions at this time because the field currently holds several theories rather than one. Psychology of the self theory, intersubjectivity theory, relational–provisional theory, and motivational systems theory all campaign under the banner of self psychology despite the fact that these theories contain differing and, at times, antithetical elements. I join the conversation now because strong currents in the discourse are carrying the field away from some older, but still useful, theoretical and technical concepts that I fear are in danger of becoming lost.

In this chapter I review several salient moments in the history of the ongoing conversation. I begin with a consideration of the value of some metapsychological concepts, despite metapsychology's current fall from favor. I begin this way because metapsychology was the conceptual tool employed to develop earlier psychoanalytic ideas, and its contributions lie at the heart of some contemporary concepts as well. I next review Freud's ideas about frustration and Kohut's innovative idea of optimal frustration. I complete this review, which forms the base from which I can then consider more current elements of the conversation, with a brief study of the metapsychology Kohut developed during the course of his work. Turning then to the contemporary conversation, I will pay particular attention to the relational–provisional perspective exemplified by Howard Bacal's concept of "optimal responsiveness" and the "provision of a corrective selfobject experience," Morton and Estelle Shane's discussion of "optimal restraint," and James Fosshage's concept of "facilitating responsiveness." I conclude by expressing a concern that the idea of provision as a central therapeutic concept has become overvalued within self psychology. This shift in emphasis deemphasizes the interpretive process and has seriously altered the direction of the conversation.

METAPSYCHOLOGY

Recent psychoanalytic writers have decried metapsychology as unsound, outmoded, and a hindrance to the further development of psychoanalytic theory (Stolorow, 1994; Gill, 1994). Although metapsychology has fallen out of conceptual favor, some useful metapsychological concepts linger in today's psychoanalytic theories, though in mildly disguised form. Metapsychology, a conceptual tool invented by Freud and expanded by Rapaport and Gill (1959), orders complex psychological data at the most experience-distant level of abstraction. Metapsychology views psychological phenomena from the experience-distant perspectives of the genetic, dynamic, structural, psychoeconomic, and topographic points of view. Like the blind men who return with different descriptions of the fabled elephant, each metapsychological perspective describes a different aspect of mental function. The genetic-dynamic perspectives remain central to psychoanalytic theory, although now they sometimes are called "the narrative." Contemporary theorists have transformed the psychoeconomic perspective from Freud's concept of quantities of energy flowing in a hydrodynamically structured mental apparatus to a view that describes issues of affect management and capacities for tension regulation. Additionally, seemingly anachronistic remnants of an ancient metapsychology linger in such clinically useful concepts as denial and disavowal. One cannot speak of these latter concepts, sometimes referred to as horizontal and vertical splits, without considering the tripartite model.

As Gedo and Goldberg (1973) have cogently and convincingly discussed, theoretical tools have no inherent value; they gain value only in their ability to perform their assigned tasks. In psychoanalysis that task is to provide clear explanations. From this perspective it is not possible for metapsychology to be either a good or a bad tool. Its value lies in its ability to explain a particular situation. I believe that metapsychology's disrepute within contemporary psychoanalytic self psychology originates not as much with the tool itself as with its history. Metapsychology has suffered a fate of "guilt by association" since psychoanalytic history has equated metapsychology with Freud's drive-defense psychology.

Metapsychology also suffers from the charge that it is an experience-distant theory that reifies the dynamic mental processes it attempts to describe. While the reification of metapsychological concepts has been a problem for the field, the problem, again, is not inherent in the tool. Reification of models, followed by a ritualization of the practices suggested by the model, is a problem for every science. The tendency to reify models is ubiquitous and seems to be an effect of the idealizing nature within the human condition. While the problem of reification rests with the idealizing scientist-practitioner rather than with the model itself, this unfortunate situation in psychoanalysis has slowed the advancement of theoretical developments for years. Because all theorists and practitioners are vulnerable to this aspect of human nature, we face the challenge of finding a position that allows us to utilize a theory for its explanatory value without becoming enslaved in an idealizing bondage to either the theorist or the theory.

Just as analysts are not neutral observers of the analytic milieu, so too, theorists are not neutral conceptualizers of the internal milieu. Personal idiosyncratic factors and an assortment of life experiences impinge upon, influence, and even help shape their conceptualizations. Theories are the expressions of theorists who attempt to explain their portion of the world as they experience and understand it. While theorists use particular and specialized words to articulate their theories, the words they use are not neutral explicators of their ideas. Rather, theorists' words carry history, and that history evokes affects. *Metapsychology,* as I have described, is one of these affect-laden words. Another is the word *frustration.*

FREUD'S CONCEPT OF FRUSTRATION: THEORY AND TECHNIQUE

Although I restate what is obvious to the informed student of psychoanalysis, it is necessary to review briefly Freud's concept of frustration since it forms the historical base against which the notion of frustration, in several conceptualizations, is compared. Frustration was central to both Freud's theory of neurotic symptom formation and his theory of treatment. With Newtonian physics as his metaphor, Freud constructed a hydrodynamic model of the mind that contained an energy he called libido. In Freud's construct, libido flowed in a forward direction within the system unconscious as long as that system was in a state of balance. Freud conjectured that the libido reversed its direction and flowed backward within the system unconscious whenever its forward flow was blocked. Such a blockade and reversal of flow occurred when the gratification of an unconscious wish was frustrated by the limitations imposed by reality. Freud named this backward flow a "regression." He further hypothesized that the backward-flowing libido reinvests the old, previously quiet, objects of childhood with a new charge of energy, which, in turn, revives the long-dormant incestuous wishes of childhood and disrupts the equilibrium of the homeostatic mental apparatus. In an urgent effort to restore the disrupted homeostatic state, the mental apparatus institutes defensive maneuvers aimed at curbing the experience and expression of unconscious drives contained in the revived incestuous wishes. Freud postulated that these defensive maneuvers were responsible for the final formation of neurotic symptoms.

Since the core of a neurotic illness lay in the disequilibrium, Freud reasoned that homeostasis would return when the intensity of the revitalized incestuous wishes was diminished. At this point Freud's theory begins to blend with his technique since his hypothesis about the etiology of neurotic illness also carries the suggestion for his cure. Because Freud, in his personal credo, valued truth and knowledge, he hypothesized that the destabilizing force of the enlivened, but still hidden, unconscious elements could be diminished if he could expose them to the rehabilitating eye of consciousness. Freud's therapeutic approach followed an elegant internal logic. His next problem was to find the technical maneuver that could force the hidden, offending elements into the open where they could be exposed to the healing eye of awareness, which, in Freud's later conceptualizations, became the neutralizing influence of the ego.

Freud found the answer to his problem in the very process that produced the neurotic symptom in the first place. He reasoned that, if a frustration revived the dormant wishes that eventuated in the neurotic symptom, he might similarly revive the offending unconscious elements by frustrating his patients' wishes as they emerged in the clinical transferences. Freud took advantage of what he understood to be the symptom-inducing process, then, by clinically frustrating his patients' wishes in an effort to create an iatrogenic illness that could be therapeutically resolved. This is the rationale for "frustration" as a technical maneuver. As Basch (1995) describes, however, the rationale behind the technique tended to be forgotten over the decades, and "frustration" remained a sacred, ritualized behavior in the therapeutic repertoire of many analysts.

In his papers on technique, Freud suggested that the analyst be "opaque as a mirror" and "cold as a surgeon" (Freud, 1912) in an effort not to gratify his or her patients' instinctual wishes. We know, however, from Freud's own reports (Freud, 1909, 1918) and from those of his patients (Grinker, 1968, personal communication) that Freud was neither cold nor removed in the course of his work. Nevertheless, his technical recommendations were misconstrued and misapplied by analysts over the years.

An extreme, but probably not unusual, example of this distortion of Freud's recommendations comes from a patient in my practice who was treated by a prominent senior analyst during the late 1960s. In an effort not to gratify any lurking wish and thus maximize the "therapeutic" frustration, this analyst did nothing for the patient but "analyze." My patient was required to write his own bill at the end of the month, place his own tissue on the pillow before lying down, close the window shade if the sun were too bright, and adjust the heat if he felt cold. My patient experienced this so-called "analytic" stance as rude, hurtful, and sadistic, but because an aspect of his illness announced itself in a deep and painful state of humiliating compliance, he was unable to do anything but acquiesce to his imposing analyst's inhospitable ways.

While this example of frustration might seem extreme, the attitude it conveys was not unique. Considered therapeutic at that time, this behavior was within the bounds of acceptable analytic technique. While today one is dismayed at such behavior, I wish to emphasize that analysts are often misled by their theories. As analysts and therapists, we tend to idealize and reify our guiding theories, a move that, in turn, entrenches our clinical blindspots. Therapeutic actions, regardless of theory, are easily and frequently rationalized to suit the unconscious needs of the clinician.

Needless to say, the misunderstanding and misuse of Freud's technique created many unhappy analytic experiences over the years. The deprivational, so-called "analytic attitude" often replicated the disruptive childhood milieu that contributed to the original deformation of the self and necessitated the patient's search for help in the first place. Many clinicians experienced this analytic deprivation in their own personal analyses. Many suffered in their training as well, as they struggled with the discrepancy between what they were taught by "teachers of frustration" and what their better judgment suggested was correct clinical behavior. For these analysts the deprivational stance of their classical training was antithetical to their own sense of humanity. Secretly uncomfortable with the ambiance their behavior created in the consultation room, they found themselves in the predicament of acting at variance with the theory they had learned and espoused. As a result of these experiences, "frustration," originally conceived as a technique designed to mobilize latent unconscious drives, is a concept that, for many analysts, has become infused with feelings of deprivation, helplessness, anger, confusion, and despair. For these analysts the word *frustration* is not a neutral explicator of a therapeutic idea. Instead, because of its unfortunate history, the word *frustration* carries the capacity to stimulate passionate affects and, I believe, has created an aversion among many self psychologists to account comfortably for the role of frustration in either their theory or technique.

KOHUT'S METAPSYCHOLOGY:
THEORY AND TECHNIQUE

The concept of clinical frustration remained largely unchallenged until 1958 when Heinz Kohut entered the conversation and created a psychology of the self that affected the course of psychoanalysis. Some of Kohut's more useful seminal ideas, however, seem to be fading as the field of self psychology evolves. Because of my concern over this development, I will briefly review some of Kohut's central concepts—"optimal frustration," empathy, internalizations, the unconscious narcissistic configurations with their concomitant selfobject transferences, and interpretation—and compare these concepts to ideas that currently seem to be gaining popularity within the field.

Optimal Frustration

Kohut's participation in the ongoing psychoanalytic dialogue began with a series of early papers and continued through the classical Freud theory course he taught at the Chicago Institute for Psychoanalysis (Kohut and Seitz, 1960). In that course, which I have described elsewhere (Siegel, 1996), Kohut discussed his understanding of Freud's concept of emotional maturation among Freud's other theories. Kohut taught that for Freud, emotional maturation required the developmental move from primary process/pleasure principle thinking to secondary process/reality principle thinking and that this move, which differentiated wish from reality, was fostered by a period of delay between the wish and its gratification. This understanding of emotional maturation was a view from the psychoeconomic perspective. It suggested that normal maturation required the differentiating delay to be of optimal duration and intensity. The delay was to be neither so intense as to be traumatic nor so minimal as to be insignificant; it had to be "just right" (Tolpin, 1971). Kohut (1972) called this "just-right" delay an optimal frustration and attributed the first use of the term *optimal frustration* to Bernfeld (1928). Discussing the origin of that term, Kohut (1972) wrote:

> For many years I have tried to trace the origin of the concept 'optimal frustration' in psychoanalysis which, as you know, I have used widely in my lectures and writings. Although I have elaborated the concept metapsychologically and have used it in, I believe, a novel way in the context of the explanation of structure formation, I always knew that (in its interpersonal meaning, i.e., as a quality of the education of children [and thus belonging to educational psychology]) I must have come across the concept elsewhere. I have never claimed any priority with regard to the term or the concept and have handled it carefully in a noncommittal way whenever I used it [pp. 867–868].

By qualifying Freud's "frustration" with the adjective *optimal,* Kohut altered the concept of frustration from a clinical intervention designed to induce an iatrogenic illness to a developmental idea that considered the *effect* a frustrating childhood experience had upon the developing psyche. As I noted previously, Kohut's concept of optimal frustration is a psychoeconomic concept. It considers the qualitative nature of the affects associated with the unavoidable frustrations, disappointments, and hurts of a child's life. Kohut asserted that, if these affects are functionally managed and contained by the objects in the child's milieu or if the intensity of a frustration can be managed by the immature psyche alone, then the frustration is optimal. Building upon Freud's (1917) idea of structuralization following loss, Kohut (1971) hypothesized that psychic structure accrued over time as minute aspects of the lost psychological function that had previously been assigned to the idealized, but now mildly frustrating, object were internalized. He asserted that each of these "optimally frustrating" micro-disappointments initiated a process responsible for the internalizations destined to become psychological structure and called this process "transmuting internalization." For Kohut, optimal frustration followed by transmuting internalization was the major route for the development of psychological structure (Kohut, 1984).

Kohut answered the process aspect of his question, "How does analysis cure?" by asserting that analysis cures through the accretion of psychological structure. While self psychologists today generally agree with this assertion, they continue to debate the specific processes involved in the accretion of psychic structure. Bacal (1985), Bacal and Newman (1990), Lachmann and Beebe (1995), Ornstein (1988), Terman (1988), and Wolf (1988), to name but a few, have questioned the validity of Kohut's concept of transmuting internalization. Nevertheless, the central question remains, "How do psychological structures develop?"

My clinical, as well as life, experiences inform me that some structures do accrue following loss. For example, the child masters the bicycle with a stable sense of internalized confidence, only after he or she has lost the steadying parental hand on the back of the bicycle seat. Similarly, the child learns to swim confidently only after the supporting parental arms are gone. Growth accompanies these frustrations. Our theory must account for the developmental role of frustration in early development and in later life as well.

Some authors assert (Lachmann and Beebe, 1995; Stolorow, 1995), and I concur, that Kohut's tenacious insistence on transmuting internalization as the *sole* route for the accrual of psychological structure reflects his enduring tie to Freud and to classical analysis. At the end of his life, however, I believe he became interested in empathy as another part of the process of internalization. It is to this issue that I now turn.

Empathy

Concepts of empathy lie at the center of Kohut's thought. Present from early on, Kohut first addressed the issue in his seminal publication "Introspection, Empathy and Psychoanalysis: An Examination of the Relationship Between Modes of Observation and Theory" (1959) where he described empathy as the instrument of observation that defined the psychological field. Eventually, feeling as though he had mined all that was of conceptual value, Kohut set the issue of empathy aside. Like an itch that doesn't quiet, however, he felt an urgent need to return to the topic at the end of his life. In his final public address, delivered at the Fourth Annual Self Psychology Conference in Berkeley, California, Kohut discussed empathy from three perspectives: as a data gathering tool; as an informer of action; and, most importantly, as a basic element in the surrounding emotional milieu that is essential for the development and maintenance of psychological health and wholeness (Kohut, 1981). In the Berkeley address Kohut said:

> I will address myself to the issue of empathy despite the fact that some couple of years ago I kept saying I'm sick of that topic. It seems to be non-productive. I hear over and over again the same arguments, and they are so far off my meaning that I had the impression that I was wasting my time, my emotions, my energy that I could use on new ideas and new work. But idiot that I am . . . despite a fairly long life, and hopefully some attainment of wisdom, that when people keep asking you the same damn question, something must be wrong!

> Something is wrong. . . . I have a sense of responsibility about the abuse of this concept. The fact again that people have acted as if I were abusing it makes me go up on a high horse and say, "These idiots, they don't read what I write!" But . . . if they misunderstand . . . other people must misunderstand too. They will claim empathy cures . . . that one has to be just "empathic" with one's patients and they will be doing fine. I don't believe that at all. . . .

> Empathy serves . . . and this is now the most difficult part—namely, that despite all that I have said, empathy, per se, is a therapeutic action in the broadest sense, a beneficial action in the broadest sense of the word. That seems to contradict everything that I have said so far, and I wish I could just simply by-pass it. But since it is true, and I know it is true . . . I must mention it. Namely that the presence of empathy in the surrounding milieu . . . whether used for compassionate, well-intentioned therapeutic, and now listen, even for utterly destructive purposes, is still an admixture of something positive [pp. 525–535].

What did Kohut mean when with one breath he said he didn't believe that empathy cured but with the next said that empathy is a "therapeutic action in the broadest sense"? I believe he was referring to the essential nature of an empathic milieu in relation to psychological survival. He was addressing the issue of the analyst's provision of the psychologically essential, but previously missing, element whereby the analyst is guided by an orienting principle that attempts to understand and explain his or her patient's experience in the most sensitive way possible. Kohut asserted that, when the analyst creates such a psychologically welcoming milieu, the patient's experiences are validated, transferences are worked through, and eventually, the enfeebled structures of the self are strengthened. The confusion Kohut was concerned about centered on the fact that, while the analyst does not set out to "do" empathy, the creation of the empathic milieu is essential to the analytic cure. As I will describe shortly, the creation of the empathic milieu via the interpretive process answers the action component of Kohut's question, "How does analysis cure?" Although Kohut did not have the time to work this issue through, it seems that his idea of empathy as "a broad therapeutic action" pointed to another route through which internalizations could occur. In this route of internalizations, the compassionate, understanding, validating, and supportive aspects of the empathic selfobjects are taken in and eventually become structures of the self. These structures create an internal attitude toward the self that is similar to the compassionate attitude of the caring selfobjects. This is a route of structure building that does not depend upon frustrations of any sort. I surmise that Kohut labored with this idea for a while but had to disavow its importance because of his overriding tie to the idea of transmuting internalization via optimal frustrations.

The Area of Progressive Neutralization: An Old Idea

I believe that evidence of Kohut's struggle over how to think about the differing routes of internalization can be found as early as 1963 in a paper entitled, "Concepts and Theories of Psychoanalysis" (Kohut and Seitz, 1963). Although that paper primarily focused on optimal frustrations and the qualities of parental behavior that made frustrations optimal, Kohut (1963) also described the "calm, soothing, loving" parental attitude that becomes structuralized as part of the self even in the absence of frustrations:

> The differences between childhood experiences of traumatic and of optimal frustration are differences of degree. It is the difference between one mother's harsh "N-O!" and another mother's kindly "no." It is the difference between a frightening kind of prohibition, on the one hand, and an educational experience, on the other. . . . It is the difference between an uncompromising prohibition, which stresses only what the child must not have or cannot do, and the offering of acceptable substitutes for the forbidden object or activity. . . .

Replicas of the experiences of traumatic frustrations and optimal frustrations (identifications) are established in the mind via introjection. The child incorporates permanently into his own psychic organization the restraining attitudes and behavior of the childhood objects who curbed his wishes, demands, needs, and strivings. If these prohibitions are of non-traumatic intensity, the child incorporates the parents' drive restraining attitude in the form of benign memory traces. . . . As a result of having introjected many experiences of optimal frustration in which his drives were handled by a calm, soothing, loving attitude rather than by counter-aggression on the part of his parents, the child himself later acts in the same way toward the drive demands that arise in him [pp. 369–370].

Written in the language of mental-apparatus conceptualizations of 1963, Kohut described a conflict-free area of the psychic apparatus that he called the "area of progressive neutralization" (see Diagram 1). This was an area, on the left-hand side of the tripartite model, where the repression barrier did not exist. Kohut's concept of the repression barrier was unique and relevant for our discussion because, for Kohut, the repression barrier reflected the environment's impact upon the child's developing psyche. Kohut conceived of the repression barrier as an experience-based protective wall that evolved as a response to multiple "traumatic frustrations" rather than as part of a static mental apparatus. It developed out of the child's unconscious protections against the frightening and overwhelming affects that were experienced when a parent responded in a harsh, seductive, or counteraggressive way (Kohut and Seitz, 1960).

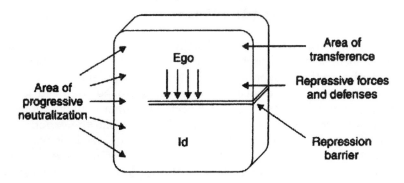

Diagram 1 (Siegel, 1996, p. 57).   Tripartite Model and Area of Progressive Neutralization

The area beneath the repression barrier is the area of transferences. The area of progressive neutralization is free of the repression barrier. It is a consequence of the nontraumatic aspects of the child's empathic caretakers. Kohut intended "Concepts and Theories of Psychoanalysis" (Kohut and Seitz, 1963) to advance the idea that the environment contributes to the child's internal life, a heretical idea in 1963. Although the emphasis in this paper is on "optimal frustration," Kohut does discuss a second route for structure building, namely the internalizations that occur via the "area of progressive neutralizations." This second route of internalizations, which Kohut neglected in favor of the concept of transmuting internalization, is similar to the more contemporary conceptualization of Stern's RIGS (Stern, 1985) and of Terman's "dialogue of construction" in which "the doing is the making" (Terman, 1988).

In *Restoration of the Self*, Kohut (1977) raised the crucial question of whether truly new structures can be formed de novo during treatment or whether the old, but enfeebled, structures are strengthened and rehabilitated during the course of analytic treatment. The answer to this question is critical since it informs the conduct of one's treatment and the answer flows, of course, from one's understanding of development and structure formation. Different answers will inform different treatment approaches. Kohut answered this question with the assertion that new structures are not formed de novo but that enfeebled structures of the self are strengthened and rehabilitated during the course of an analysis. Because this assertion flows from Kohut's ideas about the development and maturation of narcissism, I will briefly present his thoughts about the narcissistic configurations.

The Narcissistic Configurations and Their Concomitant Selfobject Transferences

In *Analysis of the Self*, Kohut (1971) describes the two well-known sets of unconscious narcissistic configurations that he hypothesized were central to the development of the self. One configuration is a set of needs, fantasies, and wishes that clusters around the need for a stabilizing union with an idealized object. The other configuration—a cluster of needs, fantasies, and wishes—forms around the experience of childhood expansiveness with its accompanying need for parental affirmation, enjoyment, and participation in the unmodified exhibitionism and grandiosity of childhood. Kohut later conceptualized a third configuration. Originally conceived as part of the cluster of grandiose feelings and fantasies that required affirmation, Kohut later conceived of the twinship transference as a separate and distinct transference that expresses the need for another who "is just like me" (Kohut, 1984).

Each unconscious configuration searches for the participation of an object to satisfy the associated needs. Kohut called these sought after objects selfobjects because, in their need-fulfilling function, they are not experienced as independent centers of initiative but rather as part of the self. The search for and the establishment of a connection with a need-fulfilling selfobject is a selfobject transference. The needs that seek a selfobject for their fulfillment are selfobject needs.

In Kohut's theory, each of these configurations has a natural course of development that, when all goes well, contributes to the formation of an intact, sturdy, productive self. Kohut hypothesized that, when development is interrupted, for any one of many reasons, elements of these unconscious configurations do not mature. Instead, they remain arrested in their development, and the self is deprived the enlivening, sustaining consequences of their natural unfolding

Kohut's theory led him to offer new technical recommendations. He departed from classical theory and its technique of "neutrality," abstinence, and frustration designed to create an iatrogenic illness when he recommended the establishment of an ambiance that accepts and even welcomes the arrested selfobject needs. Such a milieu fosters the emergence of the selfobject needs that, because they are experienced as painful, humiliating, and shameful, have been disavowed and denied. As indicated above, the surfacing selfobject needs emerge in the form of selfobject transferences. In Kohut's psychology, the self is strengthened and rehabilitated as the arrested selfobject configurations are worked through in the analytic process and resume their interrupted developmental course. While Kohut emphasized transmuting internalization as the central route of internalization, I believe it was unfortunate that he neglected the other streams of internalization he had conceived. These were the area of progressive neutralization that he described early in his work and the therapeutic action of empathy that he described at the end.

Interpretation: Kohut's Technical Tool

If metapsychology was Kohut's conceptual tool, then interpretation was his technical tool. Kohut's technical concepts flowed logically from his theory of development and illness, a theory that posits arrested clusters of unconscious selfobject needs, wishes, and fantasies as the cause of illness. For Kohut, resumption of emotional growth required the therapeutic remobilization of the arrested narcissistic configurations so that their contents could be integrated with the personality.

Kohut advocated an interpretive course of action to accomplish this task.

Kohut's sense of "interpretation" differs from Freud's "interpretation." Kohut's interpretation is not a truth-driven, intellectual construct designed to inform the ego of the toxic contents hidden in the unconscious. Rather, it is an empathic communication that expresses the analyst's deep understanding of the patient's present experience while sensitively linking that experience to the past. Kohut's interpretation consists of an understanding phase and an explaining phase. Kohut's interpretation is a therapeutic action that affirms the patient's emotional existence and provides the patient with the opportunity for a profound emotional experience. As I noted earlier, Kohut asserted that the experience of having one's existence empathically affirmed is both an essential element of psychological survival and an essential element of the analytic cure. Kohut's interpretation brings the patient a sense of being known and accepted in the deepest ways possible. Kohut (1981) writes,

> I submit that the most important point I made [in *How Does Analysis Cure?*] was that analysis cures by giving explanations; not by "understanding," not by repeating and confirming what the patient feels and says, that's only the first step; but then (the analyst has) to move on and give an interpretation. In analysis an interpretation means an explanation of what is going [on] in genetic, dynamic, and psychoeconomic terms. . . . Interpretations are not intellectual constructions. If they are they won't work; [they might work] accidentally, but not in principle. A good analyst reconstructs the childhood past in the dynamics of the current transference with warmth, with understanding for the intensity of the feeling, and with the fine understanding of the various secondary conflicts that intervene as far as the expression of these [childhood wishes and needs] are concerned [p. 533].

Through the interpretive process, childhood wishes and needs, unknown to the patient but present in their influence nonetheless, have an opportunity to come alive. They eventually become known by the patient, accepted for what they are, understood in terms of where they came from; resume their developmental course; and finally culminate in mature structures. The experience of being known in such a way becomes a new structure. In addition, the analyst's deep understanding, interpretively conveyed, provides a means by which the patient can eventually understand him or herself. This nonintellectualized experiential understanding of oneself also becomes an internal structure. The act of establishing an interpretive process fostered by the analyst's communication of his or her understanding admixed with explanations was Kohut's form of analytic provision. The discussion that follows will focus on current concepts of psychoanalytic provision.

THE CURRENT CONVERSATION: ELEMENTS OF PROVISION

Optimal Responsiveness: Bacal (1985)

Howard Bacal's paper, "Optimal Responsiveness and the Therapeutic Process" (1985), was the first in a series of papers that discuss ideas originally stimulated by Kohut's use of the word *optimal* in relation to clinical phenomena. Here, Bacal takes issue with Kohut's concept of "optimal frustration" and offers his own term, "optimal responsiveness," as an alternative idea. Bacal suggests that the concept of optimal frustration as "a central aspect of the curative process viewed from the perspective of self psychology" (p. 202) be reexamined in light of what he considers the related issue of "optimal gratification." Bacal notes that the clinical discussion of frustration versus gratification in the treatment situation inevitably freezes the conversation in an endless "either-or" debate. He states that his purpose in writing his paper is, in part, "to demonstrate the significance of the latter [optimal gratification], which until recently has been regarded with some suspicion as a form of counter-transference acting in" (p. 202). To overcome this dilemma Bacal proposes his alternative concept of "optimal responsiveness," defined as "the responsivity of the analyst that is therapeutically most relevant at any particular moment in the context of a particular patient and his illness" (p. 202).

I believe that in his discussion Bacal reads the "optimal" of Kohut's "optimal frustration" as an adverb, rather than as the adjective Kohut intended. Kohut did not use the word *optimal* to qualify the verb *frustrate.* As I stated earlier, Kohut first conceived of an optimal frustration in a developmental, rather than a clinical, context when he asserted that optimal frustrations were disruptions of psychologically manageable proportions that were essential to the structure-building process. In his developmental conceptualization Kohut was concerned with the experience and internal management of the disruptive event rather than with the event itself.

While I applaud Bacal's choice to retain such metapsychological concepts as introjects, internalizations, psychological structure, splits—both vertical and horizontal—and the psychoeconomic perspective suggested by his attention to issues of affect management and tension regulation, I find his emphasis on optimal responsiveness problematic. Kohut's *optimal,* when he used it in the clinical context, was about the inevitable disruptions that often occurred between two people who met frequently over a period of time. Kohut's clinical *optimal* was not about anything the therapist did directly. It was the analyst's ability to recognize and acknowledge the disruption along with his or her participation in its creation, followed, when appropriate, by the analyst's ability to explore the disruption's deeper meanings that made the disruption optimal, rather than traumatic. The acknowledging, validating, understanding, and explaining milieu created by these analytic actions helped contain the painful affects associated with the disruption.

In contrast to Kohut's adjectival use of *optimal,* Bacal reads Kohut's *optimal* as an adverb used to describe a therapeutic action. Bacal (1985) writes about it in the following way,

> The concept of "optimal frustration" mainly serves to give analysis respectability. It "proves" we don't think of ourselves as gratifying our patients when we treat them. Related to this image of the hard path that the patient must travel toward cure is that of fixation points of the libido and the idea that patients will adhere to these positions to which they have regressed unless confronted with reality or with the deleterious effects of their continuing to function in their archaic ways with objects. According to this perspective, unless patients are optimally frustrated and exhorted to progress they will simply be gratified by the understanding, demand more and more, and remain where they are [p. 216].

Bacal repeats this understanding in his book, *Theories of Object Relations: Bridges to Self Psychology* (Bacal and Newman, 1990), where he takes issue with Kohut's view of how analysis cures, particularly with Kohut's idea of transmuting internalization following an optimal frustration, and contrasts it with his own. Bacal and Newman (1990) write,

> The view that the curative process entails what may be called a "corrective selfobject experience" contrasts sharply with the traditional analytic view that insight is the major therapeutic factor. It is also somewhat at variance with Kohut's view of "how analysis cures." According to Kohut, therapeutic effect is mediated through the patient's experience of multiple, manageable so-called "optimal frustrations" of selfobject needs, the result of which is that the patient takes over, or internalizes—via so-called transmuting internalization—the analyst's selfobject functions for his own use. . . .
>
> There is no need to introduce "frustration" into the patient's analytic experience . . . [T]here is no analyst whose responses are so "opti-

mal" as to preclude the patient's recurrently experiencing frustrating and hurtful discrepancies between what he is after and what he gets from him [p. 258].

Bacal implies that Kohut suggested deliberately frustrating the patient, but as I have attempted to convey, deliberate frustration in the clinical setting had very little to do with Kohut's concept of an optimal frustration. In fact, Kohut opposed the classical idea of frustration as a technique and took pains to describe the properly responsive, humane milieu that he believed was essential to the conduct of a psychoanalytic treatment. In this regard, Kohut devoted an entire section in *The Restoration of the Self* (1977) to a discussion of the ambiance of the therapeutic setting. In that discussion Kohut opposed the austere, rude, hurtful, and traumatically frustrating situation created by the classical psychoanalytic technique of "frustration." He did not advocate frustrating the patient as a technical maneuver; there are several now-famous stories about how Kohut, in fact, acted in human and humane ways rather than as a cold, frustrating analyst.

Perhaps the most touching instance of Kohut's humanity and nonfrustrating manner in relation to a patient is found in a story told by an analysand who had attended the 1981 Berkeley conference I referred to earlier. At that meeting, Kohut knew he would not live to attend the next annual conference and bid a sad farewell to the audience that had gathered to hear his final words. After the meeting Kohut's analysand happened to be returning to Chicago on the same plane as Kohut. When Kohut saw him sitting several rows ahead he asked the flight attendant if she would ask his analysand to come over to his seat. The analysand approached to find Kohut obviously tired from the stress of his Berkeley presentation earlier in the day. Exhausted too from the throes of his illness, aware that death was imminent, and sensitive to his analysand's wish to say goodbye, Kohut said, "I thought you might like to speak with me" (Beigler, 1997, personal communication). This touching vignette negates the misconception of Kohut as a frustrater and underscores the point Kohut had ironically articulated about himself only hours earlier in his Berkeley address when he said, "I'm not stodgy, and I think the more one knows, the greater one's freedom. The more one knows, the less important some ritual that one sticks to anxiously, because no one knows what is appropriate and what is inappropriate" (Kohut, 1981).

Clearly, Kohut was not a "frustrater," despite subsequent attributions of active frustration to Kohut's therapeutic methods (Bacal and Newman, 1990). True, frustration did play a role in Kohut's clinical thinking, but it was not the frustration of classical analysis. As I stated earlier, Kohut was not concerned about creating an iatrogenic illness through the persistent frustration of the unconscious wish. Rather, he allowed room for his patients to be upset in the clinical encounter. He was interested in analyzing the upsets, whether intra- or extra-analytic, that occur in life. One learns most about the qualities of the self in the presence of life's inevitable distress. If an analyst moves too quickly in an attempt to prevent or alleviate psychic pain, the opportunity to learn the unique meanings of the pain is lost. As a consequence of this understanding, Kohut did not respond to the immediate wish of his patients to make things better. Instead, he strove for a position that allowed his patients the opportunity to experience their internal lives, with their inherent pain, while he remained sensitive to their needs for help in modulating affective intensities.

I find Bacal's conceptualizations in the area of developmental theory, in the burden his concept of optimal responsiveness creates for the therapist and in the absence of diagnostic distinctions about what sorts of people will benefit from his approach problematic. My primary concern with Bacal's conceptualization stems from Bacal's attempt to establish a theoretical base for his clinical ideas (Bacal and Newman, 1990), for I don't believe Bacal's clinical recommendations are adequately anchored in developmental theory. Bacal considers the optimal childhood milieu suggested by the Winnicottian "good-enough mother" and by the Kohutian appropriately responsive selfobject in his attempt to establish a theoretical–developmental base for his clinical ideas. He then, however, applies these developmental ideas to the clinical situation in a literal manner when he draws a direct analogy between the parent–infant dyad and the analyst–analysand dyad. In this analogy, Bacal suggests that, just as a "good-enough mother/responsive selfobject milieu" is essential for the development of a healthy self, so too, an "optimally responsive" therapeutic milieu is the essential element in the curative process. For Bacal, the "provision of a corrective selfobject experience" mediated through the technique of "optimal responsiveness" is the central curative factor within the analysis (Bacal and Newman, 1990).

Bacal makes an unjustified leap from his understanding of the essential nature of a child's appropriately responsive selfobject milieu to the idea of a deliberate provision of such an experience in an analysis. Bacal's clinical theory suggests that the analyst is to be active in the provision of "corrective selfobject experiences" and that such provision will be curative. Although he does not use the term, he implies that the analyst can "re-parent" a psychologically injured person through such a provision. It seems to me that Bacal's suggestion that the analyst can provide a corrective selfobject experience expresses the idea that the early optimal experience can literally be transposed into the treatment setting. This notion concretizes the early childhood experience within the treatment situation and deemphasizes the analytic approach that seeks to mobilize and explore the various transference configurations in a milieu that welcomes the affects and experiences associated with the inevitable disruptions of human discourse. Although Bacal concurs with several theorists about the import of disruptions in life, as well as in the treatment setting (Winnicott, 1951, 1958, 1963; Tolpin, 1971; Wolf, 1988), and even writes about these disruptions himself (Bacal and Newman, 1990), he deemphasizes their therapeutic value in favor of his notion of the provision of a corrective selfobject experience mediated by optimal responsiveness.

My second concern over Bacal's emphasis on optimal responsiveness addresses the psychological burden it places upon the therapist. This is especially the case for the newer therapist, who is prone to believe that there is such a thing as an optimal response and that one can and should know, a priori, what an optimal response might be for a given patient in a given situation. The concept of optimal responsiveness overlooks the fact that it is only possible to know what response is optimal in retrospect, after the patient has responded to a particular intervention. To think otherwise burdens experienced and inexperienced therapists alike by stimulating their unmodified omniscience and grandiosity. In addition, the idea of "re-parenting," inherent in the concept of the cure through provision, appeals to the therapist's own unrequited developmental and narcissistic needs. Rationalized as an intervention conducted in the patient's interest, the attempt to provide a "corrective selfobject experience" can easily slip into an unconscious enactment that vicariously fulfills a therapist's wish to be re-parented. Simultaneously, when rationalized as being in the best interest of the patient, the technique of provision can answer the therapist's unmodified unconscious grandiosity and needs for idealization, admiration, and acclaim.

In addition, I am concerned that the emphasis on provision in its varying forms fosters an overriding interest in the analyst to provide a soothing, calming, "tension-regulating" atmosphere. The potential exists, in such an atmosphere, to deprive the patient the opportunity to become upset and, in the upset, to reveal the contents and pain associated with various transference constellations.

My final concern is of a diagnostic nature. In his discussions, Bacal does not make distinctions regarding which patients will benefit from and which patients will be harmed by his proposal of the provision of a corrective selfobject experience. His proposal does not distinguish between the different levels of psychological distress and disorganization.

Instead, Bacal implies that one general therapeutic stance will be useful for all patients. He does not consider the possibility that "provision" will set a profound regression in motion for some while for others it will establish a transference bondage to the providing analyst. The diagnostic distinctions concerning who is likely to react in what way is crucial, difficult to assess, and usually impossible to know beforehand.

In reading Kohut's *optimal* as an adverb, Bacal returns the notion of frustration from Kohut's developmental conceptualization to Freud's idea of frustration as a clinical action. In so doing, I believe Bacal has affected the direction of the ongoing conversation, moving it from a consideration of developmental processes to a consideration of clinical actions.

Optimal Provision: Lindon (1994)

Another paper in the "optimal" series is John Lindon's, "Gratification and Provision in Psychoanalysis: Should We Get Rid of the 'Rule of Abstinence'?" (1994). Lindon takes issue with the dogma of Freud's rule of abstinence and the effect it has had upon the conduct of analyses. Unlike Bacal, who proposes the "provision of a corrective selfobject experience" as the curative analytic element, Lindon does not propose his concept of optimal provision as a curative technique. Rather, he addresses the issue of provision from the perspective of creating an atmosphere that enables the therapeutic exploration of the patient's unconscious arrested configurations. One might question, however, whether another unarticulated theory informs Lindon's extensive efforts in the clinical material he presents, to provide the milieu he felt was necessary to create an analytic situation for particular patients. Nonetheless, his articulated concept of psychoanalytic cure is similar to Kohut's in that it is based upon the idea that transferences are mobilized, explored, and worked through. Lindon (1994) presents his awareness of the possibility that his suggestion of "provision" might evoke countertransference enactments and closes his paper with a caveat presented by Brandchaft:

> Brandchaft (1993) warned of the danger that theory—and I believe his comments are applicable to any theory—can lead an analyst to engage in a transference enactment by supplying what he believes is seen in that theory as a needed function: "Commitment to these modalities [e.g., affective attunement, optimal responsiveness] and a belief in their *therapeutic centrality* can get in the way of the investigatory process" and thereby interferes with helping the patient first to recognize his

invariant unconscious psychological organizing principles, then to help him reorganize them and get free. . . .

I believe that what is called for is the analyst's careful, sustained, empathic exploration of the patient's subjective experiences, including the meanings of any provisions or lack of them. Provisions should be in the service of furthering the analytic work; psychoanalysis should not be subverted into becoming provision [p. 29; italics added].

Like Kohut, Lindon conceives of provision as the analyst's creation of a milieu that fosters the analytic work rather than of the analyst providing a missing psychological function that he believes is curative in itself.

Optimal Restraint: Shane and Shane (1996)

The next paper in the "optimal" series is Estelle and Morton Shane's (1996) "Self Psychology in Search of the Optimal: A Consideration of Optimal Provision, Optimal Gratification and Optimal Restraint in the Clinical Situation." Similar to Bacal, they too understand and present Kohut as a "frustrater" in relation to therapeutic technique. They write,

Bacal noted that whereas frustration and gratification are both inevitable in the clinical relationship, neither serves as an appropriate treatment goal for the analyst; the analyst should neither seek to deliberately frustrate, however optimally, nor seek to gratify. Rather the proper goal in the clinical situation is that the analyst, having understood his or her patient, should then communicate that understanding through an optimal response [p. 43].

The Shanes laud Bacal for disabusing the field of the concept of optimal frustration and for creating the new term *optimal responsiveness*. While they agree with Lindon that the rule of abstinence should be eliminated, they feel there still is need for reserve in the therapeutic process. In this regard the Shanes offer their new term, *optimal restraint,* which they define as supplying "a response within the therapeutic dyad that is neither in excess of what is needed or desired by the patient, nor so withholding or so unspontaneous that it serves to derail the process" (p. 43). They then offer guidelines for optimal responsiveness that consider diagnosis, development, and attention to motivational systems. The Shanes conclude with a restatement of their opposition to the idea of frustration in the clinical setting. They imply that Kohut advocated what I believe he actually opposed when they write: "Frustration is not a useful guide for the clinician as a method of enhancing development progression and structure building" (p. 43). In this paper, the Shanes focus on the creation of a setting in which the *optimal* refers to the therapist's action. They envision the analyst in the position of creating health through the provision of an optimal response, now mediated by optimal restraint.

Facilitating Responsiveness: Fosshage (1997)

The last paper in this series is James Fosshage's paper, "Listening/ Experiencing Perspectives and the Quest for a Facilitating Responsiveness" (1997). Fosshage concurs with Bacal, Lindon, and the Shanes about the idea of provision as a curative element in psychoanalysis. Interestingly, however, Fosshage does not distinguish between Lindon's concept of optimal provision as a provision that makes the analysis possible and Bacal's conception of optimal responsiveness and the provision of a corrective selfobject experience as curative elements in themselves. Fosshage points to a problem inherent in Bacal's optimal responsiveness, namely, the implication that a singular "optimal," clinical response exists for a given situation. Fosshage suggests that there are several possible responses in a given situation that might provide what he calls the "needed relational selfobject experience" and proposes the term *facilitating responsiveness* to overcome this difficulty. The theory that underlies Fosshage's "facilitating responsiveness" is the same as that underlying Bacal's ideas. Both theories suggest that missing developmental elements can be supplied by the analyst's corrective actions. Fosshage describes this belief in the conclusion to his paper:

> Self psychology has contributed to our understanding that an analyst must be sufficiently available so that patient and analyst can find a way of creating the necessary developmental experiences. While understanding and explaining the problematic experiences provides one basis for needed experience, patients often require more poignant interactions with analysts to create needed relational selfobject experience. . . . Accordingly, the range of responses required of an analyst has expanded far beyond the bounds of exploration and interpretation and is more adequately captured by the terms facilitative or optimal responsiveness [p. 51].

In this statement we see that Fosshage, like Bacal, understands the curative element of the analytic process as the patient–analyst co-creation of necessary developmental experiences. As I now discuss, this understanding confuses the relational experience with the selfobject experience.

DISCUSSION

I begin my discussion by restating my initial concern that some of Kohut's useful theoretical and clinical ideas are becoming lost in the current conversation that focuses heavily on the relational–provisional nature of the therapeutic process. The purpose of this chapter is not to diminish the import of the bidirectional interactive nature of therapy, for I agree that the analytic endeavor is a highly interactive process in which the two participants co-create the analytic space (Stolorow, Brandchaft, and Atwood, 1987; Ehrenberg, 1992). The dyadic inter-action inevitably becomes the stage upon which the transferences are played out. Nor do I mean to suggest that the analytic process is without a provisional element, as I will discuss shortly. My purpose, rather, is to call attention to the central role of the interpretive pro-cess, which is in danger of becoming lost to the analytic conversation.

Kohut's psychology of the self posits that analysis cures through processes that return stunted psychological configurations to their normal developmental track. In Kohut's conceptualization, the thera-peutic process creates an opportunity for these stunted configurations to resume their development through the mobilization of unconscious childhood needs, wishes, fantasies, and fears. These unconscious ele-ments are clinically expressed as the selfobject transferences. In addi-tion, old traumas, experienced with the failed selfobjects of childhood, emerge to be expressed as traumatic transferences.

The unconscious elaboration of a transference can be conceptual-ized as a vector that moves from one person to another. In the thera-peutic context the transference moves from patient to analyst as shown in Diagram 2.

Patient >————Unconscious selfobject configurations————> Analyst

Diagram 2.   Vector of the essential curative element viewed from Kohut's perspective

The patient creates the selfobject transferences that are then worked through in the therapeutic process. The internal milieu of a particular analyst can enhance or prevent the emergence of the patient's selfobject and traumatic transferences. In the latter situation a transference vec-tor moves from analyst to patient, but this is not a vector of therapeu-tic action. It is a vector of inevitable human interaction, and ideally, when recognized by the analyst, it becomes a source of information about the patient, the analyst, and their interaction.

While the relational–provisional position espouses interpretation and working through of the transference as part of the therapeutic process, it seems to me that those speaking from the provisional perspective emphasize a second vector of analytic action. The relational-provisional conceptualization emphasizes the analyst as a provisional selfobject and places the analyst's provision of a corrective relational selfobject experience, illustrated in Diagram 3, in the theoretical foreground as the essential curative element.

Patient ←————corrective relational selfobject experience————< Analyst

Diagram 3.   Vector of the essential curative element viewed from relational–provisional perspective

I believe the relational–provisionists, in equating the developmental possibilities of childhood with the developmental possibilities of the clinical setting, fail to sufficiently consider the differences between the two situations. What happens in childhood cannot be replicated elsewhere. The child is a "work in progress," who lives in a fluid state and has not yet developed the rigid structures of the older child, let alone those of the adult. Additionally, there are critical points in time beyond which it is very difficult to learn new skills and patterns. Consider, as an example, the task of learning a musical or athletic skill in childhood as compared to learning that same task as an adult. It is the rare athlete who begins training in his or her sport at the age of 20 and an even rarer musician who begins his or her work later in life. There are critical times beyond which new motor skills are acquired only with great difficulty, if at all. Can it be different with other brain functions? Can a firm self be established later in life simply through the provision of missing experiences of a healthy childhood milieu? Is that provision sufficient to accomplish the task?

I assume the relational–provisional school would assert that working through is a necessary element in the therapeutic process. My concern is that the technical approach of the relational–provisional school overemphasizes the relational element and deemphasizes the working through of the remobilized arrested configurations via an interpretative process. Answers to questions of technique are rooted in developmental theory. Self psychologists generally agree that psychological illness derives from developmental arrests that occur in toxic childhood environments where the selfobjects fail in their essential psychological functions. What therapeutic rationale follows from this theory?

As I have outlined, Kohut's therapeutic rationale was to encourage the mobilization of the unconscious configurations that were stunted by the toxic childhood milieu in order for development to resume its course. To stimulate this revival and regrowth, Kohut created a friendly, humane clinical milieu that welcomed, explored, accepted, understood, and explained the denied and disavowed shameful childhood needs and fantasies associated with the arrest. Kohut advocated a process view of the analytic cure that was fostered by an interpretive method.

Interpretation, as I noted earlier, is a technical concept that suffers from its association with Freud's drive-defense psychology. Because Freud believed that illness was the result of conflicting unconscious forces, his theory suggested that cure could be effected through an interpretation designed to bring the unconscious forces to awareness. In Freud's theory, interpretation brings "insight," and insight brings cure. The theory of psychological illness changed, however, as our field has advanced and Freud's once heralded technique of cure through cognitive insight no longer holds sway, especially among self psychologists. Because interpretation has been equated with Freud's concept of insight, the idea of interpretation as a therapeutic agent has also become devalued among some self psychologists.

I would like to state again that Kohut's "interpretation" differs from Freud's "interpretation." Kohut opposed the single-entity omniscient interpretation delivered by the removed analyst. Instead, he described an empathically informed "interpretive process" that evolved over time. Kohut's interpretive process was sequential and, as he outlined (1984), consisted of an understanding phase in which the patient's experience was empathically perceived, validated, and affirmed, followed by an explaining phase that linked the patient's current experience to its childhood origins. The interpretive process and the empathic milieu in Kohut's view are intertwined. One creates the other. The empathic milieu is created when the analyst sensitively communicates his or her empathically informed understanding of a given self-state and adds, when appropriate, an equally sensitive explanation about the childhood origins of that state. While the analyst does not set out to do empathy, the experience of being empathically perceived by the analyst is therapeutic in itself and eventually leads to the formation of a new structure.

Another structure-building element of the interpretive process is the effect the explanation has in linking the analysand with his or her own history. By providing sensitively timed and delivered explanations, the analyst links past and present. The experiential–cognitive explanation provides the patient with an orienting experience since it makes sense of what is happening now in terms of what has happened in the past. Over the course of the analysis, the experiential–cognitive explanation brings a sense of continuity to the analysand. It anchors the analysand in time and becomes a structure that enables the analysand to understand himself or herself in the absence of the understanding and explaining analyst.

The analyst's orienting therapeutic principles have a subtle, but marked, influence on the conduct of the analysis. The analyst who conceives of the essential therapeutic vector as moving from patient to analyst in the form of the selfobject transferences created from the unconscious selfobject needs pursues a process that seeks to understand and explain these transferences and their associated unconscious fantasies, needs, wishes, and fears. This position emphasizes process and deemphasizes the need for special actions perceived as necessary to effect a cure.

Proponents of the relational–provisionist school within self psychology conceive of a therapeutic vector that moves from the analyst to the patient. They are fond of citing Kohut's vignette of the deeply depressed woman to whom he offered his stabilizing fingers at a desperate moment in the analysis to support their view that special action is needed to provide missing essential experiences (Fosshage, 1997). I believe Kohut had something different in mind when he presented his now famous vignette. Here is what Kohut (1981) said about his experience of that situation:

> And now I'll tell you what is so nice about that story. Because an analyst always remains an analyst. I gave her my two fingers. She took hold of them, and I immediately made a genetic interpretation to myself. It was the toothless gums of a very young child clamping down on an empty nipple. That was the way it felt. I didn't say anything. I don't know whether it was right. But I reacted to it even there, to myself, as an analyst [p. 535].

For Kohut, the essence of analysis was the interpretive process. For Kohut, to be an analyst was to provide his patient with a profound understanding of a particular experience and then eventually to link that experience with its genetic origins. In Kohut's vignette, his action did not flow from a therapeutic orientation that suggested he could function as a selfobject and actively provide his patient with a corrective selfobject experience. The point of his story, and the difference between the two positions, is that Kohut conceived of himself as providing an empathic milieu, a milieu in which his empathy was expressed via the interpretive process. Contemporary relational–provisionists, on the other hand, suggest that empathy conveyed via the interpretive process is insufficient. They suggest that in many situations their empathy must be expressed through an action that, in turn, becomes a corrective selfobject experience.

The notion, however, that one can "provide" a selfobject experience misconstrues the essential idea of the selfobject, for the selfobject is the patient's creation. No one can actively be a selfobject. The selfobject is created out of the patient's unconscious selfobject needs as the transferential vector moves from patient to analyst. Because that vector is unidirectional, it follows that no one can "provide a corrective selfobject experience." One can be emotionally present with a patient. One can deeply understand and communicate that understanding to a patient, but that is not the same as being a selfobject. Said differently, the vector cannot be reversed.

I wish to emphasize that I would misrepresent the analytic enterprise were I to suggest that it was not a provisional experience. The analyst's response to his or her patient's search for relief from the pain that brought them for help is an implied or explicit, " I will try to help you with your suffering." That statement, made by the concerned analyst, is a profound provision of hope, support, acceptance, and nonjudgmental understanding. It is the basic analytic provision and creates an ambiance that makes the therapeutic endeavor possible. The provision of an empathic milieu, established through the interpretive process of deep understanding and sensitive explanations, constitutes the core of the corrective emotional experience.

My concern addresses the matter of vectorial emphasis. I am more concerned with the nature and conceptualization of the provisional act than with the idea of provision per se since, as I noted, provision is inherent in the analytic process. The relational–provisional school does not dispense with the concept of an interpretive process, but I worry that it emphasizes the provisional vector, that is, the provision of missing psychological experiences, and deemphasizes the interpretive process as the central curative element.

I have been endlessly fascinated by Kohut's choice of empathy and the interpretive process as the topics of his last public address (Kohut, 1981). He could have chosen to speak about new ideas. Instead, he returned to issues he had addressed nearly 25 years earlier. Why did he choose empathy and the interpretive process as topics for his farewell address? What made them such pressing issues?

Kohut returned to these issues in order to clarify the misunderstanding that developed over what he had written earlier about empathy. He was concerned that analysts had misconstrued his writings and that, "They will claim that empathy cures. They will claim that one has to be just 'empathic' with one's patients and they'll be doing fine. I don't believe that at all" (Kohut, 1981, p. 527). For Kohut, the capacity to initiate and maintain an interpretive process was the *sina* qua non of the analyst, despite his awareness that the presence of empathy in the surrounding milieu is the sina qua non of psychological survival.

The relational–provisionist school, in contrast to Kohut's understanding, emphasizes the notion of cure through the provision of a missing essential psychological element. The idea of cure effected by an interpretive process and the idea of cure effected by the active provision of a missing psychological element, represent very different positions. While it is true that "interpreters" provide and "providers" interpret, I don't believe that they mean the same thing when they use the same words. Interpreters *provide a milieu* that allows development to occur. Providers, on the other hand, believe they must *provide an action* to make development occur. Some might assert that the differences between the two positions are subtle and can be integrated while others will argue that the effect of the different positions on the analytic process is profound, which raises the question of whether these two positions are actually compatible.

In closing, I suggest that the field move from its current state of assertions "proven" by multiple brief vignettes to the study of multiple long-term analytic processes. Such studies would allow an in vivo opportunity to compare the two clinical positions over time and determine their different clinical outcomes, as well as determine whether or not they are compatible with each other. Long-term studies would also shed invaluable light on the question of whether the different conceptual positions are beneficial for different types of patients, a consideration that has been omitted from the discourse thus far. It is my hope that studies such as these would push us all—providing interpreters and interpreting providers alike—toward a deeper understanding of the complexities involved in the psychoanalytic cure.

REFERENCES

Bacal, H. (1985), Optimal responsiveness and the therapeutic process. In: *Progress in Self Psychology, Vol. 1,* ed. A. Goldberg. New York: Guilford Press, pp. 202–226.

Bacal, H. & Newman, K. (1990), *Theories of Object Relations: Bridges to Self Psychology.* New York: Columbia University Press.

Basch, M. (1995), Kohut's contribution. *Psychoanal. Dial.,* 5:367–374.

Bernfeld, S. (1928), *Sisyphos, oder ueber die Grenzen der Erziehung.* Vienna: Internationaler Psychoanalytische Verlag.

Brandchaft, B. (1993), To free the spirit from its cell. In: *The Widening Scope of Self Psychology: Progress in Self Psychology, Vol. 9,* ed. A. Goldberg. Hillsdale, NJ: The Analytic Press, pp. 209–230.

Ehrenberg, D. (1992), *The Intimate Edge.* New York: Norton.

Fosshage, J. (1997), Listening/experiencing perspectives and the quest for a facilitating responsiveness. In: *Conversations in Self Psychology: Progress in Self Psychology, Vol. 13,* ed. A. Goldberg. Hillsdale, NJ: The Analytic Press, pp. 33–56.

Freud, S. (1909), Notes upon a case of obsessional neurosis. *Standard Edition,* 10:151–249. London: Hogarth Press, 1955.

————— (1912), Recommendations to physicians practising psycho-analysis. *Standard Edition,* 12:109–120. London: Hogarth Press, 1958.

————— (1917), Mourning and melancholia. *Standard Edition,* 14:243–258. London: Hogarth Press, 1957.

————— (1918), From the history of an infantile neurosis. *Standard Edition,* 17:1–122. London: Hogarth Press, 1955.

Gedo, J. & Goldberg, A. (1973), *Models of the Mind: A Psychoanalytic Theory.* Chicago, IL: University of Chicago Press.

Gill, M. (1994), *Psychoanalysis in Transition: A Personal View.* Hillsdale, NJ: The Analytic Press.

Kohut, H. (1959), Introspection, empathy and psychoanalysis: An examination of the relationship between modes of observation and theory. In: *Search for the Self—Selected Writings of Heinz Kohut: 1950–1978, Vol. 1,* ed. P. Ornstein. New York: International Universities Press, 1978, pp. 205–232.

————— (1971), *Analysis of the Self.* New York: International Universities Press.

————— (1972), Letter, September 23. In: *The Search for the Self, Vol. 2,* ed. P. Ornstein. New York: International Universities Press, pp. 867–868.

————— (1977), *Restoration of the Self.* New York: International Universities Press.

————— (1981), On empathy. In: *The Search for the Self, Vol. 4,* ed. P. Ornstein. New York: International Universities Press, 1991, pp. 525–535.

————— (1984), *How Does Analysis Cure?* ed. A. Goldberg & P. Stepansky. Chicago, IL: University of Chicago Press.

————— & Seitz, P., ed. (1960), Kohut's unpublished course, P 200, 300, "Psychoanalytic Psychology," in Kohut Archives, located at the Chicago Institute for Psychoanalysis.

————— & ————— (1963), Concepts and theories of psychoanalysis. In: *Search for the Self, Vol. 1,* ed. P. Ornstein. New York: International Universities Press, 1978, pp. 337–374.

Lachmann, F. & Beebe, B. (1995), Self psychology: Today. *Psychoanal. Dial.,* 5:375–384.

Lindon, J. (1994), Gratification and provision in psychoanalysis: Should we get rid of the "rule of abstinence"? *Psychoanal. Dial.,* 4:549–582.

Ornstein, A. (1988), Optimal responsiveness and the theory of cure. *Learning from Kohut: Progress in Self Psychology, Vol 4,* ed. A. Goldberg. Hillsdale, NJ: The Analytic Press, pp. 155–159.

Rapaport, D. & Gill, M. M. (1959), The points of view and assumptions of metapsychology. In: *Collected Papers of David Rapaport,* ed. M. M. Gill. New York: Basic Books, 1967, pp. 795–811.

Shane, E. & Shane, M. (1996), Self psychology in search of the optimal: A consideration of optimal responsiveness; optimal provision; optimal gratification; and optimal restraint in the clinical situation. In: *Basic Ideas Reconsidered: Progress* in *Self Psychology, Vol. 12,* ed. A. Goldberg. Hillsdale, NJ: The Analytic Press, pp. 37–54.

Siegel, A. (1996), *Heinz Kohut and the Psychology of the Self.* London: Routledge.

Stern, D. (1985), *The Interpersonal World of the Infant.* New York: Basic Books.

Stolorow, R. (1994), The intersubjective context of intrapsychic experience. In: *The Intersubjective Perspective,* ed. R. Stolorow, G. Atwood & B. Brandchaft. Northvale, NJ: Aronson, pp. 2–14.

——(1995), An intersubjective view of self psychology. *Psychoanal. Dial.,* 5:393–400.

—— Brandchaft, B. & Atwood, G. (1987), *Psychoanalytic Treatment: An Intersubjective Approach.* Hillsdale, NJ: The Analytic Press.

Terman, D. (1988), Optimum frustration: Structuralization and the therapeutic process. In: *Learning from Kohut: Progress in Self Psychology, Vol. 4,* ed. A. Goldberg. Hillsdale, NJ: The Analytic Press, pp. 113–126.

Tolpin, M. (1971), On the beginnings of a cohesive self: An application of the concept of transmuting internalization to the study of the transitional object and signal anxiety. In: *The Psychoanalytic Study of the Child, Vol. 26,* ed. R. Eissler, A. Freud, M. Kris, S. Lustman, & A. Solnit. New York: Quadrangle Books, pp. 316–354.

Winnicott, D. W. (1951), Transitional objects and transitional phenomena. In: *Collected Papers: Through Paediatrics to Psychoanalysis.* London: Tavistock, pp. 229–242.

—— (1958), The capacity to be alone. In: *The Maturational Processes and the Facilitating Environment.* London: Hogarth Press, pp. 29–36.

—— (1963), From dependence toward independence in the development of the individual. In: *The Maturational Processes and the Facilitating Environment.* London: Hogarth Press, pp. 83–92.

Wolf, E. (1988), Problems of therapeutic orientation. In: *Progress in Self Psychology, Vol. 4,* ed. A. Goldberg. New York: Guilford Press, pp. 168–172.

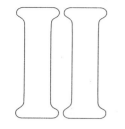

Theory of
Technique

On Boundaries and Intimacy in Psychoanalysis

Mark J. Gehrie

For many years, psychoanalytic technique reflected a general consensus about the relative positions of the analyst and analysand. The analysand came seeking insight about problems and difficulties that were brought into the analytic consulting room and presented to the analyst. The analyst attempted to maintain a position of some distance in the effort to remain "objective" about whatever was presented. This attempt to maintain some objectivity about it all seemed very important so that the analyst's skill and knowledge could be fruitfully brought to bear. This model of doctor and patient seemed impeccably rational, and deviance from it to any significant degree was usually understood to signal a difficulty on the part of the doctor—the doctor was too influenced or involved for some reason, and this was not good for the process, which required a steady hand on the rudder. Too much feeling of any type could cause a loss or disturbance of perspective and interfere with the steadiness of the doctor's focus on the inner workings of the mind of his patient. It was understood that the mind operated according to a set of principles that were generally accepted, and the patient was relying for her cure on the doctor's ability to apply these principles most effectively in order to throw light on the presumably distorted aspects of the workings of her mind. Certainly the relationship between the analyst and analysand was an issue, but primarily through one central venue: the patient carried within her a set of unconscious ideas, patterns of experience, and associated feelings from the past, which were experienced in the context of the "relationship" to the analyst.[1] This "transference" was of value primarily because it could be used to elucidate the inner workings of the patient's mind; it was understood as a re-creation of a version of an early developmental relational dynamic, heavily influenced by constitutional factors (drives) that formed the key to getting at the heart of the matter. In the service of this attempt, it remained of paramount importance that at least the doctor retain some clarity about what came from whom, that is, that there was purposely retained a (nearly) impermeable boundary between the experiential worlds of the two people in the room, specifically for the purpose of establishing clarity about what was happening by keeping the boundary as a reference point: this is about me, and this is about you. This boundary extended to interactions outside of the consulting room as well and toward the same ends: to make it possible to clarify, as much as possible, what each person's contribution to any interaction might be; to provide an opportunity for the analysand to experience the analyst in as "pure" a culture as possible, that is, with as little interference from the analyst's character as possible; and to structure an environment of relative frustration in order that underlying fantasies and longings would be stimulated and expressed in the transference.

Certainly this was an admirable goal from the modernist perspective, and when it worked properly, it often provided very useful and gratifying results. However, there were a few flaws in the argument: most prominently, of course, was the fact that, regardless of the attempt to maintain the boundary just described, it remained an impossible goal, since any and all of the experiences that were shared between the two players were of necessity intermingled with each other, and any sense of "clarity" derived from such an arrangement could also be argued as fictional. As Kohut (1984) asked, "Are there really truths of any significance and breadth that can be evaluated without regard to the observer who affirms them?" (p. 36). It gradually became apparent that the analyst's "abstinence" in service of the frustration hypothesis often unintentionally replicated pathogenic aspects of the analysand's early environment, leading to the emergence of hostility as a result of the actual transactions of the analysis, which were difficult to separate out from the transference. From this perspective, patient–doctor enmeshment seemed inevitable and therefore required a greater acknowledgement in technique.

---

[1] For some, the relationship also extended to the idea of the therapeutic alliance, although there remained disagreement about the extent to which this "alliance" was free from, influenced by, or an aspect of the transference in general.

The advent of the psychology of the self did not make the going any simpler in terms of these boundary questions. As we immersed ourselves more deeply into the experience of our patients—as we struggled to grasp, via empathy and introspection—what their experience was, and moreover, how they experienced us as aspects of themselves, it became increasingly difficult for us to maintain a sense of separateness or distance within the analytic dyad. We were compelled by the theory to adopt a technique that emphasized emotional availability, because to do otherwise made empathy impossible. Either we stood "outside" the patient's experience and examined it, or we stood more "inside" it and acknowledged our part in the creation of it. This position of the insider vis-à-vis the experience of the analysand took on even greater weight as it came to be seen as the foundation for a new, relativistic definition of psychoanalytic process and cure: our focus shifted from "keeping our magnifying glasses clean" (Kohut, 1984, p. 37) to "understand and participate in the psychological life" of our patients such that we might provide "the most crucial emotional experience for human psychological survival and growth: the attention of a selfobject milieu" (p. 37). As our role as agents in the construction and utilization of a growth process (i.e., the re-mobilization of derailed development) became more explicit, we began to question many of the heretofore untouchable principles of the analytic situation, including the idea of analytic neutrality, the principle of abstinence, and virtually everything that at base was aimed at the maintenance of distance between analyst and analysand; it became very exciting to think about how we could actively enter the therapeutic endeavor and have more influence over it in contrast to the more frustrating (for some analysts) position of waiting on the patient's free associations while limiting our interventions to illuminating interpretations about transferences or resistances.

However, as Wolfe (1992) describes, Kohut left his technique ambiguous; he did not clearly or specifically explicate how the therapeutic task as he envisioned it should be carried out. Furthermore, there evolved a lack of distinction between Kohut's theory of development and his prescriptions for the management of an analytic process. In other words, what might be a desirable position for the responsive caregiver of the developing child might not be structurally analogous to the position of the analyst in her effort to "re-start derailed development" with her adult analysand. As Wolfe (1992) notes, "The principle of responding in a manner likely to facilitate the unfolding, illumination, and transformation of the patient's subjective world has been misunderstood as implying that the analyst should acquiesce with the patient's wishes" (pp. 40–41). And, most germane to the topic at hand, she has also remarked that it is not "possible to distinguish an empathically informed response from an enactment, except by knowing more about the therapist's motives. On a practical level, it is not possible to know, in advance, which responses are necessary in order to establish a safe milieu that permits the optimal unfolding and transformation of the patient's affectivity and which will divert that process along lines dictated by the therapist's needs" (p. 42). It appears, therefore, that increasing reliance on the analyst's empathy alone, combined with a theory [such as "optimal responsiveness" (Bacal, 1985), for example, or "optimal provision" (Lindon, 1994)] that presumes that the patient will inform the analyst regarding the nature of his or her needs and therefore of the presumed "optimal" level and form of emotional involvement and that this should be relied on as a singular guide will likely result in a greatly increased pressure on the idea, as well as the fact of a boundary somewhere within the dyad. As we move along the ideological continuum toward the more now politically acceptable position of optimal responsiveness, we tend to move simultaneously toward what becomes a more psychologically acceptable position of decreasing emphasis on the relevance of the phenomenon of "boundary" or at least on how it has been defined up to this point (although it is certainly true that boundary violations have occurred between patients and their analysts of all theoretical persuasions).

Bacal (1985) indirectly addresses the question of boundary in his discussion of optimal responsiveness and the "developmental line of empathy" (Kohut, 1981). He notes that the relative emphasis that we place on "interpretation" and "relationship" as relevant to cure "has practical implications for the way we respond as psychoanalysts" (p. 213). Paraphrasing Winnicott, Bacal (1985) stresses that "the analyst's response must be commensurate with the patient's level of self–selfobject organization or the degree of intactness, defect or deficit within the self" (p. 214). Therefore, as Bacal notes, it follows that "there is no such thing as a 'parameter,' an extraanalytic, or unanalytic, measure we adopt for a time in order ultimately to return to doing proper analysis in the traditional way" (p. 215). He says, "We must respond in ways that enable us to communicate understanding to the particular patient with whom we are working. That is analysis" (p. 215). Bacal also states that optimal responsiveness is defined as "the responsivity of the analyst that is therapeutically most relevant at any particular moment" (p. 202). It refers, he says, to "the therapist's acts of communicating his understanding to his patient" (p. 202). But how is this determined? What exactly does "therapeutically most relevant" mean? And what are the guidelines for the communication of understanding? Few would argue that we must loosen the historical limits on what constitutes interpretation or how it is offered—much has been written about this over the last 20 years. But the determination of what is therapeutically most relevant is indeed the crux of the matter. Bacal suggests that, if we broaden our range of interpretations, we stand a greater chance of recognizing what he calls "the patient's bid for a creative transference relatedness" (p. 209). This leaves the impression that he believes there are instances in which the relational aspect of the process must take precedence over the interpretive one. This relates to the question of boundaries because *if we premiate the relationship over the interpretive goals, then the nature of the relationship per se is fundamentally altered; no longer is the management of the relationship just one element among others in the organization of the treatment process* (regardless of our views on what does or does not constitute "an interpretation"). Rather, it risks becoming an end in itself, managed from the perspective of what is best for it—as in nontherapeutic relationships. This, then, is an essential boundary question: does the intervention in question aim at the furtherance of a therapeutic goal or is the relationship the only therapeutic ingredient? To argue that the relationship and the treatment are inseparable or indistinguishable is tantamount to arguing that the relationship basically is the treatment. I think that to take this position essentially reduces the notion of a self from one possessing long-term structural continuity, identity, and cohesiveness to a view of the self as manufactured in the vicissitudes of moment-to-moment interaction. This position may also constitute a defensive stand on the part of the therapist for whom there may be conscious or unconscious self-enhancing countertransference engagement. There must be a conceptual middle ground that preserves the continuity of the self through time but also includes the mitigating effect of the interaction of subjective worlds. A boundary is essentially a guide that preserves the opportunity to assess interactions in terms of the goal of the therapeutic relationship and to help maintain one's focus on that goal amidst the myriad pressures of the circumstance. *The relationship is not the treatment, but the relationship makes the treatment possible if it is properly managed.*

Bacal's (1985) characterization of the nature of the analytic process, especially his emphasis on intimacy, has a powerful appeal. Or, perhaps I should say, it appeals to those of us who yearn for the analytic relationship to embody a form of relatedness that we personally value. Most of us would agree that children do better if they are raised with loving affirmation, acceptance, and encouragement, than without it. But we also agree—don't we?—that an overstimulated child may need help in calming down and that this judgment may be made externally to the child's conscious experience of the moment. It is very tempting and very easy to feel that intimacy can conquer all—as if the main challenge in the establishment and maintenance of a psychoanalytic process is a relational intimacy that is intended to be experienced in a salutary way by the patient, and to some extent this is true. Certainly we have all also learned that understanding is an invaluable tool—understanding informed by empathy and utilized with compassion—and all of us have experienced the pull toward intensified involvement as a way to ameliorate the pain that the failure to fully understand reliably engenders. *This is another essential aspect of boundary and, hence, also of boundary violation: the proper boundary is what must be maintained in the service of compassionate understanding; a boundary violation is the attempt via relational intimacy to overcome (usually unrecognized) failures in understanding in the attempt to heal a breach that is painfully experienced by both analyst and analysand.*

Most typically, boundary violations are characterized by efforts at increased intimacy as palliative, although I would argue that it is equally a violation to withdraw from appropriate levels of contact and to leave the patient in a painful aloneness. "Boundary," in this view, refers to the proper assessment—and I mean this relative to analytic or therapeutic goals—of the patient's need for psychological closeness versus distance, and it is the analyst's job to get that right.

While this is always an issue in every analysis, I do feel compelled to at least mention at this juncture that one of our greatest challenges is the training analysis. Without going into the whole history of this complex issue, suffice it to say that, most typically, we tend to train our future colleagues in an analytic environment substantially different from that of analysands who are not in such training. Some outstanding examples are termination with the knowledge of ongoing future contact of one type or another; extraanalytic contact in the training setting with the attendant grandiose fantasy on the part of the analyst that "anything can be analyzed"; and most notably, the reluctance on the part of many training analysts to analyze the idealizing transference, with the rationale that its maintenance is part of a professional identification or serves some other vital selfobject need for the candidate. These are all examples of boundary violations because they endanger a major analytic goal: that is, the fullest exploration possible of the personality and the attendant opportunity for the analysand to grow in harmony with his own internal program. Boundaries exist, in other words, both to preserve this developmental opportunity and to attempt to prevent the otherwise unavoidable corruption of the relationship with other motives. There exists an informal ethos that such "corruption" is avoidable with the proper therapeutic intent or that the analyst's wisdom will supercede the power of the transference. But when we risk replacing analytic goals with what amounts to "cure by relationship," we risk throwing out the baby and keeping the bathwater. The optimal responsiveness of the selfobject must not be mistaken for the provision of an environment that conceals certain qualities out of fear of loss of the precious tie or out of a belief that the value of the tie will be enhanced by circumventing basic principles of analytic process management.

The proper management of the archaic selfobject transference includes the analyst's constant attentiveness to the "shape" of the underlying self state and the concomitant adjustment of the relational dynamics in keeping with a focus on analytic goals, which is not always the same as keeping everything as comfortable as possible. In a recent paper, Morton and Estelle Shane (1997) address the influence of countertransference on the maintenance of boundaries and on "the creative and fluctuating tension between intimacy and boundaries in the therapeutic relationship" (p. 69). Toward this end, they emphasize their view that there are two fundamental and distinct forms of relating: the self–selfobject relationship as described by Kohut (1977) and what they call "self–other relatedness" (p. 74), the first being the more archaic narcissistic type and the second most typically described as "other-centered." From this distinction they evolve therapeutic techniques that they feel are most appropriate for each type: for the more archaic type of relating (the case of Kathy), they suggest using a technique that requires the acceptance of the patient's subjective experience, whereas for what they consider the more developmentally "advanced" type of patient (the case of Bob), they imply that interpretive interventions may be used more freely. They conclude that, depending upon the nature of the pathology and the "forms of relating" (as illustrated by their cases), boundaries should be more or less "assiduously maintained" (p. 87) or might even be seen as "synonymous with the maintenance of sensitivity and tact and the avoidance of countertransference judgement and critical response" (p. 88). In my view, this is more of a commentary on technique than on boundaries and, in essence, is a reflection of Kohut's (1984) discussion of the variable relationship between the understanding and explanatory phases in an analysis.

I would offer that there is an infinite range of relational possibilities that are a function of underlying self states (Gehrie, in prep.), none of which take precedence over the maintenance of analytic goals. The appropriate boundary questions go beyond "sensitivity and tact, and the avoidance of countertransference judgement and critical response" (Shane and Shane, 1997, p. 88) and reside on an altogether different level: *boundaries have to do with the proper assessment of the patient's self state; the integration that we seek to achieve in analytic treatment can only take place properly with the existence of boundaries that regulate the crucial balance between closeness and distance.* Without this balance, there is the risk of the appearance of integration or therapeutic progress that may not have been actually made, leading to treatments in which the continued presence of the analyst in one form or another is necessary. In other words, we as analysts have this responsibility and must make these determinations; it is up to us—countertransference pressures notwithstanding—to maintain a focus on analytic goals that will illuminate the proper boundary and point us toward the appropriate technique.

What the correct boundary is may not always be clear and may not coincide with the therapist's intuitive response to the patient. If we miss the mark too widely in this judgment, perhaps because we are influenced by a theory that favors a comfortable relational balance at the cost of keeping a firm eye on analytic goals (or for other reasons), we may inadvertently make a transition that may interfere with the very development that we are attempting to promote.

The following is an example of an instance where a therapist early on lost sight of the therapeutic goals, confusing them with relational ones from the outset of the treatment. A supervisee of mine reported on the following experience with her male patient. Slightly younger than the therapist, the patient was an intense, sincere young man who, in the old parlance, was "transference ready," implying that he was clearly eager for and accessible to an engagement in the treatment. He had been referred for ongoing relationship problems and had told the referring doctor that he liked the idea of an analysis because "that was how you could really get into things." At the outset, however, the patient hestitated to make a commitment to an analytic schedule and agreed to come twice a week "to see how things would go." My supervisee reported that she had sensed her patient's intensity early on in his response to her after only a few sessions and had felt that she had successfully engaged him. He said, "I'm already looking forward to coming to these sessions, and I really enjoy talking to you. I like how you respond to me." When I questioned my supervisee on this point, she reported that she was aware that she was responding to her patient with less of the clinical reserve than she might have maintained. She felt, she said, that she could sense the effect of this responsiveness on her patient; she didn't want him to feel turned away from, as he had in other relationships with women. She was convinced that he needed this level of responsiveness; it mediated his emotional volatility and, she felt, he could use it in a therapeutically valuable way because, she explained, without this kind of response "it seemed as if he couldn't hold on to my interpretations." Her examples of this were all in the same pattern: he would express a deep sense of affectionate longing for the therapist and would indicate that he wished to hear a similar sentiment in return. If she did not so respond or even hesitated to respond in kind, the patient would withdraw and become despairing, offering his own interpretation: "You *are* like my mother. . . . This is all one-sided, you don't really care about me." The therapist would then feel compelled to "repair" the breach by offering the wished-for reassurance. She had, belatedly, brought this case to supervision because she had finally realized that it had spun seriously out of control: as her patient's intensity grew increasingly erotized, there had begun a pattern of touching, hugging, and eventually kissing and intimate touching, although there was no sexual intercourse. "Everything but," she said. Interpretations to her patient about all this—which she had attempted to offer throughout these interactions from the perspective that "if we can talk about it, we can understand the meaning of it to you," and so on—seemed now to her to have had little value. When she eventually refused sexual intercourse, the patient again became distant and despairing, just as he had when she had in the past hesitated to respond in kind to his verbal proclamations of love. He soon left the treatment, insisting again that her refusal was "evidence" of her failure to be "with" him in a meaningful way. The point is that little had changed for this man over the course of the treatment because the primary issue had not been addressed at a level that might have afforded a therapeutic engagement. More specifically, the underlying meaning of the patient's insistence on the therapist's acquiesence was never investigated nor was the more obvious significance of the negative mother transference. The therapist, in other words, had not been able to make it possible for this patient to reflect on the nature and source of his longings and, by trying to gratify them, had confused the issue beyond repair. Eventually, of course, it became impossible to reestablish therapeutic goals in the treatment because of the unconscious implications to the patient of the therapist's actions.

In another example of the difficulty in establishing the correct boundary, a young male patient, a lawyer in a local firm, sought an analysis because of severe relational difficulties and a generalized unhappiness about nearly everything in his life. He had opted for law school as the only professional option that met the achievement criteria of his parents, but toward which he felt no noticeable emotional or even intellectual interest. He said he felt criticized for everything, by his mother in particular, and all of his accomplishments only meant that she could boast to her friends. His father seemed ineffectual to him, on the sidelines of his life and unable to offer significant emotional input. He described a feeling of "inconsequentialness" and the sense that, if he permits himself to feel cared about by the analyst, it means that, like with his mother, he feels "owned" by the analyst. The essential tie between them was like a tie of ownership, in which the patient could distinguish himself only in opposition to her. Not surprisingly, in the analysis it became imperative for this patient to feel secure that I would (somehow) respect this boundary and not press the patient in the direction of his vulnerability. This was not easy, since anything I did in the interest of the analytic work could have this quality; that is, it could (and often was) be experienced as my own agenda, even including my efforts to be cordial in an ordinary way: a pleasant greeting or smile was likely to be taken as overt seductiveness, if not manipulation, and had to be angrily fended off.

To complicate matters further, attempts to discuss this phenomenon were experienced similarly; there seemed to be no opportunity for reflective purchase on this global archaic negative transference (and, of course, in which the tie to the object was in this way preserved; see Gehrie, 1996). Everything felt to him as if I were claiming ownership of "reality." Nothing could be talked "about"—everything was an enactment of this transference, and the only venue for contact seemed to be in marginal areas that did not threaten to impinge on this "boundary": we could joke about distant things or I could listen to him complain (although if I was *too* sympathetic or understanding, that wasn't good either), but this seemed to me to have little meaningful analytic value. Sometimes I would feel compelled to offer a transference interpretation to draw him into an insight-oriented discussion about our relationship. This was reliably met with anger and hostile withdrawal and accusations that I was trying to hurt him.

Over time, I experienced a combination of intensifying frustration that little was happening in the analysis but also a simultaneous sense that, as long as I restrained myself from my inclination to go beyond what my patient offered as acceptable grounds for conversation, some kind of contact was being made and that this connection was very important to him. This I would describe as a kind of subtext or latent content in our conversations that led me to feel that contact was possible so long as I could keep myself from pursuing my agenda; it was as if there were some "space" in an otherwise closed universe. Furthermore, I felt that the pursuit of the possibility of opening up a reflective pathway required me to take this position; pursuing analytic goals in this instance meant precisely permitting a set of conditions that for me were counterintuitive but were in the interest of the development of an analytic environment.

As it turned out, I was rewarded for my efforts. About two years into the treatment, my patient, who had been sitting up, decided that he could "risk" lying down on the couch. I asked him what had prompted this, and to my astonishment, he replied, "I could see that I haven't been able to let you in. . . . When you talk about important things, I get angry and push you away. Maybe if I lie down and don't look at you, it'll be easier for me to think about what you're really saying instead of getting so scared." Nothing like this had ever been articulated by my patient before, and I had presumed that he would experience lying on the couch as too "close." As time has gone on, I've continued to marvel at his ability to "hear" things that were not possible to access before. Clearly, the boundary had shifted unexpectedly for me; I think this was the result of his ability to take in the experience of my self-restraint as a functional selfobject, gradually leading to a degree of greater self-consolidation, the experience of less vulnerability, and the resultant ability to shift the location of the boundary between us.

I would suggest that the proper assessment of the patient's need for closeness or distance may not jibe with the analyst's intuitive approach to (or avoidance of) the patient. *The boundary issue here refers to attitude in the relationship that is functionally expressed in the therapeutic process, rather than as a set of concrete limits or behavioral imperatives. This attitude should reflect an unwavering attentiveness to the maintenance of analytic goals.* Our ability to conceptualize complications (such as the myriad implications of overlapping and mutually influencing subjectivities, for example) has, I think, contributed to our loss of focus on the use of the present to grasp the past, and not simply to try to co-construct the present. To center our efforts on remaking the present changes our position from an analytic relationship to an ordinary relationship, and that is where boundary confusion originates. This confusion is often reflected in the misguided attempt to replace insight with intimacy in the effort to ward off the more painful, frustrating aspects of a process that has as its primary aim a remobilized growth experience. The proper management of closeness and distance in this effort is reflective of the analyst's dedication to and focus on the achievement of analytic goals.

In summary, I would like to present the following outline of my views on boundaries:

1. Boundaries reflect an attitude and orientation of the therapist toward what is the agent of change in treatment: is it primarily a relational dynamic, or is the relationship held in service to a therapeutic goal?
2. Most boundary violations are characterized by the therapist's efforts to repair a painful breach by efforts at increased intimacy.
3. The establishment of a correct boundary relies on the proper assessment of the patient's underlying self state and the derived judgment about the desirable balance between closeness and distance in the treatment, and will vary from case to case.

And last but not least, despite my cautions, I cannot overemphasize the value of relatedness in our therapeutic enterprise. We have no more powerful or valuable tool than the capacity to relate and no more important task than the use of this capacity to keep our therapeutic goals clearly in view.

REFERENCES

Bacal, H. (1985), Optimal responsiveness and the therapeutic process. In: *Progress in Self Psychology, Vol. 1,* ed. A. Goldberg. New York: Guilford Press, pp. 202–227.

Gehrie, M. (1996), Empathy in broader perspective: A technical approach to the consequences of the negative selfobject in early character formation. In: *Basic Ideas Reconsidered: Progress in Self Psychology, Vol. 12,* ed. A. Goldberg. Hillsdale, NJ: The Analytic Press, pp. 159–179.

——— (in prep.), Forms of relatedness: The self and the schizoid continuum in self psychology and object relations theory.

Kohut, H. (1977), *The Restoration of the Self.* New York: International Universities Press.

——— (1981), Introspection, empathy, and the semicircle of mental health. *Internat. J. Psycho-Anal.,* 63:395–407.

——— (1984), *How Does Analysis Cure?* ed. A. Goldberg & P. Stepansky. Chicago: University of Chicago Press.

Lindon, J. (1994), Gratification and provision in psychoanalysis: Should we get rid of the "rule of abstinence"? *Psychoanal. Dial.,* 4:549–582.

Shane, M. & Shane, E. (1997), Intimacy, boundaries, and countertransference in the analytic relationship. *Psychoanal. Inq.,* 17:69–89.

Wolfe, B. (1992), Problems for a rational therapeutic in self psychology. In: *New Therapeutic Visions: Progress in Self Psychology, Vol. 8,* ed. A. Goldberg. Hillsdale, NJ: The Analytic Press, pp. 29–56.

Chapter 6

Analytic Boundaries as a Function of Curative Theory: Discussion of Mark Gehrie's "On Boundaries and Intimacy in Psychoanalysis"

Linda A. Chernus

In this challenging and thought-provoking paper, Dr. Gehrie has formulated his views about boundaries in psychoanalysis. His discussion rests on the premise that boundaries are intended to further the analytic work by enhancing our capacity to effectively engage patients in therapeutically viable and growth-promoting relationships. As such, boundaries function to facilitate the analytic process both by protecting the analyst from responses that interfere with his capacity to remain empathic and protecting the patient from being injured or exploited by the analyst as a result of the analyst's own needs and vulnerabilities, which Gehrie believes to be always impacting (in subtle or not so subtle ways) on the treatment relationship.

Dr. Gehrie has appropriately chosen to focus on boundaries within, rather than around, the relationship and, in particular, on those that do not involve clear-cut legal and/or moral issues and are therefore "negotiable" by both parties. Such boundaries, inherently affected by the subjectivity of both patient and analyst, frequently present serious, if not critical, clinical challenges to us and are therefore worthy of our thoughtful exploration.

Though Dr. Gehrie does not specifically address how we come to recognize the boundaries implicit in our actual work with patients, I would suggest that perhaps we often know what the boundaries were only in *retrospect*, since we generally do not deliberately "do things" to the patient in an active sense, such as the proverbial "limit setting." In fact, when we find ourselves thinking in such terms, we are probably experiencing a collapse of our analytic selves in response to patients who cannot mirror our functions, as recently described by Bacal and Thomson (1996). Furthermore, because such "negotiable" boundaries are generally not explicit, we cannot know whether certain actions fall on one or the other side of a boundary—this depends both on the meaning to the patient of his *experience* of the analyst's action and on whether the analyst sees the action as curative in itself or as enabling the patient to make better use of him to serve needed selfobject functions. Therefore, Dr. Gehrie's views about boundary setting can only be understood in the context of his conceptualization of psychoanalysis as primarily grounded in the interpretive working through of the selfobject transference, in contrast with a conceptualization of analytic treatment as having what he terms primarily "relational" goals.

It is apparent that traditional analytic boundaries, constructed in the context of drive psychology, need to be reassessed in the context of self psychologically informed treatment. The consistent use of empathy tends to promote more analytic responsiveness and also calls into question the reasons for the most sacrosanct rules of psychoanalysis. We have less need for total anonymity and neutrality, both because we are not striving to achieve pure transference repetition and because we now all acknowledge that the patient is always affected by the analyst's responsivity.[1]

I agree with Dr. Gehrie that a new formulation of treatment as remobilizing derailed development not only challenges the reasons for

---

[1] The "intersubjective" position is not new. Bacal (1990, p. 350) credits its first formulation to Michael Balint (1949), who spoke of how clinical phenomena could only be understood as filtered through the analyst's own subjectivity, which in turn affects the patient's subjective experience. I believe that what *is* new, however, is our growing *acceptance* of the inevitability of our subjectivity, with a concomitant "de-pathologizing" of our subjective responses. This has been recently exemplified by Donna Orange's use of the term *cotransference* to replace the term *countertransference*, which has a strongly negative, pathological connotation (1995).

classical rules of neutrality and abstinence, but specifically implies a reevaluation of rules related to maintenance of analytic distance. This does not mean, however, as Gehrie points out, that what happens in analytic treatment is parallel to the responsiveness of parental selfobjects to a developing child's needs. A reformulation of our thinking about boundaries does not necessarily imply that self-disclosure or other forms of direct selfobject need meeting are helpful, let alone essential to analytic treatment. Furthermore, even if we accept that empathic understanding is inherently subjective, because we are always influenced both by our own past and by our patients' responses to us, it does not automatically follow that sharing our responses with patients will facilitate the analytic process. Perhaps, however, awareness of our total subjectivity promotes a kind of "objectivity" and provides a form of internal boundary guiding our responses to the patient.[2] Maintenance of this self-awareness is especially important in light of how easily we can regress to thinking that we are being *objective*, in response to patients who fail to silently serve selfobject functions for us that enable us to sustain our analytically functioning selves (Wolf, 1980; Brothers, 1995; Sucharov, 1995).

Believing that such actions in and of themselves promote cure represents a fundamentally different conceptualization of the treatment process than believing that it is the working through of the *meaning* of such actions, if and when they do occur, that contributes to analytic cure. Clearly, of course, there are always *some* elements of direct need meeting, even in a treatment where the analytic working through of the selfobject transference is seen as primary, since the experience of being consistently understood generally promotes self-cohesion through its mirroring function, as does the analyst's sensitivity to the patient's self state in deciding how, when, and what to communicate of his understanding. I maintain, however, that this benign form of "responsiveness" based on our empathic attunement is fundamentally different from "optimal responsiveness" as meaning employing behavioral responses whose primary purpose is to contribute to a new experience for the patient.

In recent years, it has been suggested that we replace the drive psychologically derived concept of optimal frustration with the concept of optimal responsiveness as a guiding principle for determining

---

[2] By "objectivity," I do not mean a lack of acceptance of our subjectivity but, rather, an embracing of it, along with the irony that our subjective responses are our primary tool for empathic understanding.

boundaries (Bacal, 1985, 1990, 1994). This has been interpreted by some to mean simply adapting or modifying our analytic responses to facilitate the working through process, especially with more vulnerable or fragmented patients. For others, however, optimal responsiveness has come to mean a process of responding empathically on a behavioral level that, in and of itself, is believed to bring about cure. This debate concerning optimal responsiveness, optimal frustration, and other so-called "optimal" elements in the analytic process reflects our efforts to systematize or create guidelines for our responses, in light of the inapplicability of traditional analytic guidelines in a self psychologically informed therapeutic context. It raises the issue of what it is that we *give* to patients over and above our empathically derived understanding, Furthermore, the optimal responsiveness/optimal frustration controversy raises the issue of why we decide to respond as we do to our patients, predicated (hopefully) on our beliefs about the nature of what is curative in psychoanalysis.[3]

When Bacal first formally introduced the term *optimal responsiveness* (1985), he indicated that the analyst should communicate his understanding to the patient in a manner that the patient would be most able to utilize at that particular moment in the treatment, based both on his developmental capacity and the nature of his selfobject needs. Though I agree that our empathic understanding must be grounded in attention to the state of the patient's self and the self–selfobject matrix, my interpretation of what Bacal meant is that we must *do* something special, if indeed our verbal communication of our understanding fails to ameliorate the patient's intensely painful self state.

My reading of Bacal's original position, however, is that it remained grounded in the analytic process of using empathy both for understanding and communication of our understanding, though Bacal's emphasis was on finding more effective means to do so when our usual responses do not enable the patient to feel understood. This does not necessarily mean that we must *directly meet* the patient's selfobject needs. Subsequent to Bacal's initial formulation of optimal responsiveness (1985), however, the concept has increasingly come to be incorporated into a more general trend toward making the patient

---

[3] Subsequent to Bacal's (1985) formulation, others have responded to the conceptual and clinical challenges stimulated by the concept of optimal responsiveness by suggesting a variety of other "optimal" qualities that the analyst should strive to achieve. An excellent and comprehensive review of these concepts is provided by Morton and Estelle Shane (1996).

more comfortable as an end in itself, often including direct meeting of selfobject needs.[4]

This position can be seen as a logical extension of the fact that use of the empathic mode tends to promote enhanced well-being by facilitating the integration of the patient's self. Consequently, making the patient even *more* comfortable in treatment can become an end in itself. Another factor contributing toward this trend is our working with sicker patients, who, by definition, have difficulty utilizing the usual forms of communicating our understanding to develop stable selfobject transferences.

I would like to make a few more comments about the optimal frustration/optimal responsiveness controversy. I agree with Kohut (1984, 1987) that, even when the analyst is in tune with the patient, the patient still experiences frustration of the needs that have become engaged in the transference, both because the treatment is not directly meeting these needs and because of trauma associated with them that becomes reactivated in the transference, as Gehrie (1996) has also described. In addition, of course, the patient experiences frustration secondary to our inevitable lack of perfect empathy. Though emotional suffering is unavoidable, however, we are in a sense always endeavoring to keep the patient's pain at an "optimal" level, by which I mean trying to enable the patient to tolerate the frustration inherent in the experience so that the process can continue to fruition.

Though Terman (1988) has maintained that the concept of optimal frustration is inappropriate in a self psychological context, others have redefined the meaning of optimal frustration as it relates to selfobject needs, rather than drive derivatives. Kohut himself utilized the concept of optimal frustration to refer to selfobject failures that are "comparatively nontraumatic" (1987, p. 103). "Frustration," like "empathy," can be understood as an "experience-near" concept referring to the patient's and analyst's subjective experience in relation to the patient's selfobject needs. As such, they contribute to the creation of inherent treatment boundaries since, by remaining in the empathic mode, the

---

[4] In some of his more recent formulations of the concept of optimal responsiveness (Bacal, 1990; Bacal and Thomson, 1996), Bacal defines as *optimal* those responses that facilitate a therapeutic selfobject experience. Though Bacal emphasizes the "experiential" component in Kohut's theory of cure (Kohut, 1977, pp. 30–31), Bacal nevertheless still agrees with M. Tolpin (1983) that it is the interpretation of the selfobject experience and the internalization of the selfobject transferences that lead to structure building and analytic cure. Despite Bacal's first-hand knowledge that Kohut highly valued the mutative influence of the therapeutic relationship and in particular the self–selfobject relationship, the essence of what is analytic remains "the internalization of the cohesion-fostering selfobject tie" (Bacal, 1990, p. 360).

structure of the treatment is defined by focusing our understanding on the emerging selfobject needs rather than responding directly to them. Though optimal responsiveness initially sounds more empathic because of its emphasis on being in tune with the patient's subjective experience and its disaffiliation with the concept of "frustration," optimal responsiveness, as it has evolved during the past decade (Shane and Shane, 1996), does not refer to the patient's or analyst's subjective experience but, rather, to a *technique* that is deliberately employed by the analyst based on his understanding of the patient at that moment.[5]

David MacIsaac has convincingly presented this position in his 1996 paper, in which he discusses optimal frustration in relation to a patient who was initially unable to utilize his analytic functions in order to develop a stable selfobject transference. According to MacIsaac, whether the inevitable frustrations the patient experiences are "optimal" or "traumatic" depends on whether they can be resolved analytically. This process involves two factors—the analyst's capacity for empathic attunement with the particular patient and the patient's capacity to use the analyst's empathy to serve needed selfobject functions, which, as Gehrie has underscored, is somewhat independent of the analyst's empathic capacity (1996).[6] If we focus on what response is optimal, however, rather than remaining in contact with the patient's subjective experience, we increase the likelihood that the patient will feel *traumatically* rather than *optimally* frustrated and that we will miss opportunities for deepening of our understanding.

In his chapter, Dr. Gehrie contributes to the burgeoning literature concerning the issue of what can be termed "finding the 'optimal' " in psychoanalysis. He believes that the recent emergence of a subgroup within self psychology, which regards the analyst's mode of responsiveness as determined by the patient's particular developmental needs at any given moment in treatment, is an outgrowth of the fact that the empathic mode has always tended to encourage an emphasis on emotional availability. His concern, however, is that such emotional availability, as demonstrated through the analyst's verbal and nonverbal responses to the patient, not only does not substitute for an empathically derived understanding, but also may reflect the analyst's

---

[5] As suggested earlier, I am not at all sure that this was Bacal's (1985) original intent.

[6] This position is consistent with Kohut's long-held position (1984) that optimal frustrations are *by definition* nontraumatic if they can be repaired through the analytic work in the context of a well-functioning selfobject matrix.

inability to remain in touch with the patient's subjective experience, for whatever reasons. Furthermore, Gehrie emphasizes that a primary function of boundaries is providing for an optimal degree of intimacy to facilitate analytic goals. Though I essentially agree with his position, too strong an emphasis on finding the optimal or ideal stance can distract us away from an empathic immersion in the patient's experience, through which a comfortable degree of closeness naturally emerges as the transference develops.

Dr. Gehrie concludes his chapter with a clinical example, which, at first glance, illustrates the dangers inherent in analytic approaches predicated on responding differently, depending on which mode of relating dominates the patient's transference at any given moment. He attempts to critique such a position, recently exemplified in the writing of Shane, Shane, and Gales (1997a, b), through a vignette in which the analyst responds directly to the patient's sexualized longings and increasingly becomes unable to perform an analytic function. Since the therapist and supervisor did not conceptualize the treatment based on a theoretical model of responding more personally when mutuality was the patient's primary relational need, however, and were instead conducting a treatment based on an interpretive working through of the selfobject transference, I believe it to be a clear-cut instance of countertransference acting out rationalized as necessary to promote analytic working through of the patient's abandonment issues. If indeed he was "transference ready," the analyst could have addressed this patient's ambivalence about making a commitment to analysis and his emerging fear of being turned away by her. Though perhaps she was unable to tolerate the patient's experience of her as rejecting him (and possible subsequent rage), her acting out resulted in an *actual* retraumatization by eventually "rupturing" the therapeutic relationship.[7]

Dr. Gehrie's chapter offers a powerful critique of the position of Shane et al. (1997a, b) that it is the analyst's optimal responsiveness that is curative. He strongly disagrees with them that allowing the "relational aspect" to take precedence over the interpretative one is analytic. Consequently, Gehrie believes that we should determine analytic boundaries by asking whether an intervention furthers an analytic or a purely relational goal. Dr. Gehrie eloquently concludes that, though the relationship and treatment are inseparable, the relation-

---

[7] Elkind (1992, 1994) has provided an in-depth exploration of how countertransference-based enactments frequently contribute to such "ruptures."

ship, if properly managed, is necessary for the treatment to occur but "is not the treatment."

I will briefly respond to some of Dr. Gehrie's comments regarding the optimal frustration/optimal responsiveness controversy, particularly as articulated in the writings of Shane et al. (1997a, b), because their position contrasts so sharply with and thereby helps to delineate the views of Dr. Gehrie and myself. In their writings, Shane et al. (1997a, b) identify three broad categories of boundary concerns. These include boundaries influenced by the analyst's own limitations, boundaries influenced by what they call their "theoretical postulates," and boundaries influenced by the special needs of a patient, such as one experiencing severely unintegrated self states. Their goal in relation to the internal boundaries discussed by Gehrie, which are negotiable between patient and analyst, is to identify the theoretical postulates informing the analyst's thinking and guiding his responses to a particular patient, thereby contributing to the boundaries established. They see the three clinical postulates as leading to the "co-construction of positive new experience" through the reactivation of a developmental course towards "self-consolidation" and "self-with-other-consolidation."

According to their formulation, the first clinical postulate vital to the emergence of positive new experience is the dimension of intimacy, in which the patient relates either in a "self with self-transforming other" or a "self with interpersonal-sharing other" dimension, somewhat analogous to Freud's distinction between narcissistic and mature object libido. If the patient is relating to the analyst as a separate center of initiative, they believe that a *truly analytic* response would involve, not just verbal interpretation, but genuinely giving something personal of oneself to the patient. The second clinical postulate, the relational configuration, includes three possible models describing the influence of the patient's traumatic past on his organization of present experience. Positive new experience is precluded in the first relational configuration, the "old self with old other," whereas the "old self with new other" and "new self with new other" patterns allow for positive new experience. In this, as well as the third postulate, referring to degree of consolidation of the patient's self, determination of the predominant configuration guides not only the analyst's understanding, but also the nature of this response.

Shane et al. have also introduced the idea that the analyst's response is based not only on the *patient's* wish for an intimate connection, but also on the analyst's similar wish (1997b), so that when a male patient shares his sexual feelings with his female analyst, she reciprocates by acknowledging that she finds him sexually attractive too (1997a, p. 57). If this is the only appropriate response to the "self with interpersonal-sharing other" dimension, however, what if the analyst either did not have the same need for intimate connection or felt the same need, but not toward this patient? Furthermore, in another vignette where a male patient's erotic feeling were *not* reciprocated by the analyst, the situation ended fortuitously, because the patient's true developmental needs were assessed as relational, rather than in the dimension of interpersonal sharing (Shane et al., 1997b). One wonders how this treatment would have unfolded, however, had the analyst indeed felt erotic feelings toward the patient or, alternatively, if mutuality *had* been the patient's need, but the analyst did not have similar erotic feelings. A theory of treatment based on the idiosyncratic feelings of the analyst, which cannot be generalizable, certainly poses clinical problems in such situations.

If we accept the premise that the creation of "new experiential pathways" is ultimately curative, then the idea of determining boundaries based on which postulate is in the ascendancy at any given moment in treatment makes sense. However, it is not clear how positive new experience results in permanent change in the form of new psychological structures. Furthermore, this conceptualization of analytic change is open to all of the criticisms historically leveled against the concept of the "corrective emotional experience," including concerns about pathological regression and transference cure.

In my opinion, Dr. Shane's modification of boundaries to provide the patient with a positive new experience beyond understanding alone implies an underestimation of how powerful the *positive new experience of feeling understood* can be and suggests that analytic understanding as practiced by more "traditional" self psychologists is a primarily cognitive affair (which, in my opinion, is certainly not the case). The emphasis on providing a positive new experience also implies that not responding to a patient's wish directly is equivalent to invalidating that wish, as is suggested more specifically in their discussion of the male patient whose erotic feelings were not reciprocated by the analyst. (Shane et al., 1997b).

Actually, it is precisely *through* our empathically derived understanding of a patient's transferential needs that they are validated and eventually accepted by the patient, whereas directly meeting his needs serves to extinguish his experience. Furthermore, by relegating the selfobject transference to a small, and perhaps inferior, part of one principle guiding us in determining boundaries, the Shanes and Dr. Gales deprive themselves of the benefits of the selfobject dimension, which becomes a powerful tool because it supplements the patient's self such that he is better able to tolerate painful affects and resume growth in areas of core deficits.

In conclusion, the concept of "optimal frustration" in relation to selfobject needs, when used to capture the patient's subjective experience, is in my opinion an experience-near construct referring to a dimension of the analytic relationship. If it is through our consistent use of the empathic mode of understanding that the frustrations inherent in the reactivation of archaic needs become tolerable, contributing to the development of the self–selfobject matrix and eventually leading to structural growth, then we can say that *empathy in itself serves a boundary-setting function* by making possible the achievement of analytic goals.

Though in ideal situations, such as MacIsaac's (1996), the consistent experience of feeling understood sufficiently supplements the patient's self structure that an analytic process eventually ensues, *more* vulnerable patients may require certain modifications in the treatment to enable them to develop stable and analytically viable selfobject transferences. Planned phone contacts and voicemail messages are frequently utilized for such purposes. In addition, sometimes the character structure of the patient and the nature of the selfobject transferences are such that a decision to employ some degree of self-disclosure must at least be considered, in order to more effectively maintain a viable self–selfobject matrix.[8] However, when we modify boundaries to facilitate the patient's capacity to tolerate painful affects and better utilize our selfobject functions, the benefits of so doing must be weighed against the costs in terms of limiting the depth of the patient's analytic experience and/or promoting pathological regression.

REFERENCES

Bacal, H. A. (1985), Optimal responsiveness and the therapeutic process. In: *Progress in Self Psychology, Vol. 1*, ed. A. Goldberg. New York: Guilford Press, pp. 202–226.

———— (1990), The elements of a corrective selfobject experience. *Psychoanal. Inq.*, 10:347–372.

---

[8] A recent example of such was the case of Victor, presented by Brothers and Lewinberg (1997), in which Dr. Brothers decided that complying with the patient's demand for a form of self-disclosure was a precondition for the deepening of the treatment process. She did not see the self-disclosure as an end in itself, however, but rather as enabling the patient to tolerate painful states within the transference and as providing a future opportunity for the working through of the meaning of the patient's need for such modification of boundaries.

——— (1994), The selfobject relationship in psychoanalytic treatment. In: *A Decade of Progress: Progress in Self Psychology, Vol. 10*, ed. A. Goldberg. Hillsdale, NJ: The Analytic Press, pp. 21–30.

——— & Thomson, P. G. (1996), The psychoanalyst's selfobject needs and the effect of their frustration on the treatment: A new view of countertransference. In: *Basic Ideas Reconsidered: Progress in Self Psychology, Vol. 12*, ed. A. Goldberg. Hillsdale, NJ: The Analytic Press, pp. 17–35.

Balint, M. (1949), Changing therapeutical aims and techniques in psycho-analysis. In: *Primary Love and Psycho-Analytic Technique* (New and Enlarged Edition). London: Tavistock, 1965, pp. 209–222.

Brothers, D. (1995), *Falling Backwards*. New York: Norton.

——— & Lewinberg, E. J. (1997), Exploding the myth of unilateral healing: Self psychological treatment and the analyst's development. Presented at the 20th Annual Conference on the Psychology of the Self, Chicago, November 16, 1997.

Elkind, S. N. (1992), *Resolving Impasses in Therapeutic Relationships*. New York: Guilford Press.

——— (1994), The consultant's role in resolving impasses in therapeutic relationships. *Amer. J. Psychoanal.*, 54:3–13.

Gehrie, M. (1996), Empathy in broader perspective: A technical approach to the consequences of the negative selfobject in early character formation. In: *Basic Ideas Reconsidered: Progress in Self Psychology, Vol. 12*, ed. A. Goldberg. Hillsdale, NJ: The Analytic Press, pp. 159–179.

Kohut, H. (1977), *The Restoration of the Self*. New York: International Universities Press.

——— (1984), *How Does Analysis Cure?* ed. A. Goldberg & P. Stepansky. Chicago: University of Chicago Press.

——— (1987), *The Kohut Seminars on Self Psychology and Psychotherapy with Adolescents and Young Adults*, ed. M. Elson. New York: Norton.

MacIsaac, D. (1996), Optimal frustration: An endangered concept. In: *Basic Ideas Reconsidered: Progress in Self Psychology, Vol. 12*, ed. A. Goldberg. Hillsdale, NJ: The Analytic Press, pp. 3–16.

Orange, D. (1995), *Emotional Understanding: Studies in Psychoanalytic Epistemology*. New York: Guilford Press.

Shane, M. & Shane, E. (1996), Self psychology in search of the optimal: A consideration of optimal responsiveness, optimal provision, optimal gratification, and optimal restraint in the clinical situation. In: *Basis Ideas Reconsidered: Progress in Self Psychology, Vol. 12*, ed. A. Goldberg. Hillsdale, NJ: The Analytic Press, pp. 37–54.

——— ——— & Gales, M. (1997a), *Intimate Attachments: Towards a New Self Psychology*. New York: Guilford Press.

——— ——— & ——— (1997b), Psychoanalysis unbound: A contextual consideration of analytic boundaries from a developmental systems self psychology perspective. Presented at the 20th Annual Conference on the Psychology of the Self, Chicago, November 14, 1997.

Sucharov, M. (1995), The patient's empathic understanding of the therapist: A bilateral systems view of the empathic process. Presented at the 18th Annual Conference on the Psychology of the Self, San Francisco, October 21, 1995.

Terman, D. (1988), Optimal frustration: Structuralization and the therapeutic process. In: *Learning from Kohut: Progress in Self Psychology, Vol. 4*, ed. A. Goldberg. Hillsdale, NJ: The Analytic Press, pp. 113–125.

Tolpin, M. (1983), Corrective emotional experience: A self-psychological reevaluation. In: *The Future of Psychoanalysis*, ed. A. Goldberg. New York: International Universities Press, pp. 363–380.

Wolf, E. (1980), Empathy and countertransference. In: *The Future of Psychoanalysis*, ed. A. Goldberg. New York: International Universities Press, 1983, pp. 309–326.

Chapter 7

Surface, Depth, and the Isolated Mind

Barry Magid

The language of psychoanalysis is inextricably bound up with the metaphors of surface and depth. Any attempt to review the ubiquity of these metaphors would necessarily be endless, but an outline of some of the main areas of usage might include the following: topographical distinctions between the surface of consciousness and the depth of the unconscious, the surface or manifest content of the dream versus the deep or latent content, the notion of the depth of the transference as indicated by either developmentally or functionally regressive states, and the presumption of deep psychic structures whose operation underlies or gives rise to our surface subjectivity. However, metaphors have a way of outgrowing their original uses and taking on a life of their own, entailing all sorts of conceptual consequences that go unchallenged because they go unnoticed. The reification of psychic processes into metaphors of psychic "structure," intimately entwined with those of psychic "depth," is one that has begun to undergo increasing scrutiny, and authors such as Schafer (1976) and Stolorow (1978) have encouraged us to become conscious of its implications.

This chapter explores further a few of the myriad implications of the metaphors of surface and depth and suggest ways in which our conceptualization of the mind has been entangled by their unexamined usage. I will organize my critique around Stolorow and Atwood's attempt to repudiate what they have called "the myth of the isolated mind" (1992). They have outlined three main areas of alienation from the essential embeddedness of life that are a consequence of this myth: (1) alienation from nature, including the illusion "that there is a sphere of inner freedom from the constraints of animal existence and mortality" (p. 8); (2) alienation from social life, including the illusion that each individual "knows only his own consciousness and thus forever barred from direct access to experiences belonging to other people . . . which ignores the constitutive role of the relationship to the other in a person's having any experience at all" (p. 9); and (3) alienation from subjectivity, including the "reification of various dimensions of subjectivity. These reifications confer upon experience one or another of the properties attributed to things on the plane of material reality, for example spatial localization, extension, enduring substantiality and the like. . . . Invariably associated with the image of the mind is that of an external reality or world upon which the mind entity is presumed to look out" (p. 11).

The metaphor of psychological depth, along with a preoccupation with the privacy and interiority of the self, as well as the belief in a "true," "inner," or "essential" self or nature, I propose have all been entangled with aspects of the myth of the isolated mind. This language has pervaded the psychoanalytic literature, not only in the ways delineated by Stolorow and Atwood, but regularly informs the descriptions of self-experience that are used by our patients.

In what follows I will try to supplement Stolorow and Atwood's account of the myth of the isolated mind with the perspective offered by Ludwig Wittgenstein's (1953) philosophy of language and show how his work on the notions of the inner and the outer, first- and third-person accounts of experience, and the problem of intentionality and meaning bear on our understanding of the isolated mind.

I will suggest that a renewed attention to the ordinary language usage of such words as *belief,* and *reason,* as well as what we mean by something being "deeply" felt or a "deeply" held belief, will both clarify and simplify some of the issues surrounding the metaphors of surface and depth that have worked their way into our vocabulary and help us in our ongoing attempt to disentangle ourselves and our theories from the persistent remnants of this myth.

As an example of how the myth of the isolated mind, with its attendant picture of preexistent deep psychic structure, has infiltrated, not only psychoanalysis but our broader picture of how language is acquired and operates, I will begin with the work of Noam Chomsky. Chomsky's (1986) hypothesis of universal generative structures that supposedly underlie the deep structure of language and give rise to the particulars of surface grammar and which account for language acquisition is a quintessential model of the operation of the isolated mind. Chomsky's work is very complex, and I would hardly present myself as being able to critique it fully, but I believe we can discern fundamental aspects of his theory that are incompatible with a truly intersubjective view of the mind and language.

How do we learn a language? Chomsky was right to point out that our usual use of the word *learn* is inadequate to explain language acquisition, and he (1959) famously demolished B. F. Skinner's attempt to use behavioral models of conditioning as an explanation. But Chomsky assumed that, if we didn't learn language in this conventional, behavioral sense, the only alternative was that it must somehow be innate—obviously not in the sense that we are born knowing how to speak a language, but that the brain had "hard-wired" into it the fundamentals of a universal grammar which served as a language generator. This is the Chomskian version of "deep" structure. But there is another possibility, one articulated from one direction by Wittgenstein's (1953) philosophy of language and, more recently, from connectionist theories of neurobiology (e.g., Edelman, 1987) and dynamic systems theory (Thelin and Smith, 1994). In this model, the infant brain is viewed as highly plastic or impressionable, and it is the exposure of the brain to repeated, patterned speech that actually causes neural connections and pathways to be formed. (This actually turns out to be a very old idea, one first systematically put forward by the Zeno [Diogenes, 1996] and Stoic philosophers in the 3rd century B.C.E., who said that ideas were *impressed* on the mind by sensation and experience the way that an image is impressed into wax by a seal.) The complexity of grammar is thus accounted for, not by the presence of an innate grammar generator in the brain, but rather by the complex interaction of the living language and community of speakers who use it. As Thelin and Smith (1994) put it, " 'Innate ideas' is not a biologically plausible construct. A more biologically plausible version is one in which the initial structure of the organism, the activities that structure engenders, and the typical environment in which they occur conjoin to direct development along a typical cours e. . . . The 'constraints' on development do not look like innate ideas and miniature versions of the end-state" (p. 33). This perspective, which can be found elaborated from another direction in Wittgenstein's *Philosophical Investigations* (1953) represents a truly intersubjective account of language. Chomsky may indeed have descriptively identified universal properties of grammar that seem to exist across cultures, but that simply points to the family resemblances among spoken languages and not that they have any common essence that is neurologically embodied. In other words, there is nothing—no deep structure—*behind* the phenomena of language acquisition. Our brains are the product of a process of natural selection such that exposure to language makes a certain impression on our neurological systems, and that impression serves as the only basis for future language recognition and production.

But the notion of deep structure retains a powerful intuitive pull on us. Surely, something must be the inner source of so much surface complexity. What makes deep structure so problematic?

Let me begin to answer that question by citing an example used by Gregory Bateson (1979), taken from Moliere's play *La Malade Imaginaire*. As Bateson paraphrased the story, a medieval graduate student is undergoing his oral examination, and one of his examiners asks him to explain, "Why does morphine put people to sleep?" Well, the student hasn't a clue, but thinks and thinks, and at last triumphantly comes up with the answer, "Because it contains a dormitive principle" (p. 85). What's wrong with this explanation? Just that it is no explanation at all. All the student is doing is repackaging the description of the very phenomenon he is trying to explain, sleeping, making up an abstraction, a "dormitive principle" and declaring he has discovered the "cause" of sleepiness. Now I think "deep structure" is nothing but a "dormitive principle." By invoking it, we've added nothing to what already is our description of language or psychic reality, but we've come up with a fine-sounding abstraction for what we assume must be behind the thing we're trying to explain. Wittgenstein (1953) said that the hardest thing in giving an explanation is knowing when to stop. And he meant that the temptation is always to go on to something we can't see and have no evidence for but that we are sure must be back there someplace, giving rise to all the surface complexity of our description. The most fundamental instance of it is Freud's inability to stop with a psychology of subjective experience—he felt compelled to go on and "explain" the underlying biology that must provide the "foundation" for his psychology. And so, feelings of drivenness had to have a drive behind them to explain them, and "drives" became a psychoanalytic "dormitive principle," which has taken more than half a century to shake off.

Another aspect of the problem of depth concerns our notion of an interior, subjective space to which we have priviledged access. Here depth is the counterpart to "inner"—as in the idea that a feeling or memory is located deep inside myself—an inner landscape or object that I can introspectively observe but you cannot. Again, Wittgenstein offers a radical critique of this inner dichotomy, which I believe can fruitfully extend the description offered by Stolorow and Atwood of the isolated mind's social alienation. Wittgenstein argued that we make a basic error when we confuse the grammar of first-person statements with those of third-person statements. In "I am in pain" and "Jane is in pain," *I* does not function in the first sentence the way "Jane" does in the second, a difference, as Terry Eagleton (1997) has pointed out, between "grammatical and the ontological uses" of the word *I* (p. 264). For Wittgenstein first-person statements are *expressions*, not observations, of pain, and I cannot speak of *knowing* that I am in pain the way I can speak of knowing that Jane is in pain. The grammar or use of knowing properly involves its counterpart doubt, and for Wittgenstein, to speak of knowing, if knowing is to have any sense, is to speak of something that could be doubted as well. I do not *know* I am in pain, because it makes no sense to speak of doubting whether or not I am in pain, whereas I can speak of doubting whether Jane is in pain or if she's faking it. The crucial point here is we do not make first-person statements on the basis of observation. However, we can use the word *pain* meaningfully in both instances. If we both stub our toe on the bedpost, do we feel the "same" pain? Well, we both learned the use of word *pain* in just that sort of circumstance, and we speak of knowing just how the other feels when it happens. What if someone were to say, "You can never know how chocolate tastes to me"? Our response might be to insist, "I know what chocolate tastes like." Is the taste of chocolate something inner and private, or are we able to call it "the taste of chocolate" precisely because it is an experience, that like pain, we've learned to identify and talk about in a shared and shareable context? Wittgenstein insists that a word's meaning is to be found in its use, not in its correspondence with an inner object of experience. And his emphasis on the circumstances in which we could have learned the use of a word continually reminds us to attend to the social or intersubjective dimension of language as opposed to the isolated mind's tendency to treat meaning as something that is essentially private and personal.

The temptation to use the language of observation for first-person reports is very strong. Kohut (1981) described empathy as vicarious introspection and explicitly compared it to the vicarious extrospection of astronauts on the moon radioing back to earthbound scientists a description of the lunar landscapes. But there are no inner landscapes, only first-person sentences whose grammar is deceptively parallel to the grammar of third-person sentences. The difference, as Wittgenstein would say, is really in plain view if we pay close attention to our use of language.

What may be the most clinically relevant consequence of this approach to first-person reports is that the so-called "depth" of introspection is really a function of the individual's freedom of expression. And this will in turn be a function of the intersubjective context, how free from potential injury or repetition of a traumatic scenario a person feels when they express how they feel to another person. Depth of feeling is not so much a matter of penetrating through inner layers of experience as it is a willingness or capacity to stay with the intensity of a feeling that is being felt in a particular intersubjective context. How deeply we allow ourselves to feel something is a function of where and with whom we're having the feeling.

Thus the temptation to inhabit inner landscapes may not only represent the inadvertent misuse of language in theory building, but also serve particularly defensive functions. We can see among our patients certain individuals who are more prone to try and guard against narcissistic injury by attempts to interiorize their emotional life and not leave their emotional vulnerability "visible" on the interpersonal "surface." Such individuals become preoccupied with an inner, "true" self, cut off and seemingly unknowable by others, an inner world where they imagine their real feelings can safely reside, their true potential awaiting release, their specialness awaiting recognition. But precisely because this interiority cuts off from view their emotional strivings and ambitions, they inadvertently preclude the possibility of the very acknowledgement and attuned responsiveness that they secretly crave, which leads to frustration, jealousy, reactive anger, and so on, all of which also become a part of their hidden interior landscape, but one now polluted with intense ambivalent, conflicting emotions. The temptation to reify these sequestered feelings into internal objects in an inner landscape becomes increasingly strong. But it is one thing for a patient to come to us with a pathologically interiorized sense of self and quite another for the analyst to join overtly or tacitly in believing that the patient's true self indeed lies deep within.

This perspective may be an unintended consequence of Kohut's concept of a "nuclear self." Wolf (1988) summarized Kohut's position in this way: "At the time when an individual's self first comes into being as a singular and unique specific cohesive structure, the whole configuration of poles and tension arc being laid down is the core of this nuclear self. This unique core configuration gives the self an idiosyncratic and specific direction that in its lifelong unfolding can be called a *lifeplan* for the self" (p. 51). According to this formulation fulfillment comes from being in "harmony" with the self's lifeplan, while deviating from it leads to feeling unfulfilled. He cites the example of the painter Paul Gauguin who felt unfulfilled until he abandoned a successful commercial career to become a painter. But while there may be instances of individuals like Gauguin who accurately perceive themselves to possess a talent that is lying fallow and undeveloped, far more often, I think, we encounter individuals for whom their sense of a lifeplan is, instead, an ongoing fantasy about what they imagine might bring about a sense of cohesion and direction. A young lawyer, unhappy in his work and with his partner, had successive fantasies of changing careers and being, first, a psychologist, then a doctor, then a politician. Within each fantasy he imagined himself finally relieved from the boredom, uncertainty, and self-hate that plagued his daily life. In each case he imagined he searched for and discovered his "real, inner true self," but none of these fantasies accurately portrayed any of the steps that he would eventually take to lead a more grounded and satisfying life, steps that entailed a revitalization of his ambitions and ideals within the legal profession.

The following clinical vignette illustrates the transformation of another patient's preoccupation with her inner experience. Doris was a 34-year-old artist who presented with depression, anxiety, and a highly conflicted sense of who she was, what her relationships were all about, and what she was trying to do with her life. As a young girl she had intensively trained for the ballet but, in her mid-teens, was abruptly told by her father that she could never hope to make the grade as a professional dancer and was forced to quit her lessons. She subsequently did poorly in school and refused to go on to college despite superior grades and intelligence. She seemed to renounce any career ambitions of her own but became compliantly attached to a series of highly successful older men for whom she would work as an assistant, helping to further their careers. In sessions, she was restless, had difficulty choosing a topic to discuss, often interrupting herself mid-sentence, saying it wasn't worth talking about. She said that her head was constantly teeming with intense thoughts and feelings, which she couldn't put into words and which she was sure were too confused and complicated for anyone to understand anyway. Outwardly eager for therapy, she nonetheless had a great deal of trouble arriving on time for her sessions and often became confused about the day and time of her appointments. Though outwardly devoted to her so-called mentors, she acknowledged intense feelings of jealousy and resentment that she spent all her time helping them be famous, though she quickly assured me she was unable to imagine herself pursuing any autonomous career of her own.

Over the next 2 years, Doris gradually allowed herself to display the tangle of feelings that she had previously interiorized. The content of these deeply held thoughts and feelings turned out to be little more than an elaboration of what was evident in the initial sessions, but which had then been routinely blocked, interrupted, or exposed to self-criticism. Our work together did not progress by the discovery of anything hidden; rather, as she gradually came to trust the empathic, non-critical context of the analytic relationship, she allowed her thoughts and feelings simply to exist on the surface of her consciousness without continual editing or suppression. Free association, in other words, was not so much a technique used to uncover repressed or defended aspects of herself as it was the achievement of a new baseline presentation of herself as existing right here and now, in her words and in her body. She became less identified with her "private" innermost thoughts and feelings. What I saw and heard was who she was. Inner turmoil or confusion was no longer a condition of her damaged inner self, but intrusive "background noise" that had to be handled as best she could so as not to interfere with her new sense of the real Doris who lived in a real world and was increasingly defined by her interaction with others. She joked how she was learning to be more "superficial" but that this had paradoxically made her feel more "real."

What then of the unconscious? Freud (1900) originally spoke of the unconscious as a repository of the repressed; what we could not tolerate on the surface of our consciousness was forced down into the depths. For Freud, it was our own endogenous drive-determined wishes that were unacceptable to the conscious ego and that were allowed expression only in the disguise of dreams. The intersubjective model (Stolorow and Atwood, 1992) of the unconscious as being constituted by the prereflective and the unvalidated, as well as the dynamic unconscious, has expanded our conceptualization of how experience is organized outside of conscious awareness. We need to return to the basic sense of "unconscious" as asking, "What are we unconscious of?" As psychoanalysts, too often we have been trained to reflexively focus our attention inward—whether we say we are unconscious of our own wishes or our own organizing principles. But if we ask in an ordinary sense what we are unconscious of, we might just as well list aspects of our life and of the world that we avoid facing: the fact that we will die, the unending poverty and suffering of the mass of mankind while we live in relative comfort, our insignificance and impotence in the face of the problems of the world. Mortality and suffering are two fundamental facts of life that we routinely and systematically exclude from consciousness. All are aspects of a life embedded in the world that the isolated mind avoids by a preoccupation with its own "inner" experience.

But what is excluded from our awareness is not simply what we find intolerable. We remain unconscious of a vast universe of possibility. Individually, we partake of a minuscule portion of our human cultural heritage; we experience a tiny portion of the earth's natural wonder or engage it only transiently as tourists. We remain deaf to the great symphony all around us. (The composer Charles Ives, 1970, in the preface to his *Concord Sonata,* remarked that only Thoreau had no need to travel into Boston to hear the symphony.) In all these senses, the unconscious lies not within us, but all around us. Only from the perspective of the isolated mind do we see ourselves as individuals apart from the world, using mental filters to sift its sensory input. Language, and indeed our mental life, is never private, but always communal, intersubjective, part of a shared form of life. Our minds are constituted by and in language, our sense of self co-constructed intersubjectively within its medium.

Let me now offer an example of a clinical exchange of a different sort, one that perhaps reveals a conception of unconscious process less burdened by our current conceptualizations of psychic structure.

In Plato's (1959, my translation) dialogue, *Gorgias,* Socrates is conducting a bit of group therapy, asking the participants questions that attempt to clarify what, for them, counts as a good life. Gorgias is a master of rhetoric, and the group is investigating the nature of his skill and how it might be conducive to obtaining the good life. One member, Polus, maintains that rhetoric, or the art of persuasion, is valuable since it conveys power and allows a person all the control over his fellow man that otherwise could be obtainable only by force by a tyrant. But Socrates questions the way Polus values power:

Polus. Aren't they like tyrants, who can kill or exile or rob whomever they want?

Soc. But I say, Polus, that rhetoricians and tyrants have the least power in their cities, for they don't do what they want, only what seems best to them.

Pol. Isn't it great to be able to do that?

Soc. But that's not what Polus says.

Pol. Not what I say? I just said it.

     * * * * *

Soc. But do you think it's good if someone who's lacking sense does what seems best to him? Is it great to be able to do that?

Pol. No. [466c-e]

     * * * * *

Soc. Then those doing these things do them for the sake of the good?

Pol. Certainly. [468b]

     * * * * *

Soc. Well, if we agree about that, if a tyrant or a rhetorician kills someone or exiles them or takes their money, imagining it is good for him to do so, but it turns to be bad, presumably he's doing what seems best to him?

Pol. Yes.

Soc. Then is that what he wants, if it turns out to be bad? Why don't you answer?

Pol. No, he doesn't seem to me to be doing what he wants.

Soc. Then it's true what I said, that a man can do what seems best to him in the city and not have great power or do what he wants. [468d-e]

Socrates has gotten Polus to admit that tyrants do what they think is in their best interest but that they may be fundamentally mistaken about its nature, the way someone who needs medicine instead keeps eating the rich food that he enjoys, but that may be making him sick.

At this point Callicles jumps in, profoundly upset at the implication of the argument, that we may be somehow deeply confused about the relation between our desires and our own best interests.

> Cal. Tell me Socrates are you serious, or only kidding? For if you are serious and what you say is true, wouldn't our human life be turned upside down, and everything we're doing be the exact opposite of what we should be doing? [481c]

Socrates then sums up their dilemma like this:

> Soc. If you leave this problem unaddressed, then I swear by the dog god of Egypt, that you Callicles, will not agree with Callicles, but will spend your whole life disagreeing with yourself. And as for me, my friend, I would rather that my lyre be out of tune, and my chorus out of key, and everyone disagree with me and contradict me, than I, being one man, should be out of harmony with myself and contradict myself. [482b-c]

We have in this dialogue a picture of unconscious process (one that we might characterize as predominantly demonstrating the prereflective unconscious), as well as a demonstration of two different kinds of depth, one a sustained depth of inquiry and the other the uncovering of Polus's and Callicles's deeply held beliefs about the good life, some of which Socrates shows to be in conflict with others. The version of the unconscious elucidated here has nothing to do with irrational elements per se (although the irrational was also part of Plato's [1961] tripartite model of the mind as elucidated in *Phaedrus*); rather, Socrates maintains that two conflicting ideas of the good, unless they are made explicit by this sort of dialogic inquiry, will function outside of their conscious awareness and thus give rise to conflict.

For the purposes of our discussion of surface and depth, we can begin by pointing out that the unconscious process that Socrates implies will take place in his interlocutor is entirely and adequately encompassed by the ordinary grammar or usage of the language of "belief" and requires no underlying psychic structure operating "behind the scenes" to bring about what he has predicted. It is ironic that, precisely because Socrates refrains from reifying this process into an "unconscious"—perfectly correctly in my view—commentators on this dialogue, such as Nussbaum (1994), have missed how implicit the whole idea of unconscious process is here. And what it demonstrates to us is something about the grammar (as Wittgenstein would put it) of belief.

When we believe something, when do we believe it? If I believe that Socrates was a man, am I always believing it, even when I'm not thinking about Socrates? If you ask me, I'll say I believed Socrates was a man, even if up until the moment of your question, I never gave the question any particular thought. And if then you ask me, have I always believed that, I would probably reply yes, even if I had never thought or been asked about it before, because I don't recall ever believing anything else that would contradict that statement. Where is this belief located? Inside? Does it depend on some internal image of Socrates that I've kept stored up until the time of this question, which I then retrieve and compare to another internal category of "man"? Wittgenstein asks us to do away with the assumption that we must be operating with stored samples or definitions in order to understand the maintenance of beliefs. Rather, in this case my belief is contingent on nothing more than understanding the meaning of the word *man* and the recognition of "Socrates" as a proper noun. Similarly, Polus's and Callicles's conflicting notions about the relation of power to the good life are *entailed* by their various beliefs but have no internalized unconscious counterparts in conflict behind the scenes or deep in their mental apparatus. It's simply that, if one believes A and also believes B, without ever noticing that B entails not-A, at some point trying to put into practice both A and B is going to lead to a contradiction. The "structures" of their belief may be said to be emergent in the course of the dialogue, rather than pre-existing in any psychic interior space or at any psychological depth.

What is left out of this account that a modern psychoanalyst could add to the dialogue? Primarily, I would say, questions about where Polus or Callicles *got* a particular belief, that is, the developmental history of the idea that happiness consists of the unchallenged exercise of power and, perhaps, an empathic appreciation of the grandiosity that seems to underlie Polus's envy of tyrants. But as psychoanalysts, we should note with a certain humility the power of the dialogue just as it is, to upset and challenge its participants, and not assume that no one's character was ever profoundly changed or affected before the advent of our particular theory or practice. The analyst's understanding of the patient, by means of his/her own theoretical and individual organizing principles, is never more than a first step toward the patient's feeling understood, which is the *sine qua non* of therapeutic change. What counts for a given patient as a basis for feeling understood may or may not include what we as analysts consider our dynamic understanding of the patient. But as we look across cultures and across the two millennia to the time of this dialogue, we need to be open to what counted for its participants as understanding or feeling understood in their own terms, without presuming that understanding was necessarily inadequate because it lacks elements that we, from our vantage point, would deem necessary.

Finally, I believe that we may find that a corrective to our current use of the terms *deep* or *depth* occurs when we stay close to their ordinary, experience-near use in expressions such as "to feel something deeply," "deep feeling," or "deeply held belief." And the ordinary use of these phrases is not to mean a feeling that has been hidden away in our psychic depths but, rather, allowing us simply to stay with and experience through and through a given feeling or a way we are committed to looking at the world, as Socrates asks his friends to do in this dialogue. But to take a further step and reify this use of deep into a supposed inner landscape of a topographic model of the mind or, further, to posit "deep" structures that must exist behind the scenes of consciousness to hold the feeling or belief down and keep it buried, well, all that I think only conjures up ghosts, under the pretext of uncovering the unconscious.

Sometimes progress in psychoanalytic theory may turn out to be more a matter of subtraction rather than addition. Sometimes this consists of the dismantling of elaborate metapsychological structures, as we needed to do in order to make the transition out of drive theory. Sometimes it involves a more subtle untangling of the implication of metaphors that, while not part of our theories per se, form an almost unnoticed background to our discourse.

Thomas Merton (1997), in one of his late journals, wrote, looking back on his earlier writing about the "true self,"

> The time has probably come to go back on all that I have said about one's "true self," etc., etc. And show that there is after all no hidden mysterious "real self" OTHER THAN or "hiding behind" the self that one is, but what all the thinking does is to observe what is there or objectify it and thus falsify it. The "real self" is not an object, but I have betrayed it by seeming to promise a possibility of knowing it somewhere, sometimes as a reward for astuteness, fidelity, and a quick-witted ability to stay one jump ahead of reality [p. 95].

The dismantling of old usages associated with the perspective of the isolated mind, and not the erection of new metapsychologies, may be the surest road to clarity.

As the old Zen poet Masahide once wrote (adapted from Stryk and Ikemoto, 1977):

My house burned down.
At last, a clear view
of the moon.

REFERENCES

Bateson, G. (1979), *Mind and Nature.* New York: E. P. Dutton.

Chomsky, N. (1959), A review of Skinner's "Verbal Behavior." *Language,* 35:26.

————— (1986), *Knowledge of Language: Its Nature, Origin and Use.* New York: Praeger.

Diogenes, L. (1996), *The Life of Zeno,* trans. B. Magid. Monterey, KY: Larkspur Press..

Eagleton, T. (1997), Self-undoing subjects. In: *Rewriting the Self,* ed. R. Porter. London: Routledge

Edelman, G. M. (1987), *Neural Darwinism.* New York: Basic Books.

Freud, S. (1900), The interpretation of dreams. *Standard Edition,* 4&5:1–625. London: Hogarth Press, 1953.

Ives, C. (1970), *Essays Before a Sonata and Other Writings,* ed. H. Boatwright. New York: Norton.

Kohut, H. (1981), On empathy. In: *The Search for the Self,* ed. P. Ornstein. Madison, CT: International Universities Press, 1991, pp. 525–535.

Merton, T. (1997), *Dancing in the Water of Life.* New York: Harper Collins.

Nussbaum, M. (1994), *The Therapy of Desire.* Princeton, NJ: Princeton University Press.

Plato (1959), *Gorgias,* ed. E. R. Dodds. London: Oxford University Press.

————— (1961), *The Collected Dialogues,* ed. E. Hamilton & H. Cairns. Princeton, NJ: Princeton University Press.

Schafer, R. (1976), *A New Language for Psychoanalysis.* New Haven, CT: Yale University Press.

Stolorow, R. D. (1978), The concept of psychic structure: Its metapsychological and clinical psychoanalytic meanings. *Internat. Rev. Psycho-Anal.,* 5:313–320.

————— & Atwood, G. (1992), *Contexts of Being: The Intersubjective Foundations of Psychological Life.* Hillsdale, NJ: The Analytic Press.

Stryk, L. & Ikemoto, T. (1977), *The Penguin Book of Zen Poetry.* New York: Penguin Books.

Thelin, E. & Smith, L. B. (1994), *A Dynamic Systems Approach to the Development of Cognition and Action.* Cambridge, MA: MIT Press.

Wittgenstein, L. (1953), *Philosophical Investigations.* London: Basil Blackwell.

Wolf, E. (1988), *Treating the Self.* New York: Guilford Press.

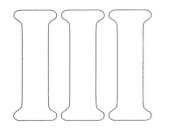

Klein and Kohut

Chapter 8

Melanie Klein and Heinz Kohut: An Odd Couple or Secretly Connected?

James S. Grotstein

Psychoanalysis has already passed its one hundredth birthday and is about to enter a new millennium. Beginning originally as "orthodox psychoanalysis" (id analysis), it gradually evolved into "classical analysis" as Freud and his followers became more interested in the repressing forces and less in the repressed. In the United States classical psychoanalysis became enriched by the concept of adaptation and by the representational world. Yet even in the classical shift of emphasis from id to ego analysis, there remained a mystifying respect for the drives, for infantile sexuality, and utmostly for psychic determinism, the last of which had profound ramifications for the fate of ego psychology in the United States. Stated synoptically, psychic determinism meant that the analysand was exclusively driven by unconscious motivation and intentionality and that only the analyst was qualified to understand that motivation or intentionality because of its unconscious status. In its zeal to maintain the mystification of the unconscious, classical analysis was unwittingly subverting the analysand's own sense of his agency and enfranchisement in the analytic enterprise. A hierarchic class system of a kind had imperceptibly become a fixed feature of the technique.

A major reaction began to take place among many classical analysts when Heinz Kohut (1971) came out, like Luther, with postulates of a psychoanalytic "reformation," one whose centerpiece was empathy and, along with it, a greater respect for the analysand's actual testimony about his lifelong plight and a explicit designation of the analyst's responsibility for failures in the self–selfobject relationship. The "class system" of orthodox and classical analysis had been overturned. Paradoxically, it was Kohut, an Austrian, who, in my opinion, forsook the tenets of a European class system that informed orthodox and classical psychoanalysis and who ultimately "Americanized" it (along with Harry Stack Sullivan). If we were to sift through all the developments that were to evolve from self psychology, Kohut's "reformational child," perhaps it would not do violence to its tenets to say that the analyst became more empathically respectful of the analysand, and the analysand commensurately became more respectable, enfranchised, and rightfully entitled retrospectively to self–selfobject relationships, which would and should have guaranteed him a basic minimum of selfobject functioning. Perhaps one of the most important subtexts of this reformation is the distinction between the orthodox/classical conception of psychical conflict and the newfound importance of psychical deficits (of selfobject structures). A cultural and sociological paradigm change had occurred.

As orthodox and now classical analysis seem to be entering their recessional in favor of self psychology, another change in analytic theory and practice needs to be mentioned. Whereas ego psychology became the main feature of the classical modification of orthodox analysis in this country as well as in England, classical analysis in Europe and South America remained closer to orthodox analysis with its emphasis on the id and on psychic determinism. In Hungary a significant new trend was to develop that was to have enormous consequences for psychoanalysis. This was the emphasis on the preoedipal infant–mother relationship, as opposed to the orthodox/classical obsession with the primacy of the oedipal phase and complex. From this new emphasis on the infant and its relationship to its mother, there emerged two new schools of psychoanalysis: the British Object Relations School (now the Independent School), whose forbears were Fairbairn and Winnicott, and the Kleinian School. Klein, a devoted but unrequited follower of Freud, had been initiated into the then revolutionary idea of the prime importance of the mother–infant relationship and of infantile dependence in her initial association with the Hungarian school—and was to extend this theme when she moved to Berlin and came under the influence of Abraham.

It is no small irony that Kleinian psychoanalysis, which today is arguably the predominant psychoanalytic school in the world outside the United States, was and still is considered heretical by orthodox and classical analysts, yet as the latter are waning in importance, it is

Kleinian analysis that best represents the authentic tradition, albeit an offshoot, of orthodox id analysis.

Thus, today there are two major psychoanalytic paradigms that seem to redefine our present conception of psychoanalytic theory, that of the Kleinian oeuvre, loyal as it still is to psychic determinism and the primacy of psychic reality (yet modified by Bion's [1959, 1962] intersubjective concept of "container/contained"), and the other is relationism, principal among which are object relations theory generally (principally the tenets of the British Independent School and the American Relational School), self psychology, and latterly intersubjectivity and constructivism. I should like to recast them as the principles of the *infantile neurosis* versus that of *developmental traumata*, a dialectic otherwise expressed as one between the psychoanalytic versions of internal reality versus external reality, of "original sin" versus "original innocence," or even of psychic determinism versus environmental deficiency and impingement, fate versus destiny, creationism versus misattunement, psychic causality versus external causality, primary process versus secondary process, or as I have lately addressed it, autochthony versus alterity and solitude versus communion. Yet the schools of psychic determinism and of relationism significantly cross over and intermix on the issues of the infantile neurosis and developmental traumata. In terms of technique one might postulate a dialectic between *bonding* and *weaning*.

It is no small coincidence that two of the doyens of this new trend are, like Freud, Austrian. Melanie Klein and Heinz Kohut, both Viennese, had other characteristics in common. They each began as loyal, dedicated, and steadfast Freudians. They each, however, had the integrity and courage to acknowledge the challenging truths of their clinical findings and to speak out—and to prevail. Notwithstanding the title, this contribution is not about their personalities, but about the revolutionary ideas that they launched, ideas that have now captured the attention of the analytic and psychotherapeutic world. Let me summarize some of the key issues that both distinguish and unite them.

THE CONCEPT OF INFANTILE SUBJECTIVITY AND DEPENDENCY OR THE TWO "INFANTS" (SUBJECTS) OF PSYCHOANALYSIS

Klein (1923, 1926), in founding child analysis, boldly abrogated the cherished orthodox/classical canon of primary narcissism and thereby not only heretically (for then) uncovered the presence of mental life in the infant. She also formulated the conception of a "virtual infant," the *"once and forever psychoanalytic infant of the unconscious,"* that consummately vulnerable aspect of the infant, child, adult, and every analysand, which constitutes a hidden order within the analysand, which continues to this very day to be the predominate clinical assumption held by all Kleinians. What has escaped notice is that, in so doing, she anticipated the postmodern enfranchisement of the "subject of and in the unconscious" long before Lacan (1966) brought it to our attention. Having discovered the early infantile subject and having detected that the Oedipus complex originates in the second oral stage, Klein thereby relegated the oedipal child of orthodox and classical analysis (in the late phallic stage) to becoming the Kleinian infant's "descendant" and a subject of an always already earlier "transference." Not only did Klein uncover the mental life of the infant and postulate the oral genesis of the Oedipus complex and of the superego as well, she also altered the orthodox/classical emphasis on autoerotism and infantile sexuality to one of *infantile dependency*, a trend that is congruent with the works of Fairbairn, Winnicott, Bowlby, and Kohut.

Kohut, surely following in the footsteps of Ferenczi, Suttie, Fairbairn, Winnicott, and Sullivan, established the foundation for another "psychoanalytic infant," one who became unconscious by default because of significant deprivation of selfobject functions from its environment. His recommendations for technique commensurately centered on the detection of these structural failures. Moreover, in emphasizing *empathy* as a technique of psychoanalytic observation and in involving the analyst in a position of responsibility for being answerable to selfobject failures in the course of the analysis, a sense of authentic affective interrelatedness began to replace the now obsolescent notion of the analyst's neutrality. There were now two equal human individuals who were partnered in the analytic enterprise. In instituting the empathic revolution, he became one of the most redoubtable spokesmen for the infant's *primal innocence* and rights of entitlement of care. In all the ways that Kleinian thinking differs from that of self psychology, it certainly agrees on the importance of the interrelationship between the *subjectivities* of the analyst and analysand and on the idea of *infantile dependency* (as compared to orthodox and classical *infantile sexuality*) but differs in their topographic emphasis of its nature and locale.

WHICH SCHOOL IS "EXPERIENCE-NEAR" AND WHICH IS "EXPERIENCE-DISTANT"?

Self psychologists frequently use the mutually differentiating notions of "experience-distance" and "experience-nearness" when discussing their differences with other analytic schools. This notion generally seems to relate to the manifest content of the analysand's associations. Kleinians, on the other hand, fervently argue that their approach—by trying to designate the operant unconscious phantasy of the "once and forever infant of the unconscious"—is "experience-near" and that self psychologists, at the extreme, operate from an "experience-distant" perspective, that is, experience remoteness from the generative unconscious infant, from which subjectivity, agency, and creativity originate. Moreover, the Kleinian technical injunction to interpret maximal unconscious anxiety before defense or impulse certainly renders it more empathic and experience-near than classical technique. Using a dual-track perspective (Grotstein, 1978, 1981), Kleinian technique and that of self psychology are each correct in their own domain and function complementarily to each other. In analysis each "infant" must be listened to and his experience validated. I personally believe that an analysis may risk being incomplete if the analyst is not informed by self psychological technique, as well as Kleinian.

DRIVES VERSUS AFFECTS

Another noteworthy difference between the schools of Klein and relationism is the major emphasis that the latter places upon affects at the expense of drives, which are currently considered subordinate to and inclusive within the conceptual embrace of the former. Kleinians, on the other hand, along with classical analysts (Opatow, 1997), still maintain the primacy of the importance of unconscious phantasy as the organizing principle of internal mental life, that they are mental representations of the drives and indivisibly include the affects.

Having said that, however, let me now state the following: It is my belief that Freud, in his desire to become scientifically respectable in the heyday of logical positivism, leaned too far to the side of absolute putative objectivity and of a narrow version of it to boot. Without compromising his theory of the drives, Freud could have stated that (a) drives are semiotic signifiers of the utterly ineffable signified within the unconscious[1] (i.e., they are the mediators of *meaning*); (b) they impart personal "mattering" and valences of "caring" to the objects of

---

[1] The "ineffable signified" would comprise Bion's (1965, 1970) concept of "O"; Lacan's (1966) concept of the "Register of the Real"; Kant's (1787) concept of the "noumenon" and the "thing-in-itself"; Ricoeur's (1970) concept of the "Ananke" (Necessity); and Matte-Blanco's (1975, 1981, 1988) concept of "absolute indivisibility," "symmetry," and "infinity." All the preceding can be understood by the current terms chaos or complexity.

their experience, and thus personal objects become subjectively "cathected" (invested) with personal subjective importance; (c) *desire*, the personally owned quintessence of the drives, declares the presence and vulnerability of the subject and thereby defines it; (d) drives are the mediators, not the promulgators, of unconscious forces; and (e) drives, the dispensers of personal meaningfulness, thereby become the authors of meaning itself and of its derivatives—all that personally matters in our subjective lives. Desire, therefore, whether positive or negative, *is* the autobiographer of the subject, whereas affect is its stenographer. Drives define us subjectively; affects describe that which drives define.

Stated further, Klein, like Freud, believed that the provenance of psychic life devolved from Kant's (1787) "transcendental analytic," that is, that the human psyche was inherently prepared with a priori primary and secondary categories whereby it was prepared to *format* (anticipate) all the experiences it was subsequently to encounter. These a priori categories are older than experience, anticipate it, and impart their preconceptual ordering or formatting to the data of raw experience. Bion (1975, 1977, 1979) calls them "memoirs of the future." These preconceptual, a priori categories determine how raw events are to become transformed into personalized, subjective experiences. Self-organization and reorganization follow upon each new iteration from that primal transcendental analytic. That is Freud's—and Klein's— legacy. Relational theory, if I am not mistaken, is empirical and begins with the raw event and conceptualizes unconscious factors as secondary to the event, a phenomenon that ultimately becomes known as the dynamic unconscious.

If we were to reread Freud today from a postmodern vertex, his "libido theory" would belong less to the concepts of energics or economics and more to the subjective investment of personal importance, unconsciously as well as consciously, to the objects cum subjects that matter—or should matter—to us. I consider *personal subjective mattering, caring,* or *counting* to be the hidden order behind the concept of drive (exclusive of affect). The other is the concept of *an unconscious sense of personal agency. Drives declare and therefore risk; affects tally the benefits and the cost of that risk-taking.* Minimizing their importance has important consequences, therefore, to the individual's felt potency as agent, which Kohut's valorization of infantile exhibitionism and omnipotence seems to aver.

Finally, the quintessential point about the importance of the drives is that they not only represent the provenance of one's subjectivity, as I have already stated, but also the provenance of one's sense of *unconscious personal agency.*

UNCONSCIOUS PHANTASY VERSUS
AFFECTIVE ATTUNEMENT OR FACTS
VERSUS PHANTASY

Now, returning to Kohut, he himself was a little unnecessarily dismissive, I believe, of the worthwhileness and appropriateness of the South American Kleinian analyst's interpretations to his patient in *How Does Analysis Cure?* (Kohut, 1984). I personally thought that that analyst was on target in defining the most proximate unconscious phantasy that was operant at that ineffable clinical moment with his analysand (Bion's [1965, 1970] "transformation in 'O' "). Kohut, true to his newfound beliefs, felt that it was that analyst's empathic rapport with his patient that was decisive, thereby in effect damning his colleague's technique with faint praise.

In this contribution I shall not make Kohut's mistake by being dismissive of a psychoanalytic school with which I have more sympathy than technical familiarity or disciplined training or experience. I *have* had some brief supervision in self psychology, but that does not qualify me to be its critic. I am more solid in my background in orthodox and classical analysis, as well as in British object relations schools, with particular emphasis on Klein, Bion, Fairbairn, and Winnicott. What follows owes its provenance to my disciplined training in their theories and techniques—and to personal analyses and supervisions commensurately. I regret that space considerations prevent amplifying my ideas with analytic case material.

PSYCHIC DETERMINISM VERSUS
ENVIRONMENTAL DEFICIENCY AND THE
IMPORTANCE OF THE HIDDEN ORDER OF
AN UNCONSCIOUS SENSE OF AGENCY
OR PSYCHIC DETERMINISM VERSUS
ENVIRONMENTAL DEFICIENCY

A significant dividing issue, as already mentioned, seems to be *psychic determinism* (inherent conflict) versus *primary environmental deficiency* and *impingement* (failures of attunement). In terms of psychoanalytic considerations of technique, this might be reflected in Bowlby's (1969, 1973, 1980) concepts of *bonding* and *attachment* as opposed to *weaning*, as I have alluded to earlier. From one point of view one can consider this to be the issue of "original sin" versus primary innocence. If nothing else, the relational schools, especially including self psychology, have gone a long way in freeing the infant (and patient) from the burden of the experience of feeling that he is inherently "bad" and needs the analyst to help him discover his unconscious "sinfulness" so that he can properly repent. Some of the basic canons of classical and Kleinian analysis inadvertently became handmaidens to the infant's severe superego and unfortunately colluded with its dictates without realizing it. In this regard the relational schools have had the salutary effect of becoming veritable champions and even ombudsmen for the hitherto unenfranchised infant and patient. Infant development findings and child abuse research have amply justified this new, enlightened position.

One of the great ironies in the Klein–Kohut dialectic is that, while self psychology, along with its relational colleagues, democratically enfranchises the infant and vouchsafes its inalienable rights for thriving via optimal attunement and loving regard by its parents and locates psychopathology as aberrances of this attunement and regard, it may potentially deprive the infant cum patient of his other inalienable right, that of believing himself to be the *agent* of his history and his destiny. I am also mindful of Kohut's validation of the infant's right to experience and express his omnipotence and exhibitionism. Yes, Kohut did affirm conscious agency, but what about *unconscious agency* and its inseparable partner, *psychic responsibility?*

I have only gradually become aware that lurking behind the classical and Kleinian concept of psychic determinism lay the hidden order of psychic motivation, that is, the infant's inalienable right to an *unconscious sense of agency for authoring his life narrative—in unconscious phantasy.* I have written about this elsewhere as the dialectic between "autochthony versus alterity," by which I mean that, following Klein and Winnicott, the infant needs to believe that he, narcissistically, is the prime mover in all causality and the creator of everything that happens—before he can comprehend a cosmic world view in which he is transitive, that is, acted upon by objects belonging to another cosmic world view in which he is barely a participant (Grotstein, 1997a). In psychopathology we call these *ideas of reference,* but in normal development we call it *egocentrism* (Piaget, 1924) or normal infantile omnipotence, a belief that characterizes the paranoid–schizoid position. It is only when the infant achieves the capacity for object separateness (in the depressive position) that he is able to contemplate a system of causality that originates externally to him (in the Other, the "nonself").

Trauma, according to this reasoning, occurs when the external world (second cosmic world view) impinges before the infant (or the infantile portion of the adult patient) has had an opportunity to "create the traumatizing object" before encountering it in his original cosmic world view. In other words, trauma is that circumstance in which the object "creates the infant" before the infant has a chance autochthonously to "create the object." That is why victims of trauma feel ashamed and why victims of family abuse characterologically protect their familiar abusers.

The concept of autochthony stands midway between absolute psychic determinism and absolute external reality. An example of this would be the following: when an analysand brings forth material that convincingly reveals misattunement on the part of a parent, the question arises, "What does the analysand believe (in unconscious phantasy) that he has done to warrant the creation of this bad mother?" Similarly, rather than promulgating the dogma of the death instinct, Klein would have been better advised, according to this thinking, to state to her analysands as follows: "I do not know whether or not you are persecuted by the activity of a death instinct. All that I can say is that you seem unconsciously to believe that you are and think, feel, and behave accordingly."

The irony that I alluded to earlier—that between the Kleinian and relational (including self psychologists') perceptions of the infant—can be expressed, consequently, as follows: whereas the relational analyst, by believing that his patient was an innocent infant whose environmental selfobjects may have failed him, may, by this very advocacy, justified as it certainly is in reality, be depriving him of his "constitutional rights" of *felt unconscious psychic agency* (Grotstein, 1997e). The Kleinian analyst, by contrast, by ferreting out the patient's unconscious infantile phantasy, which seemingly corroborates and confirms the patient's belief in his ontological culpability as putative agent, at the same time vouchsafes the sanctity of his solitude as a self but runs the danger of confirming his sense of badness. I shall return to the issue of solitude later in this contribution. Put another way, the infantile aspect of the analysand's personality must be able to self-account for the experience with the object so as to transform the *event* with object into a *personal experience*, following which, as he attains the depressive position and is then able to recognize that his object is separate from him, is *then,* and only then, able to hate the object as object or forgive the object or at least entertain a feeling of ambivalence toward it.

In summary, *I believe that the task of the analyst's interpretations is to utter to the analysand the former's ideas about the latter's own sense of causality. In other words, the analyst should interpret the analysand's own unconscious interpretations.*

BONDING/ATTACHMENT VERSUS WEANING

Yet another distinction is that between *bonding* and *attachment* on one hand and *weaning* on the other, as I have already mentioned but which I would now like to develop further. Classical and, especially, Kleinian interpretations seek in general to clarify errors of *perception* and *conception* in the analysand and consequently to facilitate his/her growing autonomy and sense of separateness through this "lens correction" as it were. Winnicott's (1963) concept of the holding environment object, as distinguished from the object-to-be used, imparted a distinction that was to cross the ocean, encounter a "sea change," and become recast as the selfobject functions, that is, background object (Grotstein, 1981) functions where the object or part-object was of less importance than the facilitating triumvirate of background functions (mirroring, twinship, and idealizing). These selfobject functions were conceived by Kohut in the light of clinical instances when he began to suspect that his patients suffered from the lack of an opportunity normally afforded by an object. Bion (1959, 1962), on the Kleinian side, made a similar observation in terms of the availability to the infant of the opportunity of having a maternal container who could accept her infant's projective identifications, that is, "announcements," of danger. The subjectivity of the infant was beginning to be recognized and acknowledged by both schools.

THE ISSUE OF PSYCHIC RESPONSIBILITY

Perhaps one of the biggest differences between the Kleinian and Kohutian infant can be understood in the dimension of the *sense* of responsibility. The Kleinian infant, at least as seen retrospectively in the analysand, is constrained, by virtue of the sense of personal agency with which he is imbued, to be a *"consulting infant,"* that is, an infant who has to be responsible enough to root to the breast-analyst and ask for help. The *abjectly dependent infant* is seen as employing regressive projective identification to fuse with the object to preclude separation and individuation and yet, simultaneously, to hold the (self-) object responsible for all that goes wrong. It is my impression that self psychologists and intersubjectivists would preferentially present the patient with an appropriate brief of the actual environmental failures that are putatively the cause of the analysand's symptomotology than deal with the putative sense of felt responsibility.

It has been my impression that the Kleinian school has been scapegoated by self psychologists, in part because of Kernberg's own idiosyncratic use—and often misuse—of Kleinian ideas that have undergone a meltdown and re-amalgamation with the concepts of Edith Jacobson and Margaret Mahler. The Kleinian attitude of dismissiveness toward self psychology may be caused in part by ignorance—as is also the case of self psychologists toward Klein—but also by the "Controversial Discussions" that took part in London at the British Psychoanalytic Institute during the war years (1943–1944) (King and Steiner, 1992). Since that time the Kleinians, afraid of expulsion from the International Psychoanalytic Association, withdrew into an inner fortress, isolating themselves from orthodox and classical analysts. This facultative, paranoia-based isolation on their part and the abuse against them by Anna Freud and classical analysts around the world resulted in an embargo on Klein's works, especially in the United States and, symmetrically, a distancing of Kleinians from the works of other schools. Thus, to this very day, London Kleinians scarcely reference non-Kleinians or, for that matter, even non-London Kleinians.

KLEIN AND HER REVOLUTION

When Melanie Klein began her career, principally as a child analyst, she had the blessings of Ferenczi and Abraham to launch her forward. Virtually idealizing Freud and the canons of orthodox psychoanalysis, she innocently, perhaps naively, sought to implement his work in the newly uncovered field of child analysis. Her intuitive observations on infants, particularly her own, and the inferences that she made from her child analyses strongly suggested to her that a hitherto unrecognized infantile mental life existed that was dominated and organized by inchoate and archaic unconscious phantasies. Her orientation was in keeping with that of her second analyst, Karl Abraham, and she framed her early work around his conception of the full panoply of autoerotic development in conjunction with corresponding and respective part-object transformations. Ultimately, she was to differ with him about the preambivalent phase of orality, suggesting that the infant was never preambivalent; rather, it felt the presence of a destructive impulse internally from the very beginning, experienced this destructiveness as annihilation anxiety, and expressed this destructiveness toward its objects from the outset. She was to place the origin of this destructiveness in Freud's concept of the death instinct, which thereafter became one of the major canons of her theoretical and clinical stance.

She immediately questioned the validity of the then predominant concept of primary narcissism by surmising that the infant experienced some degree of separateness from the object from the very beginning. This assumption was akin to Luther's posting of the 93 theses on the gate of the cathedral in Würtemberg, a heroic feat that was matched later by Kohut. The hegemony of the patristic Oedipus complex had already been placed in jeopardy by her in her now famous paper, "Early Stages of the Oedipus Conflict" (1928), where she claimed to have established its roots in the second oral phase, one that was matristically dominated. I have already mentioned that she questioned Abraham's first oral phase. With her abrogation of the validity of the concept of primary narcissism, her theoretical approach became thought of as heretical vis-à-vis orthodox tenets. What she was in fact attempting was a radical revision of the infant's developmental agenda and, with it, a new metapsychology that was based on the primacy of early object relations, both external and particularly internal, one that proceeds forward, as formulated by her follower, Susan Isaacs (1952), according to the *principle of genetic continuity.*

She was able effectively to deconstruct the enigma that underlay the concept of "*talion law*" by calling attention to how the process was set in motion by the infant's projective and then introjective relationship to an object, that is, by unconsciously projecting its destructiveness into the image of an object that, when then internalized and introjectively identified with, becomes a retaliatory superego figure with omnipotent authority, intentionality, and trajectory. As matter of fact, her understanding of the creation of the archaic infantile superego was to revolutionize the psychoanalytic conception of that structure, one whose origins and nature even puzzled Freud.

We must recall here that orthodox psychoanalysis and its successor, classical analysis, held that the oedipus complex, a late phallic developmental event, constituted the fundamental organizing principle of the infant's development. In adult analyses this canon would be promulgated as follows: even though traumatic fixations occur in the pregenital (preoedipal) phases of orality, anality, and the early phallic stage, their importance becomes secondary insofar as they become regressive elaborations as preoedipal or pregenital defenses against the awareness of the Oedipus complex, which ultimately constellates them in its hegemonic orbit.

Klein's radical reformulation of the principle of genetic continuity and her challenges to Abraham's first oral phase and especially to the canon of primary narcissism were to marginalize her and her followers for two generations, and she was condemned to live under the bane of sacrilege and of ever-threatening excommunication from the orthodox and, later, classical establishment. Time, tolerance, objectivity, the death of many zealots, and the emergence of infant development research have long since begun to heal many of these ancient wounds. Today, much of the world of analysis, especially outside the United States, is fundamentally oriented toward Klein and now also to her most famous analysand, Bion, as well as to her supervisee, Winnicott, and more recently, Lacan. She is no longer marginalized except in the United States, and even that lamentable proscription is gradually subsiding in favor of a more sanguine curiosity about her work. Moreover, many of her fundamental ideas have already found their way into common practice among practitioners in this country.

While more and more analysts and therapists have begun to think in terms of greed, envy, the manic defense, and the paranoid-schizoid and depressive positions, it is *projective identification* that has gained the greatest foothold—so much so, as a matter of fact, that its definition has undergone a veritable "sea-change" in its "Americanization" and has become illegitimately wedded to intersubjectivity, from which I am going to great lengths to rescue it to restore it to what I believe to be its rightful Kleinian heritage as primarily an *intra*-psychic phenomenon.

Perhaps one of the principle reasons why the value of Klein's work has not been valued in the United States is her belief in the clinical validity of the death instinct, that is, primal destructiveness. Stark though the idea sounds, there does seem to be some validity in her conceptualization of it, in my opinion. It is one of those ideas that one takes on faith. In my own Kleinian analysis I became utterly convinced of its existence within me. This is hardly a scientific statement, but isn't it one of the reasons why we ask candidates to be analyzed—so as to believe in the unconscious from their own personal analytic experience? This is also one of the reasons, as I have already mentioned, that I cannot critique self psychology—nor can anyone else who has not had a personal analytic experience in the techniques of that school. Space limitations do not permit an adequate theoretical defense of the clinical validity of the death instinct. I have tried to do that in other contributions (Grotstein, 1985, in press).

KOHUT'S REVOLUTION

Kohut began as an orthodox and then later as a classical ego psychologist and published a number of scholarly papers in that oeuvre until he became aware of the deficiency factor generally and of the lack of empathic affective attunement specifically in the genetic development of his analysands. It is arguable how he first really became imbued with deficiency and empathy. Certainly others preceded him in valorizing these ideas. I think of Ernst Bibring and Annie Reich as examples. Whatever is the origin of his enlightenment, once it happened, there was no turning back. Empathy became the rallying cry for a veritable psychoanalytic revolution in the United States and has gradually spread elsewhere. Once he had gotten hold of the thematics of empathy, both as an affect and as a technique of observation of the analysand's life situation, a new paradigm emerged in psychoanalytic thinking (Kohut, 1971, 1977, 1978a, b, 1984). While undoubtedly indebted more than he was able to admit to Ferenczi, Fairbairn, and Winnicott, his extension of their ideas proved to be innovative beyond their fondest dreams, and his reformulations of them in the new idiom of empathy and selfobjects represented a significant paradigm shift. Kohut enfranchised the lifetime necessity for selfobject functions and thus dependency itself, which had in the meanwhile emerged from the works of Klein and Fairbairn in terms of the emergence of the infant from infantile dependence to adult mutual interdependence.

Perhaps one of his greatest contributions was his validation of the innocence and entitlement of the infant and the infant's inalienable right to expect those selfobject functions from its caretakers. Others were his concepts of infantile rage and of shame. Self psychology became the virtual ombudsman for infant development, and its tenets have been confirmed over and over again by infant development research and childhood abuse and trauma research. Affect attunement had now become a fundamental concept in infant development and in psychoanalytic treatment as well. In that regard the emphasis that Kohut and his followers placed on the *enfeebled self* and on its affective counterpart, *shame,* became monumental contributions to psychoanalytic understanding.

Another major contribution of his, in my opinion, one that has not been significantly stressed, is his early formulation of a separate track of development for the self, one that was, in the first instance, independent of the self's relationship to objects. Klein would not have been able to understand that dimension, I believe, and Fairbairn, while strongly hinting at it, never came out and said it. Winnicott did say it in many ways but seemed to negate it with, "There is no such thing as an infant. There is only an infant with its mother," thereby reifying primary narcissism. Space restrictions prevent my discussing this vital point any further.

THE DIALECTICAL COMPLEMENTARITY
BETWEEN KLEIN AND KOHUT

Whereas the vagaries of history and the tendentiousness of politics have separated Kleinians from self psychologists, it is my belief that they each have an important place in psychoanalysis and that they both overlap in many significant areas, significantly differ in others, and complement one another overall. I have already alluded to the dual-track theorem. I also have recently submitted a paper whose title is "The Ineffable and the Phenomenal Subjects of Psychoanalysis" (Grotstein, 1997e). The former is the Kleinian subject in and of the unconscious. The latter is what I believe is the subject referred to by those intersubjectivists who have emerged from self psychology (Stolorow and Atwood, 1992; Orange, Atwood, and Stolorow, 1997).

By *ineffable* I mean the unconscious numinous aspect of the self, the one who can never be known but who represents that mysterious coherence within us that dreams our dreams, organizes our thoughts and feelings for presentation as free associations, and remains the "strange attractor" that mediates the chaos within us. It belongs to the primal unconscious and never becomes conscious, whereas the latter, the phenomenal subject, is that aspect of the ego (upper portion of the preconscious ego) that is more in contact with the external world. This complementarity represents the dialectic between instinct abuse and object abuse and what the individual from infancy onward does about them.

Another aspect of the dialectical complementarity between Klein and self psychology, one that naturally flows from the previous idea, is the valence that each school puts on the clinical material from the patient. Self psychologists and relationists, on balance, seem to be more interested in what the patient reports about what genetically occurred in his life history to account for his symptoms. The Kleinian is more interested in how the infantile aspect of the patient concretely identifies with his own version of how he, in unconsciously phantasy, autochthonously *created* his history—even though untrue—the putative damage of which became his felt obligation to own and to repair. Thus, the Kleinian, while remaining interested in "what really happened," valorizes the unconscious subject's version of the results of its own creationism and miscreationism, what I call "autochthony." In other words, while remaining interested in "what really happened" in his patient's past, he is more interested in how the patient *believes* that he created that past—as putative agent (in the stage of omnipotence; paranoid-schizoid position)—before he can gradually evolve into the depressive position, where he surrenders his omnipotence, accepts reality, and can for the first time entertain the idea of a causality that is other than, that is, external to, himself. *Then* he can comprehend the reality of abuse by others. *Then* he is ready for the self psychology version. When I say, "Then he is ready . . . ," I do not mean to suggest that the analysis should be all Kleinian at first and then self psychological subsequently; each school's technique would be constantly and continuously intermixed throughout the course of the analysis. There never is a time, in other words, when each "infant-subject" does not need to be addressed.

Put another way, the Kleinian analyst almost exclusively interprets the infantile subject's own interpretations about what was believed to have happened from the vertex of his sense of omnipotent agency—before he achieves the depressive position of object constancy (and separation) and can therefore begin to contemplate the very concept of damage emanating from a primal object who, though all-important to him, is now safely separate from him as a person in his or her own right—and therefore able to be judged—and even forgiven.

A CONCORDANCE BETWEEN KLEIN AND KOHUT

Quite recently, Dr. Allan Schore (1997), a neuropsychologist who has begun the task of integrating neurobiological and neurodevelopmental research with infant development findings, presented a paper, "The Neurodevelopmental Aspects of Projective Identification," in which he called attention to the intimate relationship that exists between Klein's concept of projective identification and the infant developmental model of self-regulation:

> Despite the controversies about Klein's theoretical constructs, her clinical concepts have offered valuable clues about working with early disordered patients, and have served as a fertile source for future theoretical elaborations by those clinical observers who are intrigued with the primitive domains of the mind. . . . I would like to re-evaluate her essential concept of projective identification in light of current scientific findings on the early development of the primitive right brain and the clinical role of primitive emotional states. . . . It has long been thought that Klein's main emphasis was on the development of cognitions in the emerging infant mind. Yet Brody (1982, in Stein) asserted that "Melanie Klein contributed to psychoanalytic thought when she described the intensities that *affects* can reach during infancy. . . ." And very recently, in a 1990 article entitled, "A new look at the theory of Melanie Klein," Stein asserts that: "The common thread running through all mental development, according to Klein, may be said to be that of "*regulation of feelings*" [p. 508].

Schore is stating that we can now use Klein's concept of projective identification to explain how the infant self-regulates unpleasant or disturbing affect states by projecting them into mother as container (Bion, 1959, 1962). According to self psychology theory the mother must optimally be able to mirror her infant. The Kleinian model can be seen as a negative mirror, one that attempts to mitigate and defuse the infant's sense of the badness and horror of its internal contents. Thus, it is a corrective mirror. It does not merely validate; it metabolizes the infant's sense of inner horror and dread.

Bion's (1959, 1961, 1962) revision of Klein's concept of projective identification deserves mention. Until his innovative leap the concept was considered to be an exclusively intrapsychic (one-person) one. He inaugurated the idea that it was also an interpersonally active one and thereby became one of the founders of our current model of intersubjectivity. In so doing, he made the analyst a fundamental participant of the analytic process.

In two recent papers entitled "Why Oedipus and Not Christ?" (Grotstein, 1997b, c), I discuss the importance of the infant's sense of innocence in the context of the practice of infant sacrifice, which I believe to be the deeper, organizing theme of the oedipus legend and complex. In that contribution I also proffer the idea of the Pietà transference-countertransference neurosis (Grotstein, 1997b, c). Briefly stated, it postulates that Mary is the archetypal mother who *must* experience both sorrow and guilt for agreeing to bear a child who was destined for martyrdom. If we abstract this sacred myth and apply it to the quotidian reaches of life, we could postulate that all parents must—or should—feel guilt or at least responsibility for bringing an innocent one into the "valley of the shadow of death" with all the agonies that it is destined to experience. The same principle applies to the analytic situation in which the analyst bears an ineradicable sense of responsibility for starting the ineluctable "conveyor-belt of sorrows" to confront the analysand, a phenomenon we analysts may all too insensitively have designated as *"regression in the service of the ego."*

CLINICAL ASPECTS

I regret that space limitations do not permit the opportunity to employ a clinical vignette with which to delineate the themes I have developed. That would have been too ambitious an undertaking for this contribution. Instead, let me present a brief summary of a generic case, one in which an adult analysand had been the victim of child abuse. In the analysis of such cases one often finds that the analysand may present a picture in which they either have denied the abuse by a parent or, having accepted the fact of the abuse, are so positioned that they are in an oppositional (understandably hateful) counteridentification with that parent; that is, they are tied to the parent by their hatred. Fairbairn (1952) theoretically and clinically portrays this situation with poignant clinical cogency. He states that the infant and/or child introjects the bad and dangerous aspects of the needed mother or father and identifies with them within himself *as* himself. The infant/ child must do this because of the unremittingness of his dependency on his object; that is, he has no choice. Fairbairn's concept of this schizoid compromise (that the infant/child is compelled to adjust to a needed parent at the expense of modifying his psychic structure in order to "launder" her/him so that they can be thought of as an adequate parent) is clearly based upon the realistic deficiency, traumatic model of childhood neglect/trauma/failure of attunement. What supports the repression of the bad objects is the infant/child's introjective identification with this bad, but needed, object. So far, the infant/child can be felt to be an innocent victim—in reality. Fairbairn then goes on to hypothesize, however, that the infant/child believes that the object would not have mistreated them if his or her (the infant's or child's) love were not *bad*.

Thus, Fairbairn, who was very much in touch with the infant's and child's realistic and justifiable feelings that they were not treated by the parent as "persons in their own right," finally resorts to an explanation that is based on unconscious phantasy (autochthony); that is, the parental object justifiably mistreats them because "their love is bad," which is the Kleinian view. Put another way, many psychoanalysts, Winnicott and Rapoport among them, have stated that Klein ignored reality in favor of unconscious phantasy. My own view is that Klein ignored external reality exactly the same way the infant does. The infant is imbued from the very beginning with "unusual logic," according to Subbotsky (1992), the Russian infant developmentalist. "Unusual logic" is his term for Freud's (1911) primary process and Matte-Blanco's (1975, 1988) symmetrical logic, two of whose mechanisms are splitting and projective identification.

In brief, the infant possesses the capacity to phantasize about the external world as a projective extension of himself—before he acquires secondary process (asymmetrical or usual logic). When that infant becomes an adult patient, the analyst must be able to detect his unconscious phantasies, but, seeing how vulnerable he is to being criticized, the analyst obligatorily must become attuned and empathic about the patient's vulnerability and be open to the verdict of pain from the conscious subject who presents himself—before he embarks on disinterring the phantasied constructions of the unconscious subject. The competent psychoanalyst, in other words, must be multilingual.

THE HIDDEN LEGACY OF SOLITUDE
(THE DEFENSE OF THE ONE-PERSON MODEL)

I should like now to address the psychoanalytic issue of *solitude*. This is my way of distinguishing the Kleinian oeuvre of the one-person psychoanalytic model from the intersubjective, relational two-person model.[2] Classical analysts, in their reaction to orthodox id analysis, seem in retrospect to have retreated from that *legacy of solitude* that once constituted a fundamental canon of psychoanalysis, and they may, in my opinion, have continued that retreat in their own reactive descendant, self psychology.

Put another way, psychoanalysis, as it was originally understood, was not the unearthing of the archive of what happened between self and Other—or what the Other did to the self. It was the archive, the imagined history of the birth and endurance of our *unconscious sense of agency,* of our sense of *psychic responsibility,* for our unwitting unconscious intentionality, of how we unknowingly yet subjectively responded to our interactions with objects, that is, how we experienced the events that confronted us as *subjects* in order to render them *personal* experiences and how we, as self-appointed agents of our ontology, our archeology, and our teleology (in the terms of Foucault), created both our internal and external worlds that we must dwell in thereafter while gradually, only gradually, begin to realize, with the sobriety of the God-Infant of *Genesis,*[3] that we are born into Ananke (Necessity) and custom, the first being indescribable, ineffable, and the second mother, father, siblings, friends, others, language.

We must come to grips with sharing our sense of agency with the Other and the others as subjects to *their* whims, as they certainly had been and shall continue to be subjects to our whims, as they had always already done since the most ancient days of their being our "objects," the raw, uninhabited, nonsubjective clay of our omnipotent molding. In short, we seem to have lost contact with that legacy of psychoanalysis that Freud had borrowed from Kant—the transcendental analytic—of inherent givens, of a priori structures and categories, of inherent deep structures whereby we unconsciously anticipate, that is, format and "create" that which we discover for the first time. Bion

---

[2] This statement may seem ambiguous since Heimann, Money-Kyrle, and particularly Bion introduced the two-person model into Kleinian analysis. The reconciliation of this seeming contradiction is that Kleinians, while certainly aware of the importance of countertransference, projective identification, and counteridentification, ultimately employ the "two-person" model within the framework of the one-person model. This means, for instance, that the Kleinian will acknowledge his own errors but does his best to contextualize his own personal feelings in terms of his interrelationship with the patient.

[3] In a recent contribution I reread *Genesis* as the birth of God, who, like all infants, believes that he creates everything he opens his eyes to, including himself, the world around him, and even his parents, Adam and Eve. When the God-infant ultimately begins to realize that it was his parents' intercourse that created him, not his autochthony, God becomes a normal infant in the depressive position (Grotstein, 1997d).

stated this Kantian principle poetically as "memoirs of the future." Psychoanalytically, this means that we put our own personal, subjective "spin" on the objects and events we encounter in order to render them as "experienced."

I come back to solitude. The human being who becomes an analysand is not only made poignantly aware of his/her unutterable solitude, subjectivity, and vulnerability; (s)he is simultaneously reminded that (s)he is the sole responsible "owner" of his/her sense of agency for running his/her life—as a "small business," so to speak, and from the earliest days of his/her life has had to go the breast-mother as a metaphoric bank to consult and from whom to obtain a "small business loan" as backup to have some foundation in learning the business of running one's life. Intersubjectivity or relationism relates to archival history. It speaks from another perspective. It represents perhaps what really happened; it does not represent how the ineffable subject of the unconscious, in confronting primal dread (Ananke [Necessity], "O," "the Real,"[4] chaos, "raw experience"), became through its solitude the sole creator, and therefore responsible agent, for its own destiny thereafter and thus became constrained to holding itself responsible for the creation and for the choreography of its history and the responsibility for its investments of caring and mattering in objects as well.

Thereafter it becomes its obligation to choose those elements from the "cafeteria of experience" with its others that it needs in order to lead an optimum life for itself—under the all-hovering shadow of unfairness. It must come to terms with its moira, its fate-bequeathed life portion. It is its obligation to get good rearing from bad parents and good analyses from bad analysts. Life is lived—and lived out—in the "shadow of the subject." That shadow is cast by the life creator, whose effable name is *projective identification*. Its agents are splitting, idealization, magic omnipotent denial, the manic and depressive defenses, personification, symbol formation, object usage, and play. Psychoanalysis becomes the autobiography of the solitude of our subjectivity, of our attempts to achieve agency, our efforts to extricate ourselves from the labyrinths we unknowingly created and miscreated and the minotaurs with which we populated them (Grotstein, 1997d)—all in order to defend ourselves from Ananke (Necessity), "O," and the demons we projectively created in order to shield ourselves from it. Thus,

---

[4] Bion's (1965, 1970) concept of "O" and Lacan's (1966) "Real" are their respective ways of talking about a register of existence that lies beyond our capacity to imagine or to conceptualize. One example would be the Holocaust.

the world that matters, psychic reality, whose dominion is both internal and external, relentlessly and continuously evolves *in* the shadow—and *as* the shadow—of the subject.

In the lifelong journey of solitude, we are accompanied by the denizens (internal objects) of our creation. When we are infants and are afraid, we abjectly expel our raw, intolerable feelings and urges into the mother—or at least our image of mother—thereby transforming her into the archetype both of the *predator* and the *prey.* We come to fear both, now at a distance. That distance is misleading. We are compelled to absorb and incorporate these miscreations of our agony—*and to become them*—via introjective identification. Thereby we become haunted by "the forever near far," to borrow from Thomas Wolfe, by forever near far demonic misrecognitions of ourselves within us and by alter egos (second selves) on the outside beckoning to us as if by déjà vu. The analysand's "mother" is fictive, a creation of his/her autochthonous imagination and should not be confused with his/her mother of actual fact, who, psychoanalytically, is more an impostor, a signifier, than is realized—when we consider that each analytic hour is a dream, and a dream reported in it is a dream within a dream.

Klein's reading of Freud's legacy is: *We are destined to become what we believe we have done to our objects. The shadow of the subject falls upon the object, whose reflected composite shadow falls yet again back upon the subject—and becomes the subject!* We are existential prisoners to our creations and miscreations. In our solitude in the journey through the valley of the shadow, we are accompanied by demons and monsters, who represent disidentified, disowned, abjected, misrecognized aspects of ourselves who persecutorily hound and haunt us from within, challengingly demanding reentry—or we may, by the grace of our gratitude and appreciation of the goodness we have received from our loving ones, acknowledge the debt and, in return, receive the legacy of our experience with that loved and loving one—and release her or him from our selfish embrace and thereby become released in turn. The legacy of that newfound covenant shines across our inner landscape as a blessing and a benediction. We now have F (Faith) to face "O" (Ananke, Necessity) in the fullness of that blessed emptiness, the absence, the "no-breast present."

Our fidelity to our solitude, our acceptance of our being-apart-from-all-other-beings, and our willingness to be solely responsible agents for what befalls us in our lonely journey constitute the consummate and truest psychoanalytic achievement and the sacred way to our self-transcendence. Its obverse, reality, ultimately is alibi, because we alone are the proprietors of our solitude and our analyst, its sacred guardian and solicitor.

Put another way, psychoanalysis is always a one-person (analysand) enterprise, which is inescapably connected in an asymmetrical two-person intersubjective atmosphere. The analyst must always seek to be neutral and objective while simultaneously respecting and acknowledging his/her own subjectivity and its impact on the analysand. The analysand, on the other hand, must be held responsible in part for how he *believes he "created" the analyst's subjective responses—before he can be able to acknowledge that they emerged from a separate, autonomous subjectivity. Psychoanalysis is clinical creationism—side-by-side with the one's merciful innocence in the face of randomness!*

EPILOGUE

I believe that there are many areas of convergence, concordance, complementarity, and differences between the Kleinian and self psychological and other relational schools of thought, yet I believe that the ideal psychoanalyst should be able to benefit from tasting each. I myself am basically Kleinian—with a Bionian accent. I speak Winnicott and Fairbairn fluently, and Lacan less fluently. But I would never want to undertake an analysis without Kohut looking over my shoulder—as one of my highly treasured guides—which is my way of saying that self psychology and relationism generally have become psychoanalytically validated within their own sphere of operations—as has Klein. It is time for the two rebels to stop rebelling, to stop proving themselves and join hands. They both are right and exist complementarily and overlappingly. As Rudolph Ekstein has sagely stated, "My father's house has many mansions, but the house is psychoanalysis."

REFERENCES

Bion, W. R. (1959), Attacks on linking. In: *Second Thoughts*. London: Heinemann, 1967, pp. 93–109.
——— (1961), A psycho-analytic study of thinking. *Internat. J. Psychoanal.*, 43: 306–310.
——— (1962), *Learning From Experience*. London: Heinemann.
——— (1965), *Transformations*. London: Heinemann.
——— (1970), *Attention and Interpretation*. London: Tavistock Publications
——— (1975), *A Memoir of the Future. Book I: The Dream*. Rio de Janeiro, Brazil: Imago Press.
——— (1977), *A Memoir of the Future. Book II: The Past Presented*. Rio de Janeiro, Brazil: Imago Press.
——— (1979), *A Memoir of the Future. Book III: The Dawn of Oblivion*. Perthshire: Clunie Press.

Bowlby, J. (1969), *Attachment and Loss. Vol. I: Attachment.* New York: Basic Books.

———— (1973), *Attachment and Loss. Vol II: Separation: Anxiety and Anger.* New York: Basic Books.

———— (1980), *Attachment and Loss. Vol. III: Loss: Sadness and Depression.* New York: Basic Books.

Fairbairn, W. R. D. (1952), *Psychoanalytic Studies of the Personality.* London: Tavistock.

Freud, S. (1911), Formulations of the two principles of mental functioning. *Standard Edition,* 12:218–226. London: Hogarth Press, 1958.

Grotstein, J. (1978), Inner space: Its dimensions and its coordinates. *Internat. J. Psychoanal.,* 59:55–61.

———— (1981), *Splitting and Projective Identification.* New York: Aronson.

———— (1985), A proposed revision for the psychoanalytic concept of the death instinct. In: *The Yearbook for Psychoanalytic Psychotherapy,* ed. R. J. Langs. Hillsdale, NJ: The Analytic Press, pp. 299–326.

———— (1997a), Integrating one-person and two-person psychologies: Autochthony and alterity in counterpoint. *Psychoanal. Quart.,* 66:403–430.

———— (1997b), Why Oedipus and not Christ?: A psychoanalytic inquiry into innocence, human sacrifice, and the sacred—Part I: Innocence, spirituality, and human sacrifice. *Amer. J. Psychoanal.,* 57:193–218.

———— (1997c), Why Oedipus and not Christ?: A psychoanalytic inquiry into innocence, human sacrifice, and the sacred—Part II: The numinous and spiritual dimension as a metapsychological perspective. *Amer. J. Psychoanal.,* 57:317–335.

———— (1997d), Klein's archaic Oedipus complex and its possible relationship to the myth of the labyrinth: Notes on the origin of courage. *J. Anal. Psychol.,* 42:585–611.

———— (1997e), Why Oedipus and not Christ?: A Psychoanalytic Inquiry into Innocence, Human Sacrifice, and the Sacred—Part II: The Numinous and Spiritual Dimension as a Metapsychological Perspective. *Amer. J. Psychoanal.,* 57(4):317–335.

———— (in press), Some considerations of "hate" and a reconsideration of the death instinct. *Psychoanal. Inq.*

Isaacs, S. (1952), The nature and function of phantasy. In: *Developments in Psycho-Analysis,* by Melanie Klein, Paula Heimann, Susan Isaacs, and Joan Riviere. ed. J. Riviere. London: Hogarth Press, pp. 67–121.

Kant, I. (1787), *Critique of Pure Reason.* New York: Bobs Merrill, 1956.

King, P. & Steiner, R., ed. (1992), *The Freud-Klein Controversies, 1941–1945.* London: Karnac Books.

Klein, M. (1923), Infant analysis. In: *Contributions to Psycho-Analysis 1921–1945.* London: Hogarth Press, 1950, pp. 87–116.

———— (1926), The psychological principles of child analysis. In: *Contributions to Psycho-Analysis 1921–1945.* London: Hogarth Press, 1950, pp. 140–151.

———— (1928), Early stages of the oedipus conflict. In: *Contributions to Psycho-Analysis, 1921–1945.* London: Hogarth Press, 1950, pp. 202–214.

Kohut, H. (1971), *The Analysis of the Self: A Systematic Approach to the Psychoanalytic Treatment of Narcissistic Personality Disorders.* New York: International Universities Press.

———— (1977), *The Restoration of the Self.* New York: International Universities Press.

———— (1978a), *The Search for the Self. Volume 1,* ed. P. Ornstein. New York: International Universities Press.

———— (1978b), *The Search for the Self. Volume 2,* ed. P. Ornstein. New York: International Universities Press.

———— (1984), *How Does Analysis Cure?* ed. A. Goldberg & P. Stepansky. Chicago: University of Chicago Press.

Lacan, J. (1966), *Écrits.* Paris: Seuil.

Matte-Blanco, I. (1975), *The Unconscious as Infinite Sets.* London: Duckworth Press.

———— (1981), Reflecting with Bion. In: *Do I Dare Disturb the Universe? A Memorial to Wilfred R. Bion,* ed. J. S. Grotstein. Beverly Hills: Caesura Press, 1981, pp. 489–528.

———— (1988), *Thinking, Feeling, and Being: Clinical Reflections on the Fundamental Antinomy of Human Beings.* London/New York: Tavistock and Routledge.

Opatow, B. (1997), The real unconscious: psychoanalysis as a theory of consciousness. *J. Amer. Psychoanal. Assn.,* 45:865–890.

Orange, D. M., Atwood, G. E. & Stolorow, R. D. (1997), *Working Intersubjectively: Contextualism in Psychoanalytic Practice.* Hillsdale, NJ and London: The Analytic Press.

Piaget, J. (1924), *Judgement and Reasoning in the Child.* New York: Harcourt Brace & Co., 1928.

Ricoeur, P. (1970), *Freud and Philosophy: An Essay on Interpretation,* trans. D. Savage. New Haven, CT: Yale University Press.

Schore, A. (1997), The neurodevelopmental aspects of projective identification. Presented at the Annual Conference of the National Membership Committee on Psychoanalysis in Clinical Social Work, Seattle, WA, September 26, 1997.

Stolorow, R. D. & Atwood, G. E. (1992), *Contexts of Being: The Intersubjective Foundations of Psychological Life.* Hillsdale, NJ: The Analytic Press.

Subbotsky, E. V. (1992), *Foundations of the Mind: Children's Understanding of Reality.* Cambridge, MA: Harvard University Press.

Winnicott, D. W. (1963), Communicating and not communicating leading to a study of certain opposites. In: *The Maturational Processes and the Facilitating Environment.* New York: International Universities Press, 1965, pp. 37–55.

Chapter 9

Insight, Empathy, and Projective Identification

Craig Powell

The title of this chapter places together empathy, one of the central topics of interest in self psychology, and projective identification, a key concept in Kleinian psychoanalysis. To what degree do they coincide or differ? What is their respective place in analytic therapy and the acquisition of analytic understanding? Before I attempt any survey of the literature, I will begin with a clinical vignette. It comes from my own experience, very early in my psychoanalytic training, so I trust you will forgive its naiveté. It was one of my first experiences of a powerful countertransference response that I was able to understand partially and use to the patient's benefit, and it remains important to me for that reason. Of course, there have been many occasions before and since when there have been countertransference responses I have *not* been able to understand or use, or even become aware of, and I am obviously in no position to talk about these.

I will call the patient Nicole. She was a young woman in her late teens referred to the government psychiatric hospital in which I worked, from a local hospital psychiatric unit in her home town some 100 km away. She had been in this unit for a month after taking an overdose. She had moved out of her highly conflicted family home to live with a girlfriend. When this girlfriend became preoccupied with a relationship with a young man, Nicole began telling people she had been diagnosed with cancer. This produced a flood of anxious concern from the girlfriend and others, but when Nicole realized she would be inevitably discovered as a fraud, she took the overdose. Just when the psychiatric unit staff were preparing to discharge her, she attempted to hang herself on the ward.

Upon arrival she presented as a thin, intense person with a withdrawn manner. She was wearing thick-lensed spectacles because of her considerable myopia. She weighed only 44.5 kg, and she revealed she had lost some 10 kg during her month in the local psychiatric unit, when she had taken very little food. There was no mention of this in the referring letter. Indeed, it appeared she had been losing weight even before the original overdose.

Thus in addition to her reactive depression and suicidality, we were faced with the problem of anorexia nervosa. She regarded herself as still too fat and was determined to keep losing more weight. She was kept in hospital on a certificate and offered analytic psychotherapy three times per week, as well as attending a psychotherapy group. In addition, a psychologist devised a behavioral management plan. It was decided that 44.5 kg was as low as her weight could be allowed to go. As long as she maintained that weight, she had full privileges. If, however, on the daily weighing she fell below that level, she was to be confined to an isolation room to one side of the ward. She would also be deprived of her spectacles, a serious punishment since she was an avid reader and too shortsighted to read without them. A nurse would come in three times a day with meals on a tray. If Nicole took the food, the nurse would sit and talk with her. But if the food was refused, the nurse would sit in absolute silence then leave after five minutes, taking the tray with her. Only her psychotherapy sessions were exempt from these conditions. I was her therapist and, if her weight was adequate, she would come to my office for sessions. If not, I would go to the ward and have the session with her in the isolation room.

For a time we fluctuated between having the sessions in the office and in the isolation room, as her weight hovered just above or below the crucial level. But then her weight kept falling steadily. Moreover, she was refusing even fluids and was starting to show signs of dehydration. A micro-urine examination revealed marked pyuria.

At this point I became quite anxious. During a session in the isolation room, I tried to point out the danger she was in. She could develop a serious urinary tract infection with possible long-term damage if it were allowed to become chronic. She remained adamant. She would not accept even tap water to give herself an adequate urinary flow. At this point I told her we might have to refer her to the general hospital for naso-gastric intubation. She replied evenly, "You can do that, and they can force fluids into me, but then they'll have to send me back here, and the whole thing will start all over again, because you can't make me do anything I don't want to."

At this moment she was seated on the edge of the bed, and I was walking up and down about a meter away from her. I had a sudden visual image of smashing a left hook into her nose. Fortunately, sanity took hold. I wondered what on earth I was doing, thinking of beating up a wisp of a girl less than half my size and weight. And then I said to her, "Right now I am feeling very angry. And I think I'm angry because I feel so helpless. And maybe this is your way of letting me know how angry and helpless you feel inside yourself."

She visibly relaxed and answered, "Of course," as though the interpretation that had cost me so much effort were the most obvious thing in the world. We talked a few more minutes, then she announced that she would like a bowl of ice cream. We called a nurse who fetched the ice cream, and Nicole slowly ate the whole plateful in front of me.

We never attempted to interpret that particular action, though I often wondered about it afterwards. In all likelihood she felt understood and thus more safe to experience her real hunger. It was also a gift she offered to me in return for the interpretation, but I could not escape the wry thought that, just as we train animals by offering food at strategic moments, so an anorexic patient may shape her therapist by taking food herself.

Her therapy proceeded very well, and on discharge from hospital, she showed no signs of anorexia or suicidal behavior. She could even acknowledge that, during her period of anorexia, she had been ravenously hungry all the time but couldn't let herself acknowledge that. It will not surprise you to learn that she took a job as assistant manager in a pizza parlor.

When I tried to conceptualize that episode myself, because of my burgeoning interest in self psychology, I thought of it as an example of my own empathic immersion in the world of the patient. Kohut wrote of introspection and empathy (or "vicarious introspection") as being the data-gathering tools of psychoanalytic therapy. I had identified my own emotions (introspection) and then, by a process of vicarious introspection, could develop an hypothesis about the inner world of the patient, which I could offer for her consideration.

A Kleinian therapist, however, might see that episode as an example of projective identification and suggest that the patient had projected a toxic part of her inner world into me so that my own emotional balance was altered and I was taken by surprise. The quality of surprise is important, indicating that what occurs is unconscious and nonverbal or even preverbal. The therapeutic response could then be seen as an example of what Bion called "container and contained" in which the patient's raw "beta elements" were processed by the therapist's thought into "alpha elements" that could be assimilated.

These two conceptualizations might be equally persuasive, or indeed equally limited, but they do proceed from a different set of theoretical hypotheses, with different implications. Now perhaps we should consider these hypotheses.

Kohut placed empathy at the center of his work in the paper that may be said to have been the beginning of self psychology, "Introspection, Empathy and Psychoanalysis," first published in 1959. He remarked, "Man and animals investigate their surroundings with the aid of the sensory organs. . . . The inner world cannot be observed with the aid of our sensory organs. Our thoughts, wishes, feelings and fantasies cannot be seen, smelled, heard or touched. They have no existence in physical space, and yet they are real, and we can observe them as they occur in time: through introspection in ourselves, and through empathy (i.e., vicarious introspection) in others" (Kohut, 1959, in Ornstein, 1978, pp. 205–206).

He went further to make the radical proposition that it was indeed introspection and empathy that defined the scientific field of psychoanalysis rather than, as earlier definitions would have it, the study of unconscious infantile sexuality or of transference and resistance (Freud, 1914, p. 16). These phenomena, indeed, could only be approached via introspection and empathy. Kohut suggested, "Each branch of science has its natural limits, determined approximately by the limits of its basic tool of observation. . . . The limits of psychoanalysis are given by the limits of potential introspection and empathy" (p. 231). The psychoanalyst may draw upon data from other fields of endeavour, such as neurophysiology, infant research, or sociology, but the clinical endeavour of psychoanalysis will always be grounded primarily in introspection and empathy.

It is important to emphasize that Kohut saw empathy as a data-gathering tool. Such data might indeed be put to malignant use, as one may observe in successful psychopaths who are generally highly empathic people. Kohut was aware of the danger of the vernacular misuse of the term. He wrote (1977), "I know in particular—to address myself first to the misgivings aroused by my emphasis on empathy—that some of my colleagues will say that by assigning a position of basic importance to empathy I am trying to bring about what others have tried to bring about before me: the replacement of the staunch acceptance of the cold facts of reality by a regressive, sentimental flight toward illusions" (p. 304). The illusions in question consisted of "nonscientific forms of psychotherapy which provide cure through love and cure through suggestion" (Kohut, 1977, p. 304). Kohut acknowledged, "We must thus be on guard about the possibility that our insights might be used as rationalizations for unscientific therapeutic activities" (p. 305). Empathy, then, is not to be conflated with kindness or sympathy. The analytic "cure," as Kohut insisted on many occasions, depended upon interpretive working through of the selfobject transference.

Projective identification is a complex term with several, often contradictory, uses, and I am indebted to Hinshelwood's *A Dictionary of Kleinian Thought* (Hinshelwood, 1989) for an excellent review of the literature. To begin with, there is no clear differentiation between simple projection and projective identification, and Spillius (1983) even suggested it was not useful to make the attempt. Nonetheless, attempts to describe projective identification commonly focus upon the analyst's experience of changes in his or her inner world linked to the current encounter with the patient. Thus a projection, in the original Freudian sense, is a phenomenon in the mind of the person doing the projecting and may have little or no influence upon the internal state of the person who is the target of the projection. But if the internal state of that person is profoundly affected then perhaps we may talk of projective identification.

Bion (cited in Hinshelwood, 1989) suggested that projective identification be categorized into normal and abnormal, and there are two alternative aims: (1) One is to evacuate violently a painful state of mind, leading to forcibly entering an object, in phantasy, for immediate relief, and often with the aim of an intimidating control of the object, and (2) the other is to introduce into the object a state of mind as a means of communicating with it about this mental state.

Similarly, Rosenfeld (1983) divided projective identification into three categories: (1) projective identification for defensive purposes such as ridding the self of unwanted parts, (2) projective identification used for communication, and (3) projective identification in order to recognize objects and to identify with them (empathy).

American authors such as Kernberg and Ogden have broadened the concept of projective identification to include observable interpersonal events, or "interpersonal actualizations," to use Ogden's term (Ogden, 1982, p. 177). This is a long way from the Kleinian meaning of the term, that it is an intrapsychic phenomenon linked to the paranoid-schizoid position.

From this brief survey, we might surmise that, if we were looking for points of confluence in the concepts of empathy and projective identification, then perhaps empathy is one of several forms of projective identification. It would coincide with Bion's concept of "normal" projective identification, something used in the service of communication and with Rosenfeld's categories of projective identification used for communication and for recognizing objects and identifying with them.

But is that so simple? Does it not neglect the capacities and responses of the analytic observer, the very fact that the analytic encounter always takes place within an intersubjective field? It is not only a function of the degree of fragmentation of the patient's psyche but also of the analyst's responsiveness as to whether the projective identification is defined as a violent evacuation with the aim of intimidating control or as a communication. To return to the earlier clinical vignette, there is no doubt that, for a brief moment at least, I did feel flooded and controlled by the patient, but fortunately did not remain so.

But let us examine the clinical vignette a little further and change paradigms in the process. From the point of view of my own subjectivity and my own selfobject needs, why might I have become so furious with Nicole? Was I motivated primarily by concern for her wellbeing? I think not. It seems more likely that my fantasies of her developing a urinary tract infection, progressing to acute and ultimately chronic pyelonephritis, arose more from my own anxiety about experiencing myself, and being seen, as a failure in my role of psychiatrist and physician. A serious threat to my self-esteem had induced a narcissistic rage. I had selfobject requirements of Nicole, that she should experience me as competent and benevolent and, indeed, that she would be glad to cooperate in what my wisdom dictated. Her refusal to provide these responses was felt momentarily to be intolerable.

In addition, I was expecting her to respond to me as a benevolent presence at the very moment that she was seated on the edge of the bed while I was standing up, quite literally looming over her. It is worth adding that Nicole described her father, a man who had lost one arm in a childhood accident, as a bullying, frequently malicious person. It is likely that she experienced my behavior as threatening a repetition of old traumas and would thus need to cling to her own psychic reality ever more tenaciously.

Each partner in the therapeutic dyad, then, was to varying degrees experiencing a danger to self-esteem and even self-cohesion and urgently requiring selfobject responses of the other. Although such selfobject strivings were largely unconscious, this intersubjective viewpoint lacks the quasi-mystical aura that sometimes attends discussions of projective identification. Admittedly, such an aura may not be inappropriate when we are struggling to conceptualize unconscious events, with their endless capacity to surprise and catch us unawares. Freud expressed open wonderment at how the unconscious of one person could seem to communicate directly with the unconscious of another, and it may be in this connection that he expresed regret at not being able to devote more time to studying paranormal phenomena.

Stolorow, Brandchaft and Atwood have written several critiques from an intersubjective stance of clinical accounts of projective identification, and I will quote two of these. The first examines Otto Kernberg's description of the Ingmar Bergman movie *Presences*. Kernberg (1975) writes:

> A recent motion picture . . . illustrates the breakdown of an immature but basically decent young person, a nurse, charged with the care of a psychologically severely ill woman presenting what we would describe as a typical narcissistic personality. In the face of the cold, unscrupulous exploitation to which the young nurse is subjected she gradually breaks down. She cannot face the fact that the other sick woman returns only hatred for love and is completely unable to acknowledge any loving or human feeling toward her. The sick woman seems able to live only if and when she can destroy what is valuable in other persons, although in the process she ends up destroying herself as a human being. In a dramatic development the nurse develops an intense hatred for the sick woman and mistreats her cruelly at one point. It is as if all the hatred within the sick woman had been transmitted into the helpful one, destroying the helping person from the inside [pp. 245–246].

Stolorow, Brandchaft, and Atwood (1987) comment that these conclusions are unjustified and would be antitherapeutic in a treatment situation.

> In the first place, there is no evidence that the sick woman is "able to live only if and when she can destroy what is valuable in other persons"; there are only indications that the sick woman does not respond in a way that the nurse-therapist wants or needs. . . . Second, there is no evidence that "the hatred within the sick woman has been transferred into the helpful one, destroying the helping person from the inside." There is, instead, every indication that the patient's responsiveness was required in order for the nurse to maintain her own self-esteem and to regulate her own psychological functioning. When frustrated, the nurse demonstrated her own narcissistic vulnerability and propensity for rage reactions. We have observed such factors at work in ourselves and regard them as to some degree universal in therapeutic relationships [pp. 113–114].

In similar vein they quote a vignette from Harold Searles working with a psychotic patient.

I had come to experience . . . a deep confusion in myself in reaction to her forcefully and tenaciously expressed delusions, which I came eventually to feel as seriously eroding all the underpinnings of my sense of identity, all the things about myself of which I had felt most sure: namely, that I am a man, that I am a psychiatrist, that I am engaged in fundamentally decent rather than malevolent work, and so on [Searles, 1965, p. 692].

Stolorow, Atwood, and Brandchaft (1988) comment,

As Searles points out, therapists who feel the mainstays of their sense of identity threatened may then be compelled to erect a defensive wall between their reality and the patients', dismissing the latter as madness, projective identification or transference distortion. . . . The resulting struggle between therapist and patient stems not from wishes to "drive each other crazy" but from their efforts to preserve the integrity of their respective psychic realities. To the extent that the therapist is drawn into such a struggle, any enquiry into the patient's subjective truth becomes thereby precluded, further accelerating and entrenching the psychotic process [pp. 107–108].

Bacal (1990) suggests that what Kleinian therapists describe as "projective identification of bad parts of the self" often constitutes

in part, a lag in attunement with the patient's need to rid himself of intolerable links with unempathic objects, including the analyst who, at that moment, may not be aware of the extent to which his lack of optimal responsiveness has contributed to the patient's "bad-object-relational" experience. Unless the analyst can "decenter" from the patient's attribution that he is the embodiment at that moment of the patient's bad objects, and therefore personally responsible for the patient's misery, he will continue to experience himself as a target for these "projections" and be unable to help his patient [pp. 259–260].

He goes on to support Brandchaft and Stolorow's contention that the concept of projective identification may be used in the service of "a presumptive questioning on the part of the analyst of the patient's perception of him and an unjustifiable attribution of the analyst's 'own unwanted or disruptive affective reactions to the hidden intention of the patient.' " But Bacal goes on to suggest, in agreement with Meltzer (1984) that there are times when "the patient may need the analyst to contain and detoxify his unbearable feelings and that he does, so to speak, also hand them over to the analyst for this purpose" (Bacal, 1990, p. 260).

We have thus far been looking at the ways in which Kleinian, object relational, and self psychological authors have tried to deal with the commonly acknowledged phenomenon that the unconscious of one person may communicate with the unconscious of another, without apparently traversing the conscious minds of either. In passing, for what such labels are worth, there is clearly an overlap between what we would call Kleinian and what we'd call "object relational" just as there is also an overlap between the latter and what we would classify as "self psychological," and I agree with Bacal that self psychology is itself an object relations theory, focusing on the self and its selfobjects.

The Kleinian view of projective identification then, put rather too simply, is that it involves the projection of internal objects and/or parts of the self, with associated affect states, into another person, thus powerfully altering that person from within, and that this is carried out with the unconscious intention of destructiveness, control, communication, or seeking containment. Just how this process is carried out is not clear and may not even be of great importance, since the focus is upon the internal state of the person receiving the projection.

Kohut defined empathy as "vicarious introspection," which thus implied, in the analytic situation, an act of projection on the part of the analyst, placing himself, so far as is humanly possible, in the subjective position of the patient. The body of theory that grew up around Kohut's early writings, which we might now call "Selfobject Theory," a term coined by Kohut's colleague Michael Basch, did not include any conceptualizing of "internal objects," certainly not of "bad objects." Indeed Kohut deliberately steered away from any theoretical constructions that he felt could justify an analyst's assuming he knew more about the inner experience of a patient than the patient himself.

But more recent self-psychological writers have felt the need for some concept of the internalization and structuralization of selfobject frustrations. Stolorow and Atwood (1992), have written of "invariant organizing principles" (1992) while Bacal (1995) has spoken of "self-distortion" via the "internalized experience of . . . (selfobject) failure . . . that is, the memory of the bad selfobject" (p. 356). It is interesting, in this context, that Bacal's original training was with the British Middle Group, while Brandchaft worked for many years within the Kleinian tradition.

The "intersubjective" approach of Stolorow, Brandchaft and Atwood sees the analytic encounter as one between two overlapping subjectivities where the principal aim is the exploration and elucidation of the subjective world of the patient. But both analyst and patient have their respective psychic realities, which neither is eager to relinquish for the sake of the other, and each has selfobject needs of the other. From this standpoint, the division of projective identification into

catagories of "pathological," for the purposes of control and destructiveness, and "normal," for the purposes of communication, seems
arbitrary, since it depends so much upon the self-cohesiveness of the
analyst at any point in time and what he finds tolerable or intolerable,
comprehensible or maddening.

Perhaps the process of "projective identification" is not so mystical
but depends upon the giving or withholding of selfobject responses
within the intersubjective field, analogous to the mutual affect regulation of mother and infant described by Beebe and Lachmann (1988).
Such responses are not mediated primarily through words, but through
tones of voice, body posture, and so on. And the motivation for this
giving or withholding has to do not only with the present responsiveness of the other, but with the identification, in each partner in the
dyad, with the gratifying and/or frustrating responses of past and
present selfobjects outside the clinical setting.

This seems an obvious, almost banal, way of putting it. Then, perhaps, we need both the obvious and the quasi-mystical, the concepts
both of selfobject responsiveness and of projective identification, just
as physicists need both the wave and particle theories of light. The
mystical element at least reminds us of the uncanny power of the unconscious and keeps us respectful of it. In this context I would like to
present a second vignette.

I will call the patient Paul. He was a law graduate who presented in
his late twenties in a state of despair because he had been unable to
establish an intimate relationship with a woman for almost a decade.
He held stringent religious beliefs and, early on, expressed anxiety
that the analysis would undermine his faith. This, not surprisingly, did
happen in time.

His experience of his mother was of a depressive, often paranoid
woman who did seem to show signs of a clinical psychosis. The father
was an unpredictably violent man who beat his children, though Paul,
as the youngest in the sib-line, received less frequent and less severe
beatings than the others. This contributed to Paul's deep sense of
guilt. Ultimately, the parents divorced, and the father removed himself
from the family and rebuffed Paul's attempts to maintain any relationship with him.

In the analysis Paul quickly established an idealizing transference in
which I became a phantasy selfobject father. It was not long before my
inevitable frustration of his archaic longings provoked rage and contempt, with concomitant persecutory anxiety. This anxiety was mutual, and there were times when I came to dread the sessions with
him. The interpretations that seemed to offer most relief were those
that addressed his profound disappointment in me.

Often, he would deal with his rage and dread by lapsing into long silences or speaking in a lifeless monotone. In one session he was talking about his mother, how oppressed he felt by her chronic unhappiness and incompetence in shaping any kind of worthwhile life for herself. We had talked about this many times before. We had related it to his difficulty in having his own life, particularly in entrusting himself to any intimate relationship with a woman, and how little use his father had been in defining the oedipal boundaries, indeed how he felt his father had wanted to keep him in a crushed, one-down position.

As I said, we had been through this many times before, and I had listened and interpreted the transference as best I could. This time I found myself bored and irritated. His dreary tone was almost lulling me to sleep. I found my mind wandering. I thought of what I planned to do on the weekend. I was going to trim the passionfruit and wistaria vines growing over the pergola by my front door. The pergola was almost covered by the passionfruit, but the flowers weren't all that attractive, and I couldn't really get much fruit from vines that were criss-crossing the pergola. Far better to cut the passionfruit back and allow more scope for the wistaria. It at least had beautiful flowers in Spring. But it was only just beginning to establish itself on the pergola, and my concern was the passionfruit would choke it off.

I caught myself with a start, realizing I was drifting away from my patient. But was I really? All the time he was ruminating on his guilt-ridden enmeshment with his mother, I'd been thinking about how well the wistaria would grow and flower, but first it had to be protected from the choking influence of the passionfruit. In some peculiar way, I'd been trying to get away from him but couldn't, just as he couldn't get away from his mother, and had been more in tune with him than I'd realized.

Perhaps that episode can be thought of in terms of the giving or withholding of selfobject responses within the intersubjective field. I only know that I felt so startled when I realized what was happening that the notion of some kind of mysterious projective identification seemed quite congenial.

Although Paul was able eventually to establish a reliable and intimate relationship with a woman and end his analysis satisfactorily, there was no improvement in his relationship with his father. To return to the case of Nicole, though, in the later stages of her therapy she did experience an improvement in her relationships with both parents, especially with her father. At one point, when she visited home on weekend leave from the hospital, she was assembling a food blender. Her father picked up the cord and held it tantalizingly close to the power point while she had her fingers on the blades. The father, it will be remembered, had had one arm amputated in childhood. But some months later, after another weekend leave, the father unexpectedly asked if he could drive her back to the hospital. She usually took the bus. The father's car was specially equipped for a handicapped driver. As they drove, he spoke for the first time of how he felt he had failed her as a father by being so remote and so bullying. Then he spoke of how difficult his own life had been since he had lost his arm, how humiliated he had felt when, as a young man, he couldn't even tie his own shoelaces. Nicole was glad to respond to these overtures and felt that this was the first time she and her father had talked in such an intimate and honest manner.

Accounts of successful therapy frequently mention a closer contact with primary objects previously felt as persecutory. This is sometimes attributed, by therapists who rely on the concept of projective identification, to a diminished projection of bad objects by the patient, as a consequence of therapy, allowing the caregivers more access to benevolent aspects of themselves.

Perhaps a more parsimonious explanation, in the case of Nicole, is that she experienced more self-cohesion as a result of the empathic ambience in her therapy and was able to use this as a basis for responding less defensively to her father. But we must also allow for initiatives proceeding from the father himself. To witness one's daughter attempt suicide twice, develop a significant eating disorder and spend a long period of time in a psychiatric hospital, would be a sobering experience for any parent. Nicole's father had, it seems, the capacity to ponder what all this could mean and what part he himself had played in it. Many caregivers would not be capable of this, and in this respect Nicole was lucky. The danger of explaining it in terms of projective identification, it seems to me, is that this could attribute some internal omnipotence to the patient, which is unwarranted.

The Kleinian concept of projective identification and the self psychological use of the term *empathy* proceed then from differing theoretical assumptions. While they have points of confluence, they can never be fully reconciled. Indeed, were such an attempt remotely possible, it would not be reconciliation at all but homogenization. While I think my own theoretical preferences are clear enough, I think we are best served by allowing both concepts to remain separate, with the potential for sparks of creative tension between them.

REFERENCES

Bacal, H. (1990), *Theories of Object Relations: Bridges to Self Psychology*, Kenneth Newman co-author. New York: Columbia University Press.

———— (1995), The essence of Kohut's work and the progress of self psychology. *Psychoanal. Dial.*, 5:353–366.

Beebe, B. & Lachmann, F. (1988), The contribution of mother–infant mutual influence to the origins of self- and object representations. *Psychoanal. Psychol.*, 5:305–337.

Freud, S. (1914), On the history of the psychoanalytic movement. *Standard Edition*, 14:7–66. London: Hogarth Press, 1952.

Hinshelwood, R. D. (1989), *A Dictionary of Kleinian Thought*. London: Free Association Books, pp. 178–208.

Kernberg, O. (1975), *Borderline Conditions and Pathological Narcissism*. New York: Aronson.

Kohut, H. (1959), Introspection, empathy and psychoanalysis: An examination of the relationship between modes of observation and theory. In: *The Search for the Self—Selected Writings of Heinz Kohut: 1950–1978*, Vol. 1, ed. P. Ornstein. New York: International Universities Press, 1978, pp. 205–232.

———— (1977), *The Restoration of the Self*. New York: International Universities Press.

Meltzer, D. (1984), What is an emotional experience? Paper presented at the 7th Annual Self Psychology Conference, Toronto, Canada.

Ogden, T. (1982), *Projective Identification and Psychoanalytic Technique*. New York: Aronson.

Rosenfeld, H. (1983), Primitive object relations and mechanisms. *Internat. J. Psycho-Anal.*, 64:261–267.

Searles, H. (1965), *Collected Papers on Schizophrenia and Related Subjects*. New York: International Universities Press.

Spillius, E. B. (1983), Some developments from the work of Melanie Klein. *Internat. J. Psycho-Anal.*, 64:321–334.

Stolorow, R. & Atwood, G. (1992), *Contexts of Being: The Intersubjective Foundations of Psychological Life*. Hillsdale, NJ: The Analytic Press.

———— ———— & Brandchaft, B. (1988), Symbols of subjective truth in psychotic states: Implications for psychoanalytic treatment. *Progress in Self Psychology, Vol. 3*, ed. A. Goldberg. Hillsdale, NJ: The Analytic Press, pp. 103–142.

———— Brandchaft, B. & Atwood, G. (1987), *Psychoanalytic Treatment: An Intersubjective Perspective*. Hillsdale, NJ: The Analytic Press.

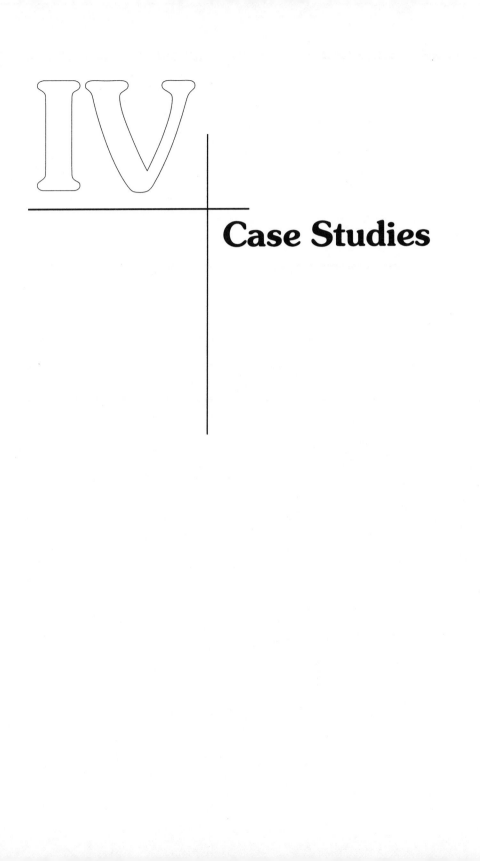

IV

Case Studies

A Life of One's Own: A Case Study of the Loss and Restoration of the Sense of Personal Agency

Dorthy M. Levinson
George E. Atwood

We are in the midst of a revolution in perspective that is transforming psychoanalytic conceptions of development, pathogenesis, and the therapeutic context. This revolution includes self psychology (Kohut, 1959, 1971, 1977), intersubjectivity theory (Atwood and Stolorow, 1984, 1993; Stolorow, Brandchaft, and Atwood, 1987; Stolorow and Atwood, 1992; Orange, Atwood, and Stolorow, 1997), and a variety of modern relational approaches (e.g., Mitchell, 1988, 1993; Bacal and Newman, 1990; Aron, 1996). From this perspective, dynamic processes, symptoms, and defenses, formerly viewed as products of an isolated mind (Stolorow and Atwood, 1992), are understood as inextricably interwoven with ties of human relatedness to vitally needed others. The development of self-experience in childhood is seen in the context of the responsiveness of caregivers. Similarly, a contextual view of the therapeutic process reveals that progressive and regressive movement in the consolidation of authentic self-experience is ex-

---

This chapter was presented at the 20th Annual Conference on the Psychology of the Self as part of a panel chaired by Stephen H. Knoblauch, Ph.D.

quisitely sensitive to and vulnerable to the analytic relationship. Oscillations in the sense of self, including the sense of agency, self-cohesion, self-continuity, and self-esteem, can be understood as organized and regulated within a system of mutual influence, both in early development and in therapy.

As the elaboration of the new paradigm in psychoanalysis continues, numerous aspects of the experience of self-cohesion, self-continuity, and self-esteem have been brought into focus and elucidated along with the ways these features of self experience are embedded in and dependent on events taking place in the relational field. The experience of self-agency, what Kohut (1977) referred to as "the self . . . as an independent center of initiative" (p. 94), has received less discussion in its own right, tending to be seen as an indispensable outcome of cohesion.

However, without the sense of agency, only a false, or "borrowed," sense of self-cohesion may be consolidated, based predominantly on accommodation to others (Brandchaft, 1993). Only seeming, rather than being, is possible when we do not experience ourselves as authors of our actions and as authentic centers of initiative. Stern (1985) writes, "The sense of volition makes our actions seem to belong to us and to be self acts. Without it the infant would feel what a puppet would 'feel like,' as the non author of its immediate behavior" (p. 77).

Through carefully detailed case studies, Brandchaft (1993) has described the compromise of the sense of agency in the context of pathological accommodation. He has illuminated the powerful resistances encountered in the treatment of patients whose rigidly consolidated sense of themselves has formed a confining "architecture for [the] spirit" based on the surrender of self agency in order to maintain archaic ties with primary caregivers. It is through sustained empathic inquiry, according to Brandchaft, that the analyst can discover the meanings of subtle shifts in affect that appear in the analytic dialogue. Such shifts signal alternations between a fleeting sense of authentic personal initiative accompanied by vitality and an immediate cancellation of such authenticity and a depletion resulting from the redefinition of self based on pathological accommodation.

Brandchaft focuses on those patients whose brief experience of self agency is immediately altered by and imprisoned in unconscious organizing principles that enshrine enslaving archaic ties. He shows that, when these invariant themes are repeatedly illuminated in the analytic dialogue, they become subject to reflection and their obliterating power as Truth is gradually diminished.

Those patients in whom the compromise of the sense of agency is even more profound pose a number of special difficulties for the psychoanalytic clinician.[1] First, in such persons the disturbance of the sense of self as a center of initiative may be so extreme as to preclude sustained acts of self-reflection (Gehrie, 1993). The inability to reflect makes it impossible for the patient to join the analyst in a traditional analytic dialogue. Such an obstacle to establishing even the rudiments of a conventional therapeutic alliance for prolonged periods of time can even lead the therapist to the judgment that the patient is unanalyzable (Brandchaft and Stolorow, 1990). When the analyst, nevertheless, persists in encouraging reflection in such patients, they tend to assimilate such encouragement as a search and destroy mission with the goal being the exposure of their fatal flaws. Second, the manifestations of agency that do appear in these instances tend to be embedded in extreme enactments that often lead to grossly destructive consequences. Included among such adventures are manic spending sprees, forming and attempting to execute glorious but ill-conceived business plans, and making death-defying journeys into the wild. The concretized form of the surviving remnant of agency is often so disastrous in its consequences that the analyst may view it as a defensive effort to avert a depressive collapse that has run out of control, or even as a sign of a malignant need to bring about self-destruction. If the therapist attempts to interpret any such motives or even expresses concern for the patient's safety, he/she tends to experience a concerted effort being mounted to eradicate the only independent action left and a humiliating demand being made for unconditional surrender. The third common difficulty for the psychoanalyst is that individuals in whom the experience of personal agency has been almost entirely nullified often resort to cutting themselves off from all personal history and declaring themselves radically independent of all the determining influences of their pasts. As analysts, our normal mode of inquiry, reflecting the present in relation to the past, thus becomes something in which these patients find it impossible to engage. If the analyst continues to pursue the roots of the present in the past, the patient usually organizes such inquiry as an effort to extract an "admission" that he/she is doomed to remain bound by inescapable enslaving archaic ties. We offer the following case study as an illustration of the ways we have approached some of these problems clinically.

---

[1] Although not focusing specifically on the disturbance in the sense of agency, a number of authors (Winnicott, 1972; Valenstein, 1973; Gedo, 1991; Gehrie, 1993, 1996) have examined early (preverbal) patterns of accommodation and the special difficulties such patterns can pose for conventional psychoanalytic treatment.

THE CASE OF ADAM

Adam was 38 years old when he began treatment, having carried the therapist's telephone number in his pocket for 2 years before he finally called. He knew he was in trouble. He said that he had been completely immobilized for 10 years following the death of his father. At first, he turned to drugs, marijuana, hashish, and cocaine. At some point he decided that he did not want to be an addict and simply stopped taking drugs. He then read self-help books, listened to Bradshaw on television, and made other efforts to improve himself and his life. The idea of directly seeking help from another human being filled him with dread. He had no reason to believe that putting his faith in *anyone* would bode well for his future. During these years Adam lived on the considerable fortune left him by his father. He spent the money recklessly and, looking back, always described his actions as deliberately trying to get rid of it. As the treatment unfolded, his therapist came to understand such acts of impulsive spending as attempts at the instantaneous actualization of a sense of agency. But now with his inheritance depleted and with no tangible results, he felt only despair. The one way he could see out of his predicament was to kill himself. With death as the option of last resort, he decided that he might as well try psychoanalytic treatment. If it did not work, he could always kill himself.

Adam's appearance was of a handsome, engaging man. Bright, cultured and articulate, he was almost poetic. This sophisticated persona made it very difficult to grasp immediately the extreme precariousness that pervaded his existence. Adam was born in Morocco, the younger son of a wealthy Jewish family he referred to as "the tribe." He had very few memories of his mother, who died when he was three years old. He always spoke of a deep bond of love and connectedness with her and believed that she was the only person in his life who loved him for himself. When she died, according to his account, his world collapsed.

Adam was never told that his mother died. His family told him only that she was recuperating from an accidental overdose of diet pills at a sanatorium somewhere in Israel. Gradually, he recognized the fact of her death. But because of the strange veil of secrecy surrounding his mother, he later concluded that she probably had no longer been able to endure the torment of living within the "tribe" and that she therefore must have committed suicide. Following her "disappearance," he was sent to stay with a series of relatives, while his brother, eight years his senior, was sent to boarding school. Only decades later, in the course of his analysis, was he able to feel these crushing losses, for he was doubly and triply orphaned, losing his father and his brother as well as his mother. Having lost all those for whom he might have existed in his own right, he lost himself.

His father had always been absent, preoccupied with business interests. A critical, emotionally cold man, he was not close to either one of his sons. After his mother "left," Adam was told that his father was suffering and that he was not to burden him. Adam's own pain and even his own questions about his mother were stifled by the entire family. He understood that he was not to speak of her, not to show what he felt. In fact, there must have been something wrong with *him* if he felt and thought things that were so unacceptable to everyone around him. His family made it very clear to him that their needs, including their need to ignore his mother's death, took precedence over anything he might feel.

Eventually, he was given to his father's childless sister Judith and her husband to bring up as their own because Aunt Judith "needed a child." She told Adam that he had no reason to feel sad, for he now had a mother, in fact a better mother. He eventually stopped asking questions and learned to accommodate her. He learned to appear happy and always to be pleasing to others, especially his aunt. But inside he felt dead. He lived in what he only much later came to identify as an "incomprehensible conspiracy of lies," in which his own authentic experience was almost entirely negated, becoming systematically subordinated to the agendas of the members of his family.

Adam recalled just two extremely brief periods of his later childhood and adolescence when he felt alive and had a sense of purpose. The first was when his fifth-grade teacher took an interest in him. He had not been a particularly good student until then. She seemed to care about him and appreciated his abilities and considerable intelligence. During the year in her class, he became confident and actually felt happy.

The second time was during his first year of high school. He was having difficulty with math, when his father offered to get him a tutor. For some practical reason, the tutoring sessions took place at his father's office. Adam interpreted this coincidence as evidence of his father's interest in him and so, once again, he blossomed. But this arrangement lasted a mere two weeks, and he then returned to "life on automatic pilot" and the associated sense of inner deadness.

No one in his family ever thought to ask what Adam dreamed of doing when he grew up. His father harshly dismissed his aspirations to be a journalist or perhaps a pilot. This persistent vote of no confidence crushed Adam's budding ambition and snuffed out his excitement over hopes for the future. At some point his father decided, without consulting him, that Adam should follow in the father's footsteps and become a lawyer in Morocco. Adam only focused on the impracticality of this plan and thought that the political situation in the country made his father's choice bizarre. Did his father not want him to succeed? Why not? Adam reached the conclusion that the only possible answer to these questions was that his father hated him. Once Adam failed to comply with his father's plan to become a lawyer, he was not sent to college. After graduating from high school, he went to live in Italy. He felt happier there, but after a few months his father began insisting that he return to Morocco. He was better able to withstand pressure from his father at a distance and refused. His father then promised him an exotic sportscar if he returned. This time he could not resist, because getting something valuable from his father meant so much to him. Of course, once he arrived, there was no car.

He traveled between Morocco and Italy for several years. Eventually, he came to live in New York and went into business with a man he liked. He did well and was very excited when, some years later, his father came to visit. He did all he could to impress his father. But when he showed him the business he had built, his father only asked, "Whose office is this?" He accused his son of lying when he said that it was his own.

At about this time, Adam fell in love with a woman who loved him. However, his continuing feeling of having no inner value was reflected in an inability to honor his own desire in any sustained way. Eventually, they drifted apart. He was unable to think of any reason for the ending of the relationship. In the course of the analysis, he came to see the ending of this relationship as a loss of something precious and as an example of a lifelong pattern of not having been able to hold on to things that had value for him. Later, he married a woman who was more like his father's family. She had a detailed agenda for who he should be and what he should do. The marriage was a turbulent one and only lasted for a few years. There was one child, his son, Philip, and he now felt that this child was his only reason for living.

When his own father became terminally ill, Adam did all he could to help him and to be with him. The last interaction he had with his father before his death was devastating. His father was concerned about the disposition of some property. For many reasons it would have been most convenient for Adam to act as his father's agent in this matter. He offered his help, and his father, unable to speak, gestured in reply by pointing his forefinger at his son and shaking it from side to side, as if to say: "Not you!"

A few months after his father died, Adam suffered a heart attack. Although he recovered physically, he remained depressed and immobilized.

HISTORY OF THE TREATMENT

From the very first session, Adam protested that he was right. He had always known the truth about his family, but no one had ever admitted it. No matter what he said or did, they only told him that he was wrong. He said that they treated him as if he did not exist, except to be used by them as they saw fit. Still, he was furious at himself for having allowed them to exploit and abuse him. Adam appeared to embrace enthusiastically his therapist's suggestion that they might together find a meaning of his paralysis and depression in relation to this family background.

As the analysis unfolded, it seemed to fall into three distinct sequences that we will call, (1) The Nine Months, (2) Amputation, and (3) The Construction Site. The events we are about to describe extended over a period of five years.

The Nine Months

The analysis began in June, just eight weeks prior to the analyst's August vacation. In immediate response to his analyst's announcement of her upcoming absence, Adam said that he had planned his own trip with his son beginning at the end of June. He was unable to speak of any emotional reaction to his analyst's leaving, adamantly denying that her taking a month off so early in their work together had any special meaning for him; nor would he entertain, even for a moment, the idea that his own trip was in part a reaction to hers. Adam's vacation plans then began to expand from two weeks to three weeks and still more. Finally, he said that he had planned a six-week trip through the Orient with his son and his ex-wife and that their work would have to be interrupted until the following September. He said that he wanted to reexamine his relationship with his ex-wife because he was feeling much stronger.

When Adam returned to the analysis two months later, following both vacations, he was profoundly disoriented. His memory was impaired, and he suffered from severe insomnia. He was extremely anxious and depressed and once again became despairing. He had expected that his ex-wife and his son would understand him and appreciate him. When he felt that they did not, he lost faith in the analysis and in himself. His therapist initially thought that Adam's state was a reaction to the two months' separation and said that he must have been very disappointed in her when the gains he had made in the three weeks of treatment did not achieve the permanent change he felt they should have. Adam angrily insisted that it had absolutely nothing to do with her and seemed profoundly disrupted by her suggestion of the possibility of such a connection.

His analyst's struggle to discern the specific therapeutic bond Adam needed with her during this period centered around several aspects of his behavior. First, he never referred to anyone by name and only described his experiences vaguely. She had no idea of the details of his life. Second, he did not remember what he felt, thought, or said from one day to the next. Yet there were moments when Adam could seem rather profound and even serene as he connected events in his life to aspects of Jewish tradition or found comfort in various works of literature. Seriously misled by his very convincing apparent thoughtfulness, his therapist repeatedly expected him to be capable of making connections between his present and his past and did not focus on what she was also seeing as their conversations unfolded, namely, that commenting in any way on what was difficult or painful for him only made him feel that she was criticizing him just as his family had done. The result was that the very difficulties she was trying to address were constantly being exacerbated.

The content of the sessions in the months that followed fluctuated between his rage at his father for having abused and neglected him, his rage at his brother for ignoring him and getting an unfair share of the inheritance from their father, his rage at his aunt, who continued to demand money from him, and his rage at his son, who seemed to be siding with his mother. The essence of his suffering was that he felt invalidated as a person when he was invariably expected to adapt to the needs of others. When his therapist showed acceptance of Adam's view of what happened in these various relationships, he grew calmer. His conversation turned once again to the 10 years since his father's death. Why had he been unable to act? Why had he not established a new business with his inheritance? He began to insist that he had squandered the money deliberately. His therapist said that in this context, the first meaning of the past 10 years might be seen as his declaration of independence; for if functioning in the world only meant carrying out his family's agenda, then inaction might represent a giant NO to a life of compliance. This way of describing the situation, emphasizing a possible constructive purpose of his paralysis, captured Adam's attention. He became hopeful about the treatment, and his affect changed markedly.

However, Adam's positive affect quickly reached great heights. At these times, he was convinced that he was cured and proclaimed, "I am no longer affected by my past. From now on everything is different!" When he invariably plummeted from these heights, he lost faith in both himself and the treatment, just as he had over the vacation. At the time, his therapist thought of these episodes as ruptures in an idealizing transference and continued to address the disappointment she believed he felt in her. He rejected these interpretations vehemently, but nevertheless, he simultaneously continued to feel sustained and calmed by the faith she communicated as she spoke of his actions as having a purpose and a meaning.

In March he told her that this was the ninth month of the analysis, bursting with delight at his own metaphor. He said that he was feeling alive again and that it was time for him to emerge into the outside world and to establish himself professionally. To do this he wanted to reduce drastically the frequency of his sessions because he would have to travel on business.

Amputation

In the midst of excitement over his plan to reduce the frequency of his sessions in order to pursue business opportunities, Adam reported a dream in which he was searching for and found his lost mother. In association to his dream, he said, in a tone that seemed filled with deep yearning and love, that he believed that he had found his lost mother in the relationship with his therapist. Responding to Adam's plan in the context of his dream, his therapist asked him whether they should understand his wish to cut back on his sessions as reflecting his feeling stronger and taking charge of his own life or whether, in addition to his new self-confidence, he experienced something that might be painful in the treatment that he wished to avoid. In response to this latter question, Adam became extremely confused and dejected. His physical bearing became awkward and disjointed. It was obvious that he had experienced the very question as a vote of no confidence. By the following day, his despair had turned into frenetic activity, and he was about to invest large sums of money in several business ventures at once with partners he had never even met. His therapist was afraid that he was in danger but knew by now that any comment to that effect would only make things worse. It was obvious that his frenetic activity, as well as his experience of her original question, could not be discussed with Adam, and it seemed very likely that the analysis and his life as a whole were on the threshold of coming to grief. Finally, after thinking back on the course of the analytic dialogue, his therapist was able to focus on the central theme that had dominated the treatment from its beginning, namely, his need that she find the constructive purpose in all his acts in order to validate the surviving remnant of his sense of personal agency. She was able to trace Adam's invariable reaction of disintegration to every instance where she understood the meaning of his words and acts in *any* other way. When she then changed her approach and began to speak of his action *solely* as an effort to take charge of his life, Adam's sense of himself became consolidated once again and they were able to continue.

However, as Adam set out to establish himself professionally, he was only interested in very grand schemes involving elaborate international travel. He said very little about these ventures until they failed. When these "big deals" turned out to be shams, he would declare: "I am glad that it happened!" He further claimed that he had undertaken the projects intentionally to prove to himself that the people he had chosen were not trustworthy, just like his family. He protested that he did not care that he had lost money; it was worth it! For, now, he claimed, the past was over: "I am no longer influenced by my family. I am no longer influenced by my father!" After every such episode, he always embarked on more extensive international travel, each trip more ambitious than the last.

As Adam protested repeatedly that he was no longer affected by his father, while intermittently expressing worry over depleting his inheritance, his therapist asked whether he thought that his spending the money might be a way in which he tried to free himself of his father's influence. He then reported the following two dreams: In the first dream he and his father were traveling together, but they were never in the same place at the same time. In the second dream, he proudly showed his father a hand of cards that turned out to be credit cards. His brother was in the room looking on and shaking his head dismissively.

He said that the first dream described his relationship with his father. He desperately wanted a connection with him, but his father was always too busy, often traveling on business. As an adult, he frequently tried to arrange to meet his father in the course of their travels. But they were, both literally and figuratively, never in the same place at the same time.

> If you are in the middle of the sea and there is no reference point, and you don't have a compass, you try to find something. I made him not a reference point, but a beacon. When my father died, I was really lost. Maybe I am still looking for him.

Of the second dream, he said only that his brother's gesture was the one his father had made on his deathbed. And so he thought that his brother represented his father in the dream. His therapist told him that, while he wanted to rid himself of his father's influence, it was understandable that he still wanted to impress him and get his attention and approval, since it was something he never received and still very much needed. He then recalled that, when his father did come to visit at his aunt's house, he spent all his time playing cards, paying no attention to Adam. The therapist suggested that showing his father the credit cards in the second dream might express a need to show his father that people did have faith in him, that he, Adam, deserved some credit. "Yes, and I still can't get it from my brother. I want to sever all those ties, to amputate them!" At the same time, he thought that his therapist's faith in him was different from anything he had ever known since his mother died, except for the year with his fifth-grade teacher.

Adam suddenly bought a small hotel in Las Vegas with two partners. With no existing written or verbal contract, he provided 75 percent of the financial investment while they contributed 25 percent in addition to their "expertise." He had never been to Las Vegas and had no knowledge of or experience in the hotel industry. Nevertheless, he saw himself as the chief executive officer who conducted the business from New York, while delegating to his partners the actual daily management of the hotel. When he soon realized that he was being swindled, he suddenly decided to move to Las Vegas, claiming that he was going to take charge of the hotel himself and run it properly. Once again, he protested that he had entered into the partnership deliberately to prove to himself that these partners, Moroccan Jews like his family, were not trustworthy. He said that he would have to stop treatment, to carry out his plan.

Once again, he experienced anything except wholehearted acceptance of his plan by his analyst as his father's, "Not you!" When she was able to restrain her powerful impulse to express concern and only spoke of his plan as a following of his own agenda, he was able to tell her that he was actually worried because he believed that he was going to hate the work he was about to undertake. He became very sad at the thought of leaving the analysis and associated his sadness with the original loss of his mother. Yet, he said, it was important for him to have his therapist's support for something he had to do.

Once he did leave, she continued to feel greatly concerned about him. She called him and left a message on his answering machine, restricting herself to asking whether they might schedule another session because she thought that there were some things that they still needed to say to each other. When he returned her call, he said, "This is the first time in my life that I have a net. You let me go, and you still care about me. You understood that I am in danger, and you came to help. No one has ever done this for me before." He said that he now realized that amputation serves a central function for him. "When I am in pain, I try to stop the bleeding by amputating the pain. I amputate people, money, anything. That's why I travel, thinking I can leave the pain behind. But always, when I come back, it is worse." The treatment now continued by telephone.

The Construction Site

The working through of the theme of amputation centered around the understanding that it was the only way he had of breaking free from the people in his family and of stopping otherwise overwhelming pain. It was in this context that Adam for the first time came to reflect about his actions and the meaning of his relationship to his analyst.

> I knew everything before I came here but I was dead. Sure! I understand why! I never trusted anyone. Even if I trust someone there are limits in my trust. But now I found someone I could trust enough to be myself. Trusting you, I have said things I have been saying only to myself. In saying them to you . . . I can go back on the road and see what happened when I took a wrong turn.

He was now able to tell about painful experiences in much greater detail and even began to refer to people in his life by name. This growing specificity, "making a short story long," emerged in the context of his therapist's unwavering focus on reflecting his sense of agency. The more he experienced her consistent devotion to finding the underlying constructive purpose in everything he said and did, the more he was able to let her into his inner world. As she was able to help him refind his fragile sense of initiative, he was able to trust her increasingly to sustain an emergent sense of himself that was still so fleeting and vulnerable to dissolution.

He now spoke of having made a terrible mistake in buying the hotel. He knew nothing about the business and felt that his partners were charlatans. He was ready to chuck his investment at any moment.

> Why did I choose uncharted territory . . . a new place to live . . . a business I've never had before . . . unfamiliar with the place . . . unfamiliar with the business?

Suddenly, Adam said amputation was over, and if his analyst kept talking about his father and the amputations, she was not listening to him. She thought, was he amputating amputation itself? After all, he had often told her that his past was behind him and no longer influenced him. She was at a loss as to what to make of what he was saying to her. She finally told him that she was obviously not hearing him. Feeling validated by these words, he replied that he liked fighting with her.

I can argue my point with you without disconnecting. . . . It is very important for me to argue for what I believe and not feel that my whole world will disappear. When you admit that you are wrong, when you admit that you were not hearing me, I feel that I have had an impact on you. It makes me feel strong.

But he was now at a difficult juncture. He felt reluctant to move forward. He said:

What I've been doing since I can remember is, instead of being, I have been seeming. To seem happy, to seem not to have any problems, not to be myself. If I go further, I will change drastically the rest of my life. And I will be stronger and feel better about myself. Maybe it's a way of not wanting to leave my childhood. Maybe I've been hoping that my father will come back, that my father will be a real father, that my brother will change. Maybe I'm waiting for something that will undo everything. Maybe I've been hoping for my mother to come back. I didn't give much importance to the life I had been living because I was always waiting for her and an ideal life.

In the next session he mentioned that he had another dream but said that he did not remember much of it and that he thought that it was of no importance:

You and I had a session on a lot, like a construction site. And the lot was surrounded by a wooden palisade. We were standing in the middle of the lot. There wasn't even a chair. We were talking just like that. There is a board that you remove to get in. But only you and I know how to get in. In this lot there is a helicopter. And you say to me, "Only you can fly this helicopter, you must fly this mission!"

She asked what kind of construction site this was. He replied that, as she asked the question, he remembered that in the dream it did not start out as a construction site, "It was a garbage dump that turned into a construction site as we were speaking." "And what was the palisade?" He continued:

You know, a palisade is a wooden structure that supports and protects so that nobody can get in and steal things . . . that board, actually, in the dream, I am the only one who knows how to get in. And you are the only one I ever let in. You know, this session is just like the dream. When I had the dream, I didn't think it meant anything. As we talk, I see that it is very important. Just like turning from a garbage dump into a construction site.

The very next day, Adam announced that he was leaving the country for a year. He had sold the hotel, without losing his investment, and now saw business opportunities overseas that he wanted to pursue.

It was very difficult and counterintuitive not to think that, having just taken the therapist into the innermost circle of his being, Adam was now fleeing the closeness he felt with her and that his planned trip was an expression of a renewal of the theme of amputation. However, the "constructive" imagery of Adam's dream was compelling and pointed to a meaning of the trip that was altogether different. In the dream, the therapist told him, "Only you can fly this helicopter! You must fly this mission!" He had used the concrete imagery of the dream to validate an elusive sense of agency sustained by her. His planned trip was an enactment, a metaphor concretizing that sense of agency in action rather than in a dream. In order to validate Adam's budding sense of himself as a center of initiative, she said, "Now that the garbage dump has turned into a construction site, you are launching yourself!" Adam then said that his plan was to travel to Italy, where his brother and his mother's surviving relatives had settled over the past 20 years. His therapist now felt convinced that, rather than a severing with the past, this journey represented a chance to find a link to his own origins.

In retrospect, it finally became clearer that each episode of international travel, every grand gesture, unwise and dangerous as it might have appeared or actually been, represented, for Adam, a desperate attempt at freeing himself from enslaving ties and reclaiming a sense of his own personal initiative.

Two weeks after the construction site dream and the interpretation of Adam's trip as a launching of himself, he described a transformation that was taking place in his experience of himself. One part of this inner change pertained to a new sense of agency and control over his life:

> I have made a deal with myself. I have greatly understood what happened in my life and I'm accepting the past. I am more sure of what I want for myself, trying to achieve it with some roadmap . . . and if I don't achieve it, I know the alternative [suicide], the choice is mine . . . the control is mine and I think that is what is making me feel so at peace with myself. Am I going to get there? I will definitely try and try hard! It's really my decision. And knowing that I have a big part of the control over it and the alternative is also under my control . . . it makes me feel serene.

A second aspect of Adam's transformation appeared in a deepening realization of how lost to himself he had been virtually all his life:

> My past was so blurry . . . I did not know who I was, and that's the difference now. When I lost my mother, I lost the sense of who I was. It

was like being stripped of my personality. When I went to live with my family, it was like being naked in front of everybody all of a sudden. That was the feeling I had when I came to Las Vegas. I lost my sense of self at that time and that is what I have found back recently . . . very recently. That is why I feel good now, even though I have no external reason.

The image of the construction site now became the central metaphor of the treatment, its organizing principle. Adam maintained contact with his therapist even while he was traveling. Whenever she did not hear from him for several weeks, knowing that he was still vulnerable to letting things of value slip away, she left a message for him saying that she had been thinking about the construction site and wanted to know all about it. Adam always called back eagerly. He could get reabsorbed in the "garbage dump" very easily, and the "construction site" would disappear regularly until the therapist reinstated it by her call and their resulting conversations. The consistent validation of his sense of purpose through the image of the construction site served as a foundation for a more enduring sense of himself, rooted in the past and in his relationship with his mother.

In Italy, Adam fell in love with a woman who loved him, and this time he married her. He could not believe that his new world was real. He was afraid that, at any moment, he might awake to find that it was only a dream. As the relationship with his wife continued to be loving and sustaining, he experienced a sense of continuity he believed he had not known since his mother died. He told his therapist:

I have unconditional love. I had it from my mother. I have had it from you. And now I have it from my wife.

Adam's developing sense of agency and continuity, replacing the theme of amputation, persisted as he repaired his relationships, first, with his brother and then with his son. He had not spoken to his brother since the death of their father, except through lawyers. Adam had filed a lawsuit (which he lost) against his brother, convinced that his brother had received an unfair portion of the inheritance from their father. In the context of the construction site, feeling loved for himself and sustained by his analyst and then by his wife, Adam realized that, in fact, he and his brother shared their fiscal, as well as their emotional, legacy from their father quite equally. He understood that they were both abandoned and invalidated by their father. If the course of his brother's life seemed to run more smoothly than his own, it was only because his brother was eight years older. Adam realized that, because his brother was 11 when their mother died, he had spent more time with her when he could experience her love and care. In addition, Adam could now see that it was because of his age that his brother was sent to boarding school and was therefore spared the unrelenting intrusions and persistent usurpation inherent in life within the "tribe." Adam was now able to develop a loving relationship with his brother, one based on mutual understanding, support, and respect.

The theme of a developing sense of self-continuity remained in evidence as Adam repaired his relationship with his son. He had always seen his own childhood self in Philip. Consequently, he repeatedly experienced Philip's attachment to his mother (Adam's ex-wife), his attempts at self-differentiation, and strivings for autonomy as a traumatic abandonment and betrayal. The depth of Adam's pain was profound, for in losing control over his son, he felt that he lost control over the totality of his own life. For years he had felt extremely precarious, poised on the threshold of a final severing of his relationship with his son.

But as the theme of the construction site unfolded in the analysis, Adam began to accept and even to enjoy his son's independence. At first, there were moments and then longer periods when he did not experience the reversals Philip suffered as his own failures. The theme of amputation continued to recede, and Adam began to understand his son's need for self-differentiation as an effort at his own construction site. Adam was thus becoming able to affirm and support his son's sense of initiative. Philip, in his turn, felt freed to express his love and appreciation of his father.

Just as Adam began to savor the new self-confidence he felt in the context of sustaining relationships, he became preoccupied with the fear that he and all those important to him would inevitably die. Never before had he been afraid of death. On the contrary, when he was recuperating from the heart attack in the aftermath of the loss of his father, he thought of dying as a welcome comfort. But now his dread of death was acute. He said:

> I never cared about living. If I were to die, it was fine with me. But now I wake up in the middle of the night terrified that something will happen to my wife, to my son, my brother. I keep running to doctors afraid that I might have a heart attack. Afraid that I might get cancer. Now that I have so much, why this?

His therapist suggested that it was precisely because he had so much; it was because he now had himself that he was afraid of dying, for he, at last, had something to lose. "Yes! Yes! Yes!" Adam replied, "I have so much, and so much to lose."

Before this time, Adam's life had not really belonged to him. It had been usurped and appropriated to serve the agendas of members of his family. Since his life had not been his own anyway, it had mattered very little to him whether he lived or died. Subsequently, the sole purpose in his every thought and deed, including that of killing himself, had been to actualize a surviving remnant of the sense of agency. Once he could begin to construct a life truly his own, the consequences of his actions became vitally important to him. The appearance of death anxiety in this context was thus a developmental achievement of the analysis (Stolorow, 1973).

SUMMARY AND CONCLUSION

In this chapter we have described a therapeutic process focusing on the specific mirroring of the sense of personal agency, something that proved to be essential to this patient for the articulation, sustaining, and consolidation of the sense of self as an independent center of initiative. The sense of agency is disturbed when the child's actions are redirected and redefined in development to accommodate the agendas of caregivers. The more sweeping the requirement to surrender a sense of personal initiative in order to maintain vitally needed ties, the more profound is the resulting disturbance in the sense of agency. We have shown that a wide array of seemingly pathological symptoms, ranging from the prolonged inability to work to manic pursuit of fame and fortune, encapsulated the patient's effort to recapture a surviving remnant of the sense of agency.

It is our experience that, when such symptoms are discussed in terms of their potential destructiveness or when they are interpreted as being a sign of defensive activity of any kind, the patient feels attacked for the only independent act left. Faced with the danger of the extinction of all volition, the patient resorts to more elaborate, more extreme, and often more dangerous enactments, designed to achieve a definitive liberation from all forms of oppression and enslavement.

In the same way one generally refrains from confronting the objective falsity in a delusion in order to understand and respond to the core of subjective truth contained within it, Adam's analyst found it necessary to avoid a focus on what appeared to be potentially or actually destructive in his various enactments in order to validate the remnant of personal agency lying at their heart. Only in the context of a therapeutic dialogue did the patient begin to reclaim a sense of his life as a construction site from the devastation that had wasted his spirit. In this validating context, his attempts to break free of enslaving ties gradually became transformed into a more enduring sense of being the author of his actions and of being in possession of a life that was truly his own. The engagement of self-reflection in the making of connections to his history, ordinarily central in the psychoanalytic dialogue, did not in this case appear as a part of this therapeutic process but, rather, came gradually into being as its outcome.

REFERENCES

Aron, L. (1996), *A Meeting of Minds*. Hillsdale, NJ: The Analytic Press.

Atwood, G. & Stolorow, R. (1984), *Structures of Subjectivity: Explorations in Psychoanalytic Phenomenology*. Hillsdale, NJ: The Analytic Press.

——— & ———(1993), *Faces in a Cloud: Intersubjectivity in Personality Theory*. 2nd ed. Northvale, NJ: Aronson.

Bacal, H. A. & Newman, K. M., ed. (1990), *Theories of Object Relations: Bridges to Self Psychology*. New York: Columbia University Press.

Brandchaft, B. (1993), To free the spirit from its cell. In: *The Widening Scope of Self Psychology: Progress in Self Psychology, Vol. 9*, ed. A. Goldberg. Hillsdale, NJ: The Analytic Press, pp. 209–230.

——— & Stolorow, R. (1990), Varieties of therapeutic alliance. *The Annual of Psychoanalysis*, 18:99–114. Hillsdale, NJ: The Analytic Press.

Gedo, J. (1991), *The Biology of Clinical Encounters*. Hillsdale, NJ: The Analytic Press.

Gehrie, M. (1993), Psychoanalytic technique and the development of the capacity to reflect. *J. Amer. Psychoanal. Assn.*, 41:1083–1111.

——— (1996), Empathy in broader perspective: A technical approach to the consequences of the negative selfobject in early character formation. In: *Basic Ideas Reconsidered: Progress in Self Psychology, Vol. 12*, ed. A. Goldberg. Hillsdale, NJ: The Analytic Press, pp. 159–179.

Kohut, H. (1959), Introspection, empathy, and psychoanalysis: An examination of the relationship between mode of observation and theory. In: *The Search for the Self, Vol. 1*, ed. P. Ornstein. Madison, CT: International Universities Press, pp. 205–232.

——— (1971), *The Analysis of the Self*. Madison, CT: International Universities Press.

——— (1977), *The Restoration of the Self*. Madison, CT: International Universities Press.

Mitchell, S. (1988), *Relational Concepts in Psychoanalysis*. Cambridge, MA: Harvard University Press.

——— (1993), *Hope and Dread in Psychoanalysis*. New York: Basic Books.

Orange, D., Atwood, G. & Stolorow, R. (1997), *Working Intersubjectively: Contextualism in Psychoanalytic Practice*. Hillsdale, NJ: The Analytic Press.

Stern, D. (1985), *The Interpersonal World of the Infant*. New York: Basic Books.

Stolorow, R. (1973), Perspectives on death anxiety: A review. *Psychoanal. Quart.*, 47:473–486.

——— & Atwood, G. (1992), *Contexts of Being: The Intersubjective Foundations of Psychological Life*. Hillsdale, NJ: The Analytic Press.

————— Brandchaft, B. & Atwood, G. (1987), *Psychoanalytic Treatment: An Intersubjective Approach.* Hillsdale, NJ: The Analytic Press.

Valenstein, A. (1973), On attachment to painful feelings and the negative therapeutic reaction. *The Psychoanalytic Study of the Child,* 28:365–394. New Haven, CT: Yale University Press.

Winnicott, D. W. (1972), Fragments of an analysis. In: *Tactics and Techniques in Psychoanalytic Therapy,* ed. P. Giovacchini. New York: Science House, pp. 455–693.

Chapter 11

An Instrument of Possibilities: A Discussion of Dorothy M. Levinson and George E. Atwood's "A Life of One's Own"

William J. Coburn

We only become what we are by the radical and deep-seated refusal of that which others have made of us.

—Jean-Paul Sartre

Kohut's revolutionary visions of the selfobject concept and the subjective experience of the self, as Levinson and Atwood remind us, set the analytic stage for intersubjectivity theory's emphasis of the way in which human relatedness to the vitally needed other is central to the consolidation of authentic self-experience. They delineate and highlight those variations in the sense of self that are organized and regulated from within a system of mutual and reciprocal, though asymmetrical, influence. These include the sense of self-cohesion, self-continuity, self-esteem, and finally, self-agency.

Levinson and Atwood conceptually reposition the notion of the individual's sense of agency into a more essential, foreground position in the organization of the individual's self-experience. Without it, they state, "only a false or 'borrowed' sense of self-cohesion" will obtain.

I wish to thank Jackie L. Legg for her critique and editorial assistance in the preparation of this chapter.

This is akin to Brandchaft's notion of structures of pathological accommodation (1994). They underscore, in other words, the importance of being able to feel that one's personal experience of cohesion across time and of self-esteem "belongs" to oneself, that one is author and owner of one's sense of esteem, efficacy, volition, and direction. Without this sense of personal agency, one's true sense of aliveness in and ownership of one's own life can often only be experienced through precariously maintained, isolated sectors of living. These sectors often are found in the realm of discrete behavioral events, sometimes of a self-destructive nature, or in overt somatization experiences and usually are tenaciously guarded.

Levinson and Atwood (this volume) cite three special difficulties for the psychoanalytic therapist posed by those patients whose sense of agency is particularly compromised. These include (a) an inability to sustain a self-reflective process, often considered a vital component of an analytic experience; (b) a propensity toward extreme enactments often with destructive consequences; and (c) a tendency to cut oneself off from all personal history, declaring a radical independence from any historical influences.

They rightly point out that the experience of agency has received less discussion than other self-enhancing experiences and selfobject functions. Indeed, few authors (e.g., Von Broembsen, 1989 and Rustin, 1997) have delved deeply into the ramifications of the sense or experience of agency. Stern (1985), though, along with the present authors, is a notable exception. He posits that a sense of agency, along with affectivity and continuity in time, is a vital component to the infant's consolidating core sense of self as a "separate, cohesive, bounded, physical unit" (p. 10). Using different languages and perhaps speaking on different levels of abstraction, authors such as Winnicott and Balint also address the notion of self-agency through the concepts of the "true self" and the "area of creation," respectively.

As with many terms in psychoanalytic history, the word *agency* conjures a variety of connotations, depending on one's background and orientation. Webster defines it as "active force; action; power; that by which something is done; instrumentality." It is useful to delineate some of the term's more specialized meanings and to clarify on which level of psychoanalytic discourse we choose to utilize it. One level, clearly in contrast to Levinson and Atwood's usage, I refer to as *agency as state*—or *agency as trait,* if considered a more ongoing, enduring pattern—and describes a *condition* of the individual characterized by apparent independence, autonomy, and authorship and ownership of one's actions. A *state* of agency might be thought of as endogenously determined but, doubtless, is largely organized around the mutual and reciprocal affective influences and interplay of the dyad.

This assumption rests upon compelling data derived from infant research (Trevarthen, 1979; Sander, 1985; Stern, 1985; Beebe and Lachmann, 1994; Lachmann and Beebe, 1996). Rustin (1997) recently commented: "The sense of agency derives from repeated experiences of having one's agency acknowledged, along with repeated experiences of efficacy so that in infancy, childhood, and adulthood one experiences oneself as a constitutive subject in the world" (p. 47).

The *agency as state* designation primarily concerns ontology and appearance. This connotation of agency rests heavily upon subjectively derived, value-laden presumptions about what constitutes agential being and action. It is necessarily reflective of the observer's personal subjectivity, however "scientifically" derived and organized, and not necessarily consistent at all with the observed individual's *experience*. This brings us to the other level of delineation, that is, *agency as experience*.

Agency as experience—the agency specifically referenced I believe by Levinson and Atwood—is more consistent with a theory and technique that highlight the notions of selfobject function and the subjective experience of the individual. This level of discourse pertains to how we *experience* ourselves, not necessarily how we *appear* to ourselves or to others. Levinson and Atwood state: "Only seeming, rather than being, is possible when we do not experience ourselves as authors of our actions and as authentic centers of initiative." This perspective is more useful clinically, as they demonstrate in their case material.

With this second perspective in mind, I wish to underscore the need to differentiate, in any psychoanalytic discourse about agency, one's subjective extrapolations about an individual's "agential behavior" from the results of a sustained assessment of an individual's unfolding experience as understood in the context of an analytic dyad. The same can be said, and has been said, about the notion of self-cohesion; that is, what appears to be a *state* of self-cohesion at a specific moment may have little bearing on that individual's *experience* of his or her self at that moment and vice versa. As always, we need to caution ourselves about confusing inferences drawn from an individual's appearance with a collaborative articulation of affective experience.

Daniel Stern (1985), from a perspective that places the sense of self at the center of scientific inquiry, speaks of *self-agency* as the sense of "authorship of one's own actions and nonauthorship of the actions of others: having volition, having control over self-generated action" (p. 71). One's nascent sense of agency at this point in development (around two to six months) is necessarily rudimentary (e.g., my arm moves when I want it to and it moves because I am willing it to do so) and provides the building materials for the more variegated, elaborate, and sophisticated sense of self-agency with which Levinson and Atwood's patient has struggled. Unlike the painful and, at times, desperate experiences of their patient, Adam, the outcome of a derailment and deficit in the more rudimentary form of self-agency, described by Stern, is characterized as a major psychosis in which the absence of agency might "manifest in catatonia, hysterical paralysis, derealization, and some paranoid states in which authorship of action is taken over" (p. 71).

The sense of agency addressed by Levinson and Atwood does not solely reside in the sensorimotor domain (e.g., I am the one who is moving my arm). It resides also in the domain of more complex, elaborate, and relationally derived affective experience (e.g., I feel I am author and owner of the way I experience and direct my cognitive/affective life and the relationally based behaviors that issue therefrom). Instead of directly correlating a severely compromised sense of agency to developmental derailments in the first few months of life, Levinson and Atwood link this problem to Brandchaft's (1994) notion of pathological accommodation, which is not necessarily bound to a specific developmental timeframe. In line with Brandchaft's perspective, they highlight that an individual's surrender of self-agency often represents an attempt at sustaining archaic ties with primary caregivers.

Levinson and Atwood (1997) present Adam, 38 years old at the outset of treatment, as a cogent and revealing illustration of the salience of an individual's sense of agency and of the ramifications and struggles inherent in that sense when it has become severely compromised. Having suffered multiple traumas and losses, "having lost all those for whom he might have existed in his own right, he lost himself." Historically, the conscious unfolding and articulation of his affective experiences in his familial context were effectively nonexistent. Adam consequently was the recipient of *two* sets of traumas: the first being the initial tragic loss of his mother and the second, perhaps more disabling, being the absence of an empathically responsive selfobject milieu, in the wake of the external losses, that might at least have inculcated some degree of affect differentiation and integration and some amount of self-cohesion and sense of agency. Stated alternatively, his experience of tragic loss, from his perspective, did not seem to exist for anyone else and, therefore, ultimately could not exist for him in any cognitively and affectively useable form. Even as an adult, he continued to experience his father as incapable of providing even a morsel of mirroring, of empathically resonating with him, or of otherwise contributing to his self-esteem in any way. This was concretized and emphasized in his father's emphatic, gestural "Not you!" in reply to his son's offer of help just before his death. This leaves us pondering the etiology of Adam's heart attack of a few months later.

We note in the beginning of treatment the therapist's attempt to articulate an interest in the patient's subjective world, especially in linking the present with the past, and to symbolize with the patient what was affectively painful and difficult for him. This was organized and experienced by the patient as a repetition of the gross empathic failures he had endured as a child. It was only when Adam's therapist demonstrated an acceptance of his own view regarding how he had felt perpetually invalidated in his relationships that he began to feel calmed and soothed. In the interest of mixing paradigms, this melioration can be conceptualized as reversing what Balint (1968) referred to as "attention-seeking interpretations" that often foreclose for the patient "the possibility of creating something out of himself" (p. 176).

We detect a second, more pronounced positive affective shift in the patient, and perhaps in the therapist as well, when the therapist comments about one of the meanings of the past 10 years, that is, that the patient's paralysis might be seen as "his declaration of independence." This helped develop a sense of hope in the patient, as it began to address his desperate need for a responsive environment and for the actualization of his sense of agency.

This segment of the analysis demonstrates well our propensities as therapists to assume, and sometimes to require, the presence of certain capacities in the patient (e.g., the reflective capacity) and to assume that the exercise of certain capacities resides in a value-free, meaning-free dimension. Often we do find, however, that the simple (if it can be called that) act of reflection carries with it profound transference meanings for the patient and for ourselves. And further, when we find, as the therapist found, our attempt to engage in a reflective process with the patient (e.g., a simple, what might this mean?) exacerbates a repetitive and fragmenting experience, we quickly locate ourselves in a steep downward spiral with the patient in which the usual and familiar means of countertransference illumination and perhaps extrication (e.g., the reflection process) are rendered useless. This case illustrates well just such a scenario and the therapist's insightful and creative means of self-righting in the service of the dyad. This theme is continually evident throughout the evolution of this case.

Later in the treatment, we are once again reminded of one of the essentials of analytic work, that is, our ongoing attempt at tracking and illuminating the patient's, and necessarily our own, subjective experience. Here the patient experienced the analyst's interpretation of his business plans (e.g., as defensively "amputating" his feelings and the relational contexts in which they occur) not just as a misunderstanding, but predominantly as a painful, repetitive enactment. As the therapist refocused on the patient's experience of his own agential behavior, conceptualized "*solely* as an effort to take charge of his life," we witness the reconsolidation of Adam's sense of self. This is a dramatic illustration of what many of us have experienced in our patients, and in ourselves as well, as the rapidly shifting, context-dependent variability of self states. We are familiar with how, for example, what we record as experientially familiar, real, and true about ourselves in one setting can transform into something novel, surrealistic, uncertain, and perplexing in another.

I wish to posit here a few important questions: Was it precisely Adam's sense of agency that was being thwarted, in repetitive fashion, by the disjunction in perspectives and the suggestion of defense, or was it some other dimension of his self-experience that was disrupted in a context of an issue that *pertained to* agential, autonomous behavior? Was it the patient's experiential sense of self-agency that was repaired as a result of reestablishing an empathic link because the derailment *pertained to* apparently agential behavior, or was Adam's sense of self-agency repaired and bolstered simply because of reestablishing an empathic resonance aside from considerations of context? In other words, does the therapist need to resonate empathically with and support the patient's experience of self-agency specifically in order to foster its development and elaboration, or is self-agency an aspect of self-experience that can reasonably be expected to emerge in the unfolding and consolidation of the self in general? Does supporting *the patient* increase his sense of self-agency, or does supporting his sense of self-agency increase his sense of cohesion and esteem? Or could it be all of the above, depending on the context of the moment? Answers to these questions will point more precisely to the peculiarities of the development of the vital sense of self around which much of our analytic attention revolves.

I would like to suggest also that it may not have been solely Adam's sense of self-agency that was felt to be derailed and at stake here, but perhaps specifically his sense of self-efficacy as well, to draw from Stern (1985). The sense of self-efficacy, perhaps a subcategory of self-agency or perhaps another aspect of one's general sense of self in its own right, was, I believe, resting in the balance here for Adam as well. What may have been constitutive and mutative for Adam was not solely his therapist's capacity and willingness to acknowledge his efforts at experientially staking out a life of his own, but also to acknowledge his need to feel efficacious, his need to approach his expansiveness with a sense of self-worth and competence, and his need to sense in his therapist some degree of conviction that he can impact his interpersonal surround in a fulfilling and constructive manner. Recall Adam's passionate observations regarding his experience of efficacy with his therapist: "I can argue my point with you without disconnecting. . . .

It is very important for me to argue for what I believe and not feel that my whole world will disappear. . . , I feel that I have had an impact on you. It makes me feel strong." This was another key component that contributed to the patient's positive developmental trajectory in the context of his analytic therapy.

Finally, I wish to underscore a crucial observation made by Levinson and Atwood toward the end of their presentation: Often it is the very capacities that we stubbornly require of our patients in the interest of conducting "true analytic work" that are not immediately or for awhile available (e.g., capacity for self-reflection, capacity for verbal articulation of affect states), but that emerge and unfold as a *result* of developmental progress in the context of treatment. Gehrie (1993) addresses this issue as well, albeit from a more objectivist, one-person model perspective, when he states that "it may be that an otherwise intractable case, approached at the outset with greater activity and flexibility of intervention, may develop so that analytic goals [i.e., the capacity for self-reflection] *become* feasible" (pp. 1092–1093). For Gehrie, however, the patient arrives at the capacity for self-reflection in a manner (via the patient's eventual acquiescence to and identification with the "analyst's empathic insistence on a reflective presence" [p. 1107]) quite different from that of Levinson and Atwood (via an empathic allowance of the patient's rudimentary attempts at self-agency experiences without necessarily the analyst's insistence on reflection).

Our proclivity for requiring self-reflective capacities in our patients during the early or middle phases of analysis parallels the notion that verbal articulation is the preferred and healthier mode of communication between analyst and analysand. This is reminiscent of Kohut's admonitions about guarding against the "health and maturity morality" common in traditional psychoanalysis. Infant research clearly demonstrates that unconscious nonverbal communication may not only represent a richer, more elaborate form of communication, but often is the only mode that is available to the analytic dyad (Knoblauch, 1997). These subjective perspectives and phenomena invite an elaborate array of countertransference conundrums and challenges for the clinician and encourage us to reorganize the more traditional notions of the psychoanalytic process and relationship. This reorganization suggests a perspective of openness to what is experientially felt by the patient as an unfolding agency and efficacy—or the patient's attempts at it—and to what *we* may envision as a defensive, self-destructive flight from analytic work. It is also helpful to remind ourselves that what may be defensive, or felt to be defensive, need not be construed as inauthentic, nonagential experience and behavior.

Sartre once commented:

I am a slave [to the Other] to the degree that my being is dependent at the center on a freedom which is not mine . . . insofar as I am the instrument of possibilities which are not my possibilities, . . . *I am in danger.* This danger is not an accident but the permanent structure of my being-for-others [Sartre, 1943, quoted in Atwood and Stolorow, 1984, p. 28].

Levinson and Atwood have provided us with a poignant clinical example of helping transform what would have been an individual's "permanent structure" of "being-for-others" into an experience of freedom, authenticity, and self-agency.

REFERENCES

Atwood, G. & Stolorow, R. (1984), *Structures of Subjectivity: Explorations in Psychoanalytic Phenomenology.* Hillsdale, NJ: Lawrence Erlbaum Associates, Inc.

Balint, M. (1968), *The Basic Fault.* Evanston, IL: Northwestern University Press.

Beebe, B. & Lachmann, F. M. (1994), Representation and internalization in infancy: Three principles of salience. *Psychoanal. Psychol.,* 11:127–165.

Brandchaft, B. (1994), Structures of pathological accommodation and change in analysis. Paper presented at the Association for Psychoanalytic Self Psychology, New York City.

Gehrie, M. J. (1993), Psychoanalytic technique and the development of the capacity to reflect. *J. Amer. Psychoanal. Assn.,* 41:1083–1111.

Knoblauch, S. H. (1997), Beyond the word in psychoanalysis: The unspoken dialogue. *Psychoanal. Dial.,* 7:491–576.

Lachmann, F. M. & Beebe, B. (1996), Three principles of salience in the organization of the patient–analyst interaction. *Psychoanal. Psychol.,* 13:1–22.

Levinson, D. & Atwood, G. (1997), A life of one's own: A case study of the loss and restoration of the sense of personal agency. Paper presented at the 20th Annual Conference on The Psychology of the Self, Chicago.

Rustin, J. (1997), Infancy, agency, and intersubjectivity: A view of therapeutic action. *Psychoanal. Dial.,* 7:43–62.

Sander, L. (1985), Toward a logic of organization in psychobiological development. In: *Biologic Response Styles: Clinical Implications,* ed. K. Klar & L. Siever. Washington, D.C.: American Psychiatric Press, pp. 20–36.

Stern, D. (1985), *The Interpersonal World of the Infant.* New York: Basic Books.

Trevarthen, C. (1979), Communication and cooperation in early infancy: A description of primary intersubjectivity. In: *Before Speech: The Beginning of Interpersonal Communication,* ed. M. Bullowa. New York: Cambridge University Press, pp. 321–347.

Von Broembsen, F. (1989), Transformations of identity: Referent location, agency, and levels of integration in the progress from potential self to existential identity. *Amer. J. Psychoanal.,* 49:329–338.

Chapter 12

Response to Coburn

Dorthy M. Levinson
George E. Atwood

We want to thank Bill Coburn for his careful and sympathetic reading of our study and for his clarifying summary of its essential points. He raises one specific question about whether our singleminded focus on the patient's sense of agency might have led us to deemphasize other important aspects of the patient's self experience, including especially self-cohesion, self-efficacy, and self-esteem. With regard to the question of self-efficacy, and self-esteem, we think of these aspects of self experience as presupposing a sense of agency, which is irreducibly a part of the very existence of the self. The loss of the sense of agency is essentially an annihilation state, and this is the danger that we came to understand as the central one in Adam's subjective world. Efficacy has to do with effectiveness, with having an impact on one's surroundings. Agency, on the other hand, pertains to the existence of will, to the experience of oneself as an abiding center of initiative. Self-esteem, similarly, presupposes the presence of a consolidated sense of self, which is then positively or negatively valued. Self-cohesion was not an issue in this patient's experience in that he did not report feelings in which fragmentation or cohesion were salient. Our specific focus on agency arose from the clinical process, because it was only when the therapist spoke of this theme that any constructive effect on Adam could be seen.

Questions and Responses Regarding Levinson and Atwood's Chapter

M. Sucharov: I want to ask a question concerning the relational and therefore the ambiguous nature of meaning. Now, Bill mentioned two levels of agency, the external observer one and a more phenomenological one, the experience of the patient. We don't always know what the experience of the patient is. Hearing this case, presented in retrospect, one might go away with the misguided assumption that it was all so clear, that it is obvious that the manic actions of the patient are his attempts to express his own self and so forth, and that it would be a disaster to address the destructive aspect. Since, in a relational field, meaning is embedded in the field, it is not clear whose experience this is. I think that one thing that was left out is the subjectivity of the therapist and how she knew what was going on. What about the resonances in her own sense of agency? So could you just make some comments on how you sort out what is going on in the middle of the session when we're not presenting it in retrospect?

D. Levinson: It certainly was not clear to me for a very long time that Adam's enactments represented the surviving remnant of his sense of agency. I had been trying to understand him in the ways that I knew and thought that I was observing ruptures in an idealizing/mirror selfobject transference that I kept attempting to repair. When Adam continually rejected such interpretations and clearly felt profoundly injured by them, I tried to find other ways of understanding him. Even the interpretation of Adam's spending his inheritance as a giant "NO" to a life of compliance, which helped him so much and which I had offered out of desperation at the time, was not based on any real understanding of his motivation, for negation and opposition never appeared as salient themes in Adam's conversation. In fact, the interpretation bore a close resemblance to his protestations of deliberate intentionality when faced with the disastrous consequences of his enactments. It was only years later, in preparing to write this chapter, that George and I understood that what Adam found so helpful in that interpretation was its implication of a constructive meaning and purpose to his acts. However, in the midst of the therapeutic sessions I paid very close attention to Adam's reactions to the interpretations I offered and made adjustments accordingly. Through this very slow process, I gradually learned that the only understanding of Adam's manic acts that seemed to help him was one that focused on agency and that he experienced any other interpretation as an annihilating usurpation. It was not until the "construction site" dream, which he reported well into the third year of therapy, that I became convinced that his enactments represented the surviving remnant of his sense of agency.

In terms of my subjectivity, my sense of it is that, rather than experiencing him as usurping my sense of agency, I was going through a parallel process with Adam. For just as he needed to free himself from the "tribe" to establish a life of his own, I was steeped in conventional psychoanalytic theory, including even self psychology theory, in which the notion of rupture and repair and the expectation that the patient will make connections from the present to the past is central, and so I had my own "tribe" from which I needed to free myself. I think that my work with Adam helped me do that, and as I freed myself from my own tribe, I was able to help him free himself from his.

J. Trop: This was an elegant presentation. My question to you concerns the fact that the moment that he left, you called him back and said that there was something that was not dealt with. Coming back to your language, he left and you made a phone call saying something was still in process. How did you know, instinctively, to call him back? He was saying, in fact, that he needed you to sustain confidence in his decision making, and your phone call seemed to be counterintuitive to that. What went on in your mind to help you see the phone call not as an intrusion that would be assimilated as a lack of support, but rather as something he could experience potentially as a reaching out? What went on in your mind? Were you just operating on instinct? It seemed to me contradictory to what you were saying earlier and yet obviously was experienced as a reaching out.

D. Levinson: I did not know that calling him was the right thing to do. I was tormented by this situation, knowing that he was in danger of letting everything that was valuable to him slip away and that, if he did that, he might very well kill himself. At the same time I knew that to call him and express any concern whatsoever would have been assimilated by him as a vote of no confidence with no possibility of reflecting on or discussing the devastating injury that would then result. My decision to make the call was not based on intuition but, rather, on the fact that I had no other choice. In fact, I agonized for quite some time over what I would say to him and finally decided on an extremely casual tone, one that conveyed the idea that he and I were two colleagues who might have a little chat because there were still some things we had to say to each other.

S. Perlman: As I listened to this wonderful presentation, I thought about what I would feel in reaction to how the patient kept leaving. I might have wondered about what I had done wrong, how bad I was, and how I had messed up the therapy yet again. It is so important that both of you are presenting because the dyad created between you must have been central throughout the treatment. A therapist working alone with the problems you have described would, I think, have enormous difficulty preventing him- or herself from imploding. Could you speak about the dynamics that developed between you, especially in containing and handling the experience of constantly being left?

G. Atwood: Dorthy and I were never completely sure of what was happening in this case, until many years had passed. What often occurred was that I would receive an emergency call from her, telling of the patient's latest planned or actual departure for distant places, usually as part of a glorious business scheme in which he seemed certain to lose all he had. She and I would review, in great detail, the circumstances and events surrounding the patient's leaving, especially in terms of what had been transpiring in the therapeutic sessions. These conversations involved sharing misery and uncertainty—she shared her misery with me and it became my misery, for neither of us felt sure he was not about to destroy himself financially and then physically.

Regarding the question of telephoning him after his leaving, we struggled over whether and when to call and also what to say once we had contacted him. Not to reach out at all seemed to involve the danger that he would still again allow something of great value to him to slip away. To pursue him with an urgent message of something being amiss, on the other hand, posed the danger of triggering his sense of being viewed as having something fatally wrong with him and therefore of being doomed. We would say to ourselves, "To call today or tomorrow would be too soon, suggesting too strongly that he needs help or otherwise has been too hasty or unwise in his decisions. To call next month would be too late, allowing him to forget the therapeutic work as he has always forgotten everything that has been important to him." So we would cut right down the middle and say: "Two weeks would be our best bet, neither too long nor too short!" Then Dorthy was able to formulate her very fine message to Adam about there still being some things they had to say to each other, a message that helped him to feel there was a safety net in his life for the very first time.

Perhaps the concept of the holding environment applies to the relationship between Dorthy and myself in the conduct of this treatment. Our frequent consultations helped us to bear together his many departures, our prolonged uncertainty regarding what was even happening, and our sense of the ever-present danger of the patient's self-destruction. As Dorthy's work with Adam and our dialogues continued, we began to see signs—faintly at first but then later more clearly, and finally unequivocally—that in focusing on agency we were on the right track.

Chapter 13

The Case of
Joanna Churchill

Alan Kindler

The treatment of Joanna Churchill was completed around 1992. During the course of her analysis, I participated in a peer consultation group to which members often presented clinical material in a raw form for discussion. To emphasize our attempt to avoid "dressing up" our clinical material as one is inclined to do in front of one's peers, we referred to our meetings as the "warts and all" seminar. The following clinical material, precirculated to the plenary session panel, was taken from notes prepared for this consultation group about one year after I had started to treat Joanna, and several months after we had begun to meet three times weekly. I took verbatim notes during the sessions reported and altered them only for clarity of verbal presentation and for brevity (I was restricted to 20 minutes, a limit rigorously and appropriately enforced by the panel chairman over the protests of my grandiose self). This required the summarizing of several sections of process and one complete session, in order to present the sequence of four sessions as they unfolded.

THE CASE

I will describe some sessions from the second year of the psychoanalysis of Joanna Churchill, a treatment completed some six years ago. She was a twice divorced woman who lived alone and worked as an account executive with a large financial institution. When we first met, I found her to be a tall, slender, attractive woman appearing much younger than her 37 years. She dressed formally and well yet at times conducted herself like a coquette. As she searched for words, she would grimace intensely, transforming her lovely face into a distorted mask of agitation. She walked stiffly, slightly bent over, as if physically disabled or crouching to diminish her stature. It was as if a vibrant beauty and a tortured soul were struggling for supremacy in the same person. Despite her obvious discomfort and her appearance of disorganization, she was able to be very specific about her experiences and to correct me precisely and assertively when I had misunderstood her in the slightest way.

I will give only a brief outline of her history.

Joanna moved to Toronto from another Canadian city about three years prior to starting treatment with me. Her move followed the termination of a 10-year relationship with her therapist, Dr. X. She ended the treatment when charges of sexual misconduct with another female patient had led to Dr. X's loss of his professional license.

Joanna had been physically intimate with Dr. X almost from the beginning of their relationship, often having intercourse, but at other times spending the session sitting on his knee, silently staring into his face. At times, Joanna described her attachment to her former therapist in idyllic terms. She admired his robust vitality, the quality of his skin, and other details of his physical being. She longed for his attention and physical presence. When she sat on his knee, she felt like a baby on her mother's lap looking into her mother's eyes. She felt and continues to believe that she made him very happy. At other times, and more so as time passed in her treatment, she resented his self-serving exploitation of her and other women.

Dr. X was angry with her for deciding to terminate and pressured her to continue treatment with him. Following the termination, Joanna became incapacitated by illness and was unable to work. She felt flooded with anxiety, and at times, fears of death prevented her from falling asleep. Her numerous abdominal symptoms were diagnosed as an ulcer. The loss of her therapist left her feeling strange, as if she did not exist. She had to carefully monitor her diet because if she forgot to eat she would feel like a body walking around, but "I was not there." Her severe bodily tensions have been eased by regular massage from a relaxation clinic she has attended over the preceding two years.

Joanna is the middle of three siblings. She has a younger and an older brother, both of whom are very successful. Her father was a cruel dominating man who physically and sexually abused her. Her mother was distant, insecure, and unavailable to her.

Joanna's history of sexual involvement with her therapists (there was at least one before Dr. X and possibly one since), her assertive sexualization of her relationship with me, and her physical attractiveness made her a serious threat to me. She quite blatantly attempted to establish physical contact with me, and in the early weeks of treatment, I had to refuse her invitations to join her on the couch and insist that she refrain from touching me and that she back away to a comfortable distance. She insisted on using the couch, despite my suggestion that she sit in a chair facing me. She also asked me to sit in my usual chair behind the couch rather than one further away. She needed to feel some physical connection, and she experienced the couch as an extension of my body. Sitting on her legs in the middle of the couch, facing me, she would often move around in a sensual and physically exposing manner, occasionally lying down briefly. As we began to meet more regularly and I was able to see her more than once a week, she seemed to become less physically and sensually expressive and more focused on her subjective and interpersonal life.

Sessions from the Treatment of Ms. Joanna Churchill

These four sessions occur on Thursday, Monday, Tuesday, and Thursday.

Session 1: Thursday

Joanna is my first patient of the day. She enters as usual, briskly placing her handbag, umbrella, hat, and scarf on the chair, moving to the couch and taking up her position in the middle of the couch, her legs folded beneath her, facing me. As she settles on the couch, she begins:

Patient: Did you see me as you entered the elevator? I was coming in the door. I know this isn't rational but I felt you were reacting to my hat. I think I fear a negative reaction.

Therapist: (I had, in fact, not seen her, but wanted to stay with her experience so I said:) Were there any gestures or signs from me that suggested I was reacting negatively to you?

Patient: No. I was too far away. I just sensed you had recognized me and had a negative reaction.

Therapist: Perhaps there is something that makes you expect a negative reaction from me.

Patient: If it's slightly cold, I cover my head with a hat to protect my sinuses. I feel odd doing it. Others don't do it, even in winter. I feel cold at night now without the heat on. It feels peculiar. After all, it's warm. It's summer. (I wondered if her self-consciousness might have made her experience me as reacting negatively to her as she approached me in the lobby, but before I could say anything, she continued with mounting intensity.)

Patient:	I saw Donald Trump being interviewed on TV. He owns the Miss Universe and Miss Teenage Universe pageants. I *like* to watch a father and daughter so I had to watch it to the end, although I'd be tired in the morning. The winner was *not as attractive* as the first runner-up, but she expressed herself very well. They showed her parents in the audience. Her father seemed stable, well adjusted. I can see these things in people—she was extremely at ease. . . . I've lost track of my point.
Therapist:	(I try to assist her regaining her train of thought.) You were telling me about your experience of watching the daughter and father together after telling me how you felt a bit peculiar.
Patient:	(regaining her momentum) I am thinking of my cousin who was a little girl when I was a teenager. Her father did whatever she wanted him to do; he was always there for her. But he rejected his second daughter. He watched her from a distance. It was as if he disliked or maybe even feared her. When I saw them later, as preteens, the older one was extremely self-assured, emotionally centered, and controlled. I noticed how Donald Trump spoke about his daughter, who looks like him. I thought she was ugly, not nice at all, but so self-assured. She has his protection and influence behind her. She is so confident; she does better than others. If it were based on physical qualities, the runner-up would have won. But the winner was more confident, and you could see it in her father. I've been thinking about my father and how he crushed my self-confidence. That's how I feel about your reaction to *me* as I came in.
Therapist:	How different your own experience of your father has been to those daughters you witnessed on TV and to that of your younger cousin. The effect on your self-confidence may have left you vulnerable to your experience of me on the elevator this morning.
Patient:	My father is so angry and depressed. He picks out the weaknesses of women. He projects his own feelings a lot. For example, he comments on homosexuals a lot and how they treat women. They design dresses which reflect their dislike of women by making them look horrible. *I* think homosexual designers make more feminine fashions. I think it is my father's attitude towards women.
Therapist:	(trying to establish clearly her meaning in the use of projection) Do you mean that he saw his own contempt for women in homosexual designers?
Patient:	Yes. His own *incompetence* with women. What do you mean by "contempt"?
Therapist:	I mean that he looked down on women, as if they were inferior.

Patient:	I think he held me in contempt, to protect himself. His anger and contempt was to keep himself at a distance from me.
Therapist:	As *I* seemed to be doing in the elevator when you came in?
Patient:	*No! I* kept *my* distance. *I* avoided the elevator—to avoid your negative reaction. I was afraid you would not accept me. It was like that with my father when I think about him with me as a little girl. I could *never overcome* it. It's depressing. *Something* in him made it impossible for him to like me. He *never* would. He just *couldn't.*
Therapist:	So there was nothing you could do because it was not coming from you.
Patient:	Sometimes I'd think about it as within myself to regain some control. I'd *even* do bad things at times. As a child, I'd simply react. I'd try to accommodate and I'd get hurt.
Therapist:	So as a child you'd assume it was you and try to change yourself.
Patient:	My *mother* supported the idea that it *was* me. She was a typical woman of her times. She degraded herself and me as a woman.
Therapist:	Your mother would make it impossible to be clear about yourself in relationship to your father because of her own low self-esteem.

The session continued with the exploration of this theme of her attachment needs, including her awareness of her inclination to turn away from someone who admires her to protect herself from the inevitable loss of that admiration.

We ended characteristically with her ritualized question: "Are you angry at me?" followed by my attempt at reassurance that I was not.

Session 2: Monday

As she takes up her usual position on the couch facing me, her face is unsteady, twitching, grimacing, gazing at me, and then looking away in a jerky nervous manner.

Patient:	How are you?
Therapist:	I am well.
Patient:	You always say that you are feeling good when I ask you. Do you really feel good all the time? Or is that something you say automatically to keep me at a distance? (She then looks away at one of my plants and abruptly changes the subject.) Do you have new plants?
Therapist:	(Uncomfortable at this confrontation about my sincerity, I take advantage of her shift of focus to my struggling plant.)

No, it is the same plant, but I have trimmed off some of the brown leaves since you were last here.

Patient: Are you angry?

Therapist: No I'm not. (said in a reassuring tone, based on the familiarity of this opening ritual.)

Patient: Are you upset with me?

Therapist: No. (Joanna's face is twitching intensely. She is grimacing grotesquely and at times smiling. Then abruptly she lies down on her back in silence for a few moments before starting up thoughtfully.)

Patient: Maybe I'm angry at you.

Therapist: Uh huh. But it *sounds* as if you're not *sure* about that.

Patient: No, I'm not sure. (She sits up abruptly. Then says defensively) I said "possibly." (Then after a pause) Is it all right for a child to be angry at aging parents? Is it all right if that child does things which actually hurt the parents, even though they are aging and helpless?

Therapist: (I was silently thinking about the question. Should I engage at the level of content, should I wait and hope for clarification, or should I ask for clarification?)

Patient: While you're thinking, I'll tell you about two brothers. One brother says to the other more successful and wealthy brother, "You're more successful than me so you should help me out financially." The more successful brother counters with, "You only think that because you need something from me." My mother and Dr. X *used and manipulated me*. (She continues angrily.) They simply thought about themselves. They rape the world, do anything they want, there's no empathy or sense of fair play, like it is with a baby. Dr. X was not *completely* like that; part of his personality was well developed and balanced and he had *some* concern about fair play. But *not my mother*; her personality was not developed at all. (Her face continues to twitch and grimace vigorously. Then with annoyance she focuses on me.) *You* are *controlling* me. As *I* become more fluid, *you* pull back and that makes me feel *I* should be more *controlled*.

Therapist: (I am silent and trying to make sense of her comment. I am aware that it probably has to do with my lack of response to her question about a child being angry at its parents. These moments of discomfort are amplified by my awareness of my intention to present some of this material to colleagues in a clinical seminar. After a pause, Joanna continues.)

Patient:	I needed to speak to you on Friday and over the weekend. I had a lot of feelings and it was very difficult.
Therapist:	Maybe your frustration with me this morning is because of my unavailability over the weekend when you needed contact. (She lies down on her back on the couch.)
Patient:	Dr. X *deliberately ignored* my wishes and feelings. When I wanted to protect myself from him, he got angry at me. On the one hand, I feel I have a right to assert myself but I need support. When he could not give me his support, I felt bad. (She pauses and then continues.) I feel very angry. I wonder why?
Therapist:	Perhaps you're angry at me for not being supportive enough and acknowledging your right to protect yourself.
Patient:	(She is puzzled.) *How* could I be angry at you about that? That doesn't make *sense*. No. I'm just wondering why you didn't answer right away.
Therapist:	(At this point I felt puzzled and, in retrospect, quite distant from the central issue of my nonresponse and its impact on her.) This three day break since we met on Thursday has been very difficult for you.
Patient:	(Joanna sits up abruptly and asks with some urgency.) Have any other analysts talked to you about me?
Therapist:	No.

This is a repetitive theme: Her concern that other analysts whom she has consulted may call me and try to influence me to stop seeing her. These concerns fill the rest of the session, switching from the possible conspiracy of other analysts to interfere with her treatment with me, on the one hand, to Dr. X and his exploitation of her, including his lack of support for her needs to protect herself from him, on the other. I was not able to connect this theme of disruption with my controlling pulling back and perhaps my comment about her uncertainty about her anger at me. The session ends with her attempting in vain to explain the nature of her need for active attuned responsiveness to enable her to feel safe.

Session 3 Tuesday

The next day she continues along the same theme. She is quite distressed and unclear about her distress. She begins to clarify her need to feel attached and her tendency to anticipate attack by the person to whom she feels attached. She describes her experience of feeling close to another analyst, then sexually excited by him, and then afraid of his anger at her. She connects this fear to her concern that any man to whom she feels attached will suddenly leave her. She ends the session expressing concern once again that a slight frown on my face suggested to her that she has done something wrong and that I was angry at her.

Session 4 Thursday

Patient: Do I look strange today?
Therapist: No. Why?
Patient: I feel sick. I'm weak. I didn't sleep last night. I've been thinking a lot about my mother. It seems to me that she has a lot of difficulty working out her emotions. She has rituals but they are not as complicated as mine. She repeats things, overstates things, cries a lot.

She describes her mother in some detail as self-centered, self-serving, and dependent on her father for everything. Her struggles to resolve her anger at her mother are constantly disrupted by her mother's intrusive style, which agitates, rather than soothes, her. As she continues, she loses track of her thoughts, and I review the themes of her resentment toward her mother to reorganize her.

Patient: I feel stuck. There is no comfortable place in my relationship with her. I called later to apologize for being so angry, but she expected me to retract my accusation. But I did not. I just apologized for my anger. She is unreasonable *all the time.* My mother tells me I am not a nice person for resenting things that were done so many years ago. *She treats me as if I am like a stain on the floor.* Gloria Steinem contrasted men and women. She said: "A man has to destroy you, take your house and your life to be considered hostile. A woman only has to put you on hold." That is how it was in my family, only *worse.*
Therapist: Gloria Steinem *really* put it into words for you.
Patient: It was *worse.* I only had to *exist* to be regarded as aggressive. My *just being there* was a problem for my father. His anger helped him keep himself at a distance. Part of my anxiety and my rituals have to do with *guilt.* I grew up being told I was evil, that I'd done something wrong, that I should not be happy and that I was being *punished* for it.
Therapist: So you have been left feeling that you are evil just for existing, just for being yourself.
Patient: You recently suggested that I have had to control my angry feelings through rituals. I was always so *alone* with my feelings. (She describes, with illustrations from her own experience and the experiences of others, her conviction

that angry feelings can be unintentionally communicated to others and hurt them.) Emotions *can* affect us. They can make us *sick*. Well, I was left all alone with my reactions. They were not accepted as normal feelings. My father would hurt women when they were fragile and needed support. He hated me as a little girl. Others found things to admire about me but he just hated me. I concluded that it was because I was female. He disliked my displays of femaleness. I could *not* have a doll or a girl's bicycle. He stayed away from me physically, as if I was dangerous. *I carry that feeling with me.*

Therapist: Perhaps that has something to do with your question of me: "Are you angry at me?"

Patient: Whenever I feel like I have been *really expressing* myself it enters my mind. I have to ask you if you are angry at me. I don't understand it.

Therapist: Perhaps it allows you to feel close and supported by me by having me actively assure you that I'm not angry. It becomes a ritual of reassurance.

Patient: (thoughtful, but doubtful) I'm not sure about that.

Session ends.

Chapter 14

Tracking Alan Kindler's Case Report: A Self and Motivational Systems Perspective

James L. Fosshage

Alan Kindler has presented fascinating clinical material. It is gripping and enticing and leaves us wishing that there was time for more.

This clinical material has been presented to enable three of us to comment on it, organizing it in our particular ways and with our special emphases. While there is probably considerable agreement between us, you the reader will decide if there are distinct differences or emphases and whether or not they are idiosyncratic or represent different models. My coauthors, Lichtenberg and Lachmann, and I (1992, 1996) add to the classical self psychological and intersubjective models, a self and motivational systems perspective. Lichtenberg (1989) has developed a comprehensive motivational model delineating five motivational systems. They are psychological regulation of physiological requirements, attachment-affiliation, sensual-sexual, exploratory-assertive, and aversive (two primary forms of aversiveness are aggression or antagonism and withdrawal). Each motivation is anchored in a basic need (for example, the need to explore, the need to protect oneself) and begins with innate response patterns that are then shaped by learning within a relational or intersubjective matrix. Personal meanings or patterned organizations accrue to each system based on lived experience with caregivers. Each system can be activated primarily from the inside or the outside. Within this framework, our motivations shift in priority, as well as typically involve several at the same time that may or may not be readily distinguishable. In the clinical arena we feel that the awareness of these different motivations and their shifting priorities potentially enhances our empathic grasp of our analysands' subjective lives. We also posit that each system needs to be functional for optimal development and maintenance of a vital cohesive sense of self. For example, aggression is crucially important in regulating our interactions and attachments and can be used for self-protection, self-delineation, and self-restoration. Aggression additionally can augment efforts of assertion when encountering obstacles. In our two books, *Self and Motivational Systems* (1992) and *The Clinical Exchange* (1996), we attempted to delineate a theory of technique or, more accurately, a theory of interaction, anchored in self and motivational systems theory, yet integrating as well as recasting self psychology and intersubjectivity theory.

Turning to Alan's clinical material, I first describe briefly those features of Joanna's inner life that stand out to me based on a close reading of the material and her expressed experience. I then follow the clinical exchange, drawing attention to particular interactive moments for what they reveal, as I perceive it, about this brief cross section of analytic work.

Joanna experienced her father as disliking her, even hating her. She decries, "He hated me as a little girl." He focused on weaknesses of women and seemed to hate her femaleness. Her father "would hurt women when they were fragile and needed support." She often felt that he was angry with her and that she had done something wrong. Based on these experiences, she had developed a pervasive sense that others felt negative and angry toward her, a transferential or organizing theme that was dominant in these sessions. She often sought relief in these sessions by asking if her analyst was angry with her.

She experienced her mother as confirming her badness, "being told I was evil, that I'd done something wrong, that I should not be happy, and that I was being punished for it." She experienced her mother treating her "as if I am like a stain on the floor." These experiences eroded confidence and further reinforced negative feelings, attitudes, and images about herself. Nevertheless, her clear articulation of these experiences conveyed an emergent perspective, undoubtedly fostered by her analysis, that demonstrated she was in the process of extricating herself from these negative self feelings.

When growing up, Joanna had felt all alone with her feelings. Self-restorative efforts at assertion and expression of anger and aggression were, in her experience, headed off with criticism and prohibition. In her family, "I only had to exist to be regarded as aggressive."

Accordingly, acts of self-assertion and aggression evoked expectations of anger from the other and were accompanied by guilt, shame, and conflict.

With this legacy, Joanna experienced intense (selfobject) longings and needs for affirmation, protection, and safety. A victim of sexual abuse by her father, which was not detailed, created a proneness for Joanna and perhaps even a confidence that she could use sexuality, unfortunately confirmed with several analysts, to connect to a man for needed mirroring and idealizing selfobject experience. In today's presentation we learned about Joanna's sexuality only as it emerged in her relationships with her analysts. With Dr. X "she longed for his attention and physical presence"; she felt "like a baby on her mother's lap looking into her mother's eyes." And with Alan, following her "assertive sexualization," she needed to feel a physical connection with him by having him sit in the chair closest to the couch. These descriptions of mirroring and idealizing selfobject experience are suffused with sensuality rather than sexuality. Joanna understandably conflates the two, for her father's distance, dislike of her, and sexual abuse, combined with her mother's repudiation, paved the way to her seeking needed sensual affirmation through sexual engagement.

Joanna's mirroring and idealizing longings entered quickly into the analysis with Alan. Successfully managing her intense efforts to use sexuality, Alan was able to co-create with Joanna the needed selfobject connection through estabishing an analytic process.

TREATMENT

As I follow the sessions provided, I will delineate what I believe is occurring. At times I will offer alternative interventions, recognizing that these alternatives are emerging not within the spontaneous heat and inevitable pushes and pulls of the clinical encounter, but within the luxuriously relaxed and reflective context of reading clinical material.

Thursday's session opens with Joanna fearing Alan's negative reaction to her hat. Following initial exploration, she reveals that she uses the hat to protect her sinuses but feels a bit peculiar wearing a hat during a summer night even though it is cold for her. Recognizing the need for physiological regulation, I might have said, "So, wearing your hat is an attempt to regulate your body temperature and protect your sinuses." My intervention endeavors to normalize physiological requirements and priorities in order to foster acceptance and to diminish self-consciousness. Simultaneously, this momentary interaction potentially creates a relational experience involving acceptance, a needed antidote to the expected criticism. [At the earlier panels the old false dichotomy between interpretation and relationship was resurrected. From today's interactional perspective it is clear that interpretation contributes to and is a part of relational experience.]

Before Alan can respond, Joanna moves on to a discussion about father–daughter relationships. Her longing for a "stable, well-adjusted" father who supports his daughter and fosters self-confidence is clear, and this selfobject striving is palpably present in the analytic relationship as well. Joanna then shifts to the repetitive experience of how her father crushed her confidence and says, "That's how I feel about your reaction to me as I came in." During the ensuing dialog Joanna spells out how she kept her distance from Alan by avoiding the elevator because of the anticipated negative reaction. She was afraid that he would not accept her and readily connects her expectations to her experience with her father. At the end of the session, Joanna asks, "Are you angry with me?" Alan reassures her that he is not. This regulatory interaction is repetitive, even "ritualized." I wonder why he moves to reassure so quickly without exploration. We can speculate that her fear of his anger was triggered both by having assertively inquired about his negative reactions to her hat and by her anger about his criticism. I also wonder if there are additional meanings about a hat that makes her feel odd-looking and if Alan and Joanna have explored her feelings and images concerning her physical appearance, which, crossing over several motivational arenas, forms an important aspect of her sense of self.

Monday's session begins with Joanna challenging her analyst's routinized response, "I am well," a possible way of his maintaining distance. Both seek momentary refuge in discussing his plants. Joanna then inquires, "Are you angry?" Alan reassures her, "No, I'm not." She inquires, "Are you upset with me?" and Alan says again, "No." Joanna's discomfort and fear of retaliation follows her assertive and perhaps antagonistic confrontation. Apart from the contribution of Alan's subjectivity, her fear of his anger apparently is sufficiently intense to pull for immediate reassurance, most likely a relational pattern that goes on with others as well. I wonder what it feels like to be the other in relationship to Joanna at this moment, what I refer to as other-centered experience (Fosshage, 1995, 1997), which would help me to deepen my understanding of her and our relational experience. This repetitive pattern, of course, needs to be opened up for mutual exploration and understanding.

Reassured, Joanna says, "Maybe I'm angry at you." Alan responds, "Uh huh. But it sounds as if you're not sure about that." Perhaps still reeling a bit from her first confrontation, Alan does not invite the anger in by inquiring simply, "What about?" Joanna experiences his response as aversive. She becomes defensive, "I said 'possibly,' " and then raises the question about the acceptability of a child's anger toward aging parents. Inquiry about acceptability to whom, namely, to her parents, to her analyst, or to her, would potentially deepen understanding of her aversiveness, its acceptability, their interaction, and related relational experience. While waiting for Alan's response, she proceeds to angrily discuss her mother's and Dr. X's manipulative behavior. She then refocuses on Alan and says, "You are controlling me. As I become more fluid you pull back and that makes me feel I should be more controlled." As she becomes more assertive and aggressive, she experiences her analyst as withdrawing. In keeping with past experience, she begins to feel that silencing herself is necessary to maintain the needed connection. Alan continues to ponder her statements and, from my vantage point, appears momentarily frozen, perhaps nailed to the wall, for it feels that he, indeed, has pulled back. All of this confirms her expectations that assertiveness and aggressiveness are not allowed.

Joanna moves on and indicates that she had needed to speak with Alan over the weekend. Perhaps experiencing this as less personally attacking, Alan quickly intervenes and connects her frustration and aversiveness to his unavailability over the weekend. She responds: "Dr. X deliberately ignored her wishes and feelings. When I wanted to protect myself from him, he got angry at me." She asserts that she has a right to protect herself but needs support for that or else ends up feeling that she is bad. She then says, "I feel very angry. I wonder why?" Alan interprets this as transferential and suggests that she may be angry at him for not sufficiently supporting her need to protect herself. She replies, "No. I'm just wondering why you did not answer right away." Feeling puzzled, Alan refers to the 3-day break. Following this misunderstanding, she begins to wonder and inquires if other analysts have intervened and have tried to convince him not to see her. Alan notes that the rupture was not mended during the remainder of the session.

From my perspective, Joanna in this session experiences and challenges Alan's distance, acknowledges the possibility of her anger at him, feels uncertain if it is acceptable, needs interpretive support, and is met with a puzzling silence. She associates to Dr. X's deliberately ignoring her feelings and to his angry reaction to her assertiveness, yet she is not quite ready to assume that it is the same with Alan. She inquires again, "I'm wondering why you did not answer right away." She is attempting to obtain from Alan a needed new responsiveness in getting answers to her questions. When frustrated, she struggles between interpreting in the old way and feeling anger and despair versus leaving it open for a different response and explanation. Assuming too quickly that the content of the patient's statements about the other, in this instance Dr. X, directly applies and is the only experience in the analytic relationship, can obfuscate a patient's struggle to remain open and to create through understanding a new experience. Joanna's use of aggression to bolster her assertiveness and to provide protection appears to momentarily immobilize her analyst. Joanna appears to be left feeling that Alan's distance means that he does not like her, a replication of her experience with her father and mother and that other analysts have reinforced his dislike of her. A possible move out of this conumdrum is a collaborative close retracking of their interplay with emphasis on her sense of his withdrawal and its origins, acknowledgment of her desire for less distance, and her need for support and its genesis when she is assertive, angry, and antagonistic. She needs her analyst to acknowledge what was happening for him on these occasions in order to better understand their interplay. If her analyst feels attacked, utilizing empathic and other-centered experiencing perspectives, he can also include in their explorations the impact of her aversiveness on him in order to expand awareness of her contribution to their interaction and to related relational scenarios.

Session 3 is summarized. Session 4 opens with Joanna asking, "Do I look strange today?" Alan responds, "No. Why?" Alan answers directly and this time quickly inquires. Joanna indicates that she is not feeling well after a poor night's sleep. She had been feeling angry about her mother's self-centeredness, agitation, and intrusiveness. She had apologized to her mother for the intensity of her anger but refused to retrack her accusation. She decries how she was so easily accused of being aggressive. Joanna further delineates how self-expression often was attacked, leading to feelings of guilt and badness. Joanna and Alan are now "in sync." Together they are facilitating her expressiveness and reflectiveness, a new relational experience that serves as a foundation for new images of self and self-with-other. She talks about her father and her feeling that he hated her. She says: "He disliked my displays of femaleness. I could not have a doll, a girl's bicycle. He stayed away from me physically, as if I was dangerous. I carry that feeling with me." (These experiences, in my view, must have intensified Joanna's need for sensual affirmation [for example, to be lovingly touched and spoken to]. Alan's attempt to protect the two of them from a sexual reenactment may have inadvertently contributed to Alan's distance, which, in combination with her proneness to experience dislike and rejection, was periodically replicating in these sessions the frustration of her needs for sensual affirmation.) In response to Joanna's last statement, Alan addresses the repetitive question so prominent in these sessions, "Perhaps that has something to do with your question of me: 'Are you angry at me?' " Joanna responds, "Whenever I feel like I have been really expressing myself, it enters my mind. I have to ask you if you are angry at me. I don't understand it." Alan interprets, "Perhaps it allows you to feel close and supported by me by having me actively assure you that I'm not angry. It becomes a ritual of reassurance." And Joanna ends the session by saying, "I'm not sure about that." Alan's focus on attachment repair with perhaps a slight pejorative note emanating from the word ritual creates a ripple of dissonance. In my view, there would have been a meeting of minds if he had described the full scenario of how self-expression in her life was often experienced as unwanted and met with anger and how she understandably anticipates that the same will be true with Alan. She keeps asking for reassurance that he is not angry, expecting that he is, yet hoping that he is not. Moreover, Alan's acknowledgement of those moments of his distance and its origins will help her to differentiate these occasions from those when Alan is more fully present and enrich the possible meanings these fluctuations may have. To understand this intricate interaction will facilitate change intrapsychically and interactively in each member of the dyad.

In these complex exchanges, elements of attachment, sensuality, sexuality, assertiveness, and aversiveness become so entangled both intrapsychically and interactively that it becomes a task for the analyst through empathic inquiry, interpretations, and other interactions to tease out the different elements along with their associated affects, attitudes, and relational experiences. This process will gradually promote expansion of awareness, psychological reorganization, and self-righting, what we consider to be the goals of analytic work.

REFERENCES

Fosshage, J. (1995), Countertransference as the analyst's experience of the analysand: The influence of listening perspectives. *Psychoanal. Psychol., 12*:375–391.

Fosshage, J. (1997), Listening perspectives and the quest for a facilitative responsiveness. *Conversations in Self Psycholgy: Progress in Self Psychology, Vol. 13,* ed. A. Goldberg, Hillsdale, NJ: The Analytic Press, pp. 33–55.

Lichtenberg, J. (1989), *Psychoanalysis and Motivation.* Hillsdale, NJ: The Analytic Press.

———— Lachmann, F. & Fosshage, J. (1992), *Self and Motivational Systems: Toward a Theory of Technique.* Hillsdale, NJ: The Analytic Press.

———— ———— & ———— (1996), *The Clinical Exchange: Technique from the Standpoint of Self and Motivational Systems.* Hillsdale, NJ: The Analytic Press.

Chapter 15

The Centrality of the Selfobject Transferences: A Discussion of Alan Kindler's "The Case of Joanna Churchill"

Paul H. Ornstein

Alan Kindler gave us some skillfully presented excerpts of his diffi-cult-to-manage analysis of Joanna Churchill. He gave us verbatim de-tails of the actual dialogue, as well as some of his own concurrent subjective experiences that influenced the nature and content of his interventions. With all of this, Alan takes us into his consulting room and invites us to reexperience with him (and with his patient) the vicissitudes of the analytic process created by its two participants. This is as it should be to enable us to learn whatever we can from the experience of the encounter between Joanna Churchill and Alan Kindler.

I shall take advantage of this exemplary clinical presentation and jump right into my exploration, with only a very few preliminary re-marks related to my approach. As is usually necessary, I had to traverse this analytic process more than once, in order to find my bearing and come away from each attempt with some additional grasp of what I had witnessed. The experiences themselves reported by Alan are not open to question; their meaning and Alan's responses to them, how-ever, are. In this endeavor I shall try to understand what Alan did and what were the discernible results of his interventions from within his

215

own and his patient's perspective (see Ornstein, 1990). I shall therefore oscillate between attempting to empathize (1) with Alan and then (2) with Joanna, and after reviewing each session, I shall step out of my vicarious introspection (3) in order to register and communicate to you my own observations of how the two participants were communicating with each other. Steps (1) and (2) require that I decenter (as far as this is possible—and I think it is both possible *and* desirable) from my own judgmental responses as an external observer and go on with my vicarious introspection regarding the experiences of both analyst and analysand. You can immediately see the complication that may easily arise in step (3). It may well interfere with my effort at decentering, if I allow myself to be deflected from returning to my empathic observational vantage point and become fixated on my extrospective findings. Not that extrospective observational data are necessarily inaccurate or invalid, but as such, they are not directly useful for our clinical interventions, nor are they sufficient for grasping the nature of the analytic process under scrutiny. Extrospective data can and should be used to enhance our efforts at vicarious introspection. The more we know about the other person, the better we can put ourselves imaginatively into his or her inner world (Kohut, 1959, 1981; Ornstein, 1979, 1995).

One additional point: Alan's concise and vivid introduction of his patient and their first meeting, along with highlights of the patient's prior psychoanalytic and psychotherapeutic experiences, as well as the brief remark about her family constellation, should serve as the available context for our understanding of the four sessions presented from the second year of the analysis. A great deal must have happened in this analysis by then, but I shall restrict my scrutiny to the text and context as given. I trust Alan's synthesis and that he captured in his presentation the essence of his own and the patient's experiences; that is, I take his text as representative of his own and of his patient's analytic experience as a whole. I have no other choice.

The Clinical Report

And now I shall turn to the clinical report. Alan immediately highlighted for us what made analysis difficult for him. I shall simply list those items that stood out for me in Alan's narrative: (1) Joanna was an attractive woman who "at times conducted herself like a coquette." (2) Another point was the details of her prolonged, sexualized relation with her former analyst—which she enjoyed while it was happening but which she resented as time went on because of "his self-serving exploitation of her and other women." (3) Another detail struck me as

highly significant: the "patient longed for his [former analyst's] attention and physical presence" and "when she sat on his knee she felt like
a baby on her mother's lap looking into her mother's eyes." (4) She
became ill after she terminated that analysis (against her analyst's wishes)
and "the loss . . . left her feeling strange, as if she did not exist." (5)
"Her father was a cruel dominating man who physically and sexually
abused her. Her mother was distant, insecure and unavailable to her."

While—as will become apparent—all of these elements of her background undoubtedly determined the meaning of Joanna's analytic behavior and experience, my attention was riveted on what Alan said
about his own reactions and responses, which co-determined the evolving analytic process. Alan, armed with the knowledge of Joanna's
prior sexualization of her analytic and therapeutic relations and experiencing her attractiveness and coquettishness, as well as her attempts
at an immediate "assertive sexualization" of their relations as "a serious threat," responded by clearly and unmistakably refusing to join
her on the couch and engage in any sort of physical contact. But
Joanna did not give up her demands easily.

This analysis thus began under a cloud: the patient's "opening gambit" on its *manifest* level was clearly unacceptable to the analyst, and
at that early point all he could do (especially since he also felt the
patient's attractiveness as a threat) was to resist the patient's demands
in no uncertain terms. They weathered the resulting tension (which
was sustained for weeks) sufficiently so that the analysis could continue. In fact, as a result of the increased frequency of the sessions
later on, the patient seemed to have become "less physically and sensually expressive"—a good omen that whatever was expressed through
these sexualized demands would ultimately yield to the analyst's understanding and explanations of their *latent* meaning.

Comments

So, what is the cloud then? When a patient's opening demands have
to be rejected, instead of accepted, understood, and explained—although not necessarily all three at once—the emergence of the pathognomonic selfobject transference may be delayed, at best, or altogether
thwarted, at worst, unless, of course, the initial (necessary) refusal of
the patient's overt sexual demands can later, in the ensuing weeks, be
translated into an acceptance of the patient's efforts at mobilizing a
selfobject transference, even if camouflaged in her sexualization of that
transference.

We are not told what Alan did or said, to make that translation at
some point during those tension-filled early weeks or, later, prior to

the sessions presented—instead of simply, steadfastly refusing the patient's sexual demands without explanation. Therefore, I shall add here—as my comment on the initial phase of this analysis—what I would have done, based entirely on the data given us by Alan and Joanna. It is, of course, easy for us now to see more clearly with hindsight and Alan's help how the translation could have been made, since Alan provides us with all the clues we need and we are not under the spell of his patient's attractiveness and unacceptable sexual demands. Under the circumstances, therefore, I might have said something like the following (not all at once, of course, but in briefer statements as our dialogue would have warranted): "I sense that the urgency and insistence with which you are expressing what you want from me contains something very, very important *that does belong here in the analysis*—but I do not yet understand what that is. What I do understand at this point is—correct me if I am wrong—that, when your analyst involved you in sexual relations, you enjoyed it, until later, when you found out that he had such relations with other women as well and you began to feel exploited. That was deeply disappointing and painful to you. You had to leave him even though he wanted to hold on to you. You told me that after leaving him you 'became incapacitated by illness and [were] unable to work. Losing him was quite traumatic and left [you] feeling strange, as if [you] did not exist.' You sort of fell apart. No wonder you now desperately want to reestablish that sexual closeness with me, hoping that it would make you feel well (and whole) again. But you are also warning me that 10 years of that kind of experience left you ultimately both physically and emotionally crippled; you are warning me not to exploit you sexually, no matter how urgently you may want it or how good it might feel for awhile. I hear your wish for a 'sexual' closeness as being very strong but so is your warning to me that it might have disastrous consequences if I give in to your demands. Am I understanding your dilemma?" I would respond in this fashion in order to avoid crossing the boundary, which might easily induce in Joanna feelings of exploitation, and to avoid a "cold" rejection.

At a later point (especially when the outlines of an emerging selfobject transference became clearer) I would add that "amidst those sexual experiences with your previous analyst, there were important, poignant moments of a very different quality: when you were sitting on his knee you felt like a baby on her mother's lap looking into her mother's eyes. Can you help me understand what we should make of that?" I might later add, if appropriate and timely, that "I had a tentative idea that you were searching for an experience you never had with your mother, whom you described as distant and unavailable to you. Could it be that both you and your previous therapists had mistaken your longing for maternal warmth, touch, and cuddling for a sexual wish? Am I on the right track?"

I shall stop here with filling in the way I would have participated in the evolving analytic process from the very beginning. I only wish to underscore again—before moving on to the sessions—that I have *not* introduced here anything other than what Alan and his patient presented us with. I simply indicated (remaining within their own perspective) how I would have elaborated what I learned from them into a coherent interpretive narrative—guided by my sense of what *function* Joanna assigned to her analyst—and would have offered my tentative understanding to Joanna piecemeal, from very early on.

What Joanna needed here, in my view, was a responsive, in-depth understanding of her needs, wishes, *and* their sources. This should have been enough until proven otherwise—a self psychologist's analytic stance, widely disregarded and disapproved of these days. Alan took the proper stance but without speaking to Joanna in the "interpretive mode" I just illustrated (P. H. Ornstein and A. Ornstein, 1996; A. Ornstein and P. H. Ornstein, 1996).

Alan presented us with a dramatic portrayal of the significant components of what he and Joanna brought to their difficult encounter. I reflected on the nature of this initial encounter in some detail as a way to focus more pointedly on what emerges later in the sample sessions. My interest is in organizing my perception around two related processes: (1) What is the patient's moment-to-moment session-to-session, week-to-week subjective experience (including her experience of the analyst)—the *microprocess* (which is strongly affected or shaped by the nature of the interaction of the two participants)? (2) What is the patient's experience over time; what psychic terrain is she traversing in the analytic relationship—the *macroprocess* (which is strongly affected or shaped by her past experiences)? We can only make analytic sense of the microprocess if we can project this onto the wider screen of the macroprocess and register what elements of the past are reenacted in the present and how the analyst responds to these. We can now turn to the four sessions in the second year of the analysis and examine what we find in them.

Session One

Joanna brings to a Thursday session an acute fear of the analyst's negative reaction to her, ostensibly evoked because of her peculiar behavior of wearing a hat in the middle of the summer. She feared that the strangeness of it caught his attention, but he turned away from her [perhaps with disgust or contempt?]. Alan, rather than introducing his own reality that he did not even notice her, quite appropriately stays with her subjective experience and explores it by suggesting that there might be something that made her "expect a negative reaction." Alan has in mind the patient's "self-consciousness" as having triggered her fear of disapproval. But before Alan could say anything, the patient embarked on a significant exploration of father–daughter relations, in the course of which Alan tuned in on and continued to pursue Joanna's subjective experiences by repeatedly reflecting—again quite appropriately—what he heard her say. The gist of Joanna's communication was that, if fathers supported their daughters and stood behind them, they turned out "self-assured, emotionally centered, and controlled." Her own father, she felt, "crushed her self-confidence" and that is how she felt about Alan's reaction to her as she entered the lobby of his office building. Alan's exploration and the patient's readiness to see the transference implications of her father–daughter stories, as well as her experiences with her own father, led here to a fruitful interchange. This is then capped off with a remarkable further insight: it was not Alan who turned away from her; she herself kept her distance and did not enter the elevator to avoid his negative reaction. It was Alan's lack of acceptance she feared, just as she never could get her father's acceptance: "It was impossible for him to like me. . . . He just couldn't." It was something in *him*—maybe his hate for women—that would explain it. Alan underscored this statement by saying: "So there was nothing you could do because it was not coming from you." In response to this simple, validating response, Joanna revealed that she often thought it was something *in her* that made her not likeable. Her mother believed that too; she degraded herself and Joanna. (This is a good example of how a simple validating response in the interpretive mode may enhance the patient's own self-reflection.)

The report of this session ends with Alan's remark that "the session continued with the exploration of [Joanna's] attachment needs, including her awareness of her inclination to turn away from someone who admires her to protect herself from the inevitable loss of that admiration." And then, in spite of a fruitful interchange, the session "ended characteristically with [Joanna's] ritualized question: 'Are you angry at me?' " To which Alan responded by attempting to reassure her.

Comments

Joanna's early, blatant sexualization of her relationship to Alan gave way in this session to her focusing more directly on her "crushed self-confidence," a part of which is her feeling "degraded" as a woman.

This appears to be a central issue in this analysis—introduced immediately by Joanna in her urgent wish and demand for a sexual(ized) relationship to her analyst. Alan's interventions and final summarizing comments at the end of the session give us no evidence that he considered Joanna's sexualization of their relations as an expression of an archaic mirror (merger) transference. I wonder why not? Instead, he spoke about "self-consciousness" (as if that would explain Joanna's "fear of a negative reaction" from him), and he spoke of exploring Joanna's "attachment needs" even while recognizing her craving for admiration and needing to turn away from such an admiring person to protect herself against the apparently inevitable loss of that admiration. Would that not indicate Joanna's efforts at mobilizing a mirror transference in her analytic struggle to build up her self-esteem by trying to get Alan to show her concretely that he valued her? I wonder whether Alan's focus on "attachment needs" (a rather bland, nonspecific term under the circumstances) felt to her as missing the mark, a misunderstanding, perhaps triggering in her some annoyance and anger—leading to her ritualized question: "Are you angry at me?"—to which Alan responds with an equally ritualized reassurance, without coupling it with some tentative understanding about the possible meaning of this repetitive question in the second year of the analysis!

My assumption that this entire experience takes place within a mirror (merger) transference is also buttressed by what I learned about Joanna's experience in her previous analysis. Aside from her sexual relations with her analyst, she described how she longed for his attention and physical presence. She fell apart when that relation ended, became ill, and has needed regular massage sessions in a relaxation clinic for the last 2 years (while already in this analysis) to relieve her severe bodily tensions. The microprocess of session #1 not only becomes more intelligible but also more sharply focused, when examined in the light of the evolving macroprocess: the mirror (merger) transference.

Session Two

Joanna arrives to her Monday session visibly anxious and testy. She challenges Alan's sincerity and forthrightness by stating that he responds to her question "automatically to keep her at a distance." (Is this a reference to the routine reassurance at the end of the previous session?) Thus she continues the theme of the Thursday session: her father distanced himself from her, and she now confronts the analyst with the fact that he is doing the same. This confrontation makes Alan uncomfortable and he loses his analytic bearing for a while. The patient senses this and asks: "Are you angry?" Alan's simple reassurance: "No, I am not" is unsuccessful and she asks again: "Are you upset with me?" Again, he responds with a simple "No" (still without any effort at engaging the repetitive, routine question but responding with a routine answer). Compliantly perhaps, because she says it with such tentativeness, Joanna turns the question around and says: "Maybe *I* am angry at you." And then abruptly—but very much to the point— Joanna asks: "Is it all right for a child to be angry at aging parents? Is it all right if that child does things which actually hurt the parents, even though they are aging and helpless?" Alan has lost empathic contact with Joanna at this point since he ponders the question and is concerned with extraneous "technical issues"; he is at a loss whether to engage the content, wait and hope for clarification, or ask for it. Joanna registers Alan's quandary and continues with her theme of having been exploited without empathy or fair play both by her former analyst and by her mother; she blames her mother even more than her former analyst. She then turns to Alan with annoyance and accuses him of controlling her (presumably with his silence) and is quite specific about her complaints: "As I become more fluid you pull back and that makes me feel I should be more controlled." Alan is at this point still not with her but is beginning to realize that Joanna's annoyance "might have to do with [his] lack of response thus far." Joanna confirms this by telling him that she needed to speak to him on Friday and over the weekend. "I had a lot of feelings and it was very difficult." His response was partially to the point since Joanna relaxed as a result and lay down on the couch. He acknowledged her frustration with him on account of his unavailability over the weekend but did not include her missing his responsiveness in this session. Joanna continues on target: complains that her former analyst ignored her wishes and feelings and when she wanted to protect herself from him, he got angry. "I feel I have a right to assert myself but I need support. When he could not give me his support, I felt bad." She felt intensely angry now and was puzzled as to why. Alan did pick this up and said: "Perhaps you are angry at me for not being supportive enough and acknowledging your right to protect yourself." Joanna rejected that: "No. I am just wondering why you didn't answer right away." So, she was more concerned about her immediate experience in relation to Alan in this session. Alan (recognizing, in retrospect, that he was still at a distance from the central issue of his nonresponse and its impact on Joanna) tries to capture the patient's experience and says: "This 3-day break since we met on Thursday has been difficult for you." But this appears to be off the mark, and the patient sits up and asks again her "paranoid" question (clearly a disruption, which lets her suspiciousness emerge in the analytic process as a "breakdown product"): "Have any analysts talked to you about me?" Alan responds with a monosyllabic "No" and tells us of the repetitive nature of this suspicious concern. He acknowledges that he was unable to connect this theme of disruption with his pulling back from her, or controlling her. He remarks that "the session ends with [Joanna] attempting in vain to explain the nature of her need for active, attuned responsiveness to enable her to feel safe." Alan is aware here of a breakdown in communication, a disruption of the transference.

Comments

Not having satisfactorily resolved the question of whether Alan was angry at Joanna at the end of the previous session or not, the second session began with Joanna challenging Alan's genuine presence and forthrightness in his responses. This put him visibly on the spot (he seems to have felt that she was right), and his efforts at capturing Joanna's subjective experience in this session remained unsuccessful, or partially successful, at best. It is at moments like this, when one loses one's analytic bearing, that theories may come to one's rescue. Having some idea about the nature of the transference may orient the analyst regarding the focal point in the session so that he/she can offer some understanding instead of direct reassurance regarding the "routine" questions. In fact, these are not routine questions, even if they are frequently recurring. Joanna either feels angry with Alan or, as is almost her chronic condition, feels that he is angry with her. At such moments she fears a rupture in their relation and needs an urgent response that all is well. But if a routine reassurance is offered, it cannot be convincing to her. Alan's tentative understanding of the meaning of the question might offer the best reassurance, in that it conveys that the analyst knows how the patient feels and is accepting of those feelings rather than censuring her for them—which is what she fears. In my view it is this lack of responding with an ongoing tentative understanding of the patient's subjective experiences that leaves this session's disruption unrepaired. Here is where a reconstruction of what the analyst said or did not say, did or did not do, to trigger the disruption would have contributed to its repair.

Joanna spells out what she needed and what would have helped, when she says: "As I become more fluid, you pull back and that makes me feel I should be more controlled." I take that to mean that the patient feels emotionally abandoned by the analyst precisely at that moment when she brings in her (most regressed? "fluid?") feelings and behavior and would need his unequivocal acceptance and validating presence—not a routine yes or no.

Session Three

The Tuesday session is briefly summarized as continuing the theme of the one from the day before. Joanna is distressed and anticipates being attacked; especially by the person that matters to her a lot. She is afraid of sudden abandonment by the person she feels attached to. At the end she is concerned "that a slight frown on [Alan's] face suggested that she had done something and that [he] was angry at her."

Comments

In this abbreviated summary, Alan confirms the continuation of the disruption and Joanna's continuing suspicion that he is angry with her. It is at such moments that one can initiate an exploration of the meaning of the recurring question by recognizing that the direct reassurance is ineffective—and asking for the patient's help in discovering the unrecognized meaning of the question.

Session Four

The last session on Thursday is filled with Joanna's complaints about her mother and father, their ways of treating her. Alan's brief responses demonstrate his attempts to capture Joanna's subjective experience by reflecting back to her what he heard her say. She claims that her mother always maligned her and treated her "like a stain on the floor." Her father hated her as a little girl, just because she was a girl: "He stayed away from me physically as if I was dangerous. I carry that feeling with me." After this last statement, however, Alan senses the possible reference of these complaints to himself, and he attempts to draw attention to this with his remark: "Perhaps that has to do with your question of me: 'Are you angry at me?'" Joanna offers a most telling response: "Whenever I feel like I have been really expressing myself it enters my mind [that you are angry]. [Then] I have to ask you if you are angry with me. I don't understand it." Alan answers: "Perhaps it allows you to feel close and supported by me by having me actively assure you that I am not angry. It becomes a ritual of reassurance." Joanna is not convinced of this explanation. Her thoughtful answer is: "I am not sure about that." Here the clinical report ends.

Comments

In this last session the tense emotional atmosphere continued. The reasons for it had become further clarified by Joanna when she said that her mother treated her "like a stain on the floor" and her "father stayed away from [her] physically as if [she were] dangerous." She added: "I carry that feeling with me." No wonder Joanna wants all of this redressed in the transference concretely by demanding physical contact as a way to get rid of the intolerable feeling of being considered dangerous—"untouchable." It is at such moments and in relation to such issues that many therapists fall into the trap of offering some sort of a "provision" as a necessary antidote, without trying the interpretive mode of response. I would have said that much to her in this session (if I had not already done so before and would have repeated it at this moment even if I had already said it before). Alan recognized that Joanna's complaints about her parents also referred to him, by suggesting that her repeated questions "Are you angry at me?" might well be connected with the fact that she is complaining about him. But this is, again, less than what could have been interpreted with reference to the specifics of both this session and the analysis as a whole thus far—in other words, how the experiences in this session could have further illuminated important aspects of the microprocess (the immediate experiences of the moment) as well as the macroprocess (the experiences remobilized in the specific selfobject transference). Nevertheless, Joanna's response adds a significant piece to our understanding of her reasons for her repetitive questions: "Whenever I feel like I have been really expressing myself, it enters my mind [that you are angry]." She is very specific but Alan offers a somewhat tangential answer, so Joanna cannot accept it. As a result, Alan and Joanna did not arrive at a mutual understanding of the meaning of their experiences in this session. Her specific response indicates that in her mind *any* honest revelation of her feelings (including, I presume, her desire for a sexual relation with her analyst) is going to evoke anger and contempt, making her feel untouchable and the like—undoubtedly a central issue in this analysis that has not been fully engaged interpretively.

Concluding Remarks

Having commented on each session essentially in terms of the details of the clinical atmosphere, the actual interchanges between patient and analyst and the nature of the transference within which the reported interactions took place, I shall now conclude with a broader statement regarding the position of Alan Kindler's clinical presentation in the ongoing dialogue among the various trends under the "big tent" of psychoanalytic self psychology.

I see this clinical report as a very important one at this juncture of our deliberations, following on the heels of the three clinical presentations last year in Washington. We attempted there to engage our current controversies in such a fashion that we could begin to listen to each other better than for some years before that conference. We succeeded at that but at a great cost: some significant issues were shoved under the rug. The three clinical presentations could not be discussed with full openness. I hope that now, dealing with a single case, all three of us panelists will be able to engage the substantive issues *sine ira et studio* (without rancor and without partiality)—admittedly a rare event among passionate psychoanalysts. I shall proceed nevertheless.

Alan's analysis of Joanna highlights for me the fact that the centrality of the selfobject concept (hence the centrality of the selfobject transferences) cannot yet be dispensed with or successfully substituted by other existing concepts at this time (Kohut, 1971, 1977, 1984, and many others). Alan's clinical presentation is important because, from here on, this particular controversy cannot be discussed in the abstract. Anyone who wishes to supplant the selfobject concept in the clinical situation, or push it out of the center—as is widely fashionable today—would have to present a sample of verbatim interchanges of a sequence of analytic sessions to show that he or she could offer the patient a richer analytic experience and to his or her colleagues a more compelling narrative, without the aid of the concept of the selfobject transferences.

I am fully aware of the fact that many rich and compelling narratives can be constructed from a variety of theoretical perspectives. But the advantages or disadvantages of any narrative would have to be demonstrated by giving us the clinical data, as Alan had done, including some of his own inner monologues. I claim to have expanded the sense Alan made of the clinical experience he presented, not only by examining microscopically the analytic dialogue, but also mainly by introducing the mirror (merger) transference as a frame within which the meaning of the details of each session could be better understood. Without the selfobject concept, I would not have been able to make sense of the patient's past history, past treatment experiences, and her current experiences in this analysis in a coherent narrative. My claim is that apparently Alan could not do so either. Whatever countertransference issues may have contributed to Alan's conduct of the analysis—countertransference issues from which none of us is immune—I see Alan's failure to put the selfobject transference into the center of his considerations as having contributed to the difficulties in this analysis (see P. H. Ornstein and A. Ornstein, 1995; A. Ornstein and P. H. Ornstein, 1995). The tense emotional atmosphere that prevailed and remained essentially uninterpreted exemplified these difficulties. So did the lack of specificity and sharpness of focus in Alan's interventions, even when he was appropriately reflecting back the patient's subjective experiences. All of these difficulties, I maintain, were to a great degree due to the absence of Alan's recognition of, and his becoming immersed in, Joanna's mirror (merger) transference.

REFERENCES

Kohut, H. (1959), Introspection, empathy and psychoanalysis: An examination of the relationship between mode of observation and theory. In: *The Search for the Self, Vol. 1,* ed. P. H. Ornstein. New York: International Universities Press, pp. 205–232.

———— (1971), *The Analysis of the Self.* New York: International Universities Press.

———— (1977), *The Restoration of the Self.* New York: International Universities Press.

———— (1981), Introspection, empathy and the semi-circle of mental health. In: *The Search for the Self, Vol. 4,* Madison, CT: International Universities Press, 1990, pp. 537–567.

———— (1984), *How Does Analysis Cure?* ed. A. Goldberg and P. E. Stepansky. Chicago: University of Chicago Press.

Ornstein, A. & Ornstein, P. H. (1995), Marginal comments on the evolution of self psychology. Response to editor's follow-up questions. *Psychoanal. Dial.,* 5:421–425.

———— & ———— (1996), Speaking in the interpretive mode and feeling understood: Crucial aspects of the therapeutic action in psychotherapy. In: *Understanding Therapeutic Action—Psychodynamic Concepts of Cure,* ed. L. E. Lifson. Hillsdale, NJ: The Analytic Press, pp. 103–125.

Ornstein, P. H. (1979), Remarks on the central position of empathy in psychoanalysis. *Bull.: The Assn. for Psychoanal. Med.,* 18:95–100.

———— (1990), How to enter a psychoanalytic process conducted by another psychoanalyst? *Psychoanal. Inq.,* 10:478–497.

———— (1995), An introduction to "Classic Article" (Kohut's introspection, empathy and psychoanalysis: An examination of the relationship between mode of observation and theory. *J. Psychother. Practice & Res.,* 4:159–162.

———— & Ornstein, A. (1995), Some distinguishing features of Heinz Kohut's self psychology. *Psychoanal. Dial.,* 5:385–391.

———— & ———— (1996), Some general principles of psychoanalytic psychotherapy: A self psychological perspective. In: *Understanding Therapeutic Action—Psychodynamic Concepts of Cure,* ed. L. E. Lifson. Hillsdale, NJ: The Analytic Press, pp. 87–101.

Chapter 16

Antidotes, Enactments, Rituals, and the Dance of Reassurance: Comments on the Case of Joanna Churchill and Alan Kindler

Robert D. Stolorow

The discussion of Kindler's challenging clinical material continues the polylogue, begun in October 1996 at the International Self Psychology Conference in Washington, among proponents of selfobject theory, motivational systems theory, and intersubjectivity theory. At the conference in 1996, I voiced my opinion that both intersubjectivity theory and motivational systems theory exist at a higher level of generality and inclusiveness than does selfobject theory, by virtue, in part, of the multidimensional nature of the former and the unidimensional quality of the latter. Intersubjectivity theory pictures personal experience as fluid, multidimensional, and exquisitely context-sensitive, with multiple dimensions of experience oscillating between foreground and background, between figure and ground, within an ongoing intersubjective system. Selfobject theory, by contrast, having originated in the study and treatment of narcissism and narcissistic pathology, primarily emphasizes the narcissistic or selfobject dimension of experience—its establishment, disruption, and repair.

As an illustration of the clinical consequences of a multidimensional versus a unidimensional theoretical perspective, consider the following quotation from *Working Intersubjectively* (Orange, Atwood, and

Stolorow, 1997), a passage highly relevant to Kindler's clinical material and the dilemmas he regularly encounters with his patient:

> It has become apparent to us . . . that the term *selfobject transference* is being used to refer to two types of relational experiences that have distinctly different origins and meanings. In one, the patient longs for the bond with the analyst to supply missing developmental experiences—what Kohut originally meant by selfobject transferences. In the other, the patient seeks responses from the analyst that would counteract invariant organizing principles that are manifestations of what we . . . call the repetitive dimension of the transference. In the former, the patient longs for something missing; in the latter, the patient seeks an antidote to something crushingly present. Making this distinction has profound implications for the framing of transference interpretations, whereas merging the two types of relational experience into an overinclusive selfobject concept obscures Kohut's clinical contribution. One's interpretive approach to a patient's wishes for mirroring, for example, will be radically different, depending on whether the patient seeks mirroring of an emerging, long-sequestered expansiveness or of a defensive grandiosity serving as an antidote to an underlying sense of defectiveness. . . . In the case of the former, mirroring experiences foster integration and developmental transformation; in the latter, addiction to the analyst's "responsiveness." It is the search for antidotes to crushing organizing principles, not for archaic selfobject functions, that leads to such clinical phenomena as addictions, sexual perversions, and aggressive, grandiose enactments [pp. 65–66].

I believe that a central, repetitive principle unconsciously organizing Joanna Churchill's experience throughout the sessions described by Kindler is her deep conviction, to phrase it evocatively, that her affective core is rotten, destructive, and utterly repugnant to other human beings. This devastating conviction materializes in the transference in every session, in the form of her constant worry—or perception—that Kindler is reacting negatively to her, is angry with her, or is distancing from her. As she herself notes toward the end of session 4, such concerns are invariably evoked when she experiences or expresses strong affect, such as angry feelings or attachment longings. For example, in session 2, during which she feels both anger and frustrated attachment need in the transference, she infers that Kindler is trying to keep her at a distance. "As I become more fluid," she says to him, referring, I believe, to her brewing emotions, "you pull back, and that makes me feel I should be more controlled." Later in that session she voices her recurring fantasy that other analysts whom she has consulted—that is, others who have been exposed to her rotten emotional core—will try to persuade Kindler to stop seeing her. The next session is pervaded by her fears that any person to whom she attaches will attack or suddenly abandon her, and she scans Kindler's face for any signs that these disasters are impending.

Sources of Joanna's crushing organizing principle can be discerned in her formative experiences with both parents. Her father is described as cruel, dominating, and physically and sexually abusive, although details are not given. "He crushed my self-confidence," she says in session 1. "He held me in contempt to protect himself. His anger and contempt was to keep himself at a distance from me. . . . Something . . . made it impossible for him to like me." Ultimately, with a little "help" from her mother, Joanna concluded that this "something" that repelled her father was within her own essence: her aggressiveness, her femaleness, her very being made her evil and dangerous to him. "I carry that feeling with me," she says in session 4, alluding to how this repetitive theme became structuralized.

Joanna's mother is portrayed as distant, unavailable, self-serving, and intrusively manipulative. With Dr. X Joanna seemed to revive early longings for a mother who took pleasure in her being, but refound instead the mother who narcissistically exploited her. Like her father, her mother made her feel evil for being angry. "She treats me as if I am like a stain on the floor," Joanna says in session 4. Clearly, her parents were a devastating one–two punch in the formation of her sense of inherent rottenness. She was left entirely alone with her painful feelings, and as she tells us, such emotional pain felt in isolation "can make us sick."

Virtually all of the concrete enactments chronicled in the case material can be viewed as manifestations of Joanna's desperate search for antidotes to the repetitive organizing principle whose nature and origins I have described. Her history of sexual involvements, her physically exposing postures and "assertive sexualization" of the relationship with Kindler, her attempts to establish bodily contact and closeness with him, either literally or symbolically via the couch—all of these can be seen as efforts, through mutual enactment, to feel desirable rather than inherently repellent, touchable rather than untouchable. The sexualization and physical enactments diminished when Kindler increased the regularity and frequency of the therapeutic sessions, because he thereby helped her to establish, however tenuously, a hope that he was not totally revolted by her being.

In place of the blatant sexualizations, Joanna and her analyst seem to have settled into a less dramatic, more comfortable pattern of mutual enactment—a ritualized dance of reassurance that they co-create at the beginning and ending of each session. Joanna asks the ritualized question, "Are you angry with me?" [read: Are you repelled by my being?], and Kindler offers the equally ritualized reassurance that he is not. Returning to my earlier remarks about the potential clinical pitfalls of selfobject theory's unidimensionality, I believe that Kindler regularly interprets Joanna's ritualistic search for antidotes as if it were an expression of selfobject need, a "need for active attuned responsiveness," as he describes it at the end of session 2, or a need "to feel close and supported" by him, as he characterizes it at the end of session 4, leaving his patient "thoughtful but doubtful." The dance of reassurance is reminiscent of Kohut's (1977) interpretation that a patient's "attempt to raise his self-esteem with the aid of his defensive promiscuity is like the attempt of a man with a wide-open gastric fistula to still his ravenous hunger by frantic eating" (p. 197). Enactments that serve antidote functions become ritualized and addictive because the underlying killer organizing principle is forever being counteracted, but never fundamentally challenged or transformed. Joanna and her analyst will dance the dance of reassurance until the cows come home, unless her unremitting sense of inherent rottenness is squarely, consistently, and repeatedly addressed.

What about Kindler's side of the intersubjective field? What organizing principle might account for his participation in the dance of reassurance? I do not know him well enough to offer anything but a generic speculation from an earlier chapter (Stolorow, 1993):

> Many people who become psychoanalysts have in their childhood histories a common element of having been required unduly to serve archaic [psychological] functions for a parent . . . , a requirement that is readily revived in reaction to patients' archaic states. . . . When empathy is equated with an ideal of [unfailing] human responsiveness and at the same time rightfully claimed to lie at the heart of the psychoanalytic process, this can exacerbate the analyst's countertransference dilemma, which takes the form of a requirement to provide the patient with an unbroken selfobject experience uncontaminated by painful repetitions of past childhood traumata—a requirement now invoked in the name of Kohut. . . . [W]hen an analyst comes under the grip of such a requirement, the quintessential psychoanalytic aim of investigating and illuminating the patient's inner experience can become significantly subverted [p. 44].

REFERENCES

Kohut, H. (1977), *The Restoration of the Self*. Madison, CT: International Universities Press.

Orange, D., Atwood, G. & Stolorow, R. (1997), *Working Intersubjectively: Contextualism in Psychoanalytic Practice*. Hillsdale, NJ: The Analytic Press.

Stolorow, R. (1993), The nature and therapeutic action of psychoanalytic interpretation. In: *The Intersubjective Perspective*, ed. R. Stolorow, G. Atwood & B. Brandchaft. Northvale, NJ: Aronson, 1994, pp. 43–55.

Chapter 17

Reply to the Three Discussions

Alan Kindler

I believe that our attempt to illustrate the three approaches to clinical material was successful and feel very pleased with the results. I experienced each of the discussants as vigorously but respectfully critical of my work with Joanna as represented in this excerpt. The thoroughness of each participant's critique spoke to the confidence that each of them felt in the value of their ideas and the safety they felt in speaking out in this context. In preparing my own comments, I have been aware of my need to avoid thinking of the process as a form of supervision. Indeed, many people in the audience seemed to be curious to know if I had been injured or pleased by the process and whether I agreed more with one of the discussants than the others. I believe that these questions were, to some extent, based on an understandable misconception of my role in the proceedings and the confusion of the panel process with supervision. I must take some responsibility for this confusion because I did refer in my introduction to my awe at the prospect of presenting my clinical material to three of my intellectual heroes, as the "mother of all supervisions."

Because of my own inclinations and those of others who were present, I believe it is worth emphasizing that this was not intended to be supervision because the discussants were there to represent their own perspectives and to use their extremely limited access to the case to demonstrate their own preferred theoretical approaches to what they were permitted to know. Their explicit goal was to inform the audience of the distinctive features and unique clinical advantages of selfobject theory (Ornstein), the intersubjective approach (Stolorow), and motivational systems theory (Fosshage). Implicit, of course, and

233

playfully accepted by all, was their natural wish to demonstrate the superiority of their approach over the other two. They had no opportunity to ask for elaboration of the clinical material, feedback on their assumptions, or more background information about the ongoing relationship between Joanna and myself. They could not ask me, the treating analyst, to elaborate or clarify what I was thinking or feeling at any time in the reported sessions and how typical or unusual this segment was. Supervision requires all of these elements expressed within a safe relationship between supervisor and supervisee (Kindler, 1998). The goals of effective supervision are the education of the supervisee and the effective treatment of the analysand, not simply the demonstration of the application of the supervisor's theory and technique to the supervisee's case.

Although we were all quite clear that this was not personal supervision of my work, all three discussants were understandably curious about my response to their comments. I understood their curiosity to be a reflection of our warm personal relationships, their identities as clinicians and supervisors, and their sensitivity to the fact that all clinical speculations require an opportunity for more information to confirm, modify, or refute them. I will take this opportunity to respond very briefly to some of their ideas about the excerpt from treatment of Joanna Churchill, bearing in mind the foregoing.

COMMENTS ABOUT FOSSHAGE'S DISCUSSION

I found Fosshage's commentary useful in several respects. He recognized accurately my "nailed to the wall" state in the second session and made some useful specific suggestions regarding my possible alternate ways of participating in the exploration of Joanna's subjectivity. For example, his simple suggestion of asking why she was angry at me, rather than focusing, as I did at the time, on her affect of uncertainty may have been more fruitful because it would have been less challenging to her. As he suggests, it would have required a more self-reflective state of mind on my part because it would have meant exposing myself to her elaboration of her anger at me, something I was obviously not ready to do. I preferred to focus on her uncertainty about her own feelings, probably as an expression of my own unrecognized shame vulnerability and an unconscious need to reverse it to protect my own self.

His use of the "other-centered" listening perspective, to complement the empathic perspective so familiar to self psychologists, seems to facilitate the analyst's efforts to regain the lost capacity for self-reflection during such difficult interchanges. This alternate listening perspective encourages the analyst to consider the impact the analysand is having on him at such times. What one does technically with the data of such a listening perspective with a patient such as Joanna is not so obvious. If I had considered Fosshage's advice at the time and thereby regained access to my own "pinned to the wall" self state, it might have been enough to allow me to recover and to participate with more animation and spontaneity. I might have been able to recognize my own shame concerns with respect to my imminent presentation to my colleagues. I might also have been able to recognize the impact on me of Joanna's sensitivity to many of my comments, triggered mainly by the tone and energy level with which they were delivered. If I was too precise and explanatory, she would experience me as dogmatic and didactic and would feel I was attacking her by insisting that she agree with my point of view. On the other hand, my tendency towards silence when I did not understand her, although thoughtful and accepting from my point of view, was nonresponsive and judgmental from her point of view and only served to confirm my angry disapproval of her.

I find that Fosshage's use of the other-centered listening perspective facilitates such understanding of the analyst's subjectivity. Had I been more familiar with it at the time, I might have been able to feel my way more effectively into her rapid shifts of mood and self states, which did, as depicted, "pin me to the wall" in a silent retreat. The conscious application of this perspective seems to offer assistance to the analyst's self-righting efforts during such disruptive exchanges.

I also agree with his analysis of Joanna's motivations and the clinically useful distinction between sexual and sensual needs and their frequent conflation with attachment needs. As he indicates, in the case of Joanna, these are in turn intertwined with aversively tinged needs for physiological regulation, combined in idiosyncratic and confusing interactive patterns. I agree also with his observation that, problematic as it seemed, the material contained evidence that she and I were in an emergent analytic process that enabled the articulation of her experiences and the progressive "disentangling of herself from these negative self feelings."

COMMENTS ABOUT ORNSTEIN'S DISCUSSION

Using the material provided and, for the purposes of this exercise, assuming that it was representative of the entire analytic process,

Ornstein demonstrates the kind of interpretive responsiveness that would correct for my failure to accept Joanna's opening gambit, a failure that he believed placed the analysis "under a cloud." He would have conveyed his acceptance of Joanna's initial offering of engagement on a sexual basis by responding interpretively to it as a manifestation of her developmentally appropriate, therefore acceptable, need for mirroring expressed as demands for sexual closeness. He then constructs a prototypic interpretation that would fully engage this central developmental need through the development of a mirroring selfobject transference. I particularly appreciated Ornstein's final interpretive example: "Could it be that both you and your previous therapists had mistaken your legitimate longing for maternal warmth, touch, and cuddling for a sexual wish?" I could not agree more with Ornstein's conceptualization of the material as he constructs it. Such an exquisitely sensitive interpretive suggestion to Joanna in those early sessions, or even at a later time, might well have facilitated a transition to the kind of stable transference configuration that Ornstein has in mind.

I do not believe that my initial understanding of Joanna was very far from that described by Ornstein. I do know that my attempts to formulate her behavior in this way were repetitively frustrated by the injuries I would inflict on her with any explanation of her behavior that departed in any way from her own immediate experience. And her immediate experience was often fragmented, contradictory and hazy. Suggestions tentatively given, comments about the meaning of her behavior as suggested by Ornstein would leave her feeling invaded and criticized. She would then become disorganized and unable to sleep or to work. In other words, the verbal content of my attempts to interpret was often overridden by her painful experience of the music and its disruptive impact on her self state.

Joanna could detect elements in my response to her, which, unknown to me at the time but expressed in my attempts to engage her in ways that were comfortable to me, drove her mad. She, in turn, I can say in retrospect, drove me slightly mad at times. I was often at a loss as to how to intervene without injuring her, often "pinned to the wall," as Fosshage depicts it. The opportunities to intervene effectively were, at times, few and far between.

It is cases like Joanna Churchill that convince me that more is needed than the categories provided by the selfobject dimension of experience, with all its complexity and subtlety so expertly demonstrated by Ornstein, to fully encompass the clinical interaction, the subjectivities of both participants, the repetitive configurations of relatedness, the disavowed subjectivities of both participants, and the dyadic systems that emerge unpredictably and inexorably in the analytic process.

COMMENTS ABOUT STOLOROW'S
DISCUSSION

I find much of interest in Stolorow's commentary, and I believe that his addition to the selfobject dimension of experience is of great value. His caveat about the risks of therapeutic stalemate associated with the gratification of Joanna's needs for reassurance is not unfamiliar. We have been concerned about this from the beginning of the self psychological revolution. The misunderstanding that the selfobject transferences were to be met by enactments that provided mirroring, idealization, twinship and so on has been an ongoing controversy in the literature, both from within self psychology (Bacal, 1985; Terman, 1988; Lindon, 1994; Shane and Shane, 1996) and from critical reviews outside of self psychology. The main objection to such provision of selfobject experience from within self psychology has been based on Kohut's emphasis on analytic cure based on optimal frustration. For Kohut (1984), the interpretation of selfobject needs, instead of their gratification, is intrinsically frustrating, and this intrinsic frustration, in the overall ambiance of empathic understanding and acceptance, is the curative element that leads to the acquisition of self structure.

Stolorow (1993), however, has moved away from the formulation of analytic cure in terms of the restoration of the defective self via the accretion of missing structure under the impact of optimal frustration. His attention to pathological structures, rather than defects, in the self, along with other critiques from within self psychology, leaves the question of provision through enactments more open to the analyst's choice or clinical judgment (Lindon, 1994; Shane and Shane, 1996).

In this shifting theoretical context, Stolorow's caveats about Joanna's needs for "antidotal experiences" require careful consideration. I was certainly not comfortable with my role in these interactions and was not unaware that the active provision of selfobject responsiveness was not likely to be of therapeutic value. The notion of antidote provision as one dimension or quality of the interactions that provide selfobject experience seems to open up new considerations in empathic understanding of patients such as Joanna. Stolorow suggests that we should now be open to the understanding of more than one kind of experiential pattern involved in the pursuit of self-strengthening responsiveness.

The traditional selfobject or developmental dimension of the transference refers to the patient's experience of the analyst as a source of responses needed, but pervasively missing, in development. In this model such unmet selfobject needs, experienced in the treatment, will lead to the new development of healthy structure resulting in a healthy self now free of the previous deficits. Such experiences will include a strengthened and expanded sense of self, and a recovery of "authentic" function, that is, abilities that feel like they belong and would have been there were it not for the "tragic" circumstances of the patient's existence. If these circumstances prevail, "addictive" demands for specific responses to sustain a continuing fragile self will not occur. Instead, the patient will describe a more flexible capacity for relatedness imbued with an exciting sense of competence triggered by the emergent awareness of new abilities. This traditional selfobject model of therapeutic progress is regarded as analogous to the process of healthy development. New structure accrues when the correct emotional environment is available.

Orange, Atwood, and Stolorow (1997) contrast this deficit model with the pathological structures existing in Joanna, structures that require her to relentlessly press, to the point of addiction, for specific responses from the analyst. They warn that these needs may be incorrectly assumed to be developmental selfobject needs. Her deeply experienced "sense of rottenness," they suggest, make Joanna continually vulnerable to crushing losses of self-organization unless she is able to elicit from the analyst a reassuring response that actively negates her relentless expectations that she is hated, held in contempt, or of no significance whatsoever. These responses do not contribute to structural change. The subjective qualities of such interactions would, I assume, include a sense of immediate relief when the urgent need for an enactment is met and the sense of self is rendered temporarily intact again. It would not include, however, the same sense of a stable acquisition of competence and of a central affective self reengaged in a genuine developmental process leading to reduced vulnerability and greater interpersonal flexibility and safety.

This dichotomizing of subjective experience seems heuristically useful but potentially empathy-distorting to me. On the one hand, it may contribute to further delineation of the varieties of relational experience hitherto assumed to be selfobject experience in the positive, that is, structure-building sense. On the other hand, it may suggest a clear-cut distinction between selfobject needs and antidotal enactments, which does not exist phenomenologically.[1] Relational experiences may include both qualities in various admixtures transacted simultaneously at different levels of communication. If we respond as if this clear-cut dichotomy is indeed so, we may be guided toward technical interventions that may not always be useful.

---

[1] As one observer commented: "[Stolorow's approach makes it seem like] we are either trying to get what we didn't get or seeking active assistance in our struggle against what we did get" (H. Tarshis, personal communication).

In the case of Joanna, Stolorow (1993) suggests that her underlying "killer organizing principle is forever being counteracted but never fundamentally challenged or transformed" (p. 6). He continues: "Joanna and her analyst will dance the dance of reassurance until the cows come home, unless her unremitting sense of inherent rottenness is squarely, consistently, and repeatedly addressed."

I assume that Stolorow and I would agree that an essential therapeutic goal in this case would include the opening up of a reflective process for Joanna so she could begin to think about her addiction, its context, its sequences, the underlying self structures that make the enactments necessary, and its generalized and repetitive effects on all her relationships. He believes that, given the clinical process to which he had access, this could never happen. He saw no evidence that her "killer" organizing principle had been "challenged or transformed." I believe that the reported material suggested that this had, in fact, happened. In the last session, Joanna wondered about her need for reassurance: "Whenever I feel like I have been really expressing myself, it enters my mind. I have to ask you if you are angry at me. I don't understand it." This indicates to me that she had begun to reflect on the repetitive experiential patterns that drove her need for active reassurance at certain moments.

While I agree with the need for attention to repetitive role enactments in the way Stolorow proposes, I am not so certain about his clear-cut prohibition and his prognostic assumptions about their existence in the clinical process. I believe that they were necessary enactments between Joanna and me at that stage of our relationship. They allowed us to keep going, to experience the repetitions and to progressively examine their meanings as they became more familiar and established safety between us. The challenge to them that Stolorow prescribes may have occurred slowly and undramatically, even as we continued to dance together "the dance of reassurance." Joanna herself began to reflect on their subjective qualities, patterns, and personal meanings. This did not stop their reemergence at times of stress, but there was a progressive lightening of our addiction to such interactions and a concomitant broadening of our self-awareness. The increased sense of familiarity with these urgent needs for specific "antidotal" responses at moments of increased intimacy and self-disclosure led to further understanding of Joanna's particular need for my stabilizing emotional availability (Orange, 1995) at these times.

CONCLUDING REMARKS

I feel honored to have been included in this seminal event in the history of self psychology. This occasion, appropriately occurring in Chicago,

was the 20th anniversary of the inauguration of the annual conferences on the Psychology of the Self. It took place 40 years after Kohut
delivered his revolutionary paper, "Introspection, Empathy and Psychoanalysis" (1959) at the 25th anniversary of the Chicago Institute
of Psychoanalysis. The comments of these outstanding clinicians will
be of enormous value as a clear record of the richness and diversity of
evolving theory at this time expressed in their three perspectives on
the clinical material.

REFERENCES

Bacal, H. A. (1985), Optimal responsiveness and the therapeutic process. In: *Progress
    in Self Psychology, Vol. 1,* ed. A. Goldberg. New York: Guilford Press, pp. 202–
    227.
Kindler, A. R. (1998), Optimal responsiveness and psychoanalytic supervision. In:
    Optimal Responsiveness: How therapists heal their patients, ed. H. A. Bacal.
    New York: Aronson, pp. 357–382.
Kohut, H. (1959), Introspection, empathy and psychoanalysis. *J. Amer. Psychoanal.
    Assn.,* 7:459–483.
———— (1984), *How Does Analysis Cure?* ed. A. Goldberg & P. Stepansky. Chi-
    cago: University of Chicago Press.
Lindon, J. (1994), Gratification and provision in psychoanalysis: Should we get rid
    of "the rule of abstinence"? *Psychoanal. Dial.,* 4:549–582.
Orange, D. (1995), Emotional availability. In: *Emotional Understanding: Studies
    in Psychoanalytic Epistemology.* New York: Guilford Press, pp. 125–140.
———— Atwood, G. & Stolorow, R. (1997), *Working Intersubjectively: Contextualism
    in Psychoanalytic Practice.* Hillsdale, NJ: The Analytic Press.
Shane, E. & Shane, M. (1996), Self psychology in search of the optimal: A consider-
    ation of optimal responsiveness; optimal provision; optimal gratification; and
    optimal restraint in the clinical situation. In: *Basic Ideas Reconsidered: Progress
    in Self Psychology. Vol. 12,* ed. A. Goldberg. Hillsdale, NJ: The Analytic Press,
    pp. 37–54.
Stolorow, R. (1993), The nature and therapeutic action of psychoanalytic interpreta-
    tion. In: *The Intersubjective Perspective,* ed. R. Stolorow, G. Atwood & B.
    Brandschaft. Northvale, NJ: Aronson, pp. 43–55.
Terman, D. M. (1988), Optimum frustration: Structuralization and the therapeutic
    process. In: *Learning from Kohut: Progress in Self Psychology, Vol. 4,* ed. A.
    Goldberg. Hillsdale, NJ: The Analytic Press, pp. 113–125.

Summation of Discussions

James M. Fisch

We have three discussions of Alan Kindler's case of Joanna Churchill by three outstanding clinicians, each of whom is identified with a specific contemporary theoretical model.

Did the three discussants differ in any substantial way regarding (1) their understanding of the central nature of the patient's psychopathology, (2) the primary clinical data that they selected in order to develop their case discussions, and (3) their recommendations for the ideal technical interventions. In my opinion, they did not. All three understood the patient's disorder as a pathologically organized self suffering from feelings of worthlessness and lack of confidence, damaged by the pathogenic early influences of both parents. They employed different evocative language to describe the problem, but they meant the same thing. They all saw the patient's seductiveness and demands for physical contact as erotization of a basic underlying need for acceptance and relational connection. They described it differently: Stolorow as an antidote to her invariant organizing principle, Fosshage as the use of sensuality to achieve affirmation of her self-worth and femininity, and Ornstein as sexualization of the wish for merger and mirroring. All three discussants saw it as imperative that the underlying motivation for the erotized behavior be discussed, which had not occurred. They all picked up on the ritualized need for reassurance as the central transference–countertransference dynamic, and all believe, as a matter of principle, that these dynamics are co-created by the dyadic pair. They alll said that bringing the reassurance ritual into the clinical dialogue, rather than through enactment, was essential to moving the treatment forward. All three discussants are self psychologists. They put the self experience of patient and analyst at the center of their field of observation, and from that vantage point they study developmental derailment and therapeutic repair.

If not in substantial ways, then were the three discussants different in any way other than style? They most certainly were, and I say, *vive la difference!* Stolorow, true to his pursuit of the most comprehensive and philosophically broad understanding, frames his discussion around the patient's sense "that her affective core is rotten, destructive, and utterly repugnant to other human beings." This is her invariant organizing principle, which dominates all her behavior in analysis. Stolorow is unwavering in his attention to this core phenomenon, pays careful attention to false "antidotes," and with his commitment to the intersubjective contextual field, is determined to understand the sources of the ritual of reassurance in both analyst and patient. His clear focus on understanding the contribution of both parties places him in an ideal position to ultimately explain the ritualized phenomena.

If Stolorow was the broadest, Fosshage was the most detailed tracker of the moment-to-moment clinical process, particularly as it affected the patient. Nobody can track like Motivation Systems theorists, coming as they do from a background of infant observation. As a small, but very special, touch, when he says to the patient, "So wearing your hat is an attempt to regulate your body temperature and protect your sinuses," I doubt that anyone else could have said that with quite the same level of acceptance and understanding. When she refers to one of the five motivational systems his response has a ring of legitimacy. Tracking the shifting motivational systems, and observing when aversiveness is deployed to deal with frustrated assertiveness, Fosshage offers a convincing explanation for the patient's defensive ritual of reassurance.

Ornstein combines the broad and the specific with his discussion of micro- and macroprocesses. His approach is anchored in the need to understand the specific configuration of the selfobject transferences. He oscillates between empathizing with analyst and patient, in answer to Fosshage's question, "I wonder what it's like to be the other in a relationship with Joanna." Ornstein offered the most explicit technical advice on dealing with the patient's sexualization analytically, rather than with behavioral control. He maintains that only his understanding of the underlying mirror transference made that possible. And he throws down the gauntlet as he challenges us to try to understand and respond effectively to this patient in a *specific* way without utilizing the selfobject concept.

Putting these differences together with my earlier impression that the three discussions were similar in substantial ways, the question of the depth of division in contemporary self psychology must remain open. There are certainly differences of terminology and emphasis which highlight different aspects of the therapeutic encounter. The practicing clinician will be the ultimate judge, over time, as to whether these are differences of substance or of style.

Chapter 18

Changing Patterns in Parenting: Comments on the Origin and Consequences of Unmodified Grandiosity

Anna Ornstein

Patterns in childrearing are intimately related to the social-cultural milieu in which family life is embedded. As the smallest social unit, it is the family that transmits the standards and values of society from one generation to the other. No wonder then that the alarming increase in violence among young children in the United States had sparked intense debates in this country regarding "family values." In these debates, many consider the demise of the nuclear family to be at the root of some of the worst mental health problems of our children.

Since it is the family that is responsible for the maintenance of the fabric of civilized society, we ought to be able to define what constitutes a family. *Webster's Dictionary* offers 22 definitions, which indicates that this simple question does not have a simple answer. Even if we had a useful definition for practical and legal purposes, from an emotional perspective, the question of what constitutes a family would be difficult to answer. This is so because in the last 40 years, drastic changes have taken place in the manner in which people congregate, live under the same roof, and share their lives. In spite of these changes, an intact nuclear family is still considered to be the ideal setting in which to raise a child. In reality, because the nuclear family (a bread-winner father, homemaker mother, and two to three children) has been relatively isolated and had little emotional support, it did not provide an ideal setting for childrearing.

From the child's perspective, a more ideal situation existed in the traditional family that best survived in the agricultural society. Children, in this preindustrial family, had a very different position from the one they occupy today. In the agricultural society where *every* member had to make a contribution to the family's survival and welfare, children were provided with a natural opportunity to develop a sense of their own value. The development of the children's self-esteem was assured because they were expected to perform certain daily chores according to their physical abilities. This may have meant carrying wood for the fire, tending to small animals, or taking grandfather for a walk. In these small but, to the family's welfare, important tasks, children had the opportunity to experience themselves as capable, competent human beings whose existence had value to the social structure in which they lived. Also, importantly, the children were not dependent exclusively on the emotional resources of their mothers and fathers; in these societies, the extended family lived nearby, consisting, at times, of several generations. Obviously, not all was well in this social setting either. In the often small physical quarters and the high level of interdependency between the generations, emotions—envy, jealousy, competition, guilt—could take on murderous proportions and many had wished for the kind of mobility that members of the industrial age families enjoy.

In today's technologically advanced society, many nuclear families are being replaced by single-parent, reconstructed, and foster families. Along with these changes in the structure of the family and at about the same time, we have been witnessing a drastic increase in teen pregnancy, drug and alcohol abuse, and child abuse and abandonment. Most destructive to child development have been situations in which secure attachment is repeatedly interfered with as young children are being moved from one foster home to another. These traumatic experiences affect development in all respects, psychological as well as neurological, creating extreme vulnerabilities in the self. The manifest symptoms related to the vulnerability may take various forms: chronically high levels of anxiety, irritability, delay in speech development, learning disability, depression, and violent temper outbursts. In these cases, the correlation between early childhood experiences and psychopathology, including violent behavior, is not difficult to establish.

However, these are not the only children therapists see because of violent and abusive behavior towards others. Over the last 10 years, I have seen children in psychotherapy with similar complaints, whose parents are anxious about their children's welfare and are heavily invested in them. Rather than suffering the consequences of neglect, abuse, or being emotionally exploited, these children appear to suffer from the consequences of being protected from experiencing frustration of any kind. The parents (frequently high-achieving professionals), in their eagerness not to thwart the development of their children's independence and autonomy, seek their opinion and approval in relation to every detail of the family's life; the children are offered a wide variety of options related to food and bedtime, regardless of their age and ability to make such decisions. As I hope to indicate, this particular parental behavior interferes with the process of idealization, resulting in a clinical picture that is not too different from those created by emotional neglect.

In previous publications, I have described various forms of parental[1] dysfunctions based on failures or partial failures in parental empathy (Ornstein, 1977, 1981; Ornstein and Ornstein, 1985). Among these dysfunctions, I had considered those to be of particular pathognomonic significance in which the child was being "used" as a selfobject for the maintenance of the parents' self-cohesion and/or self-esteem. However, in the cases I am here referring to, the children are not being "used" for the maintenance of the caretakers' self-cohesion and used only to a limited degree for the maintenance of their self-esteem. Rather, these parents' way of relating appears to be linked to their need to secure their children's love and to their anxiety that they will not be regarded by their children as "good parents."

What is the source of the parents' insecurity? What is the reason they fear the loss of their children's love—and how may this pattern in parenting be related to the industrial-technological age in which these families live today? These questions have complex answers; obviously, the various social and personal reasons have to be studied in each case, individually. However, some tentative answers can be articulated in a preliminary manner, even at this time.

The parents of young children today were raised in relatively small nuclear families, and their parents were often emotionally isolated and overwhelmed. The parents of today speak of their desire to be "better parents" than were their own parents, that is, to be more loving and emotionally available than their parents were to them. However, they

---

[1] I am using *parents* and *caretakers* interchangeably when referring to the emotional milieu created by the significant people in the child's environment. Such an environment may be limited to members of the nuclear family, or it may extend into the school or the community at large.

too are caught in the ambience of their time. The rapid economic upward mobility of the middle class and the access to higher education for women promoted the development of ambitions and ideals that created conflicts with their desire to devote their lives to raising their children. Either for economic reasons or in order to heed the call of their ambitions and ideals, today's parents enter the workforce early in their children's lives; more often than not, the children are cared for by people with whom they are in a monetary, rather than an emotional relationship.

The number of caretakers involved in the children's care creates numerous and hard to resolve conscious and unconscious conflicts for every member in this "parenting unit".[2] Manifestly, it creates a style of parenting that is characterized by material indulgences and frequent and indiscriminate praises for all of their children's activities. Indiscriminate praise is probably the most insidious in its results: the praise and exuberance that the parents exhibit at *any manifestation* of creativity or accomplishment sets up expectations in the children's minds. Disappointments in these expectations can be profound enough to create self-loathing, depression, and suicidal ideations.

Gifts and praises are "offerings"; they express an unconscious expectation that they will compensate the children for the parents' frequent physical absences and that they will secure the children's affection. The children, perceiving the need for validation and for affection, experience their parents as weak, depriving them of a developmentally crucial experience to be merged with a strong and competent caretaker.

In spite of the obvious differences between the emotional environment of children who grow up with violence and deprivation and children whose parents anxiously anticipate their every wish, the symptoms that these two groups of children develop are remarkably similar: Both groups of children are deficient in their capacity for empathic attunement and they both make use of retaliatory rage to reestablish a disturbed psychological equilibrium—the rage in these cases indicating the vulnerability of the self. Since both groups of children have difficulty adjusting to social situations that require delay and tolerance for the needs of others, they are likely to become symptomatic when they enter group situations, preschool, or kindergarten. Being deficient in

---

[2] "Parenting unit" refers to a group of people responsible for a child's care. In such a group, even when the mother and father are physically and emotionally available, they are only members of a group of people who are intimately involved in a child's life and are responsible for his/her development.

their ability to tolerate tension and moderate affect, they are quick to respond aggressively to minimal degrees of frustration. By the time a professional is consulted, the children have acquired the reputation of being "bullies," demanding of attention and readily enraged when frustrated.

IDEALIZATION AND THE TRANSFORMATION OF INFANTILE GRANDIOSITY AND OMNIPOTENCE

Kohut, similar to Freud, used concepts (such as idealization and mirroring) to describe analogous experiences that begin early in life and continue in various forms throughout development. An idealized other is an omnipotent other since his/her functions appear to alter the state of the infant's self as if by magic. While during infancy and the toddler years such experiences are primarily related to the physical strength, calmness, and power of the caretaker, later in development, caretakers and others are idealized less for their physical attributes but more because of the values, standards, and ideals that they stand for. Experientially, the two major selfobject experiences (mirroring and idealization) cannot be readily separated; their separation is a matter of emphasis. When we speak of the selfobject experience of being mirrored, the emphasis is on the *transformation* of the infantile grandiose-exhibitionistic self into a sense of pride and pleasure in who one is. Merger with the idealized caretaker, on the other hand, places the emphasis on the idealized caretaker's selfobject functions and the manner in which these become transmutedly internalized. It is important to emphasize that the "grandiose-exhibitionistic self" and the "idealized parent imago" are hypothetical psychological structures. Infantile grandiosity does not describe the children's *manifest* behavior. The arrogant and abusive behavior these children exhibit are defensive responses to an enfeebled self—enfeebled because, in the course of development, infantile grandiosity and exhibitionism had not undergone transformation into pride and pleasure in their activities. Underlying the boisterous and abusive behavior is a defective sense of self and low self-esteem.

The inability to feel merged with an idealized caretaker affects various aspects of self-development: (1) It affects the transformation of infantile grandiosity and omnipotence: the child's behavior will not be determined by phase-appropriate self-regard and self-assertion but by infantile grandiosity and exhibitionism. Because the inadequate transformation of archaic grandiosity and omnipotence also impairs the capacity to regulate affects (especially when this is co-determined by biological factors), children respond to any degree of frustration to their sense of entitlement with instantaneous expression of narcissistic rage. (2) The growing child may have to acquire and consolidate values, standards, and ideals more in relation to others than in relation to the primary caretakers. The values thus acquired may be diametrically opposed to the parents' own values and standards. (3) When the process of idealization is interfered with, mirroring experiences also become distorted; missing is the experience of being validated by an idealized other.

Early in life, the acquisition of the capacity to regulate excitation, arousal, stimulation, and tension occurs through idealization of the caretakers' physical strength. There are moments when an adult who picks up an agitated infant and holds his/her tense body firmly while speaking to him in a calm voice, can feel the tension slowly dissipating in the infant's body and can hear the desperate cry becoming a muted whimper. From the infant's perspective, these are merger experiences in which the baby temporarily "borrows" the caretaker's calmness and, with repeated experiences, will make the capacity to regulate tension, his own. Another merger experience is exemplified in situations when a toddler expresses exuberant delight in being picked up and placed on an adult's shoulders. Perched in this position, at this height, the child feels powerful, as if he/she could conquer the world. In this experience, the child is also "using" the adult as an extension of himself, but this time, the merger occurs with the adult's height and physical strength.

In the course of development, caretakers take on a "larger than life" dimension in a child's life in a variety of ways: they are experienced as all-knowing, strong, competent, and dependable; these are the experiences that provide the growing child with a sense of safety even at times when, in reality, the child is in a dangerous situation.[3]

The following clinical vignette represents a case of failed idealization in an intact family.

---

[3] Freud and Burlingham (1943) observed that children who remained in London with their parents and in their familiar surroundings had done better emotionally than children who were separated from their families and lived in the countryside during the war, in spite of the fact that the children in London had to witness the nightly bombings during the blitz. Obviously, the decisive factor here was whether or not the children were separated from their parents. However, attachment alone does not explain the almost total absence of anxiety in children who remained with their parents. Rather, I believe that idealized caretakers provide a protective shield against the child experiencing overwhelming anxiety. The shield is created by the child endowing the parents with omnipotent powers to protect them even under circumstances that, in reality, are extremely dangerous.

CLINICAL EXAMPLE

The parents of seven-year-old Robert were well intentioned people who were eager not to frustrate their son in any way and provided him with material goods as well as personal attention they themselves may not have received from their own caretakers.

Robert had a four-year-old brother, who at the time of consultation, began to have symptoms very similar to those of Robert. The father had a lucrative wholesale business. The mother had an MBA, but she has not worked since the births of the children; she stayed home to give her children the best possible start in life. Though both parents devoted every free moment of their lives to Robert, the child rarely, if ever, rewarded them with a smile—not that his parents were particularly smiling people; they appeared to endure parenting, rather than to enjoy it.

Robert was a "difficult baby," hard to comfort, easily excited. By the time he was a toddler, his parents became slaves to a strong-willed, angry and "bossy" child; his tyranny over the family had become a great deal worse at the time of his brother's birth. By then, the parents knew that the infant's life might be in danger should Robert ever be left alone with him. Robert and his parents were most distressed by the fact that the children in the neighborhood refused to play with him because he was abusive and controlling of them.

Since it was the mother who called and wanted to see me, I interviewed her first. She told me that she was at her wit's end and was afraid that, in response to the child's provocations, she might seriously hurt him. The incidents she described were truly hair-raising: when Robert did not get his way, he would call her "stupid," "a moron"; he would scream at her, saying that he wished she were dead. He also beat his mother physically; she showed me the black and blue marks on her leg and indentations that the child's teeth had left on her arm. The morning hours were nightmares because Robert refused to get up on time and would throw a temper tantrum when his mother would refuse to dress him and drive him to school. Particularly painful were incidents when he would embarrass his parents in public. In most of these, the sadistic elements of his behavior could hardly be missed.

In the initial interviews with the mother, she spent time telling me about her relationship with her own mother. She thought her mother did things for her children for her own aggrandizement; she still experiences her mother as a very insecure woman expecting gratitude and recognition for everything she does for her family. She was determined to be a "better mother" by being unselfish and making herself available to her children at all times.

Lately, she was experiencing her home as if it were her prison. All her friends are out of the home, working at various interesting jobs while she is at home, trying to "prove something." She too had a very fulfilling job before she had children. With considerable shame, she "confessed" that, when things get totally out of hand, she would lock herself into her room and would not care if the children hurt each other. During the last year, she had become depressed, feeling that she was a total failure as a mother. In previous consultations, the parents were advised to lock Robert into his room, but he is now a big boy; she cannot handle him physically. Besides, one time, when she did put him into his room, he pulled down the curtains and destroyed some of the furniture.

The father is a large, somewhat overweight man. He spoke with affection of his boys and was careful not to be critical of his wife, who, he thinks, has been "giving into" the children too much. At this time, he too was bewildered; he tried to "set limits" for the children according to the recommendations of professionals but soon realized that the measures that were recommended did not work. In fact, both parents commented that, after Robert was put into his room or otherwise separated from the family, he tended to become more sullen and more sadistic in his behavior.

The father told me about his own brother, who as a child had the reputation of being "a monster"; Robert's grandmother frequently describes Uncle Harry's behavior of being, in many ways, similar to Robert's. The grandmother herself has a "short fuse"; she too flares up quickly when feeling wronged.

Listening to this family history, I drew the conclusion that Robert's difficulty to regulate his affect, the speed and intensity with which he becomes frustrated when unable to control his environment, may well be related to having been born with a low threshold for stimulation. However, such an inborn, constitutionally determined "handicap" is not written in stone; the pliable nervous system of an infant can be modified by environmental influences. These so-called "difficult children" require caretaking that is mindful of the infant's constitutionally determined temperament and that will compensate for this by providing a low-keyed, calm environment. A child like Robert requires more than ordinary soothing and comforting in order to successfully internalize these particular selfobject functions. Robert's parents, especially the mother, were too anxious to provide such an environment.

My initial meetings with Robert were difficult, as he would frequently refuse to come. However, in the meetings that I did have with him, I could see that this was a very anxious child, vulnerable and shame-prone. At this time in his life, he also carried the heavy burden of considering himself to be "bad," the troublemaker in the family and in his neighborhood. Feeling bad about himself was poorly concealed behind an air of defensive superiority and arrogance. In his play, Robert made great efforts to control my moves and was intolerant of any suggestion I would make. On one occasion, when he ran out of my office and expected me to chase him, it was clear that he was afraid I might not come to fetch him. When I "found" him and said that I was glad I found him and he looked like he was glad also, with a tip of his head, he agreed that he wanted me to come after him. Back in my office, he went directly to the puppets and began to put on a puppet show. I was a willing and eagerly interactive audience. In response to a fight between two puppets, I suggested that the boy who started the fight looked scared and that I could imagine that it scares him too when he cannot control his anger and would hit his mother or teacher. The comment touched off a rage reaction: Robert stopped playing, threw himself into a chair, pulled his legs into his chest, and looked at me with such rage in his eyes, as if he wished to kill me. My first impulse was to move away from him. However, I realized that I was witnessing one of those moments the parents were describing to me and decided to stay close to him and said something comforting to him. At this, Robert suddenly thrust his legs out and, with great force, hit me in the chest with both feet. I took his feet into my hands and holding them so he could not hurt me, I told him he scared me; I could see that what I said made him furious. The wild look in his eyes did not disappear for a while. I also said that I could see that, when he felt reprimanded or corrected, all he could do was to strike out at the person who made him feel bad about himself. I let go of his feet as soon as I sensed his rage subsiding and he could make comfortable eye contact with me. After this episode, I thought Robert would want to leave, but instead, he suggested that we play cards. This was an activity that helped him "restore" himself since he usually won the simple games he would initiate.

[This was a fairly classical example of a "play disruption" (Erikson, 1940), a situation that may occur when the therapist fails to respond to the child within the metaphor. Obviously, had I remained within the metaphor, the puppet play could have revealed Robert's anxieties more fully. Instead, by identifying fear as the motive for the puppet's aggressive behavior and then referring to Robert who too may be scared when initiating a fight, I had exposed the very feeling the child was defending against. Though not fully aware of my mistake, I tried to recoup from the disruption by not moving away from him after he hit me in the chest. This helped in repairing the disruption and though the process had lost some ground, Robert indicated his readiness to continue our dialogue when he suggested we play some cards.]

In this brief, but emotionally loaded, interaction I witnessed the extent of this child's vulnerability and the rapid ascendency of intense rage once he felt wronged or, as in this case, exposed. I was also concerned with his self-image; thinking of himself as a "bad boy" kept perpetuating the defensively aggressive behavior. In my subsequent conversations with the parents, they told me that Robert frequently said that, because he was bad, everyone would be happier if he were dead.

I met with Robert's parents regularly. As is the case in the treatment of symptomatic children in general, I considered my first therapeutic task to be to assure that the parents do not experience me as critical of them but, rather, someone who understood their plight. Once they felt assured that I understood their disappointment in the child and in themselves, they could make contact with their sadness that they have not been able to enjoy Robert. They could also express their concern that he will grow up to be like Uncle Harry. I told them that I was glad they came for help and that I thought that Robert too could be motivated to change his relationship with them. This was hard for them to believe because Robert never apologized for his behavior.

This took us directly to the discussion of the place that rage and his abusive behavior had in the child's emotional life. Rage made the child feel—as it does everybody—momentarily powerful, but it also scared him and made him feel bad about himself: he was not only an angry, but also an unhappy, child. But, why does Robert feel so easily put down, the parents wondered, why does he not have a better image of himself? After all, they always praised him for everything he did.

I asked them to consider whether he may not have been able to make good use of their praise because his own judgment regarding his various performances may not have corresponded to theirs. Also, by having him decide what he should eat or wear, they may have, inadvertently, denied him the opportunity to look up to them as people who knew best what is good for him. Doing things for him he was able to do for himself deprived the child of developing skills that he could have been proud of; Robert, at age seven, still insisted that his mother dress him and tie his shoes. I also thought that in their eagerness to put their own lives at his service, prevented Robert from feeling respect and consideration for their needs. Obviously, now, in situations when he is expected to consider the needs and wishes of others, he does not understand why the world suddenly stopped revolving around him. It was painful, in particular for the mother, to think that her need to be "an unselfish mother" could have been part of the child's difficulties. In terms of his rage outbursts, I compared the speed and intensity of his rages to a malfunctioning thermostat and said that, very likely, Robert was born with a faulty thermostat.

These conversations with the parents had their expectable ups and downs. On the whole, they helped them consider that the aggressive, bossy behavior was secondary to Robert's feeling emotionally ill-prepared to meet the challenges of the everyday life of a 7-year-old. The father continued to think that the child ought to be made to apologize and that strict punishment eventually will "teach" him what they had failed to teach him earlier in his life. The mother, on the other hand, was better able to appreciate that only by responding to the child's *reason* for becoming so quickly enraged and not by responding to his manifest behavior alone will Robert be able to think better of himself. The mother became quite skillful in speaking to Robert in a firm voice and not withdrawing from him at times of his temper outbursts. The child's improved behavior encouraged her to continue to monitor her own rages at the child and, in spite of severe testing by Robert, to provide him with firm, but calm, responses that the child so desperately needed.

The family remained in treatment for a little over one year. At the time they terminated, Robert was not completely free of symptoms; he would still easily "lose it," but he stopped abusing his parents and younger brother. Most importantly, there was considerable improvement in his self-image; he was proud of his good grades, and he competed vigorously, but fairly, on the playground.

With progressive development, the clinical picture becomes more complicated. Twinship experiences and the internalization of idealized ideas and values attain developmental significance primarily during the elementary school years and during adolescence. Because these are the times when group affiliations provide opportunities for selfobject experiences outside of the family, children who enter the school years with poorly consolidated selves seek out groups (be these religious, political, or based on shared hostility toward adults in authority) that provide them with an opportunity to "make up" for their developmental needs. Obviously, the most dangerous are group affiliations where group cohesion is attained by shared hostility toward those who are outside of the group. When chronic narcissistic rage provides a group's cohesion, their destructive power does not only affect those outside of the group but also individual members of the group. Since these youngsters, along with poor capacity for affect regulation, also suffer from a sense of worthlessness, the propensity for destructive aggression is increased by the profound disregard for their own safety and survival.

When the internalization of values and guiding ideals are also interfered with, the combination of infantile grandiosity, poor affect control, and lack of internalized values becomes a dangerous mixture indeed. Manifestly, the difficulties related to this combination usually
peak during adolescence. However, the closer examination of adoles-
cent psychopathology is not included here. In this chapter, I only intended to draw attention to the clinical consequences of childhood
experiences in which the process of idealization is interfered with.
Such interferences may arise in relation to obvious trauma or in relation to caretakers relating to children in ways that make the child's
need to feel merged with a strong, knowledgeable, calm, and confident adult impossible.

TREATMENT RECOMMENDATION

The recommendations for treatment have to be in keeping with our
current understanding of the nature of the child's and parents' difficulties. Should the child's indiscriminate aggressive behavior be labeled
as "acting out," "limit setting" would be the most likely recommendation to correct the behavior.

Limit setting as a therapeutic measure belongs to a theory in which
psychological development was conceptualized in relation to the modification of instinctual drives, and "acting out" behavior was understood as the expression of the unsublimated, unneutralized aggressive
drive. Where "id was ego shall be" means that, in ego psychology,
limiting the expression of the instinctual drives was considered to be
fundamental for progressive development. In this theory, limit setting
in the course of development assured the transition from the pleasure
to the reality principle with all its implication for change from magical,
primary process to logical, secondary process mental functioning. In
treating conditions in which "acting out" of aggression would predominate, the recommendation of "limit setting" was in keeping with
the theory of the psychopathology.

Once the clinical picture is understood as a problem related to self-
development, specifically, to affect regulation, and the acquisition and/
or consolidation of values, standards, and ideals, then the treatment
has to be in keeping with this new understanding. However, this would
only be a theoretical consideration. More important is the frequently
made clinical observation that, rather than improving the behavior,
"limit setting" increases the child's aggressive behavior and negative
self-perception. This paradoxical response is particularly apparent when

limit setting is done by isolating the child who is in the midst of an aggressive outburst.

There are several reasons why limit setting may contribute to the further deterioration of the child's behavior. Among them is the obvious fact that it does not address the caretakers' own affects. The child's aggressive and provocative behavior creates expectable counteraggression in the caretaker; their need to retaliate can easily be disguised as "limit setting." The need to retaliate may not be manifested by harsh forms of punishment but more subtly, either in applying painful pressure to the child when attempting to hold him/her or in other, nonverbal ways. The nonverbal aspects of the caretakers' responses are crucial in these situations; much depends on the tone of voice and the firm, but accepting, manner in which a child is being held and spoken to. Stern and his team (1985) had shown convincingly that children pick up parental hesitation, anger, and ambivalence and only respond with changed behavior when the message is completely clear—when the "music" of the communication matches the verbal content. In limit setting, it is not hesitation or ambivalence but veiled hostility and rejection that enter the disciplinary measures. Isolating a child may help cool the caretaker's own rage reactions and, for this reason, may be helpful; however, as far as the child is concerned, physical isolation reinforces a negative self-image and deepens the child's depression.

Winnicott (1956), who was not a self psychologist but a therapist blessed with extraordinary empathic capacities, did not consider limit setting to be a proper therapeutic response in children with "acting out" and antisocial behavior. He considered "acting out" as a form of communication that had to be understood and responded to accordingly. I recommend that, whenever possible, the caretaker remain in close physical proximity to a child who is overwhelmed with rage and anxiety. A "faulty thermostat" can only be repaired if calming an agitated youngster is provided in the presence of "another" who now, belatedly, provides the needed, calming selfobject responses. For example, my holding Robert's feet firmly in my hands after he had hit me was a form of limit setting. However, by remaining physically close to him and continuing to talk to him in a calm voice, the child did not experience my firmness as punitive and rejecting, but calming.

As in other forms of childhood emotional problems, I recommend child-centered family treatment. In treating a young child, I rely heavily on helping the parents understand the *underlying cause* of the abusive behavior. The parents have to be helped to appreciate that the child's aggressive behavior in an attempt to regain his sense of power at times when his grandiose and omnipotent attempts to control his environment are destined to fail.

DISCUSSION AND SUMMARY

After a cursory review of the changing patterns in parenting in response to changes in the social-cultural milieu in which family life is embedded, I focused on the changes that are currently taking place in the structure of the nuclear family. I argued that violent and abusive behavior in children is not limited to overtly dysfunctional families. The pattern of parenting in these middle-class and intact families is characterized by the parents being indecisive and appearing helpless and weak, rendering them unidealizable by a young child. The case of a young child whose violent and abusive behavior towards members of his family and his peers exemplified the symptoms with which child therapists are confronted with increasing frequency.

I recommended that the treatment of these conditions ought not be restricted to setting limits to the unacceptable behavior. Rather, the underlying self-disorder has to be addressed, not only by the individual treatment of the child, but by helping the caretakers create an emotional milieu that is therapeutic. By understanding and empathically responding to the parents' confusion, anger and ambivalence when living with a child who abuses them, therapists can help them remain calm in the face of the child's provocations. A calm and firm responsiveness and a genuine appreciation of the child's anxieties, when provided over an extended period, can offer, albeit belatedly, a genuine therapeutic milieu that has to accompany the individual treatment of the child.

REFERENCES

Erikson, E. H. (1940), Studies in the interpretation of play. *Genetic Psychol. Monogr.,* 22:557–671.

Freud, A. & Burlingham, D. (1943), *War and Children.* New York: Medical War Books.

Ornstein, A. (1977), Making contact with the inner world of the child: Towards a theory of psychoanalytic psychotherapy with children. *Comprehens. Psychiat.,* 17:3–26.

———— (1981), Self-pathology in childhood: Clinical and developmental considerations. *Psychiat. Clin. N. Amer.,* 4:435–453.

———— & Ornstein, P. (1985), Parenting as a function of the adult self: A psychoanalytic developmental perspective. In: *Parental Influences: In Health and Disease,* ed. J. Anthony & G. Pollock. Boston: Little Brown and Co.

Stern, D. (1985), *The Interpersonal World of the Infant.* New York: Basic Books, pp. 181–231.

Winnicott, D. (1956), The antisocial tendency. In: *Through Pediatrics to Psychoanalysis.* New York: Basic Books, pp. 306–315.

Chapter 19

The Therapeutic Partnership: A Developmental View of Self-Psychological Treatment as Bilateral Healing

Doris Brothers
Ellen Lewinberg

Of self psychology's many transformative contributions, none has had more far-reaching clinical, theoretical, and sociocultural implications than its "decisive shift of emphasis away from a preoccupation with the pathological and toward a focus on the potentially healthy or more adaptive aspects of the personality" (Ornstein, 1980, p. 137). Elaborating on Ornstein's observation that the "new conception of health and illness" contained in Heinz Kohut's writings is fundamentally developmental, Stolorow (1980) observed that health is formulated by self psychologists "in terms of the epigenesis of self experience, the progressive transformation of archaic selfobject constellations as they evolve throughout the formative years through the requisite empathic responsiveness of caretakers to the child's changing psychological requirements" (p. 162).

We are indebted to Dr. Donna Orange for her careful reading of this chapter and her helpful suggestions.

That self psychology is essentially a developmental theory has also been compellingly argued by Marian Tolpin (1980, 1986). Reiterating Kohut's assertion that the need for selfobject experiences continues throughout life, she noted, "According to self psychology, the relationship between givens (natural endowment) and experience is a cogwheeling, spiralling interrelationship of self and selfobject. The primary connectedness of self and selfobject from birth on is taken as a point of departure in development" (1986, p. 126).

A recent paper of Tolpin's (1996) reaffirmed these ideas. Using rich case material, Tolpin demonstrated the clinical error of becoming overly involved in a hunt for pathology and missing the "forward edge," that is, the patient's search to resume development in the context of a therapeutic relationship wherein selfobject experiences are provided. In a discussion of this paper, Lewinberg (1996), drawing on infancy research, the theory of intersubjectivity (e.g., Stolorow, Brandchaft, and Atwood, 1987), the concept of self-trust (Brothers, 1995), and the work of such theorists as Suttie (1935) and Searles (1975), asserted that it is not merely the patient's development that receives a forward thrust in the course of self psychological treatment, but also the analyst's. To the extent that self psychology conceptualizes healing in terms of developmental advance, Lewinberg's assertion implies that the treatment process is essentially bilateral—a therapeutic partnership—in which the psychological well-being of both analyst and patient is enhanced during its course. This chapter is devoted to an exploration of this highly controversial notion.

First, we attempt to clarify our understanding of bilaterality from a developmental perspective. Next, we review aspects of self-psychological thinking supportive of our position, and suggest reasons that, until now, the concept of bilateral healing has been ignored, disregarded, or rejected. Finally, we provide two clinical illustrations.

BILATERAL HEALING: DEFINITIONS AND CLARIFICATIONS

Since the concept of bilateral healing is by no means self-explanatory, we must begin by elucidating our intended meaning. First, let us explain our choice of the word *healing*. According to *The Barnhardt Concise Dictionary of Etymology* (1995), the word *heal* developed from Old English *hoelen,* which meant to become whole, sound, and well. We believe this definition, which suggests moving toward a greater sense of self-cohesion and well-being, beautifully captures what Kohut (1984) meant when he spoke of cure as "the laying down of psychic structure." Such structure, according to Kohut, does not refer to any of the constituents of a mental apparatus, but to the sum total of subjectivity. This concept, he explained: "allows us to evoke, without being specific, such diverse yet defining attributes of the self as those given by our abiding experience of being a center of initiative, of being a recipient of impressions, of having cohesion in space and continuity in time, and the like" (p. 99).

As Kohut's work so persuasively demonstrates, the laying down of psychic structure occurs within the developmental context of selfobject relatedness from birth to death. Thus, we believe, healing implies a developmental progression toward an increasingly full, rich, complex, differentiated experience of self that occurs in relation to another person (or persons) whose self-experience is also undergoing developmental advance. While it may be theoretically possible for a person's psychological development to progress in the course of a relationship with another person whose development has been completely arrested, such an outcome seems highly unlikely. In other words, the self psychological concept of healing is inextricably intertwined with the concept of development, and the concept of development is fundamentally two-sided.

Second, we want to emphasize that viewing the healing process as bilateral does not necessarily mean that the selfobject needs of analyst and patient are experienced with the same degree of urgency. Nor are we suggesting that the developmental advance of both therapeutic partners will be equal or equivalent. According to *The American Heritage Dictionary of the English Language* (1980), one definition of the word *bilateral* is simply "having two sides"; bilaterality does not necessarily mean that the two sides are symmetrical or equal. Having undergone more or less successful training analyses, the self experience of analysts is likely to be relatively mature. Nevertheless, provided the analyst's selfobject needs are adequately met within a long-term, in-depth therapeutic relationship, it seems reasonable to assume that the resumption of the analyst's development is not merely possible, but likely to occur. Therefore, just as the patient's self experience stands to gain in cohesion and vitality, so does the analyst's.

Third, by developmental advance, we do not mean to imply that we endorse a view of development as proceeding in a linear fashion along lines of development or according to predetermined stages or phases. Rather, we endorse theories of development like that of Stern (1985), who posited the continuing growth and coexistence of various senses of self throughout life. In his theory one step in development does not replace the previous one. Consequently, we object to the notion of "analytic regression" when it is used to suggest that analyst and patient retrace their developmental steps as part of the healing process. We prefer to think that, under severe stress (for example, the threat of retraumatizing betrayals), either or both therapeutic partners may employ modes of experience relied upon earlier in life. When the stress is removed or alleviated, as for example, when the threat of a retraumatizing betrayal is worked through, more developmentally advanced modes may once again be employed.

Last, our concept of bilateral healing by no means holds that the analytic process is, or should be, consistently pleasurable and rewarding for the analyst. We fully acknowledge that involvement in a therapeutic relationship is likely to involve stress, conflict, and even severe psychological pain from time to time. It would be a very rare situation indeed for a patient to realize substantial gains without ever experiencing negative feelings in the treatment situation; the same, we believe, holds true for an analyst. Since the analytic process often requires that the analyst's needs for selfobject fulfillment be subordinated to the needs of the patient, the analyst may not realize any psychological benefit until the therapeutic relationship nears its conclusion. And, obviously, not every therapeutic partnership will result in healing for patient and/or analyst. Nevertheless, we believe that keeping alive the hope of feeling more whole, sound and well at the completion of the sometimes arduous therapeutic journey is equally important and beneficial for both therapeutic partners.

THE ROOTS OF BILATERALITY IN SELF PSYCHOLOGICAL THEORY

The concept of bilateral healing, that is, that a sound therapeutic relationship promotes the development of analyst as well as patient, is compatible with much existing self psychological theory. For example, it is axiomatic that Kohut's monumental discovery of selfobject experiences as essential for the development, maintenance, and restoration of cohesive selfhood pertains as profoundly to the analyst as to the patient. Similarly, analysts are not excluded from the widely accepted wisdom that psychological development is a lifelong process. Kohut (1966) observed that advancing age only ripens such fruits of transformed narcissism as creative activity, empathy, acceptance of transience, the capacity for humor, and the attaining of wisdom. And as Wolf (1979) pointed out, even a successful training analysis does not preclude the analyst's further development.

In recent years, many investigators, especially those influenced by the theory of intersubjectivity, have directed their attention to the analyst's experience of the therapeutic encounter. Sucharov (1996), for example, proposed that empathic understanding, the cornerstone of self psychological treatment, is mutual and generates selfobject experiences for both patient and analyst. A number of writers (e.g., Wolf,

1983; Brothers, 1995; Bacal and Thomson, 1996) have argued that the analyst's need to experience the patient as providing selfobject experiences is not some unfortunate manifestation of unruly countertransference; it is an aspect of every therapeutic relationship. Echoing Wolf's (1983) observation that "the analyst is in a situation very similar to that of the analysand," in that his or her selfobject needs are likely to be manifested in "selfobject countertransferences," Bacal and Thomson (1996) warn of the potential dangers that attend the analyst's failure to acknowledge his or her selfobject needs vis-à-vis the patient:

> If the analyst cannot accept the psychological legitimacy of her selfobject needs in relation to the patient, she will be affected in the same kinds of ways as the patient; her needs will intensify and she may act them out, very likely in relation to the partner who has frustrated them—her patient [p. 30].

While we agree that the therapeutic relationship should be protected from the negative consequences of an analyst's frustrated selfobject longings, we believe that accepting the legitimacy of such longings is not sufficient to maximize the healing potential of the treatment situation. To our minds, analysts must also accept as legitimate the possibility of their own developmental advancement as a direct result of experiencing their patients as meeting their selfobject needs. In certain cases, as we shall attempt to demonstrate, acceptance of the bilaterality of the therapeutic relationship on the part of the analyst may actually promote therapeutic success.

OPPOSITION TO THE CONCEPT OF BILATERAL HEALING

Few analysts would object to being told that they are likely to gain in skill and competence as a result of their experiences with their patients. Nor are they likely to quarrel with an assertion that their overall development is likely to be furthered in the course of their work. Indeed, much in the psychoanalytic literature supports such a view (see, for example, Aaron, 1974; Spielman, 1975), yet analysts have not heretofore embraced the notion that, insofar as their developmental advance constitutes healing, they, like their patients, may be healed in the course of their therapeutic relationships. Let us attempt to understand why this is so.

It is hardly surprising that traditional analysts would reject any suggestion of bilaterality; the hypothesis that the healer may also be healed by the analytic process runs counter to many of the beliefs, values, and assumptions arising out of their theory and training. Traditional theory, for example, sees a wide gulf between analysts and patients insofar as mental disorders reside solely within the patients' psyches, while analysts view themselves as opaque, "blank screens." Consequently, their self-organizations can neither affect nor be affected by the therapeutic relationship. Moreover, in traditional psychoanalysis, cure is not viewed primarily in developmental terms. Thus, the advancement of the analyst's development does not constitute evidence that healing has occurred (see Kohut, 1984, p. 95, for a review of older conceptions of cure). In addition, to the extent that bilaterality implies that analysts derive gratification from their contacts with patients, it strikes many as somehow unethical or even immoral. Here, the notion of gratification, which often disguises forbidden sexuality, is frequently confused with abuse and exploitation.

Let us not forget Ferenczi's attempt at "mutual analysis" with RN, which contributed to his fall from grace within the analytic community (Fortune, 1993) and may well have served as a warning to those tempted to conceive of analytic patients as co-healers. As Rachman (1997) observed:

> Mutual analysis was clearly Ferenczi's most controversial technique. Although he made it clear it was a time-limited clinical experiment developed to deal with an intractable resistance when standard measures were futile, critics have used his mutual analytic experience with R.N. to demonstrate Ferenczi's tendency to be a "wild analyst" [p. 405].

While the concept of bilaterality sounds obvious chords of dissonance for traditional psychoanalysts, the reasons that bilateral healing has failed to find acceptance among self psychologists, despite its harmony with many of Kohut's teachings, are less apparent. Let us now examine some of these reasons. First, clinicians who embrace self psychological theory are a widely disparate group. Some, for example, endorse the idea that a self psychological approach is enhanced by the theory of intersubjectivity, while others do not. We believe that those who oppose intersubjectivity theory are less likely to support the concept of bilateral healing. A consideration of contrasting commentaries on Thomson's (1991) chapter, "Countertransference in an Intersubjective Perspective—An Experiment" is instructive in this regard. In her commentary, Ornstein (1991), who rejects intersubjectivity theory, implicitly underscored the unilateral nature of the healing process. Criticizing Thomson's failure to attend sufficiently to emerging selfobject transferences, she called attention to the importance of the analyst's empathic immersion in the patient's inner world, which, she observed, is made possible by the analyst's efforts to "decenter" from his or her reactions. In contrast, Brandchaft's (1991) commentary on the same chapter is more congruent with a bilateral conceptualization of treatment. As one of the developers of intersubjectivity theory along with Stolorow and Atwood (see Stolorow, Brandchaft and Atwood, 1987), he predictably endorsed Thomson's "turn inward," that is, his exploration of the patients' impact on his self organization.

Brothers (1995, pp. 153–155) also commented on Thomson's countertransference experiment using a self-trust perspective. From this perspective, it becomes clear that the analysts' developmental advance may be served both by their attempts to decenter and by their willingness to turn inward. As analysts openly examine the ways in which their self-experience is affected by frustrated selfobject longings vis-à-vis their patients and identify their characteristic responses to such frustration, for example, the ways in which their trust in themselves and in others as providers of selfobject experience is changed, they are not only likely to find new ways of responding that benefit their patients, but they stand to become more whole, sound, and well in the process. Thomson's self-exploration in relation to his patients undoubtedly contributed to "the laying down of psychic structure" as he gained in wisdom, self-esteem, and greater trust in himself as an analyst. To our minds, it is not necessary for patients to participate in an examination of their analysts' experiences of selfobject failure for healing to occur as long as analysts are equally committed to turning inward and to immersing themselves empathically in their patients' experience.

Another reason that bilateral healing has been largely unrecognized by self psychologists has to do with lacunae within self psychological theory itself, specifically, its neglect of certain realms of experience, an exploration of which might have enhanced the legitimacy of this concept. These neglected realms include the need to be trusted to provide for the psychological well-being of other people and the disorders of self-experience that result from the thwarting of this need. The self psychology literature abounds with references to the patient's need for the trustworthy provision of selfobject experiences *by* others but pays little attention to the patient's need to be trusted to provide these experiences *for* others (Brothers, 1995). When mentioned at all, it is usually thought to result from some heroic effort[1] (e.g., Shane and Shane, 1989). In contrast, we believe (and much recent infancy research appears to bolster our belief) that developing capacities to provide for the psychological well-being of others involves neither

---

[1] An exception is Von Broembsen (1999), who notes that altruistic motives, expressed in caring for and contributing to the well-being of others, are manifestations of basic human strivings.

struggle nor pain. Rather, since infants come into the world equipped to provide for the psychological needs of others, these capacities are a natural, effortless product of healthy development. Furthermore, we do not equate the ability to provide for the selfobject needs of others with health or developmental advance. Consider, for example, the parentified children of alcoholics whose only hope of obtaining a modicum of predictability in their lives derived from their own trustworthy provision of selfobject experiences for others. Although many of these children develop serious self-disorders, they often retain their considerable capacity for attuned responsiveness that underlies the provision of selfobject experiences.

At this point, it is necessary to clarify our use of the concept of selfobject provision. We are convinced that, much as an analyst may wish to provide selfobject experiences for a patient, his or her attempts to do so may fail. Just as an analyst's response is empathic only to the extent that the patient perceives it as such, so the analyst's actions constitute selfobject experiences only to the extent that they result in positive changes in the patient's self-experience. Thus, a patient may not experience mirroring, despite an analyst's propensity for making affirming statements. On the other hand, an analyst who never utters a word of praise may be perceived as providing mirroring selfobject experiences. Consequently, we contend that one therapeutic partner may be said to have *provided* a selfobject experience when the other perceives this to be the case. Regardless of the partner's success or failure in providing selfobject experiences, the need to be trusted to provide them may be very strong.

On what grounds do we posit that people need to experience themselves as trusted to provide selfobject experiences for others as much as they need to trust others to provide selfobject experiences for them? First, we point to clinical examples in which the self-disorders of certain patients appear to have resulted not only from their having been deprived of selfobject experiences, but also from the thwarting of their need to be trusted as providers of selfobject experiences (see, for example, the case of James [Brothers, 1995, pp. 222–230]). Another source of evidence of the existence of this need is to be found in infancy research, which demonstrates not only that infants seem to expect to provide psychological experiences for their caretakers, but that they manifest distress when unable to do so. For example, infants invariably become distressed during the "still-face procedure" invented by Tronick et al. (1978). In this procedure, mothers who have been interacting with their infants suddenly make their faces impassive and expressionless and fix their gaze above the infants' eyes. Infants first attempt to recapture the mothers' expected responses by trying to meet their mothers' eyes and moving their bodies. When these efforts fail, they become increasingly agitated until they collapse into an attitude of withdrawal (Beebe and Stern, 1977). It is not merely that the infants have become hopeless of receiving attuned responsiveness from their mothers, they also have become hopeless about their capacity to affect their mothers. Lichtenberg (1983) makes clear that the infant becomes "the particular baby of its particular mother" through a reciprocal process in which the baby activates and alters the mother's reactions. And as Klein (1976) observed:

> An infant tends to become attached to persons who initiate interaction with him. A key factor in the attachment is the pleasure aroused in the mutuality of interaction—an interaction that seems to involve *a sensibility in the baby to the pleasure he is bringing about in the other* [p. 227, italics added].

Brothers (1995) called the dimension of trust that bears on the need to experience oneself as a trustworthy provider of selfobject experiences for others "self-as-trustworthy." The work of Beebe and Lachmann (1988a, b) and Beebe, Jaffe, and Lachmann (1994) on mutual influence support the idea that precursors of self-as-trustworthy exist in early life. "Mutual influence" refers to a process in which caretaker and infant systematically affect and are affected by the other, an important basis for the organization of self-experience. In fact, even very young infants have been shown to recognize and expect the characteristic patterns of mutual influence that develop between themselves and their caretakers. The empirical literature on caretaker–infant interaction documents mutual influence in every modality examined, including vocalization (Bennett, 1971), gaze (Stern, 1974), and general affective involvement (Tronick, Als, and Brazelton, 1977).

In order to be experienced as a trustworthy provider of the selfobject needs of others, infants should demonstrate some nascent capacity for empathy. One of the earliest indicators of this capacity is the tendency of day-old infants to become distressed when they hear another infant crying (Sagi and Hoffman, 1976). Beebe and Lachmann (1988a, b) have investigated the precursors of empathy through their focus on patterns of mutual influence in the first 6 months of life. They present data documenting the "matching of temporal and affective patterns of mother and infant" that demonstrate how the sharing of subjective states occurs. It is in the moment-to-moment mutual influence in matching and tracking the other's behavior that they find the "resonance" or "state sharing," which, in their opinion, marks the beginning of empathy. On the basis of experiencing themselves as "on the same wavelength" as their parents, infants appear to form a rudimentary expectation of providing psychological experiences for others.

Empathic caretakers do much to promote the optimal development of children's sense of themselves as trustworthy providers. They do so primarily by validating children's psychological reality and by affirming their affective expressiveness. Children who receive these "votes of confidence" are likely to experience themselves as capable of responding appropriately to the affects of others, a central feature of selfobject experience (Socarides and Stolorow, 1985).

Unfortunately, many otherwise competent caretakers fail to respond empathically to this realm of their children's self-experience, and some even deliberately stifle attempts by children to provide for their parents' psychological needs. Brothers (1995) described caretakers who misguidedly attempt to prolong their children's "carefree years" by discouraging them from carrying any of the emotional weight in the family and others who maintain fantasies of themselves as powerful providers by deriding their children's efforts at caregiving as inadequate, insufficient, unnecessary, or even inappropriate. Still other caretakers demand more than their children are capable of providing. Overburdened, such children may search for ways to avoid responding to the adults' psychological needs.

Having experienced such failures in empathic responsiveness, these children may either diminish or intensify their experience of themselves as trustworthy providers of the selfobject needs of others (see Brothers, 1995, on the bidirectionality of trust disturbance). At one extreme are those who grow up feeling reluctant ever to experience themselves as psychologically giving, while at the other are those who organize themselves exclusively around their roles as psychological benefactors (see also Miller, 1981).

Considering that the self-experience of so many analysts (including self psychologists) is weighted in the direction of providing for others rather than receiving from them, it is little wonder that they ignore or downplay evidence that relationships with patients further their own development. Acknowledging that they were helped by those in their care may disrupt highly invested selfobject fantasies of themselves as providers and produce feelings of shame and even rage. Conversely, many analysts seem all too eager to embrace suggestions that their contacts with patients might result in their own psychological pain or prove detrimental to their self-development. For example, many endorse a view of "projective identification" in which patients are thought to induce negative affects in their analysts (e.g., Kernberg, 1987). And recently, the notion of "vicarious traumatization" (Herman, 1992) of therapists who work with severely traumatized patients has gained adherents.[2]

We believe that analysts' failure to acknowledge and accept patients' efforts to provide selfobject responsiveness may actually disrupt the therapeutic relationship and impede efforts to resolve difficulties in the realm of loving and giving. There are innumerable ways in which patients' efforts to provide for their analysts' psychological well-being may be misperceived, with unfortunate consequences. For example, such efforts may be interpreted as "reaction formations" that cover hostile or envious feelings for the therapist, as maneuvers to "buy" love, or as efforts to usurp the therapist's power.

Another aspect of self psychological theory that impedes recognition of bilateral healing is Kohut's (1984) assertion that selfobject transferences arise spontaneously in the therapeutic relationship and require no active encouragement from the side of the analyst. Brothers (1995) suggested that such a view can be maintained only when the importance of trust in selfobject relationships is underestimated. She argued that analysts will not be perceived as providers of selfobject experience unless they are deemed trustworthy. Although some patients seem to make snap judgments about the analyst's trustworthiness, others do so only after prolonged periods of testing the therapeutic waters to determine if highly idiosyncratic criteria for trust have been met.

Describing the familiar clinical situation in which patients vehemently blame therapists when their condition deteriorates after an initial period of marked improvement, Kohut (1984) explained, "What happens is nothing else but the transference clicking into place. . . . The analytic situation has become the traumatic past and the therapist has become the traumatizing selfobject of early life" (p. 178). Brothers (1995) argued that patients' conditions deteriorate when the selfobject relatedness between patient and analyst is in danger of "clicking out of place." They are able to protest only in light of the fact that the treatment situation is not the traumatic past and the analyst is not the

---

[2] What Herman (1992) refers to as "vicarious traumatization," we tend to view as reactions to threats of retraumatizing betrayals of the analysts' trust within the therapeutic relationship. In other words, we do not believe that merely as a result of listening to patient's descriptions of traumas, however horrible, do therapists become subject to the dissociative alterations in self-experience typical of trauma. Rather, because treatment with severely trust-disturbed trauma survivors tends to be stormy and stressful, therapists often feel they are in imminent danger of betrayal of their trust in themselves and in their patients as providers of selfobject experience.

traumatizing betrayer. Because the therapeutic relationship was experienced as trustworthy, however briefly, patients expect their analysts to grasp the meaning of their protests and to respond in ways that will reestablish trusting therapeutic bonds. The clicking into place that Kohut described is likely to occur after patients have tested the selfobject potential of the therapeutic relationship and have found it reasonably trustworthy.

Analysts, too, continually construe events that occur between them and their patients as tests of trustworthiness. They are unlikely to experience patients as trustworthy providers of selfobject experience until much transpires to convince them that they are in little danger of retraumatizing betrayals and that their selfobject needs will be met reliably, consistently, and dependably.[3] What promotes a patient's trustworthiness for any given analyst varies according to that analyst's highly idiosyncratic criteria (see Brothers, 1995, pp. 37–38). Because of their strong bias against viewing patients as sources of emotional fulfillment, their fears of exploiting those in their care, and so on, analysts are apt to be quite mistrustful of patients as providers of selfobject experiences and, therefore, even less likely than patients to experience substantial developmental advances in brief or superficial therapeutic encounters.

PATIENT SELECTION AND THE ANALYST'S DEVELOPMENTAL STRIVINGS

The issue of patient–analyst selection has received little attention in the self psychology literature. Do analysts unconsciously select patients who are most likely to provide an opportunity for their own developmental enhancement as well as the patients'? Do patients select analysts who provide an opportunity, as Searles (1975) maintains, to give, as well as to receive, treatment? We suggest that a serious consideration of patient–analyst selection before treatment begins will greatly enhance the likelihood of therapeutic success. As our treatment cases suggest, the analyst's failure to acknowledge disappointment in the patient as co-healer can seriously impede the treatment process.

---

[3] It should be noted that just as patients may not perceive even the best-intentioned actions on the part of analysts as meeting their need for selfobject experience, so analysts do not necessarily experience mirroring when patients praise them or have their idealizing needs met by patients who achieve success or experience twinship with patients who share their values. On the other hand, even complaining, demanding, "difficult" patients may provide selfobject experiences for their analysts. For example, a patient who dares question the competence of an analyst may provide a selfobject experience for that analyst if the questioning is perceived as an indication of the patient's increased trust in the therapeutic relationship.

CLINICAL ILLUSTRATIONS OF
BILATERAL HEALING

Victor

In a concisely worded phone message, Victor, a 32-year-old married businessman indicated that he had been referred to me (DB) by Dr. A, with whom he had enjoyed a satisfying therapeutic relationship until an employment relocation forced him to terminate prematurely. Before our first meeting, I learned from Dr. A that Victor was the patient about whom he had consulted me during an impasse in the treatment. Although he had informed Victor of my helpfulness when making the referral, Victor omitted all mention of my previous involvement in his case until some time later. In any event, my hazy recollection of the consulation hardly prepared me for our first encounter.

I opened my office door to a fair-haired, slender man with intensely probing blue eyes. After a formal greeting and rather stiff handshake, Victor took what seemed an inordinate amount of time to get settled. Explaining that he had chronic back problems, he tried out all the chairs and couches in the room. He then moved the chair he finally chose to various points in the room before placing it in a spot near where I was seated. He asked my permission to remove his jacket and tie, which he did with care and then took some time to hang them in my closet. Upon ascertaining that the session would last 45 minutes, he took a small clock out of his pocket, placed it on a table nearby, and adjusted it this way and that until we could both see the time. For several minutes he stretched in his chair and swiveled his head to and fro.

"Was this some obsessive-compulsive ritual," I wondered silently to myself, "a bid for control, or an effort to master the environment?" I was so engrossed in my efforts to understand the possible meanings of his unusual behavior that I was startled when he began to speak. "I'm not at all interested in being analyzed," he said sharply. Before I could determine if he meant that he wanted psychotherapy as distinct from psychoanalysis, he explained that he would agree to form a therapeutic relationship with me only if he could feel safe with me. "In a safe relationship," he said, "one person does not assume a 'one-up' posture." In other words, he explained, one person does not presume to tell the other things about him of which he is supposedly unaware. "I grew up in a very unsafe environment," he continued, "where I was very hurt by my parents' abuse of their power and control over me. I was always told that they knew better than I about myself and that I should accept their judgments about me. Anytime I thought things or felt things they didn't want me to think or feel, I was made to suffer.

My mother wanted to use me in ways that benefitted her and not me. My father was a bigot and a bully."

"Okay," I thought to myself, "I get it. This man needs me to let him feel in charge of the therapeutic relationship. Treatment has to unfold without interpretation. Self-psychological theory will guide me. I can do this." Moreover, I felt quite drawn to Victor. I was impressed by the forcefulness of his personality, his ability to convey the central issues in his life, and his obvious intelligence. My complacency lasted all of about two minutes.

After staring intently at me for a time, Victor spoke of his wish to find a way to lead his life so that he would be free of anxiety. "How do you feel about that?" he asked. I responded that finding relief from anxiety seemed a good reason for seeking treatment. He ignored my response and repeated, "How do *you* feel about what I said? Do *you* want to free yourself from anxiety? Have *you* found a way to do that?"

Taken aback, I felt almost panicky with indecision. "If I answer honestly," I thought, "I might disrupt any of his possible idealizing needs. How can I answer until I understand the meaning of his question?" At the same time, I felt that, if I attempted to explore the meaning of his question, he might feel that I was assuming the one-up posture he warned me against. "Perhaps I should let him know that I am uncertain about the wisdom of complying with his request for an answer," I thought. "I could say that I am not clear that it would be good for his treatment if I revealed so much about myself." As my gaze met his searching eyes, I suddenly felt that it was imperative for me to answer him as directly and honestly as I could.

"I doubt that I'd know myself if I weren't somewhat anxious," I said, adding that I had not seriously considered ridding myself of all anxiety. Victor's expression suddenly relaxed, and obviously pleased by my response, he said, "Oh, that's quite different from the way I feel." He then explained that it would be very helpful if I continued to share my thoughts and feelings with him as I had just done. "If you do that, I'll feel safe with you," he said. Smiling for the first time, he indicated his wish to schedule regular appointments with me. Because of limitations of his time and finances, we agreed to meet once a week. When he asked permission to bring his own chair to my office, which he hoped to leave with me along with his clock, I felt as if I had passed an important test.

I thought of Victor frequently before our next session and with considerable anxiety. Gratuitous self-disclosure could not possibly be the right way to conduct a therapeutic relationship, I decided. Even if I no longer agreed with Freudian beliefs about neutrality and abstinance and firmly rejected the notion that the analyst must model herself after the surgeon, as Freud (1913) had urged, I tried to shape myself as a clinician in accordance with the technical principles of self psychology and intersubjectivity. Kohut, as far as I knew, never told his patients about himself. He would certainly never discuss his own anxiety with a patient. Hadn't I advised supervisees that, by addressing the meaning of their patient's questions, a la Schwaber (1984), they would find it unnecessary to answer personal questions directly? After all, Victor was paying me to help him with a painful self-disorder. How could I use time in his sessions to discuss my own experience without jeopardizing my viability as a trustworthy therapist who might come to serve his thwarted developmental needs?

The more I reflected on what had transpired during the first session, the more I resolved to find a way around self-disclosure. I said very little during the next few sessions, hoping that, through careful listening, I would resolve this thorny issue. For a time Victor seemed oblivious to my reserve. "Perhaps he just needed to know that I was willing to self-disclose," I thought with considerable relief. "Perhaps I really won't have to."

Finally, Victor addressed my silence by asking if something were bothering me. Was I feeling sad or worried? I denied having these feelings. "I'm just confused and mistrustful," I thought to myself. But still I said little. Afterwards, I noticed that Victor seemed more tense and withdrawn. He sternly criticized comments I imagined he would find empathic as pronouncements that offended him. He rejected any response that was not couched in language that clearly indicated my ownership of my own feelings. For example, when he described some problems with a fellow employee, I murmured something to the effect that the situation sounded charged and painful. Victor said my comment made him uncomfortable. "I don't need you to tell me if it was or was not painful," he said. "I'm well aware of my feelings about it. Such comments make me feel that you're trying to be the authority who knows what reactions correspond to any given situation. I don't feel safe when you do that. If you want to be helpful, tell me if you can relate to what I just described and what in your life helps you to relate to it." He roundly criticized me for not making the therapeutic relationship safe for him.

I then decided to make a concerted effort to use "I" statements in responding to him, such as,"I can understand how you feel." Victor, clearly unimpressed by these efforts, indicated that my understanding was not important to him. Still unwilling to reveal more about myself, I felt uncertain about how to communicate. Stammering and hesitant, I felt increasingly uncomfortable with him. Since Victor seemed to be in much greater distress at this point than when he began treatment,

I also felt myself in grave danger of self-betrayal. Having experienced similar reactions with other patients, I recognized the somewhat dissociated yet anxious feeling I now had in Victor's presence as the consequence of a sharp diminution of trust in myself as a competent therapist.

Finally, having reached the point of wondering if I should withdraw from the case, I realized that my strenuous efforts to avoid self-disclosure had backfired. Instead of helping to make me a more trustworthy provider of selfobject experiences for him, I had become less so. Moreover, my sense of myself as trustworthy had greatly diminished. When I finally acknowedged my misgivings about revealing myself to him, explaining that I usually tried to keep my own life out of my therapeutic relationships, Victor indicated his approval. I apologized for having made him feel unsafe and mistrustful. As if modeling for me the response he needed, Victor said he could appreciate my reluctance. He noted that he, too, often found it hard to try new ways of relating. He spoke of feeling much better and safer since I had confessed my reluctance to self-disclose.

Although delighted by his response, I nevertheless felt somewhat coerced by his unyielding insistence that I relate to him only in accordance with the manner he deemed therapeutic. In being urged to disclose my own experience, I felt pushed to relinquish a posture that had come to feel self-defining—that of a selfless healer, willing to give up my own needs in order to serve my patients. This image of myself as a therapist represented a continuation of a major childhood self-perception: the self-reliant, empathic caretaker of my parents' selfobject requirements. Despite my keen awareness that self psychologically informed analysts need not renounce their own needs for selfobject fulfillment, my training analysis had not enabled me to work through this "emotional conviction" (Orange, 1995; Orange, Atwood, and Stolorow, 1997) sufficiently.

I noticed that, when I most felt bullied by him, I would fall silent. This would invariably lead to his becoming more withdrawn, taciturn, and critical. However, when I mentioned feeling worried about not having found a mutually satisfying way to communicate with him, he seemed to relax and engage with me more openly. I realized that Victor would assume a more commanding and pushy tone with me when he felt endangered by my withdrawal. My timid experiments with greater openness, like, for example, when I shared what I believed to be innocuous memories or other thoughts about myself evoked by the material he presented, were handsomely rewarded as Victor, in turn, revealed more about himself with increasing affective force and spontaneity. It became apparent that most prominent among the selfobject experiences Victor wished me to provide was twinship, that is, an experience of essential alikeness and, perhaps even more urgently, idealized merger. He finally revealed that Dr. A had spoken highly of my efforts to get their therapeutic relationship back on track. Moreover, he had discovered, through some investigations on his own, that I had written books and was well established as a therapist. Perhaps, as he got to know me better, he suggested, I might serve as a mentor, someone who might guide him toward professional success. When he spoke of feeling touched by the lengths to which I seemed willing to go to provide him with a safe environment for exploring his inner world, I realized that one of his criteria for trusting others to provide idealized selfobject experiences was the person's willingness to allow him to dictate the parameters of relating.

As time passed, our sessions increasingly seemed to flow with an effortless give and take. I never revealed more about myself than I genuinely felt comfortable sharing with him, and he seemed content with what I offered. We often laughed together. I soon noticed that, as a result of relating to other patients with more of my newfound ease in self-disclosure, all of my therapeutic relationships seemed more pleasurable. I found my increased freedom particularly helpful in dealing with therapeutic disruptions that threatened my patients with retraumatizing betrayals, those disturbances that are usually characterized as empathic or selfobject failures. Was I imagining things, or were all of my patients becoming more relaxed and playful, I wondered. As many of them seemed to become freer in expressing their interest in me, the intensity of these therapeutic relationships seemed to deepen. Moreover, I noticed a shift in my feeling about myself as a clinician. My anxiety had noticeably subsided as I became less harshly perfectionistic in my evaluation of my therapeutic performance. In retrospect, it is apparent that experiencing Victor as providing idealizing selfobject experiences for me (I perceived him as quite special for his unique way of participating in a therapeutic relationship) had promoted my own sense of inner safety and calm. Moreover, I too enjoyed the twinship aspects of our connectedness. We were alike in our wish for an honest, open, meaningful, and unorthodox encounter.

After approximately six months of treatment, Victor described his job as becoming progressively intolerable for him insofar as it recreated the coercive conditions in which he had been raised. He felt exploited and bullied by his boss, whom he confronted on various occasions. He complained that, while his fellow workers shared his views, they had distanced themselves from him for fear that their jobs would be jeopardized if they supported his insistence on reforms. Although he wanted very much to quit, he had been unable to find another job

that required his particular expertise and fulfilled his salary requirements. As Victor became increasingly preoccupied with his unhappy
situation he filled the sessions with details of his experiences with his
boss and his coworkers. The more distressed he became, the less I
shared my experience with him. I was convinced that he needed every
minute of time in the sessions to discuss his predicament. What I disavowed at the time was my sense of disappointment and hurt at his
withdrawal of interest in my experience. And protecting myself from a
retraumatizing betrayal of my trust in myself and others, I withdrew
from affective contact with him. I could not risk discovering that what
I most dreaded about myself had been confirmed; the only basis for
trustworthy connection lay in my assuming my customary guise of
selfless healer.

When Victor, appearing alarmingly despondent, complained of sleeping and eating disturbances and what sounded like an intensification
of obsessive-compulsive symptoms, I suggested that he consult a psychiatrist for antidepressive medication. To my consternation, the medication seemed ineffective in stemming the tide of his worsening depression. Victor appeared to grow more dejected and detached. His
eyes seemed empty, and he expressed no interest in my reactions.
Our sessions once again seemed tense and uncomfortable.

One day during this period, Victor arrived with another clock. He
complained that my abruptness in ending the previous session had
made him feel that I was usurping all the power in the relationship.
Perhaps I couldn't see the face of the other clock as it was angled
between us without turning my head and squinting at it. I apologized
for my abruptness in ending the session and asked if my looking at the
clock had indicated a lack of interest in him. Victor dismissed these
conjectures as off track. At this point, I felt extremely mistrustful of
myself as a competent therapist and in him as a provider of selfobject
experiences for me. My experience of him as idealizable had all but
vanished. I wondered if his extreme sensitivity to loss of control; his
odd behaviors, such as bringing two clocks to sessions; and his depression had set his boss and the other employees against him. In the
hope of clarifying the picture, I asked questions about some negative
comments his boss had made about him in an evaluation. After several moments in which he clearly seemed to wrestle with his feelings,
Victor erupted in anger. "I have no intention of answering this inquisi-
tion," he said. "I don't think there's any point in my coming here
anymore. You're doing everything you can to put me in danger."

Stunned by his uncharacteristic outburst, I asked him to explain
how I was endangering him. "You know full well," he countered. Per-
plexed, I protested that I did not. "You've stopped sharing with me,"

he said, looking like a hurt child. "Haven't you ever been in danger of being fired? Isn't there anything you've experienced in your life that could help you understand what I'm going through? I think you're like all the other people I've tried to look up to. They judge and look down and hypocritically say, 'Oh, I understand you, you poor thing. But I am far above you.' Am I destined to go through life feeling like a freak or a monster no one can trust?"

Acknowledging that I had indeed stopped sharing with him, I let Victor know that his concern over his situation had thrown me back into an old way of relating therapeutically that felt safer for me. I also accepted responsibility for contributing to his sense of being untrustworthy. I then revealed some past situations in my life that corresponded to his. As I spoke, Victor's expression gradually softened. "Thank you," he said. "I was so worried that you thought the mess at work was all my fault. I'm so relieved."

A short time later, Victor found a new job in which he felt treated with greater fairness and respect. Very soon, his depression evaporated and he stopped taking antidepressant medication. Our exploration of the meanings of this disruption in the therapeutic relationship set the stage not only for the reconstruction of past betrayals in Victor's life that deepened our understanding of his restorative efforts, but also paved the way for the enrichment of what continues to be an increasingly trustworthy and, therefore, mutually healing therapeutic partnership. I have little doubt that my relationship with Victor contributed to my becoming more whole, sound, and well. I have felt less obliged to maintain my "selfless healer" posture and much freer to be fully myself in my work.

Monica

Monica came to see me 10 years ago, complaining of difficulty in leaving home to go to a university in a town 3 hours away. She struck me (EL) as a very obsessional and depressed late-adolescent girl. After treating her during that summer, I referred her to a colleague in the university town. I saw her during the next three summers until she graduated, at which time she returned to the city and we resumed treatment on a full-time basis.

Monica often seemed to be on the verge of total disintegration. She would cry for entire sessions without seeming to notice that her nose was dripping onto her clothes. Her obsessional symptoms were all but incapacitating: Terrified of becoming contaminated by the outside world, she would leave her "outside clothes" in the lobby so that the rest of her apartment would be "safe"; she was unable to change her hairstyle lest her hair get contaminated; and she washed her hands constantly. Moreover, she had only one friend. She reported having lost all her friends in grade 12 because of what they deemed her moralistic and judgmental attitudes, like, for example, when she adamantly insisted that it was wrong to have sex before marriage. Even a teacher she had befriended during grade 13 had gradually pulled away. This was a source of great anguish for Monica because she had no idea why it had happened. Even though she seemed to alienate and estrange others, Monica was also exquisitely sensitive to slights from other people. While claiming to work very hard at being "a good person," she often felt unliked and unappreciated.

Although my colleague had mentioned Monica's repeated outbursts of ferocious rage, I had never experienced any until we resumed full-time therapy. I soon discovered that, if she were not extremely depressed and on the verge of disintegration, she would be furiously angry. She often described waking up in a rage, thinking of either her father or work, and then going to work in "a bad mood" that she found almost impossible to shake.

Looking back, it seems apparent that, from the moment Monica first showed her rage to me, severe difficulties wracked our relationship. For most of my life, I too had struggled with anger, especially when it arose in the context of my most intimate relationships. I would often tolerate behavior that angered me for far too long before suddenly exploding. During my own analysis, I had come to understand how my behavior closely replicated my mother's—her long-suffering silences were invariably followed by explosive rages. Despite my having gained somewhat greater control of my own angry outbursts since the end of my analysis, the issues underlying them had not been completely worked through; I would still blow up.

I experienced Monica's anger as coming at me in great waves that threatened to destroy me. Overwhelmed by a sense of imminent destruction, I would fall silent, unable to think, much less speak. My failure to respond seemed to escalate Monica's rage, and she would scream, "You *have* to say something." I would eventually come up with something that sounded lame to my own ears, like, "I can see that you're very angry; something must have happened in our last session that upset you." This would enrage her even further. "You think you're so important, nothing else matters," she would snarl, insisting that her anger was meant not for me but for her father or boss or some other person in her world. Neither of us would be able to think of what might have happened between us, and she would leave completely dissatisfied and still enraged. This would last for a number of weeks, ending only when another crisis in her life eclipsed her rage at me.

Gradually, it dawned on me that my feelings of imminent catastrophe in the face of Monica's anger replicated my childhood response to my mother's rages. As a child, I would withdraw into silence, just as I did with Monica. After realizing that my silence did nothing to protect me with Monica and certainly did not help her, I decided to share my experience with her. I explained that when she screamed at me, I would feel rattled, unable to think. Feeling useless to her, I would retreat. Unfortunately, this only intensified her rage. "What am I paying you for if you can't help me?" she asked. She insisted that, if she could not express the full extent of her rage (which had included threatening to throw me against the wall, putting her fist through my wall, and kicking things in the office), I would not be able understand what she lived with every day.

After a number of months of repeated alternations of her rage-depression cycle, we discovered that her rages helped her to feel more organized and cohesive. My understanding of the self-restorative function of her rage helped me to respond differently. I found myself more willing to stay beside Monica as she exploded in anger. I would then convey my understanding that her rages arose in the context of painful experiences that had made her feel helpless and vulnerable. At first, Monica met my explanations with surprised silence. Then, she would grow calmer and discuss what had upset her in greater depth. Frequently, when she returned for the following session, she would confess that, on reflection, my way of understanding her rage had made a lot of sense to her.

On several occasions, however, I felt angry at Monica and found myself saying things that were not helpful. Distressed by the the degree to which my disruptive remarks seemed to escape my lips unbidden, I suddenly realized that I had failed to stay beside Monica out of fear that, like hers, my anger would also get out of control. I dreaded discovering that I had hurt her in anger as I had hurt others close to me. As I gradually convinced myself that, through greater awareness of my feelings, I could refrain from saying hurtful things, the situation between us improved considerably. Moreover, Monica seemed pleased by my newfound strength in dealing with her when she was most out of control.

In one session during this period, Monica discussed her need to find another managerial position in light of the extreme stress she experienced in her current job. Despondently, she confessed that she could not imagine applying elsewhere. People would not take her seriously, she complained, because her hairstyle made her look too young. I said that, when she had her hair trimmed, as she now did whenever it was needed, it would look crisp and lovely. That evening, she left an angry telephone message saying it was my fault that she had messed up an important presentation. I called back immediately asking how I had upset her. Her return message was cryptic: "My hair." I then realized that my comment about having her hair trimmed had convinced her I thought it looked bad during the session. Although I called again to apologize and assure her that I thought her hair looked fine, she did not return for three sessions. Fortunately, we had progressed to the point of being able to discuss the disruptions between us. We established that, in her rage, she had felt like killing me and had stayed away to protect me from her destructiveness.

As we spoke, I felt flooded by memories of myself as a child faced with my rageful mother. I realized that I too had feared my own destructiveness as much as I feared being destroyed. Clearly, the difficulties in our relationship were the result of this intersubjective conjunction (Atwood and Stolorow, 1984). It is hardly surprising that, after recognizing this connection, I no longer felt myself endangered by Monica's rage. And, even more importantly, I discovered that, as my reactions to Monica's rage changed, my reactions to my own ragefulness also changed. I found new and creative ways of responding to her that helped diminish the rage–depression cycle (although she still organizes herself through being angry). I also found new ways to respond in my life generally, both when I became angry and when others were angry with me.

In thinking about what produced the remarkable changes for both of us, I believe Monica's steadfastness is the most significant factor. My mother frequently abandoned me to the care of nannies or sent me off to live with my great aunt, and this reinforced my fear that my retaliatory anger was too dangerous for her. Consequently, I learned early in life that only the "other" person can be angry. My mother expressed the anger I disavowed for fear of its destructiveness. Consequently, I came to experience her as providing alterego selfobject experiences for me (Brothers, 1993). Monica reactivated this early selfobject experience. Although she often threatened to leave therapy, she never did. In contrast to my mother, she remained faithful despite my anger at her. Consequently, I came to experience my anger as less destructive and uncontrollable than I had feared. Thus, my therapeutic relationship with Monica promoted the integration of this previously disavowed, but vital, aspect of myself. Since other relationships had inadvertently reinforced my childhood disavowal of anger, I now felt more whole, sound, and well than I ever imagined possible.

SUMMARY AND CONCLUSIONS

Arguing that self psychological treatment promotes the psychological well-being of the analyst as well as the patient, we have attempted to explore factors that may have impeded recognition of the validity of our claim. Among these factors are lacunae within self psychological theory pertaining to the patient's need to be trusted to provide selfobject experiences for the analyst. Our clinical examples attempt to demonstrate that, as both partners gain trust in each other as provider and recipient of selfobject experiences, development for each is likely to advance.

As our cases hopefully make clear, we do not consider the therapist's self-disclosure a *sine qua non* of bilateral healing. In one case, the therapist's open revelations about her own experience were deemed essential to the patient's sense of safety, while in the other, the therapist's efforts to share her experience intensified the patient's mistrust.

Much therapy-outcome research finds that therapy by experienced clinicians, regardless of theoretical orientation, is likely to produce successful outcomes (Conrad Lecomte, personal communication). We suggest that these findings may reflect the enhanced self-development of experienced clinicians who have participated in many mutually healing therapeutic relationships.

We are also mindful of the potential for harm that resides in any therapeutic relationship when events threaten either partner with retraumatizing betrayals of trust. However, we believe that, to the extent that the maximization of therapeutic trustworthiness guides the therapeutic process, the analyst's needs for development enhancement will not eclipse those of the patient. Moreover, we are convinced that the analyst's failure to recognize the patient's role in enhancing his or her development is as likely to prove deleterious as the analyst's exploitation of the therapeutic relationship for his or her own advantage. We view thorough training and skillful supervision as the best assurance of bilateral healing.

REFERENCES

Aaron, R. (1974), The analyst's emotional life during work. *J. Amer. Psychoanal. Assn.*, 22:160–169.

The American Heritage Dictionary of the English Language. (1980), New College Edition. Boston: Houghton-Mifflin.

Atwood, G. E. & Stolorow, R. D. (1984), *Structures of Subjectivity: Explorations in Psychoanalytic Phenomenology.* Hillsdale, NJ: The Analytic Press.

Bacal, H. A. & Thomson, P. G. (1996), The psychoanalyst's selfobject needs and the effect of their frustration on the treatment: A new view of countertransference. In: *Basic Ideas Reconsidered: Progress in Self Psychology, Vol. 12*, ed. A. Goldberg. Hillsdale, NJ: The Analytic Press, pp. 17–35.

The Barnhardt Concise Dictionary of Etymology. (1995), New York: Harper Collins.

Beebe, B., Jaffe, J. & Lachmann, F. M. (1994), A dyadic systems model of mother-infant regulation: Implications for the origins of representations and therapeutic action. *Psychol. Psychoan.*, 14:27–33.

———— & Lachmann, F. M. (1988a), Mother-infant mutual influence and precursors of psychic structure. In: *Frontiers in Self Psychology: Progress in Self Psychology, Vol. 3*, ed. A. Goldberg. Hillsdale, NJ: The Analytic Press, pp. 3–25.

———— (1988b), The contribution of mother-infant mutual influence to the origins of self and object representation. *Psychoanal. Psychol.*, 5:305–338.

———— & Stern, D. N. (1977), Engagement- disengagement and early object experiences. In: *Communicative Structures and Psychic Structures*, ed. M. Freedman & S. Grand. New York: Plenum Press, pp. 35–55.

Bennett S. (1971), Infant-caretaker interactions. *J. Amer. Acad. Child Psychiatry*, 10:321–35.

Brandchaft, B. (1991), Countertransference in the analytic process. In: *The Evolution of Self Psychology: Progress in Self Psychology, Vol. 7*, ed. A. Goldberg. Hillsdale, NJ: The Analytic Press, pp. 99–105.

Brothers, D. (1993), The search for the hidden self: A fresh look at alter ego transferences. In: *The Widening Scope of Self Psychology: Progress in Self Psychology Vol. 9*, ed. A. Goldberg. Hillsdale, NJ: The Analytic Press, pp. 191–208.

———— (1995), *Falling Backwards: An Exploration of Trust and Self-Experience*. New York: Norton.

Fortune, C. (1993), The case of "RN": Sándor Ferenczi's radical experiment in psychoanalysis. In: *The Legacy of Sándor Ferenczi*, ed. L. Aron & A. Harris. Hillsdale, NJ: The Analytic Press, pp. 101–120.

Freud, S. (1913), On beginning the treatment (Further recommendations on the technique of psycho-analysis: I). *Standard Edition*, 12:123–144. New York: Norton, 1959.

Herman, J. L. (1992), *Trauma and Recovery*. New York: Basic Books.

Kernberg, O. F. (1987), Projection and projective identification: Developmental and clinical aspects. In: *Projection, Identification, Projective Identification*, ed. J. Sandler. New York: International Universities Press, pp. 93–115.

Klein, G. S. (1976), *Psychoanalytic Theory: An Exploration of Essentials*. New York: International Universities Press.

Kohut, H. (1966), Forms and transformations of narcissism. In: *The Search for the Self, Vol. 1*, ed. P. Ornstein, New York: International Universities Press, 1978, pp. 427–460.

———— (1984), *How Does Analysis Cure?* ed. A. Goldberg & P. Stepansky. Chicago: University of Chicago Press.

Lewinberg, E. (1996), Discussion of "Strivings of the healthy self: The psychoanalysis of normal development—selfobject transferences" by M. Tolpin. Presented at the Toronto Child Psychotherapy Conference, November.

Lichtenberg, J. D. (1983), *Psychoanalysis and Infant Research*. Hillsdale, NJ: The Analytic Press.

Miller, A. (1981), *Prisoners of Childhood*, trans. R. Ward. New York: Basic Books.

Orange, D. M. (1995), *Emotional Understanding: Studies in Psychoanalytic Epistemology*. New York: Guilford.

———— Atwood, G. E. & Stolorow, R. D. (1997), *Working Intersubjectively: Contextualism in Psychoanalytic Practice*. Hillsdale, NJ: The Analytic Press.

Ornstein, A. (1991), Selfobject transferences, intersubjectivity, and countertransference. In: *The Evolution of Self Psychology: Progress in Self Psychology Vol. 7*, ed. A. Goldberg. Hillsdale, NJ: The Analytic Press, pp. 93–99.

Ornstein. P. (1980), Self psychology and the concept of health. In: *Advances in Self Psychology*, ed. A. Goldberg. New York: International Universities Press, pp. 137–160.

Rachman, A. W. (1997), *Sándor Ferenczi: The Psychotherapy of Tenderness and Passion*. Northvale, NJ: Aronson.

Sagi, A. & Hoffman, M. L. (1976), Empathic distress in newborns. *Develop. Psychol.*, 12:175–176.

Schwaber, E. (1984), Empathy: A mode of analytic listening. In: *Empathy II*. ed. J. Lichtenberg, M. Bornstein, & D. Silver. Hillsdale, NJ: The Analytic Press, pp. 143–172.

Searles, H. (1975), The patient as therapist to his analyst. In: *Tactics and Techniques in Psychoanalytic Therapy, Vol. 2*, ed. P. L. Giovacchini. New York: Aronson, pp. 95–151.

Shane, M. & Shane, E. (1989), The struggle for otherhood: Implications for development in adulthood. *Psychoanal. Inq.*, 9:463–482.

Socarides, D. & Stolorow, R. D. (1985), Affects and selfobjects. *The Annual of Psychoanalysis*, 12/13:105–119. Madison, CT: International Universities Press.

Spielman, P. M. (1975), Twelve therapists: How they live and actualize themselves. *Internat. J. Psycho-Anal.*, 15:18–21.

Stern, D. N. (1974), Mother and infant at play: The dyadic interaction involving facial, vocal, and gaze behaviors. In: *The Effect of the Infant on its Caregiver*, ed. M. Lewis & L. A. Rosenblum. New York: Wiley, pp. 187–213.

———— (1985), *The Interpersonal World of the Child: A View From Psychoanalysis and Developmental Theory*. New York: Basic Books.

Stolorow, R. D. (1980), Discussion of "Self psychology and the concept of health." In: *Advances in Self Psychology*, ed. A. Goldberg. New York: International Universities Press, pp. 161–166.

Stolorow, R. D., Brandchaft, B., & Atwood, G. E. (1987), *Psychoanalytic Treatment: An Intersubjective Approach*. Hillsdale, NJ: The Analytic Press.

Sucharov, M. (1996), Listening to the Empathic Dance: A Rediscovery of the Therapist's Subjectivity. Presented at the 19th Annual Conference of the Psychology of the Self, Washington, D.C., October.

Suttie, I. D. (1935), *The Origins of Love and Hate*, rev. ed. London: Free Association Books, 1988.

Thomson, P. (1991), Countertransference in an intersubjective perspective-an experiment. In: *The Evolution of Self Psychology: Progress in Self Psychology, Vol. 7*, ed. A. Goldberg. Hillsdale, NJ: The Analytic Press, pp. 75–92.

Tolpin, M. (1980), Discussion of "Psychoanalytic developmental theories of the self: An integration" by M. Shane and E. Shane. In: *Advances in Self Psychology*, ed. A. Goldberg. New York: International Universities Press, pp. 47–68.

———— (1986), The self and its selfobjects: A different baby. In: *Progress in Self Psychology, Vol. 2*, ed. A. Goldberg. New York: Guilford, pp. 115–128.

——— (1996), Strivings of the healthy self: The psychoanalysis of normal development—selfobject transferences. Presented at the Toronto Child Psychotherapy Conference, November.

Tronick, E., Als, H., Adamson, L., Wise, S. & Brazelton, T. B. (1978), The infant's response to intrapment between contradictory messages in face-to-face interaction. *J. Child Psychiat.*, 17:1–13.

——— Als, H. & Brazelton, B. (1977), The infant's capacity to regulate mutuality in face to face interaction. *J. Commun.*, 27: 74–80.

Von Broembsen, F. (1999), *The Sovereign Self.* New York: Aronson.

Wolf, E. (1979),Transference and countertransference in the analysis of disorderes of the self. *Contemp. Psychoanal.*, 15:577–594.

——— (1983), Empathy and countertransference. In: *The Future of Psychoanalysis,* ed. A. Goldberg. New York: International Universities Press, pp. 309–326.

V
Affects

Affects and Affect Consciousness: A Psychotherapy Model Integrating Silvan Tomkins's Affect- and Script Theory Within the Framework of Self Psychology

Jon T. Monsen
Kirsti Monsen

One of the main hallmarks of self psychology, both in theories of development and in psychotherapy theory, is its focus on the critical importance of affect. Kohut's (1971, 1977) conceptualizations of selfobject functions and the method of sustained empathic inquiry underline the affective dimension of self-experience. Kohut viewed the integration of affect states as central to the development of self-regulatory capacities and to the structuralization of self-experience. Several authors have later made important contributions to the field of affect

This work was supported by grants from the Norwegian Research Council, Medicine and Health; The Norwegian Council for Mental Health/Norwegian Foundation for Health & Rehabilitation; and the Department of Psychology, University of Oslo.

theory and self psychology, such as Basch (1983), Stolorow, Brandchaft, and Atwood (1987), Stolorow and Atwood (1992), Lichtenberg (1989), Lichtenberg, Lachmann, and Fosshage (1992, 1996), and Stern (1985), just to mention a few of those who have inspired us in our work on integrating affect theory and theory of psychotherapy. Many of these authors, however, owe much to professor Silvan Tomkins and his advanced affect- and script theory.

AFFECTS AND AFFECT CONSCIOUSNESS

The affect consciousness (AC) concept was developed in 1983 as a part of the Tøyen study, a naturalistic outcome study with 25 personality disordered patients (Monsen, Melgård, and Ødegård, 1986; Monsen, Ødegård, and Melgård, 1989). The AC treatment model was later revised and recently tested in a controlled study with 40 chronic pain patients (Monsen and Monsen, 1998). In this chapter we will present the revised AC model, which represents an integration of Silvan Tomkins's affect- and script theory and contemporary self psychology. We will also present abstracts of the results from the first two empirical studies of this model.

The AC concept describes the mutual relationship between activation of basic affects and the individual's capacity to consciously perceive, reflect on and express these affect experiences. AC is defined and operationalized as degrees of awareness, tolerance, nonverbal expression, and conceptual expression of the nine specific affects listed in Figure 1.

A semistructured affect consciousness interview (ACI) and separate affect consciousness scales (ACS) were developed to assess these aspects of affect integration (Monsen et al., 1996). Our clinical hypoth-

Figure 1. Degree of Affect Consciousness: Scoring Form

Specific Affects	Experiencing Ability		Expressiveness	
	Awareness	Tolerance	Emotional	Conceptual
1. Interest/Excitement	1 2 3 4 5	1 2 3 4 5	1 2 3 4 5	1 2 3 4 5
2. Enjoyment/Joy	1 2 3 4 5	1 2 3 4 5	1 2 3 4 5	1 2 3 4 5
3. Fear/Panic	1 2 3 4 5	1 2 3 4 5	1 2 3 4 5	1 2 3 4 5
4. Anger/Rage	1 2 3 4 5	1 2 3 4 5	1 2 3 4 5	1 2 3 4 5
5. Humiliation/Shame	1 2 3 4 5	1 2 3 4 5	1 2 3 4 5	1 2 3 4 5
6. Sadness/Despair	1 2 3 4 5	1 2 3 4 5	1 2 3 4 5	1 2 3 4 5
7. Envy/Jealousy	1 2 3 4 5	1 2 3 4 5	1 2 3 4 5	1 2 3 4 5
8. Guilt/Remorse	1 2 3 4 5	1 2 3 4 5	1 2 3 4 5	1 2 3 4 5
9. Tenderness/Devotion	1 2 3 4 5	1 2 3 4 5	1 2 3 4 5	1 2 3 4 5

esis was that a generally low level of affect consciousness would imply a disturbance of the adaptive functions of affects in the organization of self-experience. This also includes the capacity to represent oneself interpersonally, because:

— The capacity to use affects as signals and as conveyers of meaningful information is deficient.
— Motives for actions are vague (both regarding one's own and other person's actions).
— Self-boundary formation, which implies reduced capacity to form mutual relationships, is deficient.
— Contact with a basic sense of self is lost.
— Ambitions are curbed and the pursuit of goals is thwarted.
— Reorganization of cognitive structures like central images, fixed belief-systems or rigid systems, of expectations are more difficult.

Conversely, a high degree of affect consciousness should imply that activation of affects will serve adaptive purposes and should accordingly be associated with generally sound levels of mental health.

The ACI was originally intended as a diagnostic tool, but the experience using this interview made us change our psychotherapy model as well. Let us first illustrate how we explored each of the nine affects. The ACI proceeds following the structure of the AC-scoring form shown in Figure 1. After a short introduction, the interviewer starts exploring the first of the nine affects asking the patient: "What can make you feel interested or excited?" The patient then usually starts picturing a scene. The interviewer adapts further questions and clarifies or confirms comments according to the patient's answers and attitudes. In order to obtain scorable answers during the exploration of awareness, tolerance, emotional, and conceptual expression, the interviewer uses certain standardized questions. Some examples follow.

Typical questions in exploring awareness signals and attitudes are: "How do you know that you are/feel . . . (name of affect, A1–9)?" "When you are (A1–9) how do you sense (recognize, notice) it?"

To explore tolerance: "When you are (A1–9) how does this feeling affect you; what can this feeling do to you?" "When you notice that you are (A1–9) what do you do about this feeling?" "Do you believe that this feeling can tell you something?"

To explore emotional expression: "What do you feel about showing others that you are (A1–9)?" "How do you think you show it?"

To explore conceptual expression: "How do you feel about telling others that you are (A1–9)?" "How do you typically tell others that you are (A1–9)?"

The severely disturbed patients in the Tøyen study seemed to be more involved in the dialogue during these videotaped interviews compared to the therapy sessions. They were clearly more focused and seemed to get better access to associations and connected scenes. To us, it seemed as if the consistent exploration of affect experience also had a vitalizing effect.

TOMKINS'S AFFECT- AND SCRIPT THEORY

According to Tomkins' affect- and script theory (1962, 1963, 1979, 1991, 1992), the affect system serves several functions that explain the vitalizing reactions to the interview and that, in terms of self psychology, makes affects central to the organization of self-experience. Tomkins postulated that the affect system is a prime motivating force, and the main explanation for this lies in the notion of affect as amplification. Affect, he believed, amplifies and extends the duration of any impact of whatever triggers the affect:

> Affect amplifies the source which activates them and thus makes things urgent. Without its amplification, nothing else matters—and with its amplification, anything else can matter. It combines urgency and generality. It lends its power to memory, to perception, to thought, and to action no less than to the drives [Tomkins, 1979, p. 202].

And further:

> By being immediately activated and thereby co-assembled with its activator, affect either makes good things better or bad things worse, by conjointly simulating its activator and its profile of neural firing and by adding a special analogic quality which is intensely rewarding or punishing [Tomkins, 1992, p. 8].

A very important modification of his original theory of affect as amplification was made when he discovered that affect amplifies not only its own activator, but also the response to that activator and to the affect itself. Inherent in the affect system, he believed, is a tendency to connect stimulus, affect, and response, an attribute he called "the fusion power of affects." Different experiential modalities and experiences in rapid succession fuse with the continuing affect. Like a "psychic glue" (Tomkins, 1992) affect has the power to bind ideas and sensorimotor information and functions as a unifying core behind these different modalities and sequences of experience. This connection is not learned; it arises simply from the overlap in time of the affect with what precedes and follows it.

According to Tomkins's script theory, affects are basically organized as scenes and scripts. A scene, the basic unit of analysis, is defined as a happening with a perceived beginning and end, including at least one affect and at least one object of that affect. In its fuller form the scenes become organized wholes that include people, places, time, events, bodily experiences, and more. The perception of a scene involves a partitioning of the scene into figure and ground. Differentiation of a scene involves shifting from one figure to another aspect of the same scene, which then becomes figural. Scenes may become compressed and perceived as habitual skills, which may give an informational advantage. Very small alternative samplings tell individuals all they think they then want to know about a repeated scene (Tomkins, 1995, p. 327). However, this information advantage may of course also turn into a disadvantage, like when an individual decontextualizes and generalizes its validity in different forms of transference. But, "It is only when a set of such scenes is co-assembled, thought about, and used as a base for designing strategies . . . for increasing or decreasing and/or changing the response to that family of scenes that we have a script and its magnification" (p. 322). The term *magnification* refers to the interconnection of affect-laden or amplified scenes, a process that gives structure and meaning to our experiences.

A script refers to the underlying principles for organizing scenes, that is, a compressed set of rules the individual forms in order to predict, interpret, respond to, and control families of magnified and co-assembled scenes. It reflects our attempt to maximize the order inherent in new information in a way that is consistent with prior knowledge. The main distinction between scenes and scripts is that scenes represent information of what happens, while scripts represent information of what to do with or in scenes. These two levels of affect organization are continually and inherently connected. Lived experiences are the initial basis of script formation, but later they become partially stabilized as invariant organizing principles that will shape our perception, self-experience, and interpersonal behavior in certain patterns. The organization of affects in scenes and scripts will therefore function as guiding principles for affect experiences and coping strategies. These basic organizing activities start to develop even before a child has acquired the capacity of forming symbolic representations and the use of language.

Nuclear Scripts

The numbers and varieties of scripts are an important part of the self. Some scripts clearly seem to be more central than others. A healthy self is dependent on a set of adaptive scripts that maintain the innately present vigor of the nuclear self (Kohut, 1984). Tomkins's use of the term *nuclear scripts* refers, however, to some central organizing principles that capture the most urgent, unsolvable problems of an individual:

> Nuclear scripts matter more than anything else, they never stop seizing the individual. They are the good scenes we can never totally or permanently achieve or possess. . . . If they punish us with deep negative affect, we can never entirely avoid, escape nor renounce the attempt to master or revenge ourselves upon them despite much punishment. . . . These nuclear scenes and script are relatively few in number for any individual, but are composed of very large numbers of families of such scenes [Tomkins, 1979, pp. 228–229].

Most often, "a nuclear scene is one or several scenes in which a very good scene turns very bad" (Tomkins, 1995, p. 376). The central dynamics of a nuclear script seems to be the individual's "attempts to reverse the nuclear scene, to turn the very bad scene into the very good scene again" (p. 376). These attempts will, however, result in a repetition of the organizing patterns that amplify and expand the structure of nuclear scenes.

Our experiences from the ACI and from psychotherapy focusing on AC are quite consistent with Tomkins' assumptions. The steady focusing on qualities of affect experience and how it is organized according to the four integrating functions of the AC concept seemed to give our patients better access to nuclear scenes and their formative contexts. As affects and nuclear scenes were activated, however, so were maladaptive scripts, leading to derailment of affect and fragmentation of self-experience.

CLINICAL EXAMPLE

Mr. A, a young man with a schizoid personality disorder, was asked the first question in the ACI about what could make him feel interest or excitement. He had severe difficulties in picturing a scene with this affect, stuttered back and forth for a while, and ended his first answer by saying "Why do you ask about this . . . what is the purpose . . . that I shall find . . . say . . . talk about this?"

During the further exploration of how he could experience this affect, he several times lost himself, something he once also articulated in the following manner: "I feel . . . in a way I feel like things disappear to me . . . in a way . . . your question just disappears in a way . . . what did you ask me again?"

And later during the exploration of the same affect: "I rarely succeed in anything . . . ; I'm not interested in what other people are interested in. . . . What I feel inhibits me, that I'm not able to get involved, I am standing beside myself in a way, and then I feel like I am sitting there playing, talking just to talk, smiling just to smile. I am . . . in a way . . . I must fabricate someone to be, it's awfully exhausting."

In situations where he had experienced interest together with other people, he thought it was not right to show the affect. As soon as he started to focus on something that interested him, he interrupted himself by starting to accuse himself.

His script on this affect included combinations of ruptures, derailments, and couplings with other affects:

Interest/excitement → guilt → loss of self (confusion) → shame → withdrawal

The script illustrates his lack of capacity to let the feeling impact on him, both as valid information and as an adaptive motivational force. It also inhibits him from expressing his subjective feeling of interest/ excitement interpersonally. This organizing pattern was activated in an atmosphere of empathic dialogue, while the therapist in a confirming manner tried to explore his experiences. The triggering elements seemed to be the activation of the affect itself and the therapist's expectations of him to share this affect experience and the associated scenes.

We generally also believe that this pattern was influenced by some unconscious or "silent" mental representations, shaped by invariant patterns of interaction during his early attachment relationships. Since he later had 220 sessions of intensive psychotherapy focusing on affect consciousness, we gradually came to know more about the intersubjective background for this script pattern. Both his mother and father seemed to have contributed to this script formation. For practical reasons we will just illustrate some assumed formative patterns in relationship with his mother.

The image of his mother, which he could easily and in great detail picture, was always marked with a suffering expression on her face. During therapy, he associated several scenes with his mother, who the therapist thought must have had a major depression. Upon feeling interested or excited as a child, his mother always went: "Hush!! You're making so much noise, I am getting such a headache." Or when he was a teenager and loved listening to pop-music on radio Luxemburg: Before switching the radio on, he would always turn the volume down so much that he had to put his ear close to the loudspeaker to be able to hear anything at all. He remembered one episode when he did this, and his mother, who was in another room of their house at that moment, suddenly rushed into his room and reproached him for the noise he made by pressing the "on"-button of the radio. Several other examples indicated that this had been an invariant interaction pattern between the two of them.

Gradually he began to see how his mother, by representing her own problems, had contributed to an *active derailment* of his affect experience. The activation of interest/excitement was, because of such repeated experiences, always co-assembled with guilt, the experience of self-loss, and shame. In order to preserve the best possible attachment or bond to his mother, we can imagine several analog formative scenes where he, instead of being seen, recognized, and confirmed on his own interest/excitement, had to develop something she needed, and that contributed to the best possible regulation of her self-esteem. He had to be invisible and not demand anything from her. Expressed interest or excitement was conceived of as unreasonable demands. From what he told the therapist, it seemed like his vitality may have made her feel envious or jealous. Maybe it reminded her too strongly of what she missed or was unable to have in her own life. In order to reduce her own feelings of powerlessness and shortcomings in her own life, she automatically tried to stop him whenever he was too vital.

This script is an example of a good scene that turns very bad. The interest/excitement scene turns into a guilt and confusion scene, which subsequently turns into a shame and withdrawal scene. By becoming silent and withdrawn, Mr. A tried to turn it into a good scene again. These attempts resulted, however, in a repetition of the organizing patterns that magnified the structure of these formative scenes. He felt pity for his mother and wanted to make her feel well, which in turn also would make him feel better himself. The initial good scene was lost; what he achieved was the best possible scene together with his mother, who then stopped blaming him.

A part of the intersubjective basis of the script may be understood as reflecting his mother's expressed need for him to serve selfobject functions for her, confirming her own sufferings. His awareness centered more on her and especially her expressed suffering became the focus in the associated scenes at the cost of him and his own feelings. Several unsuccessful attempts to help her by being encouraging and comforting convinced him early on that he was unable to have an impact on others and that something was basically wrong with him. During a long disillusionment process, he gradually began to see and feel the impact his mother's (and father's) narcissistic disorders had on him. After a while, he could also feel how their deficient acknowledgement, lack of confirmation, and weak self-boundary formations had influenced him to carry the moral responsibility for their problems (guilt), as well as how these patterns of affect-laden interactions had contributed to form his own self-image characterized by a basic fault (shame).

FOCUSING ON AFFECT CONSCIOUSNESS IN PSYCHOTHERAPY: THEORY OF CHANGE

This consistent way of focusing on affect also illustrates the importance of Kohut's selfobject concept. As the Tøyen therapists repeatedly kept focusing on affect and the script pattern when patients had lost themselves, this systematic way of focusing helped the patients to get back on course of their own affect experience again. Gradually, and by the assistance of the therapists' AC-focus, they started to believe in the signal function of their own affects and developed clearer awareness, better tolerance, and more differentiated and avowed ways of expressing themselves. Stolorow et al.'s (1987), Stolorow and Atwood's (1992), and Lichtenberg et. al.'s (1996) expansion and refinement of the selfobject concept furthered our understanding of selfobject experience as having a vitalizing function in the sense that selfobject functions pertain to the need for attuned responsiveness to affect states. These authors have also influenced our psychotherapy theory, and our revised theory is inspired by their contributions.

Kohut (1971, 1977, 1984) emphasized the empathic stance of the analyst, the continually strengthening of the selfobject transference bond, the transformations of this bond from more archaic to mature forms, and transmuting internalizations.

In our view, the process learning aspects during the repeated establishments of the working alliance are central in achieving structural change. A good working alliance might, as Chris Jaenicke and Stolorow et al. (1987) have suggested, be considered as a specific selfobject transference bond. The repeated establishing of an atmosphere of trust, openness to experience, reflection, and expression will in itself challenge maladaptive scripts. According to the exploratory pattern of the AC model, the manifestation of the working alliance can be described through the following four integrating functions of a process we have called "personal reflection."

1. The patients must, first of all, learn to pay attention to emotional responses within themselves. Gradually, they will expand the range of awareness signals until they reliably recognize and distinguish distinctive affect states.

2. In attaining greater tolerance, the patients will allow themselves to be "moved" in such a way that the content or information inherent in the affects can be integrated. As Stolorow et al.

(1987) pointed out: Rather than rupturing the continuity of self-experience, affects can become employed in the service of its preservation. Containment and modulation of affects also enable the use of them as signals to oneself.

3. Steady decoding of the informational aspects of affects promotes acquisition of interpersonal knowledge and maturation. Transforming affect states into concepts also facilitates articulation of self-experience.

4. More direct, differentiated, and avowed expressions of affects provide the individuals with clearer and more differentiated responses from their surroundings. This is an essential requirement for all further development.

Working through these four integrating functions also facilitates identification of nuclear scripts and their formative contexts.

If it takes several repetitions of invariant interaction patterns to form psychic structures like scripts, it also takes several variant repetitions to change scripts. A structural change implies both better access to content of experience, for example, affects, ideas, and scenes, as well as increased knowledge of how it is organized at a script level. The underlying working pattern in the AC model can be summed up in Figure 2.

When focusing on a theme or a scene, affects are always activated. The therapist systematically tries to read the affect information and invites the patients to explore their affect experiences and to start or get on with the process of personal reflection. Keeping this repeated affect exploratory process alive will increase the patients' ability to

Figure 2. Working pattern/process learning aspect of psychotherapy focusing on affect consciousness

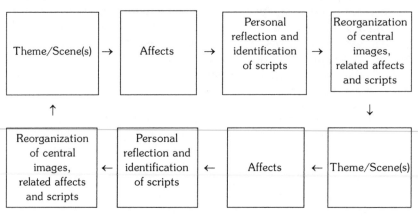

know, show, and articulate their affect experiences, a capacity that is a primary component of a healthy self.

An important step further in this treatment model is the development from gaining access to affects, scenes, and central images to the identification of scripts. Identifying scripts is most of all important because a nuclear script with negative affect scenes will expand by the construction of new analogs (Tomkins, 1979). The patient may have become more self-conscious, but without an identification and reorganization of the nuclear script, new analogs may still seize him.

The crucial distinction between content of experience and how it is structured must therefore be directly focused on in the treatment process. Mr. A, from the clinical example above, could, for example, easily and in great detail picture his mothers' suffering face (concrete symbol, conscious thematic content). He had, however, no conscious experience of how her repeated expressions of suffering had influenced his organization of affect experience (structural level, script). Since this pattern could be observed during the ACI, in therapy sessions, and in other current relationships, this demonstrates how a script that originally was shaped in one particular relationship gets structuralized and then becomes decontextualized and generalized. It is still regulating the individual's affect experience and participation in new interpersonal relationships in predictable ways. The script will consolidate and stabilize one's self-experience in a way that is consistent with prior experience.

The nuclear script is an example of an invariant organizing principle that, according to Tomkins, expands by the construction of new analogs. Analog elements in a new scene, that is, with similar elements from earlier, formative scenes, may activate anxiousness about a possible repetition of the bad scene. The patient

> characteristically does not know why he feels as he does. He is victimized by his own high-powered ability to synthesize ever-new repetitions of the same scene without knowing that he is doing so. This is one reason why insight psychotherapy so often fails to cure—because no amount of understanding of the past will enable the individual to become aware of his new analogs before they are constructed [Tomkins, 1979, p. 231].

In the first version of the AC model, we labeled the last box in figure 2 "insight." Later experience and further readings of Tomkins (1991, 1992, 1995), Lichtenberg et al. (1992, 1996), Stolorow et al. (1987), and Stolorow and Atwood (1992), however, influenced us to change this label into "reorganization of central images, related affects and scripts." More specifically, this refers to symbolic transformations of parental images, self-image, related affects, and unconscious representations of the relational systems that were shaping the organization of affect experience.

As was the case with Mr. A, transformations of parental images most often included disillusionment and mourning processes. Increased affect tolerance facilitated his capacity to mourn and renounce the attempts of turning the very bad scene into a very good, idealized scene again, a central dynamic in his script. The transformed images gradually became more differentiated and separate in a way that validated *his* own affective experience and contextualized his script. Even if he sometimes could feel pity for his mother, he could now also see her as demanding, self-centered, jealous, and disturbed. The restoration process included recovery from his lost sense of being and how this was connected to his most problematic self–selfobject experiences, in which self-awareness, tolerance, and expression of his own affects was dangerous and threatened the needed bond to others.

Structural change in psychotherapy, which includes a restoration of the sense of self, seems to be facilitated by increased affect consciousness and reorganization of maladaptive scripts. The following conditions are most likely necessary in the achievement of such an aim:

1. Establishing contact with and forming concept about own affects;
2. Identification and contextualization of formative, nuclear scenes. This means attaining an experience of connection between nuclear scenes and unintegrated affects to which people, objects or themes are linked;
3. Symbolic transformations of parental images, self-image, and unconscious representations of the relational systems that formed the scripts;
4. Obtaining conscious experience of nuclear scripts and changing the pattern of this organizing activity.

This last point is probably quite decisive in attaining lasting change. The patient usually needs to get to know the same affect in different scenes, with different intensities and with several variant repetitions before the conditions in point four are met.

INITIAL RESEARCH ON THE AFFECT CONSCIOUSNESS MODEL

The AC model has been tested in two different studies: the Tøyen study and the Norwegian Hydro study. Details of the first study have been published elsewhere: changes in personality characteristics (Monsen et al., 1995a), psychosocial changes (Monsen et al., 1995b), and empirical validation of the AC concept and the psychometric properties of the ACS (Monsen et al., 1996). The Norwegian Hydro study has recently been completed and has been presented at research conferences (Monsen and Monsen, 1998), and details of this study will be published later. The main findings from these studies will therefore be reported here in shortened form.

The Tøyen Long-Term Psychotherapy Study

The AC model was first developed and tested in a psychiatric outpatient clinic in a naturalistic, prospective follow-up study of 25 individuals with severe personality disorders and psychoses. The mean treatment duration was 25 months, and the mean follow-up interval was five years. Change was assessed using standard psychotherapy research scales.

At termination, there were substantial changes in AC, characterological defenses, and symptoms. Seventy-five percent of patients no longer fulfilled DSM-III-R axis I diagnostic criteria. Seventy-two percent no longer met axis II diagnostic criteria. High levels of stability persisted at follow-up. Patients showed improved capacity to establish and tolerate intimate relationships, better relationships with friends, improved socioeconomic status, and reduced use of health- and social services. At follow-up, HSRS and SCL-90-R scores suggest that 76 percent of patients reached psychosocial and adaptation levels that can be defined as "no-caseness."

Norwegian Hydro Short-Term Psychotherapy Study

Forty patients with pain disorders participated in a controlled, matched, and randomized study conducted in the company health service setting at Norwegian Hydro, a large Norwegian company. Most patients were well educated, and all of them worked full-time. Twenty patients were treated for 36 sessions, and the control group received treatment as usual. All patients were tested before and at the end of treatment, and at one year follow-up with the ACI, a test for muscular tensions, patterns of respiration and postural characteristics (MRPC), subjective feeling of pain, MMPI, SCL-90-R, and IIP-64.

The findings show a significant and substantial change in the treatment group on affect consciousness, pain (50% no pain at all, 35% on the lowest level), somatization, denial, anxiety, social withdrawal and increased assertiveness. The most pronounced changes in bodily characteristics were observed in muscular tensions, patterns of respiration, and flexibility in the columna (back)/neck. All these findings seem to indicate increased capacity to express affects. The stability of these changes during follow-up was high with no relapses in the treatment group. The treatment group continued to improve on interpersonal problems (IIP), especially on assertiveness and the tendency to feel too responsible.

Summary of the Initial Research

Patients with the kinds of problems we have focused on in these two studies clearly seem to profit from psychotherapy focusing on affect consciousness and interpersonal relations. Both studies show effect sizes that are larger than what is common for similar patient groups. In both studies, the largest change was found on AC, which also was the main focus in both therapies. The design of these studies does not, however, allow us to conclude that the AC focus is a significant causative factor. To answer such questions, one needs a randomized, controlled design with comparable psychotherapies, but which differ in their affect focus. We do believe, however, that AC may be a central component of the opening of more effective pathways to the establishment of functional self–selfobject bonds.

SCRIPTS, AFFECT CONSCIOUSNESS, AND SELF PSYCHOLOGY

How is Tomkins's affect- and script theory and the AC model connected to self psychology? We will try to elucidate some central connections to self psychology by discussing the relationship between selfobject functions and integration of affects, and affects and organizing principles.

Selfobject Functions and Integration of Affects

Kohut (1971, 1977) underlined the need for specific selfobject ties of mirroring, twinship, and idealization and showed how integration of some affects states is crucial for the consolidation of self-esteem, empathy, and self-soothing capacity. Pride, expansiveness, efficacy, pleasurable excitement, strength, security, and calmness are examples of such central affect states. Stolorow et al. (1987) pointed to how Kohut (1977) seemed to be moving toward a broadened selfobject concept, beyond his earlier formulations of mirroring and idealizing selfobject ties, by emphasizing the parental empathic responsiveness to the feeling states characteristic of the oedipal phase.

Stolorow et al. (1987) expand the selfobject concept further in the direction of affect integration: "It is our contention that selfobject functions pertain fundamentally to the integration of *affect* into the organization of self-experience, and that the need for selfobject ties pertains most centrally to the need for attuned responsiveness to affect states in all stages of the life cycle" (p. 66). Attunement to the whole variety of affect states and requisite affirming, accepting, differentiating, synthesizing, and containing responses is seen as essential selfobject functions. Kohut's three specific selfobject ties are viewed as "important special instances of this expanded concept of selfobject functions in terms of integration of affects" (Stolorow et al., p. 67). Stolorow et al. argue that central affect integrating functions like affect differentiation and self-articulation, synthesis of affectively discrepant experiences, affect tolerance, and the use of affects as self-signals and desomatization and cognitive articulation of affects all contribute to the structuralization of an individual's sense of self.

Tomkins's (1995) descriptions of good scenes are quite equivalent to Kohut's descriptions of selfobject ties of mirroring, idealization, and twinship. The good scenes typically evoke "excitement or enjoyment at others who provided either models, mirrors, stimulation, guidance, mutuality, support, comfort and/or reassurance" (p. 379). At the formation of maladaptive, nuclear scripts, such good scenes turn bad, and Tomkins' illustrations of such bad scenes are, in our opinion, all examples of selfobject failures. Tomkins categorizes the bad scene as "either an intimidation, a contamination, a confusion or any combination of these that jeopardizes the good scene" (p. 379). He describes some typical examples of affective communication patterns in bad scenes in the following manner:

1. Intimidation scene: Excessive terror, shame, or distress is evoked by excessive violence or threat via anger or disgust.
2. Contamination scene: Excessive distress, anger, shame or disgust is evoked by:
   — excessive overcontrol;
   — indifference, distancing, or threat of withdrawal of love;
   — character flaws of the other that contaminate the idealized image of the other as model, mirror, guide, provider of mutuality, support, or comfort;
   — humiliation by the good other;
   — excessive piety of that good other that evokes guilt, distress or conflict;

— the death of the good other;
— any triangular rivalry.
3. Confusion scene: Extreme lability of action and affect is evoked by:
  — both multiple affects from the good other and by the self in response to the creation of excessively turbulent scenes;
  — extreme lability of affect and action by the good other.

Turbulence and confusion are compounded whenever there are too many possible sources of blame for good scenes turned bad and whenever one does not know whether it is the self or the other or some complex combination of both that is responsible for catastrophic problematic multiple good scenes turned bad in different ways (Tomkins, 1995, pp. 379–380).

The coupling of good scenes that turn bad may be examples of ruptures in the continuity of self-experience, especially if significant others and their affect expressions tend to come to the fore in the scenes in a way that does not validate the individual's own affects. Tomkins's examples illustrate some types of affective interplay that typically represents selfobject failures because the individuals lose their sense of selves, that is, the experience of their own affects. If both the pleasant affects in the good scene and the unpleasant affects that were triggered when the good scene was turning bad were recognized and validated by others, we would not consider this as a selfobject failure. The integration of negative or unpleasant affects is, of course, as necessary as the integration of positive affects to preserve a sense of self-cohesion (Monsen et al., 1986; Stolorow et al., 1987; Lichtenberg et al., 1996).

The AC concept, which we regard as an operational elaboration of self psychology theory, distinguishes four central affect integrating functions of the self that make possible the identification of which affect integrating functions are intact or disturbed. Our experiences from the ACI and the AC-therapy model are quite consistent with Stolorow et al.'s (1987) assumptions that "selfobject functions pertain fundamentally to the integration of affect into the organization of self-experience" (p. 66). The AC therapy model undoubtedly facilitates the establishment and maintenance of the affect focus in psychotherapy. Therefore, it also seems to strengthen the therapists' selfobject functions.

Affects and the Organization of Self-Experience

According to Tomkins's affect- and script theory, the affect system has certain properties that make affects central to the organization of self-experience. The theory of affect as amplification and fusion power refer to how affects fuse, both simultaneously and sequentially, the cognitive, perceptual, and the motoric aspects of an experience with the continuing affect(s). These properties of the affect system give affects a central status in the organization of self-experience: It connects large amounts of experiential information and serves as a unifying core behind all these variants and as the "psychic glue" in the formation of scenes and scripts.

Consider Mr. A in our previous clinical example. The specific coupling of interest–guilt and shame connects and sustains the organization of his self-experience, including the automatic or unconscious conviction that he would cause harm to others whenever he became interested or excited. His mother's excessive reactions to his expressions of interest were amplified by and fused with this affect-sequence and became a central part of this script.

Self psychological concepts that refer to similar organizing activities are the motivational theorists' use of model scenes and Piaget's schema concept (Lichtenberg et al., 1992, 1996). A script might also be described as a specific pattern of self–selfobject relating with a tendency to form a particular form of selfobject transference (Kohut, 1984). The intersubjectivists' notion of organizing principles (Stolorow et al., 1987; Stolorow and Atwood, 1992) is however, in our opinion closest to Tomkins' script concept, because of the way it emphasizes the role of affects in the organization of self-experience.

Organizing principles refer to "emotional conclusions a person has drawn from lifelong experience of the emotional environment, especially the mutual connections with early caregivers" (Orange, Atwood, and Stolorow, 1997, p. 7). The parallel to Tomkins's script concept is striking. As scripts, organizing principles may be flexible and adaptive or rigid and maladaptive; they include expectations and convictions and are most often automatic or unconscious. By emphasizing the emotional aspects of experiences and convictions, they accentuate the role of affects in the formation and continuation of organizing principles. Implicit in their conception is the assumption of the affect system serving as a basic, preverbal, signaling and communication system.

If affects influence the formation of organizing principles, this may also imply, as Tomkins has suggested, assumptions of some kind of connecting force or fusion power that serves the purpose of amplifying and combining ideas, images, affects, and sensorimotor impressions simultaneously and sequentially. While the principle of affect as amplification accounts for only the short-term importance of any experience, psychological magnification increases the duration, coherence, and continuity of affect experience by co-assembling and relating amplified scenes to one another. The role of cognition is assumed to be incidental in the evocation of affect as an amplifier but plays a major role in psychological magnification. However, magnification presupposes amplification and is a mixture of memory, thought, imagination, and affect-driven amplification. As far as we know, the intersubjectivists do not offer hypotheses or explanations at this level of specificity. Their emphasis on context as a co-determinant to which principles that will be called on to organize the experience is also a parallel to Tomkins' concept of script expansion according to the principles of analogs and variants.

It is our impression that the transference concept partly seems to be replaced by concepts like organizing activity or organizing principles. As Stolorow et al. (1987) and Fosshage (1994) have pointed to, transference is neither displacement, distortion, or projection, but rather, an expression of the continuing influence of activated organizing principles. As old inferences, such organizing principles will "thematize the sense of self," including "convictions about the relational consequences of possible forms of being" (Orange et al., 1997, p. 7). If the central aim in psychotherapy is to form new organizing principles, Tomkins's script theory and its clinical application through the AC model concretize such efforts.

The AC model, we believe, is clearly embedded within the frameworks of self psychology and has, as we have shown, several similarities with contemporary self psychological models. The selfobject and the repetitive dimensions of transference are both understood as codetermined by the patient's scripts and the therapist's capacity for attuned responsiveness. We follow the general principles in self psychology, viewing empathic disjunctions or ruptures as constructive potentials for deeper understanding by exploring the discrepancy of the subjective experiences. We also emphasize focusing on external relationships and scenes from the patients' daily life that may activate maladaptive scripts that are more pressing in the patients' social environment than within the empathic atmosphere in the therapeutic relationship.

The main difference seems to be the continuous focus on affects through the four AC functions and scripts. This way of focusing more frequently makes affects and the four central affect integrating functions figure in the psychotherapy process, which may be viewed as a series of new formative scenes. The AC concept facilitates exploration of affect experience, in a consistent manner. Such repeated explorations make it easier to achieve conscious experience of earlier unvalidated affect experiences as well as changing maladaptive scripts.

We believe that the continuous oscillation between exploration of content of affect-laden experience and how it is structured at a script level makes the therapy more effective. In our experience, the operationalization of AC is most helpful clinically, and it also moves psychotherapy research closer to what may be truly relevant variables in psychotherapy.

REFERENCES

Basch, M. F. (1983), Empathic understanding: A review of the concept and some theoretical considerations. *J. Amer. Psychoanal. Assn.*, 31:101–126.

Fosshage, J. L. (1994), Toward reconceptualising transference: Theoretical and clinical considerations. *Internat. J. Psycho-Anal.*, 75:265–280.

Kohut, H. (1971), *The Analysis of the Self*. New York: International Universities Press.

———— (1977), *The Restoration of the Self*. New York: International Universities Press.

———— (1984), *How Does Analysis Cure?* ed. A. Goldberg & P. Stepansky. Chicago: University of Chicago Press.

Lichtenberg, J. D. (1989), *Psychoanalysis and Motivation*. Hillsdale, NJ: The Analytic Press.

———— Lachmann, F. & Fosshage, J. L. (1992), *Self and Motivational Systems: Toward a Theory of Psychoanalytic Technique*. Hillsdale, NJ: The Analytic Press.

———— ———— & ———— (1996), *The Clinical Exchange: Techniques Derived from Self and Motivational Systems*. Hillsdale, NJ: The Analytic Press.

Monsen, J. T., Eilertsen, D. E., Melgård, T. & Ødegård, P. (1996), Affects and affect consciousness: Initial experiences from the assessment of affect integration. *J. Psychother. Pract. & Res.*, 5:238–249.

———— Melgård, T. & Ødegård, P. (1986), Vitalitet og psykiske forstyrrelser belyst ved begrepene "opplevelsesevne" og "ekspressivitet". [Vitality and psychological disorders elucidated by the concepts "experiencing ability" and "expressiveness."] *Tidsskrift for Norsk Psykologforening*, 23:285–294.

———— Ødegård, P. & Melgård, T. (1989), Major psychological disorders and changes after intensive psychotherapy: Findings from the Tøyen project, Oslo. *Psychoanal. & Psychother.*, 7:171–180.

———— Odland, T., Faugli, A., Daae, E. & Eilertsen, D. E. (1995a), Personality disorders: Changes and stability after intensive psychotherapy focusing on affect consciousness. *Psychother. Res.*, 5:33–48.

———— ———— ———— ———— & ———— (1995b), Personality disorders and psychosocial changes after intensive psychotherapy. A prospective follow-up study of an outpatient psychotherapy project, 5 years after end of treatment. *Scandinav. J. Psychol.*, 36:256–268.

Monsen, K. & Monsen, J. T. (1998), *Pain disorders, affect consciousness and psychodynamic, body therapy: A controlled study*. Paper presented at the annual meeting of the International Society for Psychotherapy Research, Snowbird, Utah.

Orange, D. M., Atwood, G. E. & Stolorow, R. D. (1997), *Working Intersubjectively. Contextualism in Psychoanalytic Practice*. Hillsdale, NJ: The Analytic Press.

Stern, D. (1985), *The Interpersonal World of the Infant: A View from Psychoanalysis and Developmental Psychology*. New York: Basic Books.

Stolorow, R. D. & Atwood, G. E. (1992), *Contexts of Being: The Intersubjective Foundations of Psychological Life*. Hillsdale, NJ: The Analytic Press.

———— Brandchaft, B. & Atwood, G. E. (1987), *Psychoanalytic Treatment: An Intersubjective Approach*. Hillsdale, NJ: The Analytic Press.

Tomkins, S. S. (1962), *Affect, Imagery, Consciousness, Vol. 1: The Positive Affects*. New York: Springer.

———— (1963), *Affect, Imagery, Consciousness, Vol. 2: The Negative Affects*. New York: Springer.

———— (1979), Script theory: Differential magnification of affects. In: *Nebraska Symposium on Motivation—1978, Vol. 26*, ed. H. E. Howe, Jr. & R. A. Dienstbier. Lincoln: University of Nebraska Press, pp. 201–236.

———— (1991), *Affect, Imagery, Consciousness, Vol. 3: The Negative Affects: Anger and Fear*. New York: Springer.

———— (1992), *Affect, Imagery, Consciousness, Vol. 4: Cognition: Duplication and Transformation of Information*. New York: Springer.

———— (1995), Script theory. In: *Exploring Affect. The Selected Writings of Silvan Tomkins*, ed. E. V. Demos. New York: University of Cambridge Press.

Chapter 21

The Self and Its Past: On Shame and the "Biographical Void"

Martin Gossmann

In this chapter I shall discuss the effect of disruption of transgenerational continuity on the developing sense of self. I shall view the influence of "tradition" on development, as well as on the ability to maintain the integrity of the self even at times of crisis, from within a self psychological perspective.

Heinz Kohut referred to the sense of psychic continuity as one of the central hallmarks of the cohesive self.[1] Traumatic experiences that cannot be integrated into the fabric of the self interrupt the sense of continuity. Repression and disavowal are defenses by which such disruptions are mended. However, these defenses are also responsible for the symptomatic elaborations of these traumatic disruptions. Repression and disavowal create "empty pages in one's life's narrative" that may unexpectedly and intrusively call attention to themselves.

The painful retrieval of hitherto repressed traumatic memories and the following integration into the biographic narrative is here of central

---

[1] Kohut (1984) summarized the different aspects of continuity and the relation to the development of the self as follows: Throughout his life, a person will experience himself as a cohesive, harmonious firm unit in time and space, connected with his past and pointing meaningfully into a creative-productive future, only as long as, at each stage in his life, he experiences certain representatives of his human surroundings as joyfully responding to him, as available to him as sources of idealized strength and calmness, as being silently present but in essence like him, and, at any rate, able to grasp his inner life more or less accurately so that their responses are attuned to his needs and allow him to grasp their inner life when his is in need of such sustenance (p. 52).

importance. The individual may choose different ways to accomplish this task,[2] and it may become the central tasks of an analytic dialogue.[3]

In the following I shall focus on clinical observations that are related to a trauma experienced by a whole nation, nevertheless constituting disruptions within an individual's own psychology. Many of my patients reported a loss of their sense of continuity in response to traumatic experiences that lay outside their individual, but within their collective, national or family histories. The traumatic events of the Third Reich and its demise had led to disruptions, not only in the biographies of those who lived through these traumatic events, but had a further disruptive effect on their children's sense of psychic continuity as they were denied authentic recollection of their forefathers' experiences.

Listening to my patients, the question I had to answer was this: What kind of therapeutic experiences could undo the impasse that became established between the generations resulting from the traumatic events during and following the second World War? The working through of the impasse is of importance since it was this impasse that led to the "biographical void" and the ensuing difficulty in development among the members of the post–World War II generation. This is why I would maintain that moments of collective remembrances, be they part of family life, be they part of the community life or a nationwide event, constitute an important contribution, not only to a nation's history, but to the establishment of a coherent narrative of the individual.

Rather than viewing "the contemporary Germans" as "obsessed with the Holocaust"[4] I would say that this process of repossessing the

---

[2] Marcel Proust's (1913–1928) detailed recollections of his early childhood memories constitute a poet's effort to reestablish a meaningful narrative interrupted by experiences of desperate loneliness. Kohut (1977) pointed to the psychological function of these minute descriptions of his experiences saying that "Proustian recovery of childhood memories constitutes a psychological achievement significantly different from the filling in of infantile amnesia, which as Freud taught us, is the precondition for the solution of structural conflicts and thus for the cure of a psychoneurosis. The Proustian recovery of the past is in the service of healing the discontinuity of the self" (pp. 179–180).

[3] Anna Ornstein (1994) exemplified in what ways an artist's work may address individually, as well as collectively, endured trauma.

[4] Maxim Biller (1996), the Israeli Author of (Germany) "The Country of Perpetrators and Traitor's" on the occasion of the 50th anniversary of the *Reichskristallnacht*, Nov. 1996 questions the necessity to commemorate this event, an event in which in the night from the 9th to the 10th of November, 1936, almost all German synagogues were destroyed in a coordinated act of violence and mass destruction of which much more was to come. Biller questions the need to commemorate this event in today's Germany altogether and the motives that may lie behind this commemoration in particular. It sounds almost like a reproach when he writes: "the contemporary Germans are obsessed with the Holocaust." Instead of letting go of a past "of which any other country would be embarrassed" he says, they take "Auschwitz as the basis for a new German identity" (p. 6).

past, however difficult and painful this may prove to be, is a necessity. When Biller (1996) says that, instead of letting go of a past "of which any other country would be embarrassed," the young Germans "take Auschwitz as the basis for a new identity," I feel that it is indeed this search for "identity" that is at the heart of the contemporary struggle exemplified in the clinical material presented here. It is in this area that continuity, that is, the establishment of biographic continuity overarching one's life span, is of greatest importance.

CLINICAL EXAMPLES

"Disruption"

Mr. Albert was the youngest of three children and the most talented one among his siblings. As a young student, he participated in international exchange programs and at the time he left high school he was fluent in three languages. Later in law school he was regarded as a very promising student with great career chances ahead of him.

During his third year in law school he took a job in an office that dealt with the international property market and was so good at it that the company offered to take him on after his bar exams. It was only after he had finished school and had accepted the position that he felt increasingly isolated behind his desk, finding himself working long hours without a sense of fulfillment but at times just "doodling" along. Maybe he was successful in the eyes of others, but in his own opinion what he did was not meaningful at all. It was this search for meaning, a strong wish to "have a place in life," that led him to seek out psychotherapy.

After entering my office and introducing himself, he quickly began to describe his search for what he called an "inner connectedness" with everything he did, especially his job. He tended to start new projects with great enthusiasm. But after a short while, he would lose his enthusiasm and wonder whether the task was really of importance. His sense of disconnectedness was not primarily an interpersonal one; we immediately established a very cordial, even if professional, relationship. His sense of disconnectedness was more a sense of not belonging, of being without context.

A dream he had early in the treatment represented this feeling: "In this dream I go back to my former high school for some kind of reunion. In the school yard there is a desk full of pictures of students and their families. There are photos of my own parents, too. But for some reason the background is foreign; the city looks as it did before the war. But I myself was certainly born later and these were supposedly photos from my school years." This mystery deepens as he initially cannot find a picture of himself at all. Finally, he recognizes a photo of both his parents and a young boy that must be him. "But why can't I see my face? There is some kind of a hole in the picture, or a blank spot of some sort."

The dream leaves him with a sense of alienation, a feeling similar to his experience sitting behind his desk wondering about the value of his work. Who was he within the institution he worked for? How did he know that his contributions really mattered? His superior was interested in reaching the company's expectations and he obviously contributed to that end because he frequently got positive feedback. Was that good or bad? He felt he was walking on unsafe grounds. Nothing really obviously wrong, just a sense of certainty was missing in a profound way. He did not experience a stable sense of himself and where he belonged—just like the picture in his dream where time and space were unrelated. It did not make sense that his parents would be standing in front of pre-war façades when they had met after the war and he was been born even later. As if they somehow belonged to a different time.

What did he know about his parents' past—their experiences before or during the war in particular? It turned out Mr. Albert had often been told episodes concerning these times, but in a way, he had never been able to picture his parents as the young adults they had been during the Third Reich. Since his father was born in 1924 and his mother in 1927, they were young children when Hitler came to power and were adolescents when the war broke out. His mother came from a small town where her own father had a small shop. She was an only child and had spent most of the war in the country with her family where they were spared many of the hardships of the war. Mr. Albert's father came from a family that cherished the values of the aristocracy, which had a long history of contributing to the higher ranks in the military. As a young boy, his father had wanted to be a General one day. Growing up, though, he did not have what it took to become a leading soldier like his older brother, and this deeply hurt his sense of pride. When the war broke out, he was therefore stationed on the home front. Although at the time suffering from a sense of inferiority compared to his brother who had been accepted into a more prestigious regiment, he was "glad that he did not have to fight." Later, it dawned on him that he may have owed his life to this supposed "weakness." At the end of the war, both brothers returned home safely, and his family felt that, in light of that, the loss of the home, which had been burned down in an airraid, was unimportant. Mr. Albert's grandparents were eager to see their sons get a good education, and his father was proud to be accepted at one of the old universities and decided to go into law.

Mr. Albert remembers his father explaining to him that, after several years in private practice, he had been asked to take up a position in the executive branch of the newly formed federal government but had declined. Why? He felt that he "did not want to get too deeply involved with the government" because he was afraid that "what had happened before might happen again," and he did not want to "ever be part of anything like that."

Mr. Albert had always felt that his father, by staying in his own office, had in fact functioned below his potential. He explained that he had accepted this as his father's way of coming to terms with his war experiences, of which he himself did not know much. His father remained vague in what he shared with his family, and Mr. Albert felt he had to be read between the lines. It sounded like: "I am glad that is all over and I will always make sure not to become part of a system which looks like it is striving for important goals and then one day you find yourself unwillingly contributing to something you do not overlook anymore. Stay away from people who have too much power, who knows what they'll use it for."

What at first sounded like a clear message and a set of parameters that may have given his father directions for his own life melted away when looked at more closely and as a means of guidance for his son: "Power can always be abused" and "Beware of hidden dangers" may turn into: "Do not feel safe with anything you do."

Mr. Albert clearly felt that there was something in his father's past that had led to this profound uncertainty, but he could not identify it. All he knew was that it must have happened before 1945, and he always felt that his father did not really know it himself. Maybe he once knew, but he certainly did not share it with his children: "It was like my parents carried their own experience and their knowledge around like an object enclosed in a piece of amber. You could not really get to it, but it was always visible in some way, and somehow I always felt that this brought into question my right to live a free life; I could not distance myself from these feelings, I could not say, "this is the burden my father is carrying around because of his own experience when he was young. It affected me very directly; it was part of who I felt I myself was allowed to be."

Mr. Albert felt that the person he could become was defined, not by the context of his own life, but by the lives of his parents. The development of his self was confined and determined by his father's past and the manner in which he parented his son. In his treatment it became clear to what degree Mr. Albert could not free himself of his father's experiences and "identified" with them in the sense of "feeling determined by them."

A second case shall further illustrate this point: Mr. Bertram, a young scientist in his early thirties and in the midst of a promising career, was suffering from a similar sense of "burden," or an overall sense of "inhibition," which was very difficult for him to describe and even more difficult to trace to its origins. It seemed so paradoxical to him: No, it was not a sense of having done anything wrong, but at the same time he wondered if what he did was right, anyhow. It was not that he felt as if he were to be blamed for anything in particular; nevertheless, he was "unable to feel good about himself." It was in a rather indirect way we were finally able to understand this sense of "doom" he always felt hanging over him. He was on a recent business trip, the airplane had taken off, and they had reached travel altitude. All of a sudden, he wondered what would happen if there were an accident, if the plane crashed? He could not brush it off. And to his surprise he realized that he was actually intrigued with the idea, not fearing for his life, but fantasizing that he would be rescuing others from the burning wreck. Wondering why this image was so enticing, he realized that his phantasy was that under such conditions he would finally have the chance to prove that he was capable of being "a hero," that he was not condemned to feel ashamed because of an unnamed defect in himself for the rest of his life. As we now understood, he felt he "was not allowed to lead a happy life until he was able to prove that he was a good human being."

What had created these deeply felt doubts about his value as a human being? Why would he have to prove that he was capable of being a hero? Was it that he was not heroic enough in his own life, or was he trying to free himself of assumptions he could not yet name? It seemed to me that, although he had not done anything wrong in his life, he felt he had been regarded as at least potentially evil until proven otherwise.

Yes, this made sense to him. He explained that, indeed, he had often asked himself what he would have done during the Third Reich. He always asked himself how he would have acted: Would he have had the courage he admired in those who had risked their lives by protecting others, hiding Jews in their homes, for example, sharing with them their own food rations? His parents had often talked to him and his siblings about their lives as adolescents during the Third Reich; his father had been too young to be drafted or to be sent to the front at all. He was glad he did not have to think of him as a soldier. Who knows what he might have gone through or might have done to others. He had heard so much about the terrible experiences others had gone through, and of course, he knew a lot about the atrocities that had been performed by German men and women. He did not know much about his grandparents' lives either. And it seemed to me that it was exactly this lack of information that created the "biographical void" and that was more disruptive and traumatic than factual information might have been. The void acted as a vacuum that became filled with fears and hopes of which the fears expectedly were more troublesome.

Unknowingly, he had felt that, since his grandparents and parents had not stood up to the Nazi regime, it was up to him to prove that he was not the son and grandson of cowards, cowards who had passively contributed to the horrors of the Third Reich, who had obviously been guilty of silent collaboration. After all, were they not guilty since they did not do anything to fight the regime?

Now he understood that his hope "to prove one day his ability to be good" would have implied that, no matter what his grandfathers may or may not have done, he himself was not guilty of cowardice and that he therefore did not need to be ashamed of being German anymore.

"Repair"

Isaac Bashevis Singer's "The Little Shoemakers" (1982) explores the process by which a person is "determined" by his ancestors; it describes ways in which the meaningful tradition of values and of membership, of a sense of belonging to a valuable transgenerational lineage, can be a source of pride in happy times and a source of reassurance in times of crisis.

"The Little Shoemakers" is the story of Abba, the head of the household and a devout Jew. He is the oldest in the current generation of shoemakers, the latest in an endless chain of renowned shoemakers in the little village of Frampol in Poland. He lives in the Diaspora, but he accepts his faith willingly. He holds the values and ideals of his Jewish family tradition highly, and they give him meaning and a sense of direction in life. We get a short glimpse of his rather peaceful attitude toward life in the following description of his Sabbath:

[Abba] knew the story of Joseph and his brothers by heart, but he never tired of reading it over again. He envied the ancients because the King of the Universe revealed Himself to them and performed miracles for their sake, but consoled himself by thinking that from him, Abba, to the Patriarchs, there stretched an unbroken chain of generations—as if he too were part of the bible. He sprang from Jacob's loins; he and his sons were of the seed whose number had become like the sand and the stars. He was living in exile because the Jews of the Holy Land had sinned, but he awaited the Redemption and he would be ready when the time came [p. 40].

Abba knew himself to be privileged to belong to the lineage described in the Bible, as he knew himself to be the offspring of a family that over several generations, had taken pride in being famous shoemakers, renowned for their craft, as well as their distinguished contributions to the community. Yes, the Jews of the Holy Land had sinned, and this was the reason for his living in exile, but he nevertheless knew that, by holding on to the holy traditions, he was a member in the chain of generations reaching all the way back to the Patriarchs. And this gave him the strength to face the day and trust God, as well as foresee a better future.

Terrible times set in, though: First, his sons decide to leave the rather poor living conditions in Eastern Europe and to emigrate to the United States where they successfully establish a modern shoe industry. But Abba holds on to the piece of land passed on to him by his ancestors. After his wife's death, the pogroms of anti-semitism finally reach his village, and he is forced to leave everything behind to save his life. Shortly after his arrival in the West, he becomes severely ill. He becomes "clinically depressed." Removed from his familiar context and exposed to a world he does not know and that does not include those traditions that had provided him with a sense of continuity and meaning in his prior life, he withdraws into himself.

When spring came and he was no better, the daughters-in-law began to hint that it wouldn't be such a bad idea to put him in a home. But something unforeseen took place. One day, as he happened to open a closet, he noticed a sack lying on the floor which seemed somehow familiar. He looked again and recognized his shoemaker's equipment from Frampol: last, hammer and nails, his knife and pliers, the file and the awl, even a broken-down shoe. Abba felt a tremor of excitement; he could hardly believe his eyes. He sat down on a footstool and began to poke about with fingers grown clumsy and stale. When [his daughter-in-law] Bessie came in and found him playing with a dirty old shoe, she burst out laughing.

"What are you doing, Father? Be careful, you'll cut yourself, God forbid!" That day Abba did not lie in bed dozing. He worked busily till evening and even ate his usual piece of chicken with greater appetite. He smiled at the grandchildren when they came in to see what he was doing. The next morning, when [his son] Gimpel told his brothers how their father had returned to his old habits, they laughed and thought nothing more of it—but the activity soon proved to be the old man's salvation. He kept at it day after day without tiring, hunting up old shoes in the clothes closets and begging his sons to supply him with leather and tools. . . . After the Passover holidays the brothers got together and decided to build a little hut in the yard. They furnished it with a cobbler's bench, a stock of leather and hides, nails, dyes, brushes—everything even remotely useful to the craft.

Abba took on new life . . . [p. 55].

Singer exemplifies, with the help of Abba who stands for the East European Jewry, the value of traditions: they are a source of direction and pride in Abba's life and serve as a confirmation both in times of peace and in times of crisis. To be able to lean on traditional values and ideals allows for the individual to organize his/her life accordingly, feeling part of a larger transgenerational family line one can be proud of. Passing these values on to the next generation completes this sequence very meaningfully. Initially, both these processes seem to be crushed: Abba's sons decide to leave their parental home in order to emigrate to the new world. It is difficult for Abba to let them go, but he decided it to be best to hold on to the house he had inherited from his forefathers and to continue living according to the traditions they had also passed on to him. But then the pogroms force him to leave everything behind. Although he is able to find refuge in the country to which his sons had emigrated, he does not recover but gets more and more depressed. Being with his family does not provide him with what he needs to be able to pick up a new life. It is, however the ability to reconnect with his past and with his traditions in particular that revitalizes him at last. Picking up the old tools, literally as well as metaphorically, enables him to rediscover meaning in his life. Being able to reestablish this kind of continuity reconnects him with his own sense of self and proves to be curative.

Reading Singer's exemplification of the process of traumatic disruption and successful repair via the reestablishment of continuity with the lost past, I wondered how the young German generation would be able to accomplish this in light of the profoundness of the disruption of the collective national as well as the individual family history. I wondered if the way in which the young Germans were raised to believe that their history belonged to a new era that was bare of any connections to the dreadful past might in fact interfere with such a reparative process altogether.

I shared my understanding of the importance of meaningful continuity with Mr. Albert, pointing out that I felt that it is this need for the sense of belonging to a transgenerational lineage that encompasses one's own biography. This is missing in the lives of young German men and women because they have been robbed of their family's past.

I feel it is this need for continuity and connectedness that establishes the "identification" with our parents' and grandparents' lives, that in order to understand our own place in life, we need to place it within the frame of our own family history. In this process the tradition of values and ideals, as well as the understanding of an uninterrupted biographic continuity, serves as a source of reference in the search for direction and meaning. In order to be able to fill the biographical void and for young Germans to be able to create a coherent narrative of their own lives, they need to be able to place such a narrative within the context of their families.

He laughed when he came in the next week: "You got me here—talking about the biographical void. You'll love to hear a dream I had since then: I am in an old city again, but this time I know it is the city where my father grew up. I am my age and first I walk around the house by myself—but then I am at the front entrance again and my father is there, too. It is not clear whose house it is. Probably the house of the family. The front door is unusable, but there is a side entrance which can be used by walking across a plank bridging a narrow but deep cleft. As we enter the house, I see that the floor has large gaps between the beams, but my father seems not to notice. Therefore I make sure he stays close to me as we walk through the house. One room overlooks a valley. I think this part is all in black and white. Or rather dark colors. And then the scenario changes somewhat. A procession of people in costumes comes dancing in, but then I realize, they are different kinds people of who seem to be having a good time whilst refurbishing the house. One of them, I do not know exactly why, reminds me of you".

The dream indicated that the process of repair was now in progress. This reparative process was also occurring in Mr. Bertram's life. It was by accident that he passed by a little antique shop and saw an old chest. He was so taken by it that he had to inquire about it and learned that it had been made in the second half of the 18th century. He immediately liked it, and scratching together all the money he had available at the time he bought the old piece and felt he had found "a treasure."

With a gleam in his eye, he explained: "You know, my grandparents lost everything during the war when their homes went up in flames. I actually often wondered how people could give away what they had inherited from their ancestors because we had nothing that really belonged to us. My grandparents fled from what is now Poland, but as I said, they did not leave anything behind either. What they had was destroyed, and they started all over after the war. First, I thought I was trying to make up for their loss by buying something old. Someday, I will be able to pass on to my own children something which stems from the times of their great-grandparents, even if it had not belonged to them personally. But you know, I think what made me buy this piece was even something more important than the material aspect. This chest appeared to me to be so "innocent." It was built in 1770 and it survived the Second World War and other dangerous times. It is a wonderful idea that it may have been around when Mozart was travelling across Europe composing the operas we still listen to today. Taking care of this chest gives me a sense of having something to pass on to my own children or even grandchildren one day, which is free of the terrible times in-between. It is as if I had been able to preserve something from the past which was not under the spell of the Third Reich. It is as if I could thus write a piece of family history where otherwise there was only a gap."

"You know," Mr. Albert said at our last meeting a few months later,[5] "the tragedy of what you referred to as the biographical void is that I could not take my father and grandfather as examples and go about life in the tradition they passed on to me; they did not pass anything on; their goal was indeed not to pass on the thinking of the Third Reich they had grown up with and had seen leading to the greatest catastrophe of the twentieth century. Thus they actually avoided passing anything on to us apart from the warnings they gave us. And because they did not know otherwise; they just pretended we were starting all anew. Yes, that did not give us the support of family traditions. The positive aspect, though, and the real challenge may be that we are very aware of making our own decisions. These decisions may turn out wrong one day, but at least there is the great chance for us to find our own way by trusting our own ideas and feelings. And maybe that is even the best we can do and isn't that fair enough?"

CONCLUDING REMARKS

In self psychology psychic development is placed into the experiential sphere of the self–selfobject matrix. In order to develop and maintain a cohesive self, the individual depends on nurturing and reassuring selfobject experiences. To express this succinctly, I shall quote from a recent publication by Ornstein and Ornstein (1996):

According to Kohut there are three sets of developmental needs and experiences that are paramount for the development of a healthy

---

[5] He accepted a job outside the country, and we had to terminate earlier than we otherwise would have.

self. . . . The availability of "mirroring" [as he called the first set] establishes a healthy self-esteem and its reliable regulation during the inevitable vicissitudes of daily existence. It safeguards the capacity for the enjoyment of one's mental and physical activities and the uninhibited pursuit of one's goals and purposes: feeling pride in one's self. . . .

The second set of experiences (Kohut called them idealizations) requires the availability of idealizable caregivers, and later others, whom one can put on a pedestal and "borrow" their assumed power, values, and ideals in the service of acquiring and internalizing them. Once acquired, these ideals and values lead to the capacities for internal tension regulation through the containment of affects, for channeling of drive-needs, and for being able to maintain enthusiasm for life—to be able to invest emotionally in higher ideals outside of oneself.

The third set of experiences (Kohut called them alter-ego or twinship experiences) is the matrix within which skills and talents develop [pp. 12–13].

Where in this set of experiences do we place the need for continuity and for membership in a group?

The tradition of values and customs from one generation to the next provides selfobject experiences both in the area of idealization and merger, as well as in the area of mirroring and alterego selfobject experiences. The stabilizing sense of belonging to a transgenerational lineage with shared ideals and ambitions is beautifully portrayed in "The Little Shoemakers." He reacted to the pogroms and the loss of family ties with a sense of disorientation, depressive withdrawal, and life-threatening apathy.

The retrieval of his tools, practically and figuratively, allowed him to reconnect with his past and to pick up the continuity that had been so pervasively severed. It had been severed on both poles of the bipolar self. He was taken away from his home, which he knew would be destroyed with all the cultural meaning it had had for him and his forefathers, and was placed within a new sociocultural environment to which he had no inner connection; he was herewith deprived of the inherited value system that he had been able to idealize and of which he felt to be a part himself; in addition, he lost the opportunity to be the successful shoemaker who served his community, which had provided him with a sense of the meaningful pursuit of his own goals and ambitions.

Now in the New World, picking up his "trade" therefore allowed him to overcome his severe depression by bridging the gap in his own biography, as well as in his transgenerational lineage, and by reconnecting with his set of inherited ideals and own ambitions. Going back to his cherished activity passed on to him in pride from his forefathers revitalized him and filled him with a joy in which his children and grandchildren joined him happily.

Mr. Albert's father must have experienced a similarly traumatic severage of his own ideals and ambitions when the societal system he had grown up in was defeated and his county destroyed at the end of World War II. He had grown up with ideals and ambitions, which now proved to have contributed to the devastating regime that had led the world into the biggest catastrophe of the century, if not of mankind. How could he possibly be proud of his earlier hope to be a good soldier, how could he hold on to the sense of being a member of a valuable nation that, as he came to realize it, had built the concentration and extermination camps now opened and shown to the horrified world? In light of these revelations and realizations, it is understandable that he and his fellow Germans were determined to break with the past and start new at a supposed Hour Zero. No, they would not allow any ties back into the Third Reich, and they would raise their children as the members of a new society.

Mr. Albert therefore grew up on the other side of a deep chism, on the other side of a biographic gap that was not supposed to be bridged ever. His parents, out of the inability to tolerate the overwhelming reality of their own recent past could and would not provide him and his sibling with the recollections that would allow him to see and understand his roots. Learning, at the same time, more and more about the Third Reich through history books and documentaries, among other sources, he could not help but fill this biographical void with phantasies, assumptions, and certainties. This is where the biographical void acts as the vacuum which we have to fill because we have to re-establish a past which provides us with the context within which we can understand our own lives. As no word can have meaning without its context, the individual life lacks meaning and direction when it cannot define its own context, of which the transgenerational lineage with the heritage of ideals and values is a constituent part.[6]

In addition to being robbed of the inheritance of stable values as such, Mr. Albert also experienced his parents' inability to address their past and therefore his transgenerational context as a weakness on their sides. This deprived him of the merger selfobject experiences

---

[6] Georges Perec, co-director of a documentary on the history of Ellis Island and the immigrants that passed through it, was asked why he—a French citizen—was interested in this subject: He feels that, as a Jew growing up in France, he owes his life to the existence of a Diaspora as much as those who emigrated to the United States and passed through Ellis Island. But he gives us even further insights when he says: "Somehow I am a stranger in relation to myself; I am 'different', but not different from others, but different from 'my own people': I do not speak the language my parents spoke, I do not share the memories they may have had, nor anything that they may have owned and which resulted in them being who they were: their culture, their beliefs, their faith, their hopes, they were not passed on to me."

otherwise provided by our parents whom we can idealize as omnipotent and omniscient.

The lack of a shared value system and a rather coherent community further deprived him of mirroring and alter-ego selfobject experiences otherwise provided by parents and social groups. They are provided by parents who are able to identify their ambitions as worthy and are therefore able to discern in the child his own capacities and goals and can support him accordingly.

Within the therapeutic relationship, Mr. Albert experienced mirroring and alter-ego selfobject functions provided by his analyst who was able to reflect back to him his understanding of his dilemma (from own experience) of having to come to terms with the lack of transgenerational continuity and its multiple functions. This allowed him to enter the healing process so poignantly pictured first in the dream showing a group of craftsmen joyfully going about refurbishing the damaged family home and later in the identification of his own room within the newly renovated family home.

Mr. Bertram had found his own way of bridging the gap to his family's past by acquiring a piece of furniture, which he knew had been built before the war and had survived it undamaged by the horrors of the Nazi regime. To be able to pass it on one day to his children and grandchildren provided him with a sense of transgenerational continuity with an idealizable past and a meaningful future.

REFERENCES

Biller, M. (1996), 50 Jahre danach. Die Zeit, Zeitmagazin, Nov. 8.

Kohut, H. (1977), The Restoration of the Self, Madison, CT: International Universities Press.

———— (1984), How Does Analysis Cure? ed. A. Goldberg & P. Stepansky. London: University of Chicago Press.

Ornstein, A. (1994), 1994 Kohut memorial lecture. Trauma, Memory, and Psychic Continuity, Progress in Self Psychology, Vol. 10, Hillsdale, NJ: The Analytic Press, pp. 131–146.

Ornstein, P. & Ornstein, A. (1996), From prejudice to genocide: Vulnerabilities of the group-self—A psychoanalytic perspective; Presentation at the Conference Sept. 18–19, 1996, Washington, D.C., "Prejudice Past and Present: Case Studies of Historical Memory and Everyday Experience" cosponsored by The Woodrow Wilson Center for Scholars and The U.S. Holocaust Museum.

Proust, M. (1913–1928), Remembrance of Things Past. New York: Random House, 1934.

Singer, I. B. (1982), The little shoemakers. In: The Collected Stories of Isaac Bashevis Singer. New York: Farrar, Straus, Giroux, pp. 38–56.

Chapter 22

Death and the Self

Charles B. Strozier

Heinz Kohut lived his last decade in the shadow of death. In the summer of 1971, at 58 years of age, just after the huge triumph of the publication of *The Analysis of the Self*, his doctor discovered in a routine medical examination that he had an enlarged spleen. Kohut decided, somewhat fatalistically, to delay further diagnostic testing and take his vacation as usual that summer in Carmel, California, though he talked morosely at times about it as his last. When he returned to Chicago in September, he went in for tests and was diagnosed as having lymphoma (or lymphatic cancer), which is similar to, but not the same disease as, leukemia.[1] The cancer never really went into remission but spread slowly and seemed largely under control until the middle of 1977.[2] In those first six years of cancer, Kohut's most serious complaint was it affected his immune system and he often got colds and flus. The worsening of his disease from 1977 on, however, ground him down in general and resulted in the need for more aggressive treatment. First, the doctors tried a round of chemotherapy in the summer of 1977, which gave him a sore throat, aching feelings, pain on the top of his eyeballs, and a mounting fever. Needless to say, the

---

[1] Interview with Thomas A. Kohut, November 1 and 2, 1996. Felix Kohut, Heinz's father, died at 49 years of age in 1937 of leukemia. The preferred technical term is "lymphoma," but the more colloquial usage is "lymphatic cancer." Lymphoma, one of the four major types of cancer, affects the lymphatic system and can assume different forms (including Hodgkin's disease) with varying prognoses. Note from Heinz Kohut to John Van Prohaska, May 27, 1965, which suggests Kohut had long worried whether he was a "bleeder" and had something wrong with his blood.

[2] John E. Ultmann to Kohut, June 6, 1977. All cited letters and other materials, unless otherwise noted, are unpublished and in the Kohut Collection of the Archives of the Chicago Institute for Psychoanalysis.

drugs were discontinued within two months.[3] A year later, in the fall of 1978, he received some radiation treatment for which he had to prepare by having weekly blood tests.[4] Then came a relentless series of shocks. On January 12, 1979, Kohut had double by-pass heart surgery, which was followed by serious complications (and more surgery) that spring from which he almost died.[5] Just as he was recovering, he developed inner ear trouble that was to recur periodically over the next year.[6] Meanwhile, his cancer spread relentlessly. It had not responded to the chemotherapy or radiation, nor had his heart surgery jolted it into remission, something that occasionally happens and which he had hoped would occur in his case.[7] In the late fall of 1980, within days of returning from the Boston Self Psychology conference, he again almost died from type 3 pneumonia in both lobes that required two full months of convalescence.[8] In the last couple of years, Kohut also got increasingly weak and began seriously to lose weight. By the summer of 1981 he was bone-thin and down from his customary 128 pounds to 100 pounds. He developed edema, or severe swelling throughout his body, for his heart was simply unable to push things around any more. When he died on October 8, 1981, some 20 percent of his weight was in the form of cancer tumors spread throughout his body.[9]

---

[3] Kohut's notes to himself in his medical record and in a letter from Dr. Donald Sweet to Kohut, July 3, 1977. Sweet was standing in for Ultmann, who was away on vacation until October 4.

[4] Dr. Donald Sweet to Kohut, July 23, 1977, and Kohut's notes to himself in his medical records.

[5] During the operation, Kohut contracted a virus that led to his hospitalization in March. While in Billings an attendant drew blood from Kohut with a dirty needle and he contracted a "purulent phlebitis with staphylococus septicemia" which led to high fever and more surgery to remove the infected veins in his arms all the way from his wrist to his chest. He was in the hospital until the end of May and his weight dropped to 107 pounds (see Kohut to Melvin Sabshin, June 10, 1979). Note also James E. Bowman (the supervisor of the labs in the hospital who had been severely criticized by one of Kohut's doctors) to Kohut, May 25, 1979, and Kohut's reply to Bowman, June 8, asking him not to be so defensive but to "think his way into the situation."

[6] Heinz Kohut to Nathaniel London, July 17, 1979.

[7] Interview with Thomas A. Kohut, November 1 and 2, 1996.

[8] Heinz Kohut to Jacques Palaci, December 11, 1980, in a collection, "Letters to Jacques: Selected Letters of Heinz Kohut to Jacques Palaci" (see Reppen and Reppen, 1997). Kohut also wrote Douglas Detrick on December 6, 1980: "[After the Boston Self Psychology Conference in October] I came down with a serious, life-threatening pneumonia shortly after returning to Chicago from Boston" (see Cocks, 1994). If a letter from the archives, as this one, has also been published in Curve, the published citation will be given.

[9] Interview with Thomas A. Kohut, November 1 and 2, 1996. In the interview, Thomas Kohut first said the autopsy revealed 40 of his body weight was in the form of tumors. When I expressed my surprise, he said that maybe it was 20 percent, but was in any event an astonishing amount.

It would be difficult to overstate the narcissistic injury that getting cancer had for Kohut. He took a good deal of pride in his body and its physical shape. He had not smoked in over a decade.[10] He had also long since transformed his rather pudgy personna, when in 1964 (that is, just after turning 50) he went from close to 160 pounds to his ideal weight of 128 pounds. His diet, which he rigorously followed, involved eating extremely little during the week but allowed for full meals with his beloved wine on the weekend.[11] He exercised regularly and grew particularly fond of running the mile, which he did in under seven minutes.[12]

Cancer shattered Kohut's personal myth of invincibility. In his moment of greatest glory, he was brought low by a disease that was completely outside of his control. His first reaction that summer and fall of 1971 was to assume he was on the verge of death. In the hospital he also raged at various people, including the internist who told him early on that his rock-hard spleen suggested a malignancy. Kohut felt that was an unempathic communication. Kohut also spun out some rather wild fantasies under the stress of trying to adjust to his illness. He told John Gedo, who was one of only three friends whom he allowed to visit him in the hospital, that the cancer was caused by his exposure, 30 years earlier, to radiation leaks from Enrico Fermi's then-secret experiments to reach nuclear fission in the abandoned stands under Stagg Field. Gedo (1997) felt Kohut was acting paranoid, though he added, interestingly, that the thought of Kohut unravelling made him "dizzy with anxiety."

In trying to understand Kohut's response to having cancer, one should keep in mind its larger cultural associations. As Susan Sontag, (1978), who herself had cancer, has so aptly argued, this disease, unlike any other, is our culture's metaphor for the ugliness of death. Cancer is unseemly. You rot from within, your body awry in some fundamental disjunction. There is nothing elegant or even tragic about cancer. It is, on the contrary, shameful. Not all diseases have such cultural associations. In the 19th century, for example, there was something exotic about tuberculosis, and any number of novels from the time have beautiful maidens in white, lounging on couches with bloodied handkerchiefs dangling from their delicate fingers as they tragically expire. Furthermore, sanatoria, where privileged TB patients often spent years in good condition with clean air, could be sites of deepened self-awareness, as Hans Castorp discovers in Thomas Mann's

---

[10] Kohut to Sydney J. Harris, July 5, 1960, in Cocks, 1994, p. 72.

[11] Interview with Thomas A. Kohut, November 1 and 2, 1996.

[12] Kohut to Ignacio Matte-Blanco, August 21, 1969.

The Magic Mountain, Kohut's favorite book as a young man.[13] Heart disease, to take another example, has cultural meanings of mechanical breakdown, of a body moving toward death but in a natural sequence that connects life processes with endings. Not so with cancer. People often cannot even say the word and refer obliquely to "the big C" or use any number of euphemisms to avoid direct confrontation with it. Only AIDS in our day has begun to assume some of the opprobrium that cancer carried in the early 1970s.[14]

Even from his hospital bed Kohut moved to contain the knowledge of his cancer. He insisted that no one in his family tell anyone. It was a "deep and dark secret," his son says. Only within the bosom of the family for the next decade did Kohut allow himself to talk about the anxiety of the latest blood results or the terrors of an upcoming round of treatment. It brought them close but also created a "kind of hell" for the family. As he became more driven and obsessed with his health, he sucked them into the vortex of his anxiety. They all awaited the latest news, sure that it was for the worst. It did not help that his doctor, Ogelsby Paul, was rather apocalyptic himself. As Tom Kohut says: "He and we would wait for the next blood test, and he was constantly having blood tests, checking the platelet counts, etc." The reason for all the secrecy, Kohut explained to his son, was ostensibly to protect his patients. But Kohut was aware there was more to it than that, and he would at times talk to his family about how there was "something a bit shameful about his disease, something unpleasant," and how injured he was by having his body attack itself in that way. "My father," says Tom Kohut, "was very intolerant of weaknesses on his part."[15]

For all of Kohut's efforts to keep the knowledge of his cancer secret, it was in fact quite widely known. He told his old friend, Siegmund Levarie,[16] and though the documentation is lacking, he must have told Robert Wadsworth, his best friend since March 5, 1940, the day of his arrival in Chicago, and Charles Kligerman.[17] Kohut also told Anna Freud of his illness.[18] Even some of Kohut's junior colleagues knew of

---

[13] Kohut read much of *The Magic Mountain* out loud to his first girlfriend in America, Barbara Tweedle, in the early 1940s. Interview with Barbara Tweedle, January 2, 1983.

[14] Note Sontag (1989).

[15] Interview with Thomas A. Kohut, November 1 and 2, 1996.

[16] "Barring news [to] the contrary," Levarie wrote Kohut on May 3, 1972, "I happily assume that all is well with you. I interpret the scare of last fall as tribute you paid to the Gods in advance to ward off any further evils."

[17] John Gedo to me on September 9, 1998, says he is fairly certain that Kligerman visited Kohut in the hospital.

[18] Kohut to Anna Freud, December 25, 1971, in Cocks, 1994, p. 260.

his illness. Paul Ornstein and John Gedo had both visited him in the hospital. They knew what the diagnosis had been.[19] Kohut himself later told Michael Franz Basch, who was a close colleague and had once been an analysand, about his cancer.[20] Others found out through the rumor mill, which began grinding out the story almost as soon as Kohut entered the hospital. Kohut was, after all, the leading psychoanalyst in Chicago with an international reputation when he got sick. Roy Grinker, the dictatorial head of psychiatry at Michael Reese for many years, found out right away and seemed to stop people in the halls to let them know. That is how Arnold Goldberg first found out.[21] In time, everyone close to Kohut knew he had something like leukemia. Even many patients knew. He was quite open and honest about his sickness with one female patient of whom he was particularly fond,[22] and others found out by rumor. In the group, there were often discussions about Kohut's illness and concern that he might be sicker than he let on.[23]

And, yet, astonishingly, the knowledge of Kohut's cancer in his circle and within the psychoanalytic community in Chicago after 1971 was largely disavowed. John Gedo, out of friendship, kept his own counsel before 1974 and was out of the loop after that. Others, like Roy Grinker, lacked a reason or the desire to confront the issue. Still others, like his special patient, treasured the secret knowledge they possessed and would not even consider compromising him. But how the others dealt with the knowledge of Kohut's life-threatening illness, as well as the power of his charismatic presence in their lives, says much about the human capacity to dissociate when confronted with something decidedly unpleasant. Paul Ornstein had only happened on Kohut in the hospital. Kohut gently said matter of factly that he would really prefer if he would not tell anyone about his cancer. Ornstein not only obliged but entirely forgot himself what he had seen with his own eyes in 1971. For an entire decade, Ornstein, himself a medical doctor, wondered about the "mystery" of Kohut's recurrent colds and flus that were clearly systemic and related to the spreading cancer.[24] Others in the group kept their information about Kohut's illness as a kind of

---

[19] Interview with Paul Ornstein, May 20, 1996; Gedo, 1997, pp. 306–307 and 573n. John Gedo to me, September 9, 1998, notes that he was not told the diagnosis at the time but came to understand it later.

[20] Interview with Arnold Goldberg, January 14, 1997.

[21] Interview with Arnold Goldberg, January 14, 1997.

[22] Interview with Gail Elden, November 3, 1995.

[23] Interview with Arnold Goldberg, January 14, 1997.

[24] Interview with Paul Ornstein, May 20, 1996.

middle knowledge, which is how many deal with anything touching death.[25] They all knew at some level about the cancer and yet it was not known. They continued to act with each other and, probably even more importantly, with themselves as if he were fine and would live forever.

Kohut, of course, fed this process in a variety of ways. He had specifically instructed Paul Ornstein to keep the knowledge of his illness to himself. To others he acted as though he weren't sick at all. He kept running, writing books, and becoming more famous. He also fended off the occasional question about the cancer by completely obscuring his answer. When Arnold Goldberg once asked him about it directly, he said: "Who knows who has leukemia," and "What's leukemia, anyway?" Another time he told Ernest Wolf that he had had a spleenectomy but said it had nothing to do with leukemia. Perhaps he rationalized both answers on the grounds that he actually had lymphoma cancer rather than leukemia.[26] Kohut in general was unapproachable about personal issues, unless it was something he first brought up. He might, for example, regale you with a story from his childhood in Vienna but bristle at a question that hinted of self-revelation. He gave out clear signals you were not to ask about things he did not want to talk about. Furthermore, in the 1970s his close colleagues in Chicago who knew at some level about his cancer were all decidedly younger, in structurally weak and dependent relationships to him, some were in treatment (or had been), others had been or were still in supervision, and all were in thrall in his presence.

Sometimes, however, Kohut's ruses failed. Then he flat-out lied. One analyst, who was in treatment with Kohut in the late 1970s, heard a rumor that Kohut had a malignant tumor. At his next session this analyst directly asked Kohut whether he had cancer. Kohut denied that he did and asserted that the rumor was untrue. Kohut said his protracted illness resulted from an infection secondary to his cardiac problems and that, though it had proven difficult to treat effectively, it was not a malignancy. This analyst was puzzled, but convinced, by this answer. And he continued to think that those who maintained that Kohut had cancer were misinformed and malicious. When, after Kohut's death, this analyst finally learned that Kohut had, indeed, had cancer—and had not told him the truth—he was quite surprised. He is

---

[25] The term *middle knowledge* was first used in connection with people who were actually dying. (See Weisman and Hackett, 1961.) Needless to say, it has broader meanings. (See Lifton, 1979, p, 17.)

[26] Interview with Arnold Goldberg, January 14, 1997, and interview with Ernest Wolf, March 3, 1996.

quite certain he would not have been undone by the truth, does not think Kohut thought he would have been, and cannot believe that Kohut doubted he would have kept quiet about it in deference to those who did not know (Robert Leider, 1996, personal communication).

The attempt to contain the knowledge of his illness created other problems as well for Kohut. He was notorious throughout the country, indeed in the world, for turning down invitations to speak in the 1970s with flimsy excuses, which gave him the reputation of someone unwilling to defend his controversial ideas.[27] But even closer to home, the stories got exceedingly complex. When Ernest Wolf was organizing the 60th birthday celebration for Kohut in the spring of 1973, he naturally asked Kohut if he would speak sometime during the planned symposium and evening banquet. Kohut begged off with an absurd story about how he had developed a hysterical symptom that made him choke sometimes when he was talking. Whenever it happened, he said, he could not continue speaking. He was afraid he might be in the middle of a presentation and have to beg off in what would be very embarrassing circumstances. In the end, Kohut agreed to be listed on the program after the banquet as giving "Some Thoughts in Response." His supposedly modest comments became in fact a full-length presentation, which he worked on quietly throughout the winter and spring and was a blend of the personal and scientific perfectly suited for the event.[28] In retrospect, Wolf is quite certain Kohut's hesitation about presenting had to do with his uncertainty about his health. He did not yet know what would be the course of his illness and how long he would last.[29]

Kohut's relationship to death, in other words, was heavily split and disavowed. As with issues surrounding his identity, that is, his Jewishness, as well as his sexuality, he tended to compartmentalize things that required confabulation to maintain and to create personal

---

[27] See Malcolm (1981, p. 119) where Aaron Green speaks with disdain of the way Kohut sends his "emissaries" out to defend his ideas and won't go himself. Another example was when Martin Bergman's New York study group on second generation survivors wanted Kohut to talk with them about his case of Mr. A (who had been born in Poland in the 1930s and whose family had to flee Nazi persecution) that appeared in Kohut, 1971, pp. 57–73, 78, 84–85, 168, 193, 240, 289. He curtly refused, saying his patient's problems had nothing to do with the Holocaust. Interview with Judith Kestenberg, September 30, 1990. He even cut back on clinical matters, especially supervision; see Heinz Kohut to John A. Lindon, May 27, 1980.

[28] The highly worked-over draft of his talk (Kohut, 1973) is in the archives. It is clear he spent many months preparing his comments, which he then memorized and delivered apparently extemporaneously.

[29] Interview with Ernest Wolf, August 30, 1996.

myths that took on oddly separate lives.[30] This was a basic personality trait from a childhood filled with the presence of an overbearing, intrusive, and quite paranoid mother. At several levels of consciousness, he sought to control his feelings and tuned out those that threatened his equilibrium. He, of course, knew that he was sick, and at least until the end could talk about it quite rationally with the members of his family. But he also lived out a myth of health. He could lie about it convincingly because at some level he had convinced himself that he was an immortal genius struggling to complete his appointed task. In everything he became more focused and self-absorbed, alternately incredibly generous with friends, colleagues, and patients and impossibly narcissistic.

The reality of illness and death, however, could not be ignored. It was with Kohut every moment of his life. His life-long tendency toward compulsivity, for example, became exaggerated. He started tracking his weight every day to within a quarter of a pound and kept meticulous records on small pieces of paper that he stapled together.[31] And the sicker he got, the more he lived in denial. With only weeks to live, he talked enthusiastically with his family about a vacation to Greece. He had never been there and always wanted to tour the sites he had read so much about as a child. The plans got quite real, with maps laid out and cities selected.[32] He was being indulged, of course, but he actually came to believe in the trip. Sometimes, he talked directly, if cautiously, about death. He told me when I interviewed him in the spring of 1981 that death is not feared if the self is intact and one can retain selfobjects. His example, typically, was from literature, that is, The Death of Ivan Ilyich by Tolstoy, in which Ilyich's intense loneliness at the end is eased by his relationship with an empathic peasant on the estate who rubs his painful legs.[33] To be without empathy, Kohut believed, is to be without life. To be cut off from others, to be unconnected with human or symbolic selfobjects, to be utterly unto oneself or locked within the self as in psychosis, is to be dead. As he put it in 1973 at his 60th birthday banquet speech: "From the moment when man is born it is empathy, the wordless psychological extension of the human environment to the baby which separates him from the inorganic world: from death, from the meaninglessness of

---

[30] Note the odd section on lying in Kohut, 1971, pp. 109–112; compare a similar section in Kohut, 1984, p. 72.

[31] In Kohut's medical file that he put together, the stapled papers on which he recorded his weight every day for three complete years, from 1977 to 1979, have survived.

[32] Interview with Thomas A. Kohut, November 1 and 2, 1996.

[33] Leo Tolstoy, The Death of Ivan Ilyich. Kohut could also be quite kind and helpful with friends about dealing with death; see Kohut to Siegmund Levarie, October 30, 1956.

racing solar systems, from incomprehensible spaces, and from the even more incomprehensible vastness of endless time. . . . It is this expansion of the self beyond the limits of the individual which is the barrier to meaninglessness, to pessimistic despair" (Kohut, 1973).[34]

Death for Kohut, in other words, was the absence of empathy, a negation, a black hole in psychological life. But he never developed these ideas in any systematic way. He never wrote a paper or book chapter on death. He dealt with it glancingly, as in his paper "On Courage" (Kohut, 1985) or in the last section of "Forms and Transformations of Narcissism" (Kohut, 1966).[35] There was not really a conceptual room in Kohut's many-storied mansion for death.[36] His is a theory of beginnings and development, of healing and change, of self and culture, of endless possibilities warding off dark potentials. But it is not a theory of endings. Kohut skirted at the edges of the psychological, philosophical, and spiritual meanings of death. In this, self theory, as in so many other ways, was an extension of Kohut's own personality.

Yet death worked in some mysterious ways to shape Kohut's creativity during his last decade.[37] The constant (and mounting) threat of ending on an incomplete note opened Kohut up to primal matters. In this perhaps his splitting aided him. He reached new levels. It is easy to forget that until the mid-1960s Kohut was a man of more potential than dynamic reality. He had written one really remarkable essay on empathy; a number of good, but mostly forgettable, papers on applied psychoanalysis; and several positively pedestrian reports for various committees of the American Psychoanalytic Association.[38] He was

---

[34] Heinz Kohut, "A Reply," unpublished draft of speech at banquet celebrating his 60th birthday, May 13, 1973, later edited and published as "The Future of Psychoanalysis" in Ornstein, 1978–1994, pp. 663–684.

[35] Kohut, 1985, 1966. As far as I can tell, Kohut only once discussed death theoretically in a letter and that was not particularly illuminating (see Kohut to Harry Slochower, April 7, 1965, in Cocks, 1994, pp. 117–118). Note Kohut (1976) comments to David M. Moss.

[36] In this, of course, Kohut was not much different from other psychoanalysts. "The omission of the fear of death in clinical case reports, to take one example, is so blatant that one is tempted to conclude that nothing less than a conspiracy of silence is at work," is the way Yalom (1980) expresses it (see his discussion of the sources of Freud's own personal and theoretical avoidance of death, 59–74). Note also Becker (1973) and Lifton (1979). The principal philosopher who shaped this debate was Heidegger (1962).

[37] I am indebted to Robert Jay Lifton for some valuable insights into Kohut's relationship to death in a conversation January 9, 1997.

[38] The empathy paper is "Introspection, Empathy, and Psychoanalysis: An Examination of the Relationship Between Mode of Observation and Theory." Probably his most interesting example of applied psychoanalysis is "Death in Venice by Thomas Mann: A Story About the Disintegration of Artistic Sublimation," though his paper with Siegmund Levarie on music is also noteworthy: "On the Enjoyment of Listening to Music." His most forgettable paper may be "The Psychoanalytic Curriculum." All these papers are in Ornstein, 1978–1994, Vol. 1.

overly involved in administrative leadership of American psychoanalysis and served one term as President of the American from 1964–1965. After that, he was determined to direct his energies to research and writing, which he largely accomplished, though even as late as 1968 he toyed actively with the utterly distracting idea of making a run for the Presidency of the International Psychoanalytic Association because Anna Freud encouraged him. He let his name get floated and had begun to plan his program and policies as president. It was only when he realized he did not have the votes and would lose to Leo Rangell that he pulled out of contention.[39] What really focused Kohut's energies just after that was the truly transformative impact of his mother's psychological fragmentation in the late 1960s.[40] He was quite explicit with his family at the time that the confirmation of her paranoia liberated him from years of self-doubt and the Freudian nonsense of his training analyst, Ruth Eissler, that his hesitant belief in his mother's craziness was a defense against oedipal strivings.[41] More than anything, the psychological death of Else Kohut underlay the writing of *The Analysis of the Self*.

It may well be that Kohut's great discoveries were all clinical in nature and made before he got cancer. These include his recognition that analysts had been shaming their patients in the guise of offering interpretations, that neurotic pathology is often a mere cover for narcissistic issues, that idealization is not a defense, that mirror transference needs are ubiquitous, and that rage is a by-product of self fragmentation.[42] But much can be said for Kohut's later work. In classical psychoanalytic terms, 1971 marked a turn for Kohut from clinical theorizing to his later, more metapsychological phase in which he built a general theory of psychology. Though I think the distinction is valid, it tends to obscure both the important lines of continuity in his thought, which have been developed most completely so far by Paul Ornstein in his lengthy "Introduction" to the first volume of *Search for the Self*,[43]

---

[39] Kohut to Ruth Eissler, February 16, 1969. Note also the letter that covers the same ground and uses much of the same language, though is a little more circumspect, to Anna Freud, February 16, 1969, in Cocks, 1994, pp. 230–231.

[40] Interview with Thomas A. Kohut, November 1 and 2, 1996.

[41] Interview with Thomas A. Kohut, November 1 and 2, 1996.

[42] John Gedo helped clarify for me that these ideas are essentially clinical in nature. I would have to disagree with his further observations that Kohut was unable to theorize after he got sick, that he became like a "quarterback who can't see his receivers," largely because he was separated from Gedo himself. Interview with John Gedo, August 29, 1996.

[43] Paul Ornstein emphasizes the continuity in Kohut's thought in his long introduction to the first two volumes of *The Search for the Self* that came out in 1978. Ornstein's concern at that point was to clarify the "underlying unity" of Kohut's ideas and to show that his early

and the fact that in any clinical formulation there is an implicit metapsychology, just as coherent theory-making worth serious consideration has a sound empirical basis. While carefully noting these qualifications, I would nevertheless argue more for the discontinuities, the changes and transformations in Kohut's thought, especially the break associated with his illness in 1971.

In the years of preparation for greatness before 1971 Kohut pursued the meanings of narcissism within the strict confines of Freud's structural model. In retrospect his early work is more of a piece than was apparent at the time. His 1957 paper on Thomas Mann's *Death in Venice* (that was actually written in 1948) leads logically to the 1959 empathy paper, and from there to the 1966 "Forms and Transformations of Narcissism." The culmination of this line of thought is, of course, *The Analysis of the Self*. The self, in that way of thinking, is an experience-near "content of the mental apparatus," not an agency of the mind (as are id, ego, and superego) but a structure within it that is "cathected with instinctual energy" and has "continuity in time" and is "enduring" (Kohut, 1971). *The Analysis of the Self* realizes the structural model, both for Kohut himself and in a sense for psychoanalysis, while it subtly contradicts the essence of that tradition. The more Kohut sought to toe the line, the more his ideas took him into new arenas. The language remained almost quaintly conventional and for many beginners now is incomprehensible, while the ideas and their implications were altogether new in psychoanalysis. The book, in other words, stands ironically as a profound indictment of the very drive theory it attempts to bolster. *The Analysis of the Self* is as much the end of something as its beginning, though such implications took much further reflection to develop.

It was no mean feat what Kohut accomplished after *The Analysis of the Self* (1971)—and cancer. In 1977 he published his most readable and accessible book, *The Restoration of the Self* and, in the two years before his death completed his more obscure, but extremely important, posthumously published book *How Does Analysis Cure?* (1984). as well as worked on some of his earlier essays on history and culture that I put together after his death and brought out as *Self*

---

papers and presentations helped "sharpen his own clinical and theoretical grasp" and "test out his formulations" that had become increasingly clear over time. Ornstein's rather complicated schema attempted to identify three themes in Kohut's thinking that developed into three major lines of thought that moved through several "nodal points." The key interpretive point of the essay, however, is the teleological one of continuous forward movement that he sees in Kohut's thinking, of ever-deeper understanding and clarity as he created a "new paradigm" (see Ornstein, 1978–1994, Vol. 1, 1–106).

Psychology and the Humanities (Strozier, 1985). In other arenas, he wrote his autobiographical case of Mr. Z (1979),[44] fostered the creativity of those in his immediate circle and oversaw the *Casebook* that began as a project in 1974 and was published in 1978 (Goldberg, 1978) and wrote thousands of letters and provided leadership for a movement of national and international significance of which we are all a part. At the center of this latter phase in Kohut's thinking was a clear and explicit break from Freud and drive theory. He changed his understanding to an all-embracing definition of the self in the broad sense. The self-found agency, one might say, in the Jamesian sense as Kohut found his voice. Even something as seemingly small as taking the hyphen out of selfobject in 1977 marked a rather large conceptual shift in his thinking.[45] Death, I would say, forced Kohut toward the more radical (and creative) implications of his thinking. It allowed him to come out from under the shadow of Freud and the tyranny of orthodox psychoanalysis. Death forced Kohut to think for himself.

Death also kept Kohut alive. He had a mission. Kohut's clear sense of his own immortality lay within self psychology. That was the arena in which he felt he could permanently leave his mark. His unusual talents and insights put him in touch with the pulse of the historical moment. Drive theory was dead, but no one before Kohut had found a way to question its basic assumptions while retaining the intellectual and spiritual core of psychoanalysis.[46] Kohut knew he had solved that problem but that his explanation was only half clear by 1971. Illness threatened completion of that project. There is no question he talked about his illness and his work in these terms, at least to his family.[47] His fear, as death loomed, was of leading an incomplete life, of not finishing his work. Perhaps we all share such fears, but the dread of not finishing may well be that much more acute for the talented and perhaps agonizing for the genius. Kohut knew he was shaking up psychoanalysis in a profound way and that only he could carry through

---

[44] Interview with Thomas A. Kohut, November 1 and 2, 1996; the case was published first in the German translation of *The Restoration of The Self, Die Heilungs die Selbst,* tr. Elke vom Scheidt (Frankfurt, 1979), and then in English as "The Two Analyses of Mr. Z," *International Journal of Psychoanalysis* 60:3–27, reprinted in Ornstein (1978–1994) Vol. 4, pp. 395–446.

[45] Kohut began to consider taking out the hyphen in the spring and summer of 1977. The event was then celebrated first with the Wolfs over a Flemish "Pot en feu" on October 29, 1977, and somewhat later with the Goldbergs and Tolpins at the Wolfs. Interview with Ina Wolf, August 28, 1996, and with Connie Goldberg, January 14, 1997.

[46] Michael Franz Basch, comments at the Memorial service for Heinz Kohut, First Unitarian Church of Chicago, October 31, 1981.

[47] Interview with Thomas A. Kohut, November 1 and 2, 1996.

the revolution. His sense of himself required a fierce devotion to complete the task, which was now potentially compromised by premature closure.

To extend that point further, Kohut's urgent need to complete the task of his calling lent his project a transcendent purpose. He felt touched by fate, or history, or God.[48] It is not that Kohut had not always been grandiose, something his critics had long criticized him for, as though those who were close to him were not aware of his narcissism; it was rather that he had to be endured and sometimes suffered him to get the gift of what he had to offer. But in his last decade, all of what he was got concentrated and exaggerated as he took on the task of openly and coherently challenging Freud. It was a process for Kohut of heroic self-fashioning in the context of dreaded incompleteness.

One consequence of this self transformation was that Kohut's friendships radically altered. Lionized for years as the logical successor to Heinz Hartmann and one of four or five people in the world at the epicenter of the psychoanalytic movement, Kohut found himself shunned by Anna Freud and Kurt Eissler as they became more aware of the implications of *The Analysis of the Self* and the directions in which he was moving. Another old friend, Martin Stein (1979), charged at the front of the orthodox minions from New York by lambasting *The Restoration of the Self*. Sometimes, people who had known him for decades literally turned their back on him at meetings.[49] At the Chicago Institute the old guard, amazingly enough, even voted him off the Council in 1977 because he was not sufficiently Freudian (at least so they said). Kohut felt as though he had been kicked out of his own family, surely evoking for him the trauma of being forced out of his beloved Vienna by the Nazis because he was Jewish.[50] The depth of his suffering at these rejections should not be underestimated. Since hard-core Freudians are now something of an anachronism, it may be difficult to remember the extent to which Kohut's challenge threatened the foundations of orthodoxy. The dominant theme in hundreds of letters he wrote during his last decade was the surprise and pain at the establishment turning against him.

---

[48] See Rank (1952). See also Storr's (1996) very interesting recent study. I have also had many discussions on this general topic with Robert Jay Lifton in the last decade at our Center on Violence and Human Survival at John Jay College. Note his recent research in this regard on the Japanese cult, Aum Shinrikyo. His first paper from that study is "Reflections on Aum Shinrikyo," in a book I edited with Michael Flynn (Strozier and Flynn, 1997).

[49] Interview with Bernard Brandchaft, October 21, 1995.

[50] Kohut to Lotte Kohler, June, 1978, in Cocks, 1994, pp. 368–371.

His adaptive solution to the rejection by old friends was to find new ones. This was a process that began before cancer—the first group was formed in 1969—but accelerated in scope and significance during the 1970s. The first group reinvented itself in 1974 to produce the *Casebook*, expanded into a monthly Saturday seminar by 1977, and after 1978 reached out to the world in the self conferences. People came and went and there were bitter fights, most notoriously between John Gedo and Marian Tolpin in 1974, but a core group of what Ina Wolf called the "sacred seven" formed the immediate supportive circle that confirmed Kohut's messianic purpose and concretized his charisma.[51] The group listened raptly to every word of his latest drafts as it self-consciously modeled itself on Freud's followers (some roles were unclear, but in the early days all knew that John Gedo was the resident Carl Jung). Nobody worked harder than Heinz Kohut to foster and nourish those relationships. He responded with deep empathy to the special needs of each core member of the group, designating Arnold Goldberg, for example, as the chosen successor in ways that recognized his brilliance while giving him lots of room to be cantankerous, or taking Marian Tolpin into analysis, or strongly encouraging Michael Franz Basch to be intellectually rebellious but personally almost obsequious, or creating just the right dose of closeness with Paul Ornstein and Ernest Wolf. He only failed with John Gedo, though one wonders if that relationship was doomed from the start. The general point, however, is that Kohut clearly understood that his heroic mission would be incomplete without these devoted followers whom he needed to support him psychologically and to carry forward the work.

One important point to keep in mind is that the meanings of death worked in Kohut's self as a process that changed over time. Until about 1978, death was a kind of Jungian shadow in Kohut's life, the significance of which is only apparent in retrospect. But after heart surgery in early 1979 and the more rapid spread of the cancer, Kohut's struggles with illness were more apparent, more visible to the world, and the urgency with which he worked and related to others more marked *and* more emotionally comprehensible. The heart surgery and subsequent infections, the inner ear problems, and general aches and pains also gave Kohut an opportunity to talk openly about his health—without having to deal with the cancer. One senses in Kohut's letters after 1979 almost a kind of liberation for him from the tyranny of secretiveness. With his old friend from medical school, Jacques Palaci, he was able to begin talking openly about death.[52] He also reached out

---

[51] Ina Wolf, personal communication, November 15,1997.
[52] Interview with Jacques Palaci, October 10, 1990.

to his childhood friend, Siegmund Levarie. In the summer of 1979, for example, he fussed to Levarie about how he tired easily and felt seasick from his inner ear problems, but "when I consider where I was about three or four months ago, I have good reason to be pleased with the progress I have made."[53] The next year, when Levarie's grandchild was born, Kohut called to congratulate him and was enthusiastic, warm, and friendly (and as Levarie told me this in an interview in 1985 he fought back a tear and broke into the present tense, as though Kohut were still alive). "I will never see my own grandchild," Kohut lamented to Levarie.[54]

In this same period Kohut wrote detailed descriptions of his ailments (though nothing about the cancer) to Douglas Levin, Martha Louis Little, and Nathaniel London.[55] Six months later, he reported to Levarie feeling better but still "woozy," "unsteady," "lightheaded," and "feeble," but "the brain is working in the important tasks I am putting it to."[56] That summer he told his son: "My mind is ok, my courage unbroken, my work proceeds."[57] It was Kohut's mind that really mattered. He told Paul Ornstein: "How much time do I have? I want to live as long as I have ideas. When I no longer have ideas, I don't care. I am not afraid to die, but I am afraid I will run dry and not have ideas and not be able to think straight."[58]

For all the pain and suffering, he always kept thinking straight. In fact, one of the most important and moving talks of his life came at the fourth Self Psychology Conference in Berkeley on the cusp of death. For most of that fall weekend in early October 1981, Kohut was a very sick man, holed up in a hotel room. No one from Chicago had seen him in months and therefore had no idea of just how close he was to the end. Friends anxiously consulted each other and tried to pry more information out of Mrs. Kohut. But no amount of whispered huddling at the margins of a busy conference brought forth any more concrete information about Kohut's physical state. Kohut had, however, invited Jacques Palaci to visit him Saturday at the hotel. Warm and outgoing, Palaci had made it a point to travel from Paris for the meetings since they first began in 1978. Kohut always tried to do something special for Palaci, and they had established a tradition of

---

[53] Kohut to Siegmund Levarie, August 11, 1979.
[54] Interview with Siegmund Levarie, October 7, 1985.
[55] Kohut to Douglas Levin, June 23, 1979; to Martha Louis Little, May 8, 1979; and to Nathaniel London, July 17, 1979.
[56] Kohut to Siegmund Levarie, February 21, 1980.
[57] Kohut to Thomas A. Kohut, August 17, 1981, Cocks, p. 433.
[58] Interview with Paul Ornstein, May 20, 1996.

visiting for a day or so after each conference. It is not surprising Kohut chose Palaci to visit him that Saturday. Palaci was Kohut's link to the past, to his youth, to their medical studies together in Vienna. Nothing would be compromised by revealing to Palaci how sick he really was.

Betty Kohut's look when she greeted Palaci at the door was his first indication of just how serious things were with his old friend. But nothing could have prepared him for what he saw when he came to Kohut's bedside. Palaci instantly recognized the imminence of death in the pallor of Kohut's skin, the edema that caused his belly and legs to swell, the major loss of weight that left him an empty shell, and the odors of the sick room. The mere fact that Kohut stayed in bed when Palaci walked in suggested to him the seriousness of the situation. A man of boundless enthusiasm, Kohut hated to appear helpless or sick.

Motioning Palaci to his side, Kohut greeted him warmly. He did not deny to this friend how sick he really was. He brought him up to date quickly on his various ailments. He also shared how awful the night before had been. "If I have to go through that again," he said, "I don't want to live any longer." Then he gossiped with Palaci for over an hour about his followers and shared his serious concern for the future of self psychology. Who among his key followers, he asked rhetorically, might lead the movement after his death? Where would it all go? What would happen when he died?

But there were also more immediate concerns, especially his determination to speak the next day at the conference. Palaci asked whether Kohut was really up to making such a presentation in his condition. Indeed he was, asserted Kohut. All these people had gathered to honor him, to examine his ideas, and to see him. He couldn't disappoint them. Besides, he had a plan. He would remain in bed until the last minute and then get hooked up with a vial of adrenaline dripping directly into a vein near his heart. He planned for an ambulance to transport him to the lecture hall just before he was supposed to speak. Palaci could only shake his head in amazement. He knew, when set on such a course, Kohut was not to be dissuaded.

The night went badly. Bernard Brandchaft happened to spot Kohut aimlessly walking the hall of the hotel outside his room in clear distress. When he offered to help, Kohut waved him off, probably most upset at revealing his state to a friend and colleague.[59] But somehow he made it through the night. The next morning, after dressing slowly and painfully, he set off for the conference hall. On the way, he stopped with Betty Kohut for a brief lunch at a McDonald's, which he boasted

---

[59] Interview with Bernard Brandchaft, October 21, 1995.

of later to his son. He loved such symbols of America, his beloved adopted country.[60] In the late morning, just as the four other panelists wound up their comments, the ambulance arrived at the plaza outside the Berkeley campus lecture hall. A curious crowd gathered instantly near the ambulance. The driver removed a folded wheelchair, and after opening it up, Kohut got out of the front seat of the car to sit in it. He had a grim, set look on his face that baffled many who knew him. He seemed to look through them. He was completely focused. He even ignored Palaci, who was standing nearby and greeted him as soon as the ambulance arrived. Kohut waved him off without even looking in his direction. Palaci had never been ignored by Kohut, and it momentarily hurt his feelings. But he could also appreciate as no one else in the crowd what it took for Kohut to summon up the strength to get through his presentation. Bruised a bit in his feelings, but recognizing that something larger than himself was unfolding, Palaci pulled back and faded into the crowd. A silent parting of those gathered near the ambulance made room for Kohut to pass, with his wife at his side, and approach the entrance to the lecture hall.

Kohut had sent out advance word that he would definitely make it for a few brief comments at the end of the morning session. The panelists on stage and most of the conference participants in the lecture hall thus knew that the stir at the back of the room signaled the arrival of Kohut. Arnold Goldberg, the last speaker at the long table covered with a white cloth, instantly ended his comments. Everyone turned to the door. Some stood in their seats to get a better view. Deliberately, Kohut stepped out of his wheelchair at the entrance to the room and walked alone and firmly down the long aisle, up the three steps to the proscenium, and took his place at stage right at the far end of the table.

His appearance, while suggestive of the seriousness of his medical condition, in no way gave it away. He was pale, to be sure, even ashen, and it was clear he had lost weight, for his neck looked scrawny and his high cheekbones were sharply accentuated. But everything else disguised his state. The reddish hue in the florescent illumination of the room partly offset the sickly tone of his complexion.[61] He had on a white dress shirt and a dark tie, slightly ajar, that enhanced the formality and professionalism of his appearance. He wore a tan sports coat and underneath it a V-necked sweater; these various layers added

---

[60] Interview with Thomas A. Kohut, November 1 and 2, 1996.

[61] In the extant videotape of Kohut's talk the color balance has been adjusted to make him look normal, which has the curious and misleading effect of making the other panelists on the stage look disarmingly ruddy.

substance to his frail frame. The layers of clothing also completely covered over the apparatus dripping adrenaline into his heart. His high forehead faded into a shock of bright white hair. His black frame glasses seemed too heavy for his nose, and he often had to push them up or scrunch his nose to position them properly.

The anxiety about his absence that had hung in the air during the conference now completely dissipated with him actually in the room, seated at the long table on the stage. He was alive, and without too much denial, one could be convinced he even looked well. Hadn't he walked into the room on his own? And when he started talking, he was clearly the familiar Kohut of everyone's memory and imagination: the high-pitched voice that ranged from a comforting sing-song in what almost seemed a musical key to a sharp whine or a kind of cackle to express his irritation at the stupidity of some critic; the soft and appealing lilt of his Viennese accent that had entered into the transferences of a thousand patients in the three decades of his psychoanalytic practice; the gestures with his hands to mark certain points; the self-deprecating jokes that filled the room with laughter throughout the talk; the warmth and human energy that he radiated; and, surely, the charisma, whatever it is, that filled the room and instantly changed the atmosphere of the conference. Everyone felt the charisma.

The topic of Kohut's lecture was empathy.[62] He apologized for taking up the subject again, both in the lecture and in his recently completed draft of *How Does Analysis Cure?* (Kohut, 1984). In both contexts he was returning to the subject, despite the fact that he had decided a couple of years ago that he was "sick of that topic." He had written himself out about it. Yet people kept criticizing him "over and over again" with the same arguments and profound misunderstandings. It wore him out. "I was wasting my time, my emotions, my energy,"

---

[62] For the most part the text of Kohut's extemporaneous lecture that I use here is the transcribed and edited version, later titled "On Empathy," published in Ornstein, 1978–1994. Paul Ornstein, the editor of the four volumes of the papers, notes that he, in turn, relied in part on an earlier transcript provided by Robert J. Leider. I have, however, watched the videotape of the lecture more times than I can count and made many further corrections to the published transcripts, as well as noting Kohut's appearance, gestures, tics, mannerisms, and in general the physical surround of the room. Ornstein himself was deeply ambivalent about publishing the lecture. The reasons have to do with both content and style. In a footnote (p. 525) he addressed style: "These remarks would undoubtedly have been carefully edited by him [Kohut] afterward, to meet his standards for publication. They have only been minimally edited here, to enhance clarity by deleting some repetitious phrases, a few extraneous asides, and in order to maintain proper grammatical standards. Editing was also held to a minimum, so as to retain the immediacy, informality, and emotional impact of Kohut's delivery, even at the expense of some 'inelegance' of style."

he said. He felt he should get on with some new ideas. But "idiot that I am," he said with a slight smile, he eventually came to feel that "when people keep asking you the same damn question, something must be wrong!"

Lacking myself time to analyze the talk in detail, I will only note that Kohut's main point was to affirm, with all due qualification, that empathy in and of itself heals. The mere act of being empathic with someone else has beneficial effects. Empathy is a therapeutic action in the broadest sense. Even if nothing else happens with a patient, if there is empathy from the analyst, healing occurs. Kohut was fully aware of the radical implications of such an idea for someone like himself who was so deeply ingrained in the Freudian tradition. It muddied the waters of inquiry. "I wish I could just simply by-pass it," he said shrugging. But "since it is true, and I know it is true" it is an aspect of his topic that deserved the closest attention. He had to mention it.

And yet empathy per se, Kohut says, constitutes only the first step toward cure. There must also be explanations, or "interventions on the level of interpretation." Such interventions are not simply the repetition and confirmation of what the patient says and feels. That must occur, but it is "only the first step." At some point psychoanalysis cures because the analyst gives an interpretation, which means "an explanation of what's going [on] in genetic, dynamic, and psycho-economic terms." An interpretation, in other words, works at several levels and connects meanings across time, in depth, and in the context of their full emotional intensity. Such a move, furthermore, from understanding to explanation in most cases must be sequenced in that order. The analyst must first empathically reflect back to the patient his or her feelings and images. Only then is the analyst in a position to interpret, which Kohut called "a higher form of empathy."

Clearly tiring, having spoken half an hour, Kohut announced he wanted to close. His head was beginning to tilt slightly forward, as though its weight was difficult to support. He looked, if that were possible, even paler than he had at the beginning of the lecture. His gestures with his hands had become muted and the scrunching of his nose and adjustment of his glasses less pronounced. The eyes seemed sadder. Everything spoke of a profound exhaustion.

But in fact he had trouble stopping. He knew it was his last lecture. And so, first, he reiterated that empathy must not be abused for vaguely supportive measures and that it must be appreciated on its various levels of development. He uttered that pronouncement, even though he knew immediately it had the tone of a hard and fast rule. He hardly wanted to go out on a fussy note. So, he added quickly, by way of qualification: "Certainly, I'm not stodgy." The more you know, the freer you can be to experiment and find your own truth and avoid "some ritual that one sticks to anxiously." We don't really know yet how to treat people with serious self disturbances. But with time and care and patience we will discover the best approaches and the most effective ways to blend empathy and explanation.

That thought brought to mind a clinical example. Many years ago, Kohut had been involved in a long analysis treating a severely disturbed woman. After abruptly leaving another analysis, she lay down on the couch her first day and said it felt like she was in a coffin and that the top was about to close with a click. Kohut mimicked the sound by opening his mouth widely and twice loudly clicking with his tongue. He had always been good at such imitations. He was a natural actor, which early on he learned to turn to professional advantage. As a resident in neurology at the University of Chicago School of Medicine in the 1940s, for example, he was famous for being able to act out perfectly the odd neurological ticks that are described in the textbooks and must be memorized for boards. That double click was one of his great moments of performance. Watching it made you feel the coffin closing.

Over the years of treatment with the woman, Kohut noted that she was so deeply depressed there were many times he thought he would lose her and she would commit suicide. Once he was even spontaneously moved to ask if she would like to hold onto his fingers while she talked. "Maybe that would help you," he said to her. It was a "doubtful maneuver," he added, and he was not recommending it in general. But he was desperate. So he pulled his chair closer and reached out and gave her two of his fingers to hold. The patient clasped Kohut's fingers tightly. It made him think of the "toothless gums of a very young child clamping down on an empty nipple." That was his thought, indeed his interpretation. He did not say it. That would come later. But he thought it. It was fully formulated in his mind. And that is what made it a psychoanalytic interpretation.

Then Kohut really did end. "I'm quite sure this will be the last self psychology meeting that I will attend," he said gravely, as many in the audience of 500 began to cry, aware now more than ever that he was announcing his own end. "I wanted to do my utmost to be able to go through with my promise [to attend]. So, let's all hope for a good future for the ideas embodied in self psychology." And he said good-bye.

The applause was tumultuous now, the tears abundant. Kohut raised his hands: "Enough, enough. I know your feelings. I want to take a rest now."

Four days later, on October 8, 1981, Heinz Kohut died in Chicago.

REFERENCES

Becker, E. (1973), *The Denial of Death*. New York: The Free Press.

Cocks, G., ed. (1994), *Curve of Life: The Correspondence of Heinz Kohut, 1923–1981*. Chicago: University of Chicago Press.

Gedo, J. (1997), *Spleen and Nostalgia: A Life and Work in Psychoanalysis*. Northvale, NJ: Aronson.

Goldberg, A., with the collaboration of Heinz Kohut. (1978), *The Psychology of the Self: A Casebook*. New York: International Universities Press.

Heidegger, M. (1962), Dasein's possibility of being-a-whole and being-toward death. In: *Being and Time*, trans. J. Macquarrie & E. Robinson. New York: Harper and Row, pp. 279–311.

Kohut, H. (1966), Forms and transformations of narcissism. In: *The Search for the Self: Selected Writings of Heinz Kohut: 1950–1994, Vol. 1*, ed. P. Ornstein. New York: International Universities Press.

———— (1971), *The Analysis of the Self: A Systematic Approach to the Psychoanalytic Treatment of Narcissistic Personality Disorders*. New York: International Universities Press.

———— (1973), The future of psychoanalysis. In: *The Search for the Self: Selected Writings of Heinz Kohut: 1950–1994, Vol. 4*, ed. P. Ornstein. New York: International Universities Press, pp. 663–684.

———— (1976), Narcissism, empathy and the fragmentation of the self: An interview. *Pilgrimage*, 4.

———— (1977), *The Restoration of the Self*. New York: International Universities Press.

———— (1979), The two analyses of Mr. Z. In: *The Search for the Self: Selected Writings of Heinz Kohut: 1950–1994, Vol. 4*, ed. P. Ornstein. New York: International Universities Press, pp. 395–446.

———— (1981), On empathy. In: *The Search for the Self: Selected Writings of Heinz Kohut: 1950–1994, Vol. 4*, ed. P. Ornstein. New York: International Universities Press, pp. 525–535.

———— (1984), *How Does Analysis Cure?*, ed. A. Goldberg & P. Stepansky. Chicago: University of Chicago Press.

———— (1985), On courage. In: *Self Psychology and the Humanities: Reflections on a New Psychoanalytic Approach*, ed. C. B. Strozier. New York: Norton.

Lifton, R. J. (1979), *The Broken Connection: On Death and the Continuity of Life*. New York: Basic Books.

Malcolm, J. (1981), *Psychoanalysis: The Impossible Profession*. New York: Knopf.

Ornstein, P., ed. (1978–1994), *The Search for the Self: Selected Writings of Heinz Kohut: 1950–1994*, 4 volumes. New York: International Universities Press.

Rank, O. (1952), *The Myth of the Birth of the Hero: A Psychological Interpretation of Mythology*. New York: Brunner.

Sontag, S. (1978), *Illness as Metaphor*. New York: Farrar, Straus & Giroux.

———— (1989), *AIDS and its Metaphors*. New York: Farrar, Straus & Giroux.

Stein, M. (1979), Review of *The Restoration of the Self* by H. Kohut. *J. Amer. Psychoanal. Assn.*, 27:665–680.

Storr, A. (1996), *Feet of Clay*. New York: The Free Press.

Strozier, C. B., ed. (1985), *Self Psychology and the Humanities: Reflections on a New Psychoanalytic Approach*. New York: Norton.

——— ed. with Michael Flynn. (1997) *The Year 2,000: Essays on the End*. New York: New York University Press.

Reppen, J. & Reppen, F. (1997), Letters to Jacques: Selected letters of Heinz Kohut to Jacques Palaci. *Psychoanal. Rev.*, 84:822–837.

Weisman, A. & Hackett, T. (1961), Predilection to death: Death and dying as a psychiatric problem. *Psychosomatic Medicine*, 33.

Yalom, I. (1980), *Existential Psychotherapy*. New York: Basic Books.

Author Index

Subject Index